GLASGOW OBSERVED

Edited by
SIMON BERRY
and
HAMISH WHYTE

JOHN DONALD PUBLISHERS LTD
EDINBURGH

ISBN 085976 189 4

Exclusive distribution in the United States of America and Canada by Humanities Press Inc., Atlantic Highlands, NJ 07716, USA

The publishers acknowledge the financial assistance of the Scottish Arts Council in the publication of this volume.

Phototypeset by Print Origination, Formby, Liverpool.
Printed in Great Britain by Bell & Bain Ltd, Glasgow.

CONTENTS

ACKNOWLEDGEMENTS

The anthologists would like to express their appreciation of the help and encouragement received from the following when looking for suitable material for this book: Derek Dow (Greater Glasgow Health Board archivist), Andrew Jackson (Strathclyde Regional Council archivist), Elspeth King and staff of The People's Palace, Linda Mackenney and the Scottish Theatre Archive, Alison Ferguson (Glasgow Museums & Art Galleries librarian), Michael Moss and staff of the University of Glasgow archives department, Jean Grail and staff of Glasgow District Council planning department, Eleanor Murdoch (CWS archivist), Cliff Hanley, Jack House, Kevin McCarra, George Oliver, Tom Moulds and Hazel Wright. Special thanks are due to the tireless efforts of Joe Fisher, Anne Escott and all the staff of the Mitchell Library's Glasgow Room without which *Glasgow Observed* would never have developed into more than a good formula for a different kind of book about the city. Any errors, omissions or opinions expressed in the book are, of course, not of their making.

Particular gratitude is due to Winifred and Colleen who did not discourage us from perservering with our task of illuminating 200 years of Glasgow history.

For permission to reprint copyright material the editors and publisher gratefully acknowledge the following: the extract from *Boswell's Journal* is printed with permission of Yale University and Wm Heinemann Ltd; Roy Gillespie, Librarian of The Mitchell Library, for extracts from The Journal of a Frenchman and David Willox's Diary; the extract from *The English Notebooks* is reprinted by permission of the Modern Language Association of America © 1941; Strathclyde Regional Archives for the extract from the Anderston Case Book; Glasgow Museums and Art Galleries for extracts from the Harrington Mann papers; Elizabeth Lauder Hamilton for an extract from *Roamin' in the Gloamin'*; Ronald Mavor for an extract from *One Way of Living*; Brian D. Henderson (Hon. Sec. The Old Glasgow Club) for extracts from *A Tour in the Calton*; Pluto Press and Harry McShane for an extract from *No Mean Fighter*; H.V. Morton and Methuen and Co. for extracts from *In Search of Scotland*; Mrs Hamilton for an extract from *Scotland the Brave*; Glasgow University Press for extracts from Compton Mackenzie's rectorial address and from *Homes in High Flats*; Prof. Christopher Blake for an extract from *The Heart of Scotland*; Gavin Muir for extracts from *Scottish Journey*; Mary Brogan for extracts from 'The Glasgow Comedians' and 'The League and the Cup'; the Glasgow branch of the EIS for 'Report of Glasgow Speech'; Charles Oakley for extracts from *The Second City*; Naomi Mitchison for an extract from *The Bull Calves*; Augustus Muir for an extract from *Scottish Portrait*; Anne Cluysenaar for an extract from J.B. Singer's 'Glasgow'; Jack House for extracts from 'Community Life' in the *Third Statistical Account*; J.F. Sleeman for extracts from 'Transport in Glasgow' in *The Glasgow Region*; Edwin Morgan for extracts from 'Signs and Wonders' in *The New Statesman*; *The Observer* for extracts from 'Anatomy of a Contemporary Gang' by Ken Martin and from Edward Mace's 'Travel Talk'; Charles McKean for an extract from 'Motorway City' in the *Architects' Journal*; Jimmy Reid for an extract from *Reflections of a Clyde-Built Man*; Cliff Hanley for an extract from 'A Drop of the Hard Stuff in Humour'; Mary Brennan for an extract from 'Their Very Own Mayfest'; *New Society* for an extract from 'Estates of Another Realm' by Andrew Broadbent; Scotmedia Magazines and Ruth Wishart; Billy Connolly for an extract from 'I'm Telling Ye We're the Big Yin of Arts' in *The Sunday Times*; Sean Damer for extracts from 'Wine Alley'; and Brian Barr for an extract from *The Scottish Daily News*.

Every effort has been made to secure permission to include passages in this anthology; the editors and publisher apologise for any error or omission in the above and will take note of any additional information supplied to them.

Simon Berry
Hamish Whyte

Introduction

I

More than three hundred years ago people were writing about Glasgow, and they have continued doing so to the present day. Early observers like Daniel Defoe (in the 1720s) were extremely complimentary: to him the town had an almost Mediterranean appearance and was 'the cleanest and beautifullest and best built city in Britain'. Fifty years later another traveller, Thomas Pennant, described Glasgow as 'the best built of any second-rate city I ever saw'.

Two centuries later Edwin Muir, returning to the city where he had lived as a young man, could only record the truly appalling conditions that most people lived in. 'The London slums are dreary,' he wrote in *Scottish Journey*, 'but the Glasgow slums always hold a sense of possible menace; they take their revenge on the respectable and the rich . . . ' Ever since, the city's name has been used by sociologists as a totem for every kind of modern urban horror.

The problem for the Glasgow anthologist is not shortage of material (although the same passages have tended to occur with numbing regularity in recent accounts of the city's growth), but knowing just where to start. We have decided on the 1780s as our main jumping off point, but we have taken the liberty of beginning with Boswell's account of his and Johnson's visit in 1773 to the 'elegant' city. Built, in Pennant's words, with 'good taste, plain and unaffected', Glasgow was still a merchant city, the domain of the Tobacco Lords.

1776 marked the peak of the Virginian and Maryland tobacco trade; thereafter the merchants needed to look nearer home to repair their fortunes. In 1783 they invited Arkwright the inventor to a banquet and at least one of their number, David Dale, immediately saw the immense possibilities in the machine production of cotton cloth. It was the rapid growth of industrialisation that made the first major changes in the appearance of the small town by its bleaching green. Men (and women and children too) were needed to tend machines; in the fifty years from 1781 to 1831 the population quintupled and with the coming of steam power the modern city was born.

It was in the 1780s too that the Town Council commissioned engineer John Golborne to start building the jetties which gradually led to the deepening of the Clyde right up to the Broomielaw. Early in the new century steam power took to the water in the shape of Henry Bell's first *Comet.* By the time Victoria was on the throne new docks were being planned on the waterfront as the way was thrown open to transatlantic trade once again. By the mid-1800s ships of iron and then of steel were being built, a new technology that the Clyde was to dominate up until the First World War.

The last two hundred years have seen a number of peaks and troughs in Glasgow's fortunes, and the present time shows her in a considerable state of economic and social distress. Perhaps it is simple-minded to refer back to periods like the late 1840s when starvation stalked the city's streets or to the misery caused by the City of Glasgow Bank crash of 1878. But somehow, with a mixture of far-sightedness, energy and considerable ingenuity, Glasgow has always pulled through, usually turning apparent liabilities to her own advantage.

We hope that the hundred and fifty or so passages in this collection, drawn from a wide range of sources, will perhaps give the flavour of two hundred years of Glasgow's history—during her darkest moments as well as in her days of resplendent glory.

II

Isolating themes or motifs in a city's history can be seen as imposing a pattern on events that only exists in hindsight. Nevertheless, Glasgow's story does contain a number of recurring themes that give a clue to the prevailing character of her citizens.

In the history of every person, every enterprise and every nation there must be an all-important 'T'-junction where one course is firmly fixed on rather than another. With Glasgow that point was surely the discovery, towards the end of the eighteenth century, of the plentiful supplies of coal and ironstone to the south and east. Both were essential materials for the Steam Age and the consequent rapid growth of industrialisation.

Even with the natural resources to hand, even with the Clyde opened to the sea, even with Watt's demonstration of the more efficient use of steam power, there was no ordained path to Glasgow's Victorian role as the European centre of heavy engineering and shipbuilding. In 1770 she was a prosperous city of merchants investing in and speculating on labour undertaken two thousand miles away, almost exclusively given over to the leisurely pursuits of trading. Most of her ships were built and berthed twenty miles downriver.

Fifty years later she was a city of industrialists, investing heavily and employing vast numbers of hands, quick to see new markets and discover new manufacturing processes to make goods that would be needed in ever-increasing quantity. The coming men were no longer those equipped with a good classical education, but those who had first-hand experience of technology and how theory could be put into profitable practice. This was the making of the archetypal Glasgow engineer, breathing the same smoke produced by the machines he had brought into being.

Unlike Birmingham, the only rival (outside London) to her industrial might in the nineteenth century, Glasgow was a city of vast undertakings which required the rapid redevelopment and expansion of the city. A single lifetime would see the appearance of textile mills, large foundries and associated engineering shops, the growth of carpet-weaving factories, large breweries and maltings, huge bonded stores, chemical works of all descriptions holding aloft needle-like stacks, and finally the construction of vast engineering shops to build pressure boilers and locomotives. By the 1860s the first generation of shipyards were already proving too limited and the seaward drift began, with new keels being laid at Linthouse, Whiteinch, Fairfield and Scotstoun.

Glasgow's response to the industrial challenges of the nineteenth century produced spectacular wealth and an equally spectacular destruction of the living environment. The ubiquitous soot-laden smoke that lends a touch of *chiaroscuro* to early photographs of the city also gave a greenish tinge to black felt hats. But over and above the mixed blessing of massive industrial development, and the rapid transformation of the city's skyline, these changes are typical of the many ambitious schemes that the city has witnessed over the last two centuries. From the seemingly impossible dream of deepening the Clyde up to the city's quaysides (largely achieved during the 1780s) to the conception and planning of the Garden Festival (continuing a century-long tradition of staging large-scale exhibitions and luring millions of visitors) is undoubtedly a long leap over two centuries. But it shows that the Glasgow Man, memorably anatomised in Charles Oakley's indispensable *The Second City*, as well as having a cool head and a tidy mind, still possesses a vision of the future. That way he is imperishable.

Of course, much of Glasgow's physical upheaval this century has been municipal in origin, a valiant attempt to relieve the terrible congestion bequeathed by the Victorians. Yet, despite the social conditions for which the city has long (some would say far too long) been notorious, the citizens have always known that change must come. From the Calton Weavers to the Upper Clyde Shipyard Workers Glasgow people have always been too thrawn to lie back and take the medicine that has been prescribed for them. Often this refusal has taken violent form—witness the events of the 1837 Cotton Spinners strike, the Chartist agitation for electoral reform and the pressure for a forty-hour working week in the aftermath of the First World War—but the aims of those involved have usually been justified by history. More recently there has been the irrepressible Glasgow chauvinism, described by a recent commentator as 'a formidable if sometimes ill-founded kind of sub-nationalism (though Glaswegians would demur at the sub)'.

Finally, what must strike any student of Glasgow's history (and perhaps reduce him or her to despair) is the impossibility of making neat generalisations that stick. There is an unpredictable quality to the place, a heterogeneousness amongst her people, a feeling that change is always in the air (never more so than in the 1980s) and that events—whether triumphs or disasters—will probably happen with dramatic suddenness. It takes an exception like the Burrell Gallery to prove the rule.

The city's sons and daughters have inherited a large degree of warm heart in their make-up as well as having canny heads. This quality is discernible in the most revered self-made figures like David Dale or Thomas Lipton as well as in the most notorious—even Madeleine Smith's worst detractors could not claim she lacked passion. It is this unpredictable rogue strain (perhaps the product of successive waves of Celtic immigration?) that has in the past thrown up an Alexander Smith, a John Maclean, a Charles Rennie Mackintosh, a James Bridie out of the most unlikely circumstances. Where else in mainland Britain does religious adherence still swing votes in local politics? Who else would have spent £60 million restoring the Underground—and still talk about bringing back the trams to the city centre? Who else is so quick to make legendary heroes out of her sportsmen, her political misfits, her creative artists, her bloated plutocrats?

If David Dale appeared, Rip Van Winkle-like, in George Square tomorrow he probably wouldn't recognise the city created by the processes he helped set in motion. On the other hand, we like to think he would know exactly where he was once he started to talk to people. And in no time at all he would be eating fish suppers, walking on the Green, popping into the Third Eye Centre, or even watching an Old Firm game—in his case, probably from the Directors' Box. Glasgow cherishes her deserved reputation for making the stranger welcome. In the past this has been cited as a compensation for her lack of other attractions; now it can be used as an added lure for tourists and visitors.

III

The passages selected for this anthology have come from a wide variety of contemporary sources: Acts of Parliament, official reports, newspapers, periodicals, guidebooks, pamphlets, diaries, letters, memoirs, novels and poems—both published and unpublished. History books have been resorted to only in the absence of other sources or where the author had first-hand knowledge or provided a contemporary account.

The aim of the anthology is not primarily to provide a source book for a history of Glasgow (although it could be used as a first step) but to illustrate, as far as possible from contemporary documents, events and moments in the lives of the people of Glasgow over the last two hundred years, triumphs and disasters both public and private. (Some obviously key events have had to be excluded, on the grounds of either over-familiarity or the unsuitability of the material found: the City of Glasgow Bank crash, the two Ibrox disasters, the *Daphne* sinking, the 1911 Exhibition, the launch of the two *Queens*, for example, but the diligent reader should turn for guidance to the list of further reading.) The idea was to reflect the life of the city as seen and felt at the time, retaining the inevitable bias and prejudice that this implies: how people lived, how they worked, how they spent their spare time, and how they were viewed by outsiders, the see-Glasgow-in-one-night journalists, curious literary folk and tourists from abroad.

The selected extracts are, whatever else besides, 'foreground' material with all the benefits of immediacy and emotional colour, but also containing the liabilities caused by individual partiality and selectivity. For example, Dorothy Wordsworth reached Glasgow clearly not in the best of spirits in 1803. The following day she said it 'rained very hard' (this from a Lake District dweller) and she was depressed. Two marvellous incidents—the sight of the merchants in the Tontine coffee house and the boys running beside their carriage—stand out all the more vividly. On a different note, Alexander Smith's account of the 1848 riots betrays the conflicting feelings of a man who in the twenty intervening years has climbed the social ladder and cannot condone the violent behaviour of the 'operatives'. Even so, it is a lively, almost cinematic account, conveying something of what it must be like to be on the wrong end of a bayonet. So many of these passages hardly need the intrusion of notes or an introduction—they speak for themselves, as in the heart-rending diary entry by David Willox on the death of his young son in 1886. The first-hand and eye-witness accounts are naturally the most vivid, but other more dispassionate pieces—newspaper reports, official statements, rules and regulations even—have value too, providing atmosphere and detail. Indeed, it is remarkable how much suppressed emotion can be detected in a factual report like the firemaster's on the Cheapside Street fire. They are all the stuff of history, helping us get a sense of people's lives, to make contact however limited, with the social fabric of Glasgow over the past two hundred years.

This anthology is a modest attempt to reassert the value of personal observation and description in understanding the past. The passages chosen vary greatly in style and approach. They have been selected not on any grounds of personal celebrity or literary achievement but rather for the quality of the observations—whether of great events or everyday life. The passages are arranged chronologically rather than by category—the index caters for the latter approach. Each extract has a brief introduction providing biographical and background detail. Minor elisions from passages have not normally been indicated but major ones are indicated by . . . The occasional spelling mistake (as Dickson's for Dixon's, for example) has been corrected; otherwise the passages have not been tampered with. The source of each passage is given at the end of each extract. Much of the material may be consulted in The Mitchell Library, Glasgow.

I

The Beautifullest City (1773–1800)

Introduction

Visitors to Glasgow in the last quarter of the eighteenth century were still struck by its village-like appearance. Even though Mennon's map shows that by the 1780s the building of the New Town (known rather grandly as 'the extended Royalty') was well under way, there were still extensive open bleachfields and washing greens within the city limits. Jamaica Street marked the westward boundary and there were few mansions in existence north of the present line of George Street until well into the new century. Sheep were allowed to graze in George Square and the newly-opened St Enoch Square (1783).

Rapid urbanisation was due to begin with a growing flood of immigrants, mainly from the West Highlands, coming to work in large cotton mills under construction near the city boundaries. Glasgow's population was around 28,000 in 1763; by the turn of the century it was 47,000, with another 30,000 living in adjacent suburbs to the south and west.

By the 1790s the population was increasing at the rate of about 2,000 a year (despite the enlistment of thousands of men for the Napoleonic Wars). As merchants and fledgling industrialists moved away from the High Street area to new mansions further west, so their place was taken by the incomers. Living conditions in the overcrowded wynds were increasingly favourable to the spread of contagious diseases. Smallpox was the major killer, with more than 40% of children under two dying from it until free vaccination was introduced in 1801.

In 1792 the Royal Infirmary was built to offer basic surgery and medical care, supported by public benefactors like David Dale. Water was still drawn mainly from public wells, often discoloured by iron and other mineral impregnation. Piped water, although adopted in eighteenth-century Edinburgh, had to wait in Glasgow until the new century when water from the Clyde was raised by a steam pumping engine. Sewage was still deposited in back courts to await collection by horse and cart. For the better-off the first sewer was laid between George Square and St Enoch in 1790, beginning the growing pollution of the Clyde. The Town Council began a series of projects designed to deepen the Clyde up to the Broomielaw, but nothing was done to counteract regular flooding of the Saltmarket area.

With the outbreak of the Napoleonic Wars European trade was always uncertain and demand for cotton goods fluctuated. Conditions in the mills were harsh; workers experienced further misery when wages were cut and later there was a harvest failure.

At the other end of the social scale there was a flourishing club life. Some of these clubs, like the Hodge Podge, had pretensions to being debating societies but most were colourful throwbacks to the leisurely lifestyle of the tobacco lords. The home life of the new middle classes became more refined, in keeping with the fashionable new mansions they occupied. Intoxication in the dining room was being replaced by the tea urn and piano recitals in the drawing room.

Eventually with the development of the iron-framed power-loom and the increasing use of steam power the new cotton industry became urbanised. Large mills for spinning, weaving and dyeing cotton were put up in Anderston, Mile End and Hutchesontown, employing thousands of men, women and children under the same roof. In the eastern districts of Calton and Bridgeton cotton yarn was being produced on spinning jennies in the home, but this method would become outmoded in the next century.

Associated industries like bleaching and printing were thriving. Fortunes were made by the new cotton kings like Henry Monteith. Other traditional industries, often situated along the waterfront, also prospered. It was a time when there was a steady confidence once again after the sudden demise of the tobacco trade. A contemporary observer remarked that young men in Glasgow 'endeavour to seem extremely busy . . . distressed by an extensive correspondence or the management of a multiplicity of affairs'.

1773: Boswell and Johnson at the Saracen's Head

Boswell and Johnson put up at the Saracen's Head Inn on their way to the Western Isles. Boswell must have been delighted to be able to defend Adam Smith in his praise of Glasgow's elegance. Smith's lectures at Glasgow University on Rhetoric and Belles-Lettres had made a lasting impression on him during 1759–60 (when he was supposed to be studying Civil Law). Smith in turn regarded Boswell favourably, complimenting him on his 'happy facility of manners' (a compliment Boswell typically never tired of repeating). Johnson seems to have been disappointed of any learned or interesting conversation either from the professors (Thomas Reid, Moral Philosophy, and John Anderson, Natural Philosophy) or from the University printers (Robert and Andrew Foulis), the former too wary and the latter too inquisitive and lacking in respect.

This extract is from the original manuscript of Boswell's journal, discovered only in 1930 in an old croquet box in Malahide Castle.

Friday 29 October. The professor of the university being informed of our arrival, Dr. Stevenson, Dr. Reid, and Mr. Anderson breakfasted with us. Mr. Anderson accompanied us while Dr. Johnson viewed this beautiful city. He had told me that one day in London, when Dr. Adam Smith was boasting of it, he turned to him and said, 'Pray, sir, have you ever seen Brentford?' This was surely a strong instance of his impatience and spirit of contradiction. I put him in mind of it today, while he expressed his admiration of the elegant buildings, and whispered him, 'Don't you feel some remorse?'

. . .

Professors Reid and Anderson, and the two Messieurs Foulis, the Elzevirs of Glasgow, dined and drank tea with us at our inn, after which the professors went away; and I, having a letter to write, left my fellow-traveller with Messieurs Foulis. Though good and ingenious men, they had that unsettled speculative mode of conversation which is offensive to a man regularly taught at an English school and university. I found that, instead of listening to the dictates of the sage, they had teased him with questions and doubtful disputations. He came in a flutter to me and desired I might come back again, for he could not bear these men. 'O ho! sir,' said I, 'you are flying to me for refuge!' He never, in any situation, was at a loss for a ready repartee. He answered, with quick vivacity, 'It is of two evils choosing the least.' I was delighted with this flash bursting from the cloud which hung upon his mind, closed my letter directly, and joined the company.

We supped at Professor Anderson's. The general impressions upon my memory is that we had not much conversation at Glasgow, where the professors, like their brethren at Aberdeen, did not venture to expose themselves much to the battery of cannon which they knew might play upon them.

Boswell's Journal of a Tour to the Hebrides with Samuel Johnson, ed Frederick Pottle and Charles Bennett (1936).

1775: The Deepening of the Clyde

John Golborne, a civil engineer from Chester, was commissioned by the Town Council in 1768 to study the possibility of deepening the Clyde from Dumbuck Ford, near Dumbarton, right up to Broomielaw quay. His ingenious suggestion was that transverse jetties should be built from both banks to speed up the flow of the Clyde and cause it to scour its bed. This work began in 1773 and two years later (when 117 jetties were completed) Dumbuck had nearly 7 feet of water at low tide, while at the Broomielaw there was 14 feet. Golborne was rewarded with an *ex gratia* payment of £1,500 subscribed by the city's merchants. This is part of his initial report.

The River Clyde is at present in a state of nature, and, for want of due attention, has been suffered to expand too much; for the sides in most places being much softer than the bottom, the current has operated there, because it could not penetrate the bed of the River, and has by that means gained in breadth what is wanting in depth.

I shall proceed on these principles, of assisting nature when she cannot do her own work, by removing the stones and hard gravel from the bottom of the River where it is shallow; and, by contracting the channel where it is worn too wide, for quantities of sand brought down by the spates form banks in the channel, to the great detriment of the navigation.

. . .

By these means, easy and simple in themselves, without laying a restraint on nature, I humbly conceive that the River Clyde may be deepened so as to have four or perhaps five feet depth up to the Broomielaw at low water; and I am humbly of opinion, that, by removing these several obstructions, the surface of low water will be lowered considerably. Let us suppose one foot only. By general estimation, there is a difference of two feet only between the rise of spring and neap-tides in the River Clyde; but at the Broomielaw there is a difference of near three feet, and I shall endeavour to account for it. The tide at full and change, flows till twelve o'clock at Port-Glasgow, and till two at the Broomielaw; hence, there is two hours difference in the time of high water at those places; or, in other words, it has ebbed two feet at Port-Glasgow before it is high water at Broomielaw. Now, the spring-tides flowing much quicker than the neaps, rise three there; but the latter, not being impelled with that force, are languid and do not flow so quick, and consequently are not raised so high, and the great breadth of the River contributes not a little to this evil, because the tide having but a given time to flow, cannot fill that large space before the reflux comes on. When the River is confined to a proper breadth by jetties, the intermediate space will be filled up with sand carried down by the spates and the fitts brought by the tides, and become firm land; in proportion, then, as this happens, the neaps will rise higher at the Broomielaw, so as to bear a due proportion with the other parts of the River. I have before observed, that the surface of the low water would be lowered one foot; and the neaps flowing one foot higher, these added to four feet, the depth at low water, make six feet at neap, and nine feet at spring-tides at the Broomielaw. From the observations I made during my short stay, I am induced to think that the tide coming from the sea has not an ample and sufficient communication with the Frith of Clyde. Could a better inlet be given to it, I humbly conceive that it would flow considerably higher at the Broomielaw;—this is a matter worthy of attention.

Reports on the Improvement and Management of the River Clyde and Harbour of Glasgow 1755–1853 (1854).

1782: Glasgow's Urine Put to Good Use

An anonymous manuscript journal in French of a tour in Scotland is now thought to be by the French naturalist Pierre Auguste Broussonet (1761–1807). As usual he came armed with letters of introduction to the local scientists and like Faujas de St Fond (*see 1784*) was more interested in the scientific aspects of a place than the tourist sights. Like most visitors in the eighteenth century, however, he could not help being impressed by the appearance of Glasgow. His only *faux pas* is in attributing the Cathedral to the work of Saxons.

Arrived in Glasgow at eight o'clock. The town has a lovely appearance. The streets are wide, clean and the houses elegantly built for the most part, with vases on top of the facade. They are very elegantly built and several have window frames gilded on the outside. The river doesn't carry large vessels, but business is done through Greenock which is also close to the sea at the estuary of the river. The products are considerable, above all in gauze which is exported to Russia and to several places on the continent. Considerable business is done with America and most of the streets have the names of places in America eg. Jamaica Street, Havannah Street, Virginia Street etc. There are two bridges on the river with five new arches. One has a balustrade. The high church is an ancient church built by the Saxons with a quantity of small windows. There are forty to fifty thousand inhabitants.

Tuesday 11th. I went to the college and handed in a letter to Professor Anderson who showed me the library etc. He has a very nice collection of machines, among which I saw a pneumatic machine used by Newton. He has a machine which collects water on his roof which flows down a tube into his room. On the menu planche he has a thermometer, barometer and wind indicator. I gave a letter to Dr Stevenson who is one of the leading practitioners here, the brother-in-law of Dr Hope, another to Dr Hamilton teacher of anatomy who is a young man—I saw Dr Irvine, teacher of Chemistry. They collect the lichen *omphabrily* and *rupertris* here and by a secret they colour especially curtains with it, which have a lovely colour as of sorrel. This manufactory collects all the urine in the town and distils it in an alembic which contains more than 2000 gallons. It is reduced to powder, which is used for printed calico. Dr Irvine told me he had intended to publish something on indigo—The kelp here gives 20 and 25lbs of alkali per quintal. One acre of ground at the sea-side gives three pounds sterling. Large stones are dumped in the sea to allow the sea wrack to grow on top. I promised to send him some antimony. He makes artificial agates. There are sixty students here in medicine. He would like to do some experiments on soft sulphur which he cannot explain by his theory of heat. There is an equestrian statue of William III in the main street. The High Church cemetery surrounding the church is very large, on the slope of a hill all covered with large flat gravestones. A river flows over an artificial cascade at the back, and beyond is a hill covered with pines. The church, the cemetery and the walls, painted black, have a particularly gloomy air.

Journal of a Frenchman (unpublished manuscript in The Mitchell Library, Glasgow. Translation by Norman Bett).

1784: The Women of Glasgow

As Louis XVII's Commissioner of Mines the geologist Barthélemy Faujas de Saint Fond (1741–1819) travelled extensively throughout Europe. On his tour of Britain he made a point of visiting the eminent scientists of the day and important geological features (including Fingal's Cave). Two things impressed him about

Glasgow: its geology ('The environs of Glasgow present a fertile field of observation, by assemblages of pitcoal, freestone, calcareous stones, and volcanic productions, within very short distances of each other.') and its women.

I was astonished, in a climate so cold and so humid as that of Glasgow, to see the greater part of the lower class of females, and even many of those in easy circumstances, walking about with their heads and feet bare, their bodies covered only with a jump, and a gown and petticoat of red stuff, which descended to the middle of their legs; and their fine long hair hanging down without any other ornament than a crooked comb to keep back that part which would otherwise fall over their faces. This garb of the females, simple as it may be, is not destitute of grace. As there is nothing to fetter their movements, they display an elegance and agility in their gait so much the more striking, as they are in general tall, well made, and of a charming figure. They have a clear complexion, and very white teeth. It is not to be inferred, because they walk barefooted, that they are neglectful of cleanliness; for it appears that they wash frequently, and with equal facility, both their feet and their hands. In a word, the women of Glasgow will be always seen with pleasure by the lovers of simple nature. The children and young folks go also barefooted.

The vicinity of the mountains draws a great number of Highlanders to this city. Their antique vestments, very much resembling those of the Roman soldiers, form a remarkable contrast with the dress of the women and other inhabitants.

In the environs of Glasgow there are considerable coal-mines of excellent quality. They make trade and manufactures prosper; and thereby increase the happiness of the inhabitants.

B. Faujas de Saint Fond, *Travels in England, Scotland, and the Hebrides* (1799).

1787: The Calton Weavers

Calton was an eighteenth-century suburb given over mainly to handloom weaving of cotton. An attempt by the manufacturers to cut rates by 25% led to a four-month strike. Non-cooperators were forcibly restrained by having the work they had done cut out of its frame and burnt. Eventually the magistrates (who later rewarded the soldiers with free shoes and stockings) decided to show a strong hand. The shooting took place near the Drygate bridge and three weavers died immediately, three others later. Many were severely wounded. The Calton weaver's combination was certainly 'daring' but not strictly illegal. The day after the shooting the authorities tried to calm the atmosphere by posting the following proclamation, but more troops had to be brought in before peace was restored.

PROCLAMATION

By the LORD PROVOST and MAGISTRATES of the City of Glasgow, and the SHERIFF of the County of Lanark

WHEREAS a great number of operative weavers, and other evil-disposed persons in the city of Glasgow, and the suburbs thereof, have, of late, formed a most illegal and daring association, assembling together in great crowds, and forming resolutions subversive of all peace and good order; have violently entered the houses of many peaceable inhabitants, and forcibly cut, and carried away, webs from their looms, though they were willing to have wrought them in terms of their bargains with the manufacturers. AND WHEREAS the Lord Provost, Magistrates and Sheriff DID, yesterday, the third day of September current, repair to a place about a quarter of a mile without the city, (where several hundred of people were then employed in the foresaid unlawful and daring offence of cutting webs out of looms) with an intention to apprehend and imprison the most guilty persons, and to endeavour to persuade others to return peacably to their lawful employments; or, at least, to refrain from these unwarrantable practices—Instead, however, of complying with these admonitions, which were delivered with temper and moderation, the said mob attacked the Magistrates, Sheriff and their attendants, in a most daring and unmerciful manner,—who, being overpowered by numbers, were obliged to retreat back to the city; into which they were pursued, many of them being severely wounded and bruised. That the said mob having continued, for some hours afterwards, to keep their station upon the ground they had at first taken up, threatening to carry their outrages to a still greater height than they had formerly done, the Magistrates, attended by a party of the 39th regiment of foot, proceeded to the said ground, in the vicinity of which they found the said mob still assembled, who, without the smallest provocation on the part of the Magistrates and their attendants, made a most furious attack upon them by throwing stones, brickbats and other missile weapons; to defend themselves against which, the Magistrates were reduced to the disagreeable necessity, after due publication of the act against riots, of ordering the military to fire, by which some of these infatuated people were unfortunately killed or wounded. That although the Magistrates and Sheriff deeply regret the disagreeable necessity to which they were reduced, and are exceedingly sorry for the unfortunate individuals who have suffered upon the occasion; yet, as they are informed that the operative weavers are still continuing the before-mentioned lawless and unwarrantable practices, the Magistrates and Sheriff think it their duty to give this public intimation that they are determined to continue their utmost exertions to suppress these daring combinations, by every legal means within their power, whatever the consequences may be to the unfortunate individuals who may suffer by these exertions: ALL PERSONS, therefore, within the said City, are hereby strictly prohibited and discharged from the continuation of these daring combinations and practices and from gathering together, in crowds, upon the streets, particularly in the night time, CERTIFYING to all persons who

transgress, after the publication of this Proclamation, that they will be punished with the utmost rigour of law. And parents and masters are hereby strictly required to keep their children, servants and apprentices within their quarters, in the evenings and in the night time, as they shall answer at their highest peril.
Council-Chamber, 4th Sept. 1787

The Glasgow Mercury 12 September 1787

1788: The London-Glasgow Mail Coach

In 1784 a Mr Palmer of Bath established, with Government backing, what was to become a nationwide system of mail coaches to speed up journeys and make delivery of mail safer. Four years later the new system linked Glasgow with London in three days rather than five. The mail now went under armed guard in the coach rather than with a mounted postboy, and merchants no longer resorted to cutting bank bills in two and sending them by separate posts. These descriptions of the London Mail are from the long memory of Peter Mackenzie, editor of *The Reformer's Gazette.*

We may here stop for a little, and not go much out of our way, to observe, that the London Mail Coach then arrived pretty regularly in Glasgow, at or about five o'clock of the morning, containing of course, the usual mail bags, with some eight or ten passengers, not more, because the Postmasters-General at head-quarters—there were *two* of them in those days in London—viz., the Marquis of Salisbury and the Earl of Chichester, with salaries of £5000 each (not bad for the Post-Office Department),—those high potentates would not permit more than *four* inside, and *six* outside passengers to travel together in the Mail between London and Glasgow. This was absolutely all the direct conveyance between London and Glasgow at that time, occupying three long days' and two nights' journey! And truly it was frequently ludicrous to see some of those weary mail coach passengers as they arrived at their long journey's end, with their faces besmeared, and almost as black as ink, from want of being dressed, shaven, or shorn; and their legs benumbed with cold, or nearly paralysed with heat, according to the seasons: and yawning and sneezing, and rubbing their eyes, as if they had just awakened from a long, dreary and comfortless slumber, but still mustering strength sufficient anxiously to inquire for all loving friends, so long away, and—what news?

. . .

The Mail Coach had the 'Royal' arms conspicuously painted in gold letters on both of its side doors. The Guard thereof in his rich scarlet livery had allotted to him for his own special use a queer projecting seat stuck up *behind* the coach, dangling with a goat's-skin, and also with a bear-skin, to cover his legs or wrap up his 'outward man,' in a wet or a frosty day, but with sufficient space from his high altitude, to see everything before him in or around the coach. He was armed with sword and cutlass at his side; and had also two large carbines, or brass 'blunderbusses,' always ready primed and loaded, within his immediate grasp, for the Mail Coach was sometimes invaded in this country, but oftener in Ireland in those days. We remember a rather exciting scene which took place one evening, just as the coach was about to start from its well-known position near the Tron, at the foot of Nelson Street. An unfortunate gentleman had neglected, or was not able to take out his seat for London in sufficient time; in fact, all the seats had been already pre-engaged and occupied; and it was often the case, that if any lady or gentleman—few ladies travelled so far in those days—really wished, or were required, or necessitated to go from Glasgow to London by the Mail, it was deemed prudent, or essentially necessary for security's sake, to have the seat taken out, and the passage money paid, at least eight or ten days before the journey commenced. No one was permitted to travel in the Mail Coach without being regularly booked,—name and designation written down in 'the way bill,' a duplicate whereof was ready to be given to the Guard for his guidance and government upon the journey. On that occasion, the gentleman alluded to was in a most agitated state, grieving and mourning that he could not be booked in the office, for he had been charged with some important domestic business or other to London, admitting of no delay; so he rushed despairingly out of the office and made his way to the steps of the coach, got up to the very top of it, and squeezed himself underneath the legs, or seat of the driver, into whose hands he had slipped something not at all disagreeable to that person, who soon spread one of his oily coats kindly over him. The accustomed and well trained horses, as if they really understood everything that was going on, were now prancing to get away—the whip and reins of the driver were adjusted, the Guard himself began to sound the last blast of his official horn, as he always did, whether on arriving or departing from Glasgow; but he got his sharp eye instantly fastened on *one* he thought too many on the coach for that journey. He therefore commanded the driver to pull up and wait; and down the Guard came from his seat, requiring the passengers each and every one of them to answer to their names, as he read them aloud from the 'way bill' in his hands. Of course he soon detected the above unlucky gentleman, and required him immediately to dismount, and quit the coach.

Peter Mackenzie, *Reminiscences of Glasgow*, Vol. II (1865).

1789: Rules of the Debtors' Prison

Before its demolition in 1814 the Tolbooth served both as Town House and Prison. The debtors' prison was a superior suite large enough for about twenty 'persons of good character' (Rule 7). As staunch club men the inhabitants drew up strict rules for admission, day-to-day administration and election procedure for a committee headed by a 'Provost'. The practice does not seem to have continued when the new Police Office was opened in Bell Street, but the record book was preserved. A favourite pastime of these gentlemen felons was to toss out into the street a coin that had been heated in a brazier.

RULES AND REGULATIONS TO BE OBSERVED BY THE DEBTORS CONFINED IN THE UPPER STOREY OF THE TOLBOOTH OF GLASGOW

Rule 1st—The provost, collector, and clerk are to be chosen by a majority of the members. It is the duty of the provost to summon the members to attend a court upon the admission of new members, or any other case of emergency. The collector's duty is to receive and take care of the funds, and to see they are applied to a proper use, agreeable to these rules, and to keep a regular account of his disbursements which are to be open to the inspection of the members at all times.

Rule 2nd—The Sabbath-day shall be kept holy, and prayers be said in the forenoon, afternoon, and evening. Every member shall preserve a proper behaviour, and whoever deviates from it shall be severely fined.

Rule 3rd—Upon application being made by any person incarcerated for a civil debt to become a member of these rooms, the provost shall call a court, and take the opinion of the members one at a time; and if no fraud or other crime be alledged against him, it shall then be put to the ballot whether he shall be admitted a member. The manner of balloting shall be as follows:-Every member shall be furnished with a red card and a black one; one of these he is to put in a hat, and the provost shall take them all out. If there are a majority of red, he is admitted a member; if a majority of black ones he is rejected. By this means disputes will be prevented, for no person will know who is *for*, or *against* the candidate.

Rule 4th—Every person admitted a member must immediately pay into the hands of the collector the accustomed garnish of 3s 6d, if between the 15th of September and the 15th of March, and 2s 6d during the remainder of the year, otherwise he cannot be admitted a member, unless he deposits something into the hands of the collector in security, or one of the members of the court become caution for him. The members having been frequently ill used by persons admitted on their promise or that of their friends, when they have been liberated in a short time for the debt, and very dishonestly left the garnish unpaid, it is now made an unalterable rule that if they do not instanly comply with the above terms they cannot be received as members, and accordingly handed down stairs.

Rule 5th—The funds arising from the garnish is to be applied to the furnishing the prisoners with coals, candles, pens, ink, soap to shave with, salt, pepper, and mustard, wafers, and other little necessary articles.

. . .

Rule 9th—Every member, when liberated, shall treat his fellow-prisoners with one shilling's worth of what liquor they think proper. But as it is not meant to take advantage of *poor* persons, it will not be exacted, if they declare upon *their word of honour* to the members that they cannot afford it.

Rule 10th—The smoke of tobacco being very disagreeable to many people, no member of these rooms shall smoke, provided three or more members object to it.

Rule 11th—If any member shall have any of his property stolen, he is at free liberty to search any of the members he may suspect, without giving offence. And if any member is convicted of having robbed his fellow-prisoner, he shall instantly be expelled, and never again be admitted a member.

Rule 12th—The youngest prisoner is to take upon himself the business of officer; his duty is to warn the members, by desire of the provost—to attend courts—to fasten the door before the court is opened—to inform every member of the determination of the court—and to turn down stairs persons who have no business in these apartments . . . .

. . .

Rule 16th—If any quarrel or dispute shall arise among the members, the party offended shall table sixpence, upon which the provost must call a court, within two hours, to hear the parties. And if the pursuer is found in the right, he may lift his sixpence, and the defender must submit to such fine as the court shall inflict.

. . .

Rule 22nd—It is firmly and irrevocably agreed upon, that the members of these rooms shall not permit the jailor or turnkeys to force any person or persons into their apartments, who are thought unworthy of being admitted.

Rule 23d—Seeing that debtors suffer sufficient punishment by being imprisoned, it is unanimously agreed, that if any creditor or creditors shall presume to come into these apartments and insult any of the members, it shall be made a common cause, and every one shall aid and assist to turn such creditor down stairs with sufficient marks of indignity . . . .

At a Court held in the Upper Storey of the Tolbooth of Glasgow, upon Tuesday, the 10th day of February, 1789.

James Pagan, *A Sketch of the History of Glasgow* (1849).

1792: 'Nothing but spires, buildings, and smoke'

Robert Heron's *Observations* is a fairly mundane Scottish travelogue, made interesting by his often fierce asides on manners and morals (e.g. 'Yet, I say not, that in great towns, it is better for the children of the poor to be idle than to be employed: If there be a choice between two such evils, I would rather employ them, work them to death, than send them wandering about the streets, as blackguard boys and infant-strumpets.'). Heron (1764–1807), a Kirkcudbright weaver's son with aspirations to the ministry, exemplifies the eighteenth-century hack: devilling for Sir John Sinclair on the Statistical Account; translating the Arabian Nights; writing a history of Scotland, a life of Burns, a System of Universal Geography, etc, etc: and spending much of his time in and out of the debtors' prison. The account of his Scottish tour was a success, going into a second edition in 1799. The picture of Glasgow it presents is of a city beginning to lose its merchant elegance in manufacturing smoke.

> From Paisley, we continued our journey to Glasgow along a crowded highway. On either hand appeared a cultivated country: Villas, gardens, and decorated fields covering its whole face; with hardly a cottage to be seen. Those fields were nearly, but not entirely bare of their crops. The larger divisions of the fields were formed, for the most part, by well-built walls of stone and lime; the subdivisions, by ditches and hedges . . .
>
> Near Glàsgow a cotton-work was pointed out to me, the machinery of which is wrought by steam. It is impossible to conjecture how far human ingenuity may yet advance in appropriating the powers of inanimate nature, no less than in taming the ferocity and instructing the stupidity of the inferior animals!
>
> Glasgow being situate on a high-lying plain, does not afford such a comprehensive prospect of its extent from any place in the immediate neighbourhood as if it were seated either in a low vale, or on a rising hill. The traveller approaching this city, beholds before him, nothing but spires, buildings, and smoke, spreading out, without any definite limits. Yet, is the prospect grand and interesting. It suggests naturally to the recollection, all that dignity and those honours which man derives from the most splendid exertions of Art, and the happiest social union . . .
>
> The merchants and manufacturers of Glasgow are proprietors of most of the cotton-works through Scotland. This is the centre from which the spirit, the energies of manufacture are spread out over the whole kingdom. Hence is the whole of Renfrewshire and a great part of Lanarkshire in some sort one large straggling manufacturing town. With their manufactures, the providers of the raw materials, and the exporters of the manufactured goods have necessarily increased. The numbers of those who have acquired fortunes have increased with the numbers of those who are busy in the acquisition. The artisans who furnish the necessaries of life; the ministers of elegance and of luxury have all become more numerous. The buildings have been amazingly enlarged. The modes of life have become more luxurious: and Glasgow has increased to

be one of the largest towns in Britain, and one of the most elegant in
Europe.

Robert Heron, *Observations Made in a Journey through the Western Counties of
Scotland in the Autumn of MDCCXCII* (1793).

1792: The Tontine Hotel

The Rev. John Lettice (1737–1832), vicar of Peasmarsh in Sussex and later
chaplain to the Duke of Hamilton, was yet another indefatigable traveller in
Scotland during the last quarter of the eighteenth century, following in the wake of
Johnson and Boswell.

The Tontine Hotel opened in 1783, next to the Council meeting house beside
the Tolbooth on Trongate, and made a speciality of catering for travellers. The
coffee room (opened in May 1784) was used as the Exchange by Glasgow
merchants and there was an assembly room for balls and the like. Despite the
Glaswegian penchant for burning down places of entertainment the Tontine
building lasted until 1912 before succumbing to the flames.

At length . . . we found ourselves under the lofty tower of the Tolbooth; and,
alighting at the piazza which joins it, supported by handsome columns, we
entered the tontine hotel behind them; a house of public accommodation,
worthy of this magnificent city. Its name imports that it was built by
subscription, raised on the modern scheme of survivorship: and no small sum
must have sufficed to carry this establishment to its present state; although the
new stables, and some other of its appendages, are yet incomplete, or remain to
be added. Several apartments, consisting of large dining-rooms, bed-cham-
bers, &c. neatly furnished, and fit for the reception of the most distinguished
travellers, occupy a considerable portion of a large court; removed backward
from the noise of the street. The rest of the house branches out in different
directions; and contains an infinity of rooms and offices on the several stories.
But all were nearly full, or else previously engaged on our arrival, yesterday
afternoon; and we were uncertain, for some hours, whether beds could be
found us within the precincts of the hotel. But an unexpected departure, or two,
toward the evening, fortunately made room.

We had time this morning to examine at leisure an important member of our
hotel, which had, yesterday evening, excited our curiosity, as we contemplated
it from our dining room window opposite. A grand bow, lighted by five lofty
sashes, projects into the court of the hotel: all we could then perceive through
them, was a space apparently considerable, with a number of figures sitting,
standing, or walking about. On entering, we found a room of seventy or eighty
feet in length, with corresponding dimensions of height and breadth; having
another vast window on one of its sides, mingling its auxiliary light with those
of the bow. This was no other than the great subscription coffee-room;

supported by certain annual contributions of more than six hundred of the principal citizens of Glasgow, and members of the university. Half the newspapers of London, the Gazettes from Ireland, Holland and France, and a number of provincial journals, and chronicles of Scotland and England, besides reviews, magazines, and other periodical publications, are objects of the Subscription. At the daily arrival of the post, a more stirring, lively, and anxious scene can hardly be imagined. But no part of the day passes without some concourse of subscribers, or of strangers at the hotel, whom their liberality permits freely to partake the benefit of the room. At those hours, when the news of the morning may be said to have grown cold; the monthly publications claim attention in their turn; or people meet for the sake of looking up their acquaintance, or of engaging in casual parties of conversation.

John Lettice, *Letters on a Tour through various parts of Scotland in the year 1792* (London, 1794).

1791-5: Extracts from the first Statistical Account of Scotland

The first Statistical Account was published (in 21 volumes) in the 1790s, based on a questionnaire circulated to all parish ministers and other well-informed people by Sir John Sinclair, the agrarian reformer.

The City of Glasgow

The following account was assembled from 'the Communications of several respectable Inhabitants'. By now water-powered manufacturing was well established and in 1783 the Glasgow Chamber of Commerce and Manufacturers had been set up. This picture of solid prosperity is perhaps a little premature, since, on the outbreak of the Napoleonic Wars in 1793, most of the city's banks had to suspend dealings.

The variety of manufactures now carried on in Glasgow, which have extended in almost every branch, are very great; but that which seems, for some years past, to have excited the most general attention, is the manufacture of cotton cloths of various kinds, together with the arts depending on it. For this purpose cotton mills, bleachfields, and printfields, have been erected on almost all the streams in the neighbourhood, affording water sufficient to move the machinery, besides many erected at a very considerable distance; and though the number of these mills have increased greatly of late, yet they are still unable to supply the necessary quantity of yarn, required by the increased manufactures, as a considerable quantity is still daily brought from England. This trade not only employs a great number of persons in Glasgow, but is extended over a very large tract of country in the neighbourhood, many weavers being employed by the Glasgow manufacturers, 20 and 30 miles from the city. In 1791, it was computed, that they employed 15,000 looms; that each loom gave employment to nine persons at an average, including women and children, in the different stages of the manufacture, from picking the cotton wool, until the goods were brought to market, making in all 135,000 persons; and that each loom, at an average, produced goods to the value of £100 *per ann.* making £1,500,000. The increase, since that calculation was made, has been very great; but to what extent it is at present carried on, cannot be said with any precision, for want of sufficient data.

. . .

About the year 1760, a very extensive brewery was erected near Anderston, from which large quantities of ale and porter were exported to Ireland and to America. Since that time, a number of others of the same kind have been erected in the city, and so great is the additional increase in the use of malt liquors, that most part of what they now manufacture, is consumed at home. As porter brewed in the city, and its vicinity, is now much more drunk in public houses by tradesmen, than formerly, it has consequently diminished the consumption of whisky, that article so destructive to the health and morals of the people; though still it is to be lamented, that so much of it is yet made use of.

. . .

The increased population of the city, arising from the various branches of manufactures established in it, has necessarily occasioned a greater dissoluteness of manners and more crimes; and hence the necessity of a bridewell, or workhouse, for the punishment and correction of lesser offences, became evident. This institution was begun in the year 1789, when, in order to try the effects of plan of solitary confinement and labour, some buildings belonging to the city and formerly used as granaries, were fitted up as separate cells, for the confinement of persons guilty of crimes meriting such punishment. These have been gradually increased to the number of 64, where the prisoners are kept separate from one another, and employed in such labour as they can perform, under the management of a keeper, and under the inspection of a committee of council, who enquire into the keeper's management, &c. The members of the town council, also, in rotation are appointed to visit, not only this, but the prison and cells near the hospital, once every week, and report whatever appears to them proper, either to be rectified or altered. The keeper has a record of the sentences, on which each prisoner is confined,—keeps an exact account of the wages of their labour, and after defraying the expence of their maintenance, the surplus is paid to them, when the period of their confinement expires; and some have received from £5 to £7. Experience in this and other great towns, where this institution has been established, has demonstrated, that of all the species of punishment for offenders of a certain description, solitary confinement and labour is not only the most humane, but the best calculated to answer one great end of punishment, the amendment of the offender.

As to the manners of the people in general, they are, for the most part, industrious, and *still* economical. They are in general contented and happy in their situation. They grumble at taxes, and the high price of provisions; and some of the more ambitious wish for some more political consequence, than they at present enjoy, under the laws of the Scottish burghs; which they consider as confining the presentation of ministers, and the power of election and offices to a few, in exclusion of the rest, and these they wish to have put on a broader bottom. As they are getting rich, this desire will increase among the people; yet, notwithstanding, there is at present much difficulty to get proper persons, of the merchant rank, to accept of the offices of councillors and magistrates, almost every year furnishing instances of their paying a fine rather than serve.

Riches in Glasgow were formerly the portion of a few merchants. These, from the influence of the manufactures, are now diffusing themselves widely among a great number of manufacturers, mechanics, and artisans. This has made an alteration in the houses, dress, furniture, education and amusements of the people of Glasgow within a few years, which is astonishing to the older inhabitants; and has been followed by a proportional alteration in the manners, customs, and style of living of the inhabitants. And as many of the merchants have of late years been engaging in manufactures and trade, the distance in point of rank and consequence, between merchants and tradesmen, has now become less conspicuous, than it was before the American war.

The Statistical Account, Vol. V

The Parish of Govan

Until 1771 Govan included the village of Gorbals, the land being jointly owned by the Trades Council, the Trades House and Hutcheson's Hospital. Both were extensive, with a combined population of nearly 5,000, and feus had been laid out for building town houses around Gorbals. As this extract reveals, at this time the ground was mainly given over to farming to supply the Glasgow markets.

The lands of Govan are generally well enclosed and divided; and a considerable proportion of those on the S. side of the river is farmed by the proprietors themselves. With the industry and activity of the farmers, which are nowhere more conspicuous, several other circumstances have evidently concurred, in bringing this parish to its present state of improvement. Its vicinity to Glasgow, which, till lately, has, for a number of years, been increasing with astonishing rapidity, procures a sure and ready market for its produce, and furnishes a most convenient and plentiful supply of the best manure; and as no less than 4 branches of the King's highway run through the parish, the carriage to Glasgow of the articles it produces, and of the manure brought from thence, particularly on the S. side of the Clyde, is attended with no sort of difficulty.

. . .

The draught horses in this parish, are mostly above the common size. The mode of farming generally practised renders this necessary. Not to speak of the heavy carts of dung brought out of Glasgow, the plough used in the greater part of the parish is drawn by 2 horses; and it has, of late, been found, that 2 harrows, so constructed and joined together, as to take an equal hold of the ground, may be drawn by 2 such horses managed by one man, and do nearly as much execution as 4 unconnected with one another, drawn by 4 smaller horses, which require 2 men. From the richness of the pasture, in general, it is likewise found expedient to keep milch-cows, of a pretty large size. The number annually fattened in the parish, is not great. They are of a smaller size, and are usually brought from the Highlands. There is only 1 sheep farm in the parish, which consists of about 108 acres. The inundations of the Clyde prevent it from being profitably kept in tillage.

The Statistical Account, Vol. XIV

Cathcart

The Reverend David Dow sums up the situation of Cathcart, a village of nearly 700 souls, mainly living on small farms. Although clearly dependent on the nearby city as their market, they are deeply suspicious of any attempt to set up new industries within their parish. Within a few years the population would be over 1,000 as the village was engulfed by the spread of manufacturing and mining.

Business.—This parish may be considered almost entirely as an *agricultural* district. While the manufactures, of Paisley and Glasgow, have diffused themselves through all the neighbouring parishes, to a much greater distance, they have as yet made but inconsiderable progress in Cathcart. How long this may be the case, it is difficult to determine. Indeed, manufacturers have little encouragement to settle here, from the hopes of finding a cheaper market; as every article of provision sells as high as in Glasgow, with the additional expence, of sending to that town, for those necessaries which the parish cannot afford. There is neither butcher, brewer, nor baker, within its bounds: At the same time the parish abounds with many other articles, essentially necessary to the manufacturer, and without which indeed, he cannot go to work; such as coal, lime and water. Upon the Cart, there are many favourable situations for erecting machinery for cotton spinning; it is not to be expected, that they will much longer remain unoccupied. Indeed, we believe, proposals have already been made, by one of the chief adventurers in that business, for erecting a work of this kind. How far such works may ultimately prove beneficial to the persons immediately concerned, time alone can determine; but persons living in the neighbourhood have no great reason to wish for their establishment, as, by all accounts, they bring along with them, many causes of disturbance, and many other inconveniencies.

. . .

Manners and Character. —The manners and character of the people here, as well as in all other parishes, are various. It would be doing injustice to many individuals of every station, not to make many favourable exceptions; but, at the same time, it must be acknowledged, that the neighbourhood of so great a city as Glasgow, has, perhaps unavoidably, a very pernicious influence on the morals of the inhabitants. The frequency of their communication with that town, has extended their knowledge, at the expence of their virtue; and they have acquired a taste for many of those vices, which flourish luxuriantly in so rank a soil. Conversing, not with the moderate and rational part of the citizens, but with the violent and intemperate, they imbibe their notions, which they transplant with them into the country, greatly to the annoyance of their more peaceable neighbours. Thus, there is reason to lament the decline of that primitive innocence, and simplicity of manners and character, by which people, living in more remote situations of the country, are happily distinguished.

The Statistical Account, Vol. V

II

Fervent in Business (1800–1870)

Introduction

1800 to 1870 was a further period of spectacular growth, with Glasgow pushing its way to the position of Second City of the Empire, Workshop of the World. The old city boundaries could not contain the expansion. By 1830 the population had quadrupled since 1800 to 200,000, and by 1870 it was half a million. Building schemes went on apace: private, like the new merchant city around George Square, the 'new town' occupying agricultural land to the west and the development of the residential estate of Laurieston to the south; public—infirmaries, asylums, theatres, court house, bridges—the beginnings of Victorian civic architecture; and industrial—springing up round the city were cotton weaving and spinning mills, chemical works, iron foundries, warehouses, many of them concentrated in the Port Dundas area. The face of Glasgow was changed also by the railway companies, whose lines and stations drove great wedges into the heart of the city. The street pattern as we know it today was now established.

Change was not merely physical. Politically Glasgow was hot for reform, as the demonstrations in the early 1830s with their banners of *Liberty or Death* showed. The Reform Act of 1832 was received with jubilation, and in the following year the Reform of the Royal Burghs Act ensured a more democratic way of electing town councillors.

This was the Age of Progress, and from one point of view Glasgow was certainly prospering. Her ability to keep moving, to turn her hand to a new industry as an old one began to fail, served her well: from textile to chemical manufacturing, from iron-founding to shipbuilding. The speed of progress too was amazing: in just seven years, from 1856 to 1863, iron shipbuilding on the Clyde produced 636 vessels, with a tonnage of 377,176.

Just as Glasgow in its present post-industrial phase is being promoted as a tourist attraction, so it was in the early part of the nineteenth century—a place with its own delights and a starting point for excursions, such as going 'doon the watter' in the new steamboats or treading the banks of Loch Lomond. But it was not only pastoral scenery that attracted visitors—high spots of any visit were the wonders of the industrial age: bleaching works, chimneys, chemical factories, mills (especially New Lanark, where the visit also included the Falls of Clyde). Literary tourists came as well: the Wordsworths, Southey, Hawthorne, Harriet Beecher Stowe and others. Trade and tourism, aided by improved transport (revolutionised, in fact, by steamboats and railways), led to the building of more hotels. By the second half of the century the tourists had become sensation-seekers, venturers into the Dark Places of Glasgow.

For there was an obverse side to the success story. As the city grew and immigrants flocked from the Highlands (in the wake of the Clearances) and Ireland (in the Hungry Forties) to seek work in the factories and on the railways, the pressure on available housing became more and more acute. Once-large houses were divided up into single-room flats; the notorious backlands appeared. The overcrowding bred disease: the first major typhus epidemic was in 1817, there were two cholera outbreaks in 1831–32 and 1848–49. Attempts were made to combat the overcrowding, the squalor, the disease, the crime—this period saw the creation of temperance and anti-vice societies and the growth of civic responsibility for police, a fire service, public health, water supply and sewage disposal, street lighting, cleansing—all the things taken for granted today.

It was during this time too that Glasgow began to have a recognisable literature of its own: histories, guides, statistical accounts appeared, including some of the most famous Glasgow books written, such as Hugh Macdonald's *Rambles Round Glasgow* and John Strang's *Glasgow and its Clubs.* There was a realisation that the growing city itself could provide raw material for creative writing—for novels rather than poetry: the only poet who seized on the new Glasgow of shrieking trains, blazing apocalyptic foundries, and harbours forested with masts, was Alexander Smith in his poem 'Glasgow' (1854)—this kind of poetry had to wait another hundred years to be exploited. However, the Glasgow novel developed, from episodic beginnings in Galt's *The Steamboat* (1822) and Thomas Hamilton's *Cyril Thornton* (1827), through Dickensian sagas like George Mills's *The Beggar's Benison* (1866), to melodramatic social commentary in David Pae's *The Factory Girl* (1868).

Glasgow, then, was fervent in various kinds of business: its industrial success creating problems and the problems in turn needing urgent solutions, and providing the background for the consolidation of the city's reputation both as the greatest city in Britain, outside London, and the most fearsome.

1800: The Watchman's Duties

After two previous attempts to set up an official force to combat increasing lawlessness, the Glasgow Police Act established Britain's first police brigade in November 1800. At first it comprised only seventy-five men armed with staves and rattles under a Master of Police for a population of nearly 48,000. Street scavenging, lamplighting and firefighting also became police duties. The Police Act re-drew the map of Glasgow, establishing twenty-four administrative wards. These did not yet include areas like Calton and Anderston (still in the Barony parish that took in large areas north of the Clyde). This account is by Dr John Aitken, later the city's Commissioner of Police.

> Our first start with a police force took place in 1800, in the Laigh Kirk session-house, which was the first office. We had 68 watchmen and 9 day officers; and our impression was, that this force was so large and overwhelming, that it would drive iniquity out of the city as though by a hurricane. On this first night great-coats and staves were served out to each watchman—the latter not the ordinary sticks which were recently in use, but joiner-made staves, about four feet long, painted of a chocolate-brown colour, and the running number painted on each. Each man's number was also painted on the back of the great-coat, between the shoulders, in white-coloured figures, about 6 inches long, and of a proportionate breadth. A lantern and two candles were also served out

to each man—the one lighted and the other in reserve, it being understood that the 'candle doups' became the perquisite of the man himself. This first turning-out of the force was a great event, and before being told off to their respective beats, a number of the men exercised their lungs in calling the hours, to show how rapidly they had acquired proficiency in this important part of the watchman's functions. It is proper to state, that before beats were assigned to the watchmen, or lights served out to them at all, they did duty a little while after they were embodied, by patrolling the streets in squads of a dozen or more, headed by officers. Our staff of officers, as contradistinguished from watchmen, amounted actually to only nine, and even these were divided into three divisions of three men in each, namely, a sergeant and two officers. The duties of the sergeants, so far as they went, were exactly similar to those now performed by the lieutenants of police. The clothing of the officers consisted of blue cloth coats as at present, with blue vests and blue knee breeches, but the seams were welted over with red stripes, and the sergeants were distinguished from the common officers by having shoulder-knots of red and blue mixed worsted thread.

. . .

Our second police-office was up one stair in the locality long known as the *'Herald Office'* Close. It was on the north-west corner of Bell street, with a front to Candleriggs. Our third office was in Candleriggs over the Mainguard House; and here we got on swimmingly, for, not content with one large room as before, for sergeant, officers, and prisoners, we had two large walled presses or closets, one for males, and the other for females, into which the refractory might be locked up. But more than this, we had a large room underneath, in which no less than seven wooden cells were constructed, sufficient for the accommodation of seven different prisoners. We thought there was no danger of us running short of space now, and that we had provided prison accommodation to serve us for a generation. But our business increased amazingly, so much so, that in two years we were obliged to remove to more commodious premises, viz., an old packing-box and joinery establishment, situated exactly on the site of our present police buildings. In about fifteen years, however, our trade had increased so tremen-dously, that we conceived the bold intention of pulling down the joiners' shop, and rebuilding entirely from the foundation

. . .

At the commencement we had no fire brigade—that department being specially under the charge of the magistrates. Neither had we any separate scavenging squad. The watchmen were engaged to do the duty of scavengers on two days of the week, and for two hours each day. In the summer mornings, they were relieved at four o'clock, but instead of going to bed they plied the broom till six. In the winter mornings, they knocked off at six, when they immediately went to bed for a comfortable sleep, and, with renovated strength they commenced their sweeping operations at twelve noon. As there were no fewer than sixty-eight of them, they went rapidly over a large extent of ground, and two hours each day, for two days in the week, were found quite sufficient for the cleansing operations. The squad was superintended by one of the officers, who appeared on duty in a short blue coat with a red neck. This jacket was manufactured out of the uniform coat of last year, which had been turned, and had the tails rumped off; and, in this way he preserved the uniform of the current year, in which to make a figure before the citizens.

There was no causewaying squad, originally, under the charge of the police. The magistrates managed this department and kept it up from a small assessment called 'road money.' I may also add, that when the fire brigade was under charge of the magistrates, before being added to the police, the superintendent of the fire engines was a master slater, carrying on his business in town and country as a slater, and residing within the city, wherever he might please to choose a dwelling-house. In those days the fire drum was beat off from the Mainguard House, Candleriggs, by the regimental drummer on duty; on midnight alarms he was escorted by two men of the military guard; and it was usual for the guard to turn out to assist at the fires, by keeping the ground clear, and, on occasions of large fires, and of several hours' continuance, we had a reinforcement of sometimes two or three hundred men from the infantry barracks, for the same purpose, viz., to keep a clear space and course for the men employed.

In these early times the officers and watchmen assumed a discretion in the performance of their duty, which would look rather queer at the present day. It was nothing uncommon then for a watchman to take a man to the office and lock him up for a few hours, and then let him out again, without any charge being entered, or any record kept of the proceedings. I remember well a stern old pensioner, named Jaikey Burns, who officiated as an officer. Jaikey had a mortal antipathy to Irishmen, and whenever, in the case of any street disturbance, he heard the brogue uttered, he was sure to take the unhappy owner of it into custody, whether he was the assaulting or assaulted party, holding it to be sufficient evidence of guilt that the man was a Patlander. In fact, it was alleged, that in these times many a poor fellow was locked up for no other offence than that he was an Irishman.

. . .

Each watchman had a wooden box, called a sentry-box, for resting in when he felt fatigued, or when the weather was cold and rainy. The wild youths of the town used often to lock Dogberry in his nest altogether, and sometimes they even tumbled the box over on its face, in which position the poor fellow lay till relieved by his fellow-watchmen. In these times there was no regulation to prevent all the watchmen in the city being in their boxes at one and the same time; and it was well known that many a snooze they took in these retreats, while the city took care of itself. This system would be considered the height of absurdity now-a-days; but when (fully 40 years ago) it was resolved that not more than every alternate watchman should take shelter in his box, this modified arrangement was thought to be one which savoured of inhumanity. The watchmen went on duty at 10 in summer, and came off at 4; and at 9 in winter, and came off at 6. As there was no retiring muster-roll called, however, these hours were not, by any means, strictly observed, and many a one was snug in bed, when his betters believed him to be on duty. There were no detective or criminal officers in those days, as distinguished from common policemen.

A Sketch of the Incorporation of Masons, ed. James Cruikshank (1879).

1803: Dorothy and William Wordsworth

Dorothy and William Wordsworth found Scotland in general a very foreign country: 'we were reminded ten times of France and Germany for once of England'. They were accompanied by Coleridge who disliked the open Irish carriage they travelled in—and who, wet and ill, parted from the others at Arrochar. Dorothy displays here not only her powers of observation—sharp and practical—but also her affinity with children (a *fantoccine* was a puppet show).

> *Monday, August 22nd.* Saw nothing remarkable after leaving Bothwell, except the first view of Glasgow, at some miles distance, terminated by the mountains of Loch Lomond. The suburbs of Glasgow extend very far, houses on each side of the highway,—all ugly, and the inhabitants dirty. The roads are very wide; and everything seems to tell of the neighbourhood of a large town. We were annoyed by carts and dirt, and the road was full of people, who all noticed our car in one way or other; the children often sent a hooting after us.
>
> Wearied completely, we at last reached the town, and were glad to walk, leading the car to the first decent inn, which was luckily not far from the end of the town. William, who gained most of his road-knowledge from ostlers, had been informed of this house by the ostler at Hamilton; it proved quiet and tolerably cheap, a new building—the Saracen's Head. I shall never forget how glad I was to be landed in a little quiet back-parlour for my head was beating with the noise of carts which we had left, and the wearisomeness of the disagreeable objects near the highway; but with my first pleasant sensations also came the feeling that we were not in an English inn—partly from its half-unfurnished appearance, which is common in Scotland, for in general the deal wainscots and doors are unpainted, and partly from the dirtiness of the floors. Having dined, William and I walked to the post-office, and after much seeking found out a quiet timber-yard wherein to sit down and read our letter. We then walked a considerable time in the streets, which are perhaps as handsome as streets can be, which derive no particular effect from their situation in

connexion with natural advantages such as rivers, sea, or hills. The Trongate, an old street, is very picturesque—high houses, with an intermixture of gable fronts towards the street. The New Town is built of fine stone, in the best style of the very best London streets at the west end of the town, but, not being of brick, they are greatly superior. One thing must strike every stranger in his first walk through Glasgow—an appearance of business and bustle, but no coaches or gentlemen's carriages; during all the time we walked in the streets I only saw three carriages, and these were travelling chaises. I also could not but observe a want of cleanliness in the appearance of the lower orders of the people, and a dullness in the dress and outside of the whole mass, as they moved along. We returned to the inn before it was dark. I had a bad headache, and was tired, and we all went to bed soon.

Tuesday, August 23d.—A cold morning. Walked to the bleaching-ground, a large field bordering on the Clyde, the banks of which are perfectly flat, and the general face of the country is nearly so in the neighbourhood of Glasgow. This field, the whole summer through, is covered with women of all ages, children, and young girls spreading out their linen, and watching it while it bleaches. The scene must be very cheerful on a fine day, but it rained when we were there, and though there was linen spread out in all parts, and great numbers of women and girls were at work, yet there would have been many more on a fine day, and they would have appeared happy, instead of stupid and cheerless. In the middle of the field is a wash-house, whither the inhabitants of this large town, rich and poor, send or carry their linen to be washed. There are two very large rooms, with each a cistern in the middle for hot water; and all round the rooms are benches for the women to set their tubs upon. Both the rooms were crowded with washers; there might be a hundred, or two, or even three; for it is not easy to form an accurate notion of so great a number; however, the rooms were large, and they were both full. It was amusing to see so many women, arms, head, and face all in motion, all busy in an ordinary household employment, in which we are accustomed to see, at the most, only three or four women employed in one place. The women were very civil. I learnt from them the regulations of the house; but I have forgotten the particulars. The substance of them is, that 'so much' is to be paid for each tub of water, 'so much' for a tub, and the privilege of washing for a day, and, 'so much' to the general overlookers of the linen, when it is left to be bleached. An old man and woman have this office, who were walking about, two melancholy figures.

The shops at Glasgow are large, and like London shops, and we passed by the largest coffee-room I ever saw. You look across the piazza of the Exchange, and see to the end of the coffee-room, where there is a circular window, the width of the room. Perhaps there might be thirty gentlemen sitting on the circular bench of the window, each reading a newspaper. They had the appearance of figures in a fantoccine, or men seen at the extremity of the opera-house, diminished into puppets.

I am sorry I did not see the High Church: both William and I were tired, and it rained very hard after we had left the bleaching-ground; besides, I am less

eager to walk in a large town than anywhere else; so we put it off, and I have
since repented of my irresolution.

Dined, and left Glasgow at about three o'clock, in a heavy rain. We were
obliged to ride through the streets to keep our feet dry, and, in spite of the rain,
every person as we went along stayed his steps to look at us; indeed, we had the
pleasure of spreading smiles from one end of Glasgow to the other—for we
travelled the whole length of the town. A set of schoolboys, perhaps there might
be eight, with satchels over their shoulders, and, except one or two, without
shoes and stockings, yet very well dressed in jackets and trousers, like
gentlemen's children, followed us in great delight, admiring the car and longing
to jump up. At last, though we were seated, they made several attempts to get
on behind; and they looked so pretty and wild, and at the same time so modest,
that we wished to give them a ride, and there being a little hill near the end of
the town, we got off, and four of them who still remained, the rest having
dropped into their homes by the way, took our places; and indeed I would have
walked two miles willingly, to have had the pleasure of seeing them so happy.
When they were to ride no longer, they scampered away, laughing and
rejoicing.

Dorothy Wordsworth, *Recollections of a Tour Made in Scotland A.D. 1803*, ed.
J. C. Shairp (1874).

1803: Sabbath Observances

The Rev. James Hall was yet another travelling clergyman (educated at St
Andrews, he became chaplain to the Earl of Caithness), but he chose to see
Scotland 'by an unusual route'—round the coast—with the intention of compar-
ing 'the notions, customs and follies of the people'. His account is enlivened by his
admitted 'propensity to prattle'. The Wordsworths seem to have missed the kind
of goings-on on the Green that Hall relates here, with obvious fascination.

> ...it being Sunday when I landed...on one side of the street,
> almost in every house, I heard psalms singing and fervent prayers ascending to
> the father of the universe, while, on the other, there was nothing to be heard but
> swearing, blaspheming, and the most obscene and abusive language. In short,
> the one side of the street, if appearances were not false, might be called the
> temples of the Holy Ghost; the other, in the language of Rowland Hill, the hot-
> beds of the devil. And it was astonishing to see in some places a set of drunkards
> and debauchees reeling from the bagnios, and, at others, numbers going
> leisurely home with their Bibles under their arm, from places of worship, to
> their peaceful habitations.
>
>   . . .
>
> There are, it seems, notwithstanding the profligacy of many in this city, near
> a hundred praying societies, each of them consisting of about thirty members,

who meet weekly; and, once a month, there is one elected from each of these societies to attend another society or prayer meeting, composed of a member from each of the rest. And, as at each of the particular societies they not only read, pray, and sing psalms, but also converse over religious matters, keeping regular minutes of what is done; so, at each general meeting, they pray, read, and sing psalms, and not only converse on religious subjects in general, but consider of appeals, cases of conscience, and other religious matters laid before them from the societies in the city and environs, of which this is composed. A clergyman, it seems, is always in the chair, at the society composed of delegates from the others. There are certain funds belonging to these societies, appropriated for purchasing religious books, hiring rooms, providing for sick and poor members, paying physicians and apothecaries to attend any of the members when taken ill; and defraying the funeral expense of any deceased member when necessary.

As the different corps of volunteers, the officers in the army, navy, &c. &c. have uniforms, so some teachers of religion here think that, like those that went to the crusades, the different sects of christians should be distinguished in the same manner. This idea has been in part adopted in Glasgow; and some of the various denominations of christians are about to be clothed in uniform. One sect of christians have chosen a green short coat for the men, with green buttons. Though a certain uniform is pointed out to the ladies in it, which is a green skirt and jacket; yet, as they are making some remonstrances, that not being the fashionable colour at present, I understand they are partly to be allowed to dress as they please; provided their bosom and neck are properly covered. So that it is probable, as the Quaker is known by his broad brimmed hat, and his lady by her plain grey bonnet, the Davidalites, the Unitarians, the Anti-trinitarians, the Haldanites, the Universal Redemptionists, &c. &c. will all be known, on Sunday, and perhaps on other days, by the uniform and badges of their peculiar sect.

. . .

The prosperity of Glasgow is truly astonishing, and shews what industry can do.

. . .

But commerce and manufactures have their inconveniencies, and there is too good reason to conclude, that though the external circumstances of the common people are considerably bettered by them, yet their morals are not. The manners of the common people here were certainly never so profligate; and their high wages but serve to furnish too many of them with the means of becoming more wicked; and, owing to the mixture of the sexes at the manufactories, infant prostitution is, it seems, not uncommon; and so audacious have some of the little wretches of both sexes become, that if a girl is solicited to go to a manufactory, she will ask if any boys are to work along with her; and a boy, if girls; making these conditions of their engagement. For there are some manufacturers, it seems, who keep their boys and girls separate.

Certain it is, that a high preference is given to servants, labourers, clerks, &c. from the country; as too many of those brought up in the city and its environs, as is too often the case about all great cities, are debauched, and not to be trusted. Nay, so abandoned are some of the lower orders about Glasgow, that, on a Sunday afternoon, in the green, which is a large meadow, with public walks, belonging to the citizens at large, and where hundreds were assembled, (after having, for the special purpose, formed a ring, only a few yards diameter) one of the inhabitants, with an abandoned woman, that had agreed to it, while his companions, and those forming the ring, continued to shout and applaud him, did what, even cats, elephants, and many other of the inferior animals avoid in public, for a Scotch pint of gin.

James Hall, *Travels in Scotland* (1807).

1805: The Merchant City

This is indeed a pleasing picture of the new merchant city being planned and built in the vicinity of George Square, often employing classical forms. Surviving examples include the Trades House in Glassford Street by Robert Adam and Hutcheson's Hospital by David Hamilton. Not so well covered are the new industries appearing on the city's fringes—steam-powered weaving and spinning mills, the Phoenix iron foundry and the warehouses to the north in the area of Port Dundas. Nor is there much said about the populous Calton and Bridgeton districts. The author of this account, Robert Forsyth (1766–1846), trained as a lawyer, but made his living as an author and also by contributing to the first *Encyclopaedia Britannica.*

The city of Glasgow ... contains a vast multitude of beautiful private buildings erected of hewn stone, and in the finest style. At the same time, as these are in a less degree set aloof upon a particular spot, and separated from the ancient buildings, than occurs with regard to the New Town of Edinburgh, their appearance is not that of a great effort of the community, but rather of individual riches. At the same time these very circumstances, that is the position of the new buildings in the nearer vicinity of the old, their situation on different sides of the Clyde, and their separation from each other by ancient buildings, probably operate as a matter of convenience in a commercial and manufacturing city, where most persons are engaged in the pursuits of active life. It also gives to the city an aspect of greater extent and variety to the eye of a stranger. All the streets are well paved with blue basaltic stone or whin-stone, universally used for that purpose in Scotland. Besides this sort of pavement, which is called the *causeway*, and occupies the centre of the street, intended for the use of wheeled carriages and horses, all the principal streets of the ancient part of the city, and the whole streets which have been more recently built, are furnished with a spacious side-pavement for the use of foot-passengers, consisting of great flat free-stones accurately jointed together. The town is at all times, well lighted, and the streets preserved in the best order.

Robert Forsyth, *The Beauties of Scotland*, Vol. III (1805).

1806: David Dale

David Dale was the epitome of the self-made Glasgow man. He owned factories (like the famous New Lanark mills, founded in 1786) employing men, women and children, yet his heart seems often to have got the better of his head. He began working life as an Ayrshire herd-boy, then tried the weaving in Paisley and Hamilton before coming to Glasgow. His first shop was in Hopkirk's Land near the foot of the High Street; from these humble beginnings he never looked back. His portly figure with cocked hat and cane was apparently the inspiration for Scott's Baillie Nicol Jarvie in *Rob Roy*. This extract from an obituary of Dale reveals that he had an original approach to religious observance and believed in good works.

At an early period of life, he was religiously disposed, attended prayer-meetings, and went to Cambuslang, at the time of the striking revival of religion there. Dissatisfied with the Established Church, a few friends united with him in founding a Church on the Independent plan; and he became one of the preachers. In this capacity he continued to officiate statedly till his last illness. With no fluency of eloquence, he was a plain, serious, and very scriptural preacher. To enable him the better to expound the Bible he received some instructions in the Hebrew and Greek languages. In his own temper and conduct, appeared much of the humble, meek, and forgiving spirit of Christianity. When only a journeyman weaver, it has been said that he appropriated a part of his earning to the poor. When his resources were greater, during a time of scarcity, he imported a large quantity of meal, and sold it to the poor at a low rate. That he was the general patron of generous and laudable undertakings, the Glasgow Infirmary, and Missionary and Bible Societies, among many other public institutions, can thankfully bear testimony. We have much pleasure in adding that Mr Dale has left at least 100,000l. to his family, after having appropriated, in his life time, more than twice that sum to purposes of the purest benevolence.

'Biographical Account of Mr David Dale', *The Scots Magazine* (1806).

1807: Plans for a Dock at Windmill Croft

The narrowing of the Clyde meant that winter floods in the city were fairly common. Apart from damage to property, ships tied up at the Broomielaw also suffered. A 'wet-dock' (with lock-gates to maintain a constant water level) was proposed for vacant land on the south bank by the Windmill Croft quay opposite Broomielaw. The famous Scottish engineer John Rennie was commissioned to produce a report on the best site. Windmill Croft was soon found to be too small and was replaced by Kingston Dock in the 1860s.

In regard to giving additional berth-room for vessels lying at the Broomie-law, the most simple and least expensive mode would be to extend the present quay-wall farther down the River, and to raise the whole sufficiently high to be above the height of moderate floods. The present quay-wall is only about 1,120 feet in length, which is by much too short to afford convenient room for vessels to get to the quay to discharge their cargoes speedily: they often now lie in three or four rows abreast of each other, by which great inconvenience is experienced, as well as much detention in the discharging and loading of their cargoes; but, besides this, during floods, particularly at the breaking up of a frost, they are so crowded together, that much damage, as I am informed, frequently ensues, and always much tear and wear. Extending the quay-wall, therefore, farther down the River, would not obviate all these objections; by this plan, no doubt, further quay-room for the berthing of vessels would be obtained, and vessels would thereby be enabled to extend farther downward; of course, they would not be so apt to sustain injury during floods as they now do, there being more room for the floods to pass off; but still, considerable damage would often take place, although perhaps not quite to the extent it now does. The rising and falling of the tide is also an inconvenience to vessels while lying alongside of a quay, by varying the height of their decks so much; whatever improvement, therefore, could be made in this way, would not give the advantages to the vessels frequenting the Port of Glasgow at the Broomielaw, that its importance demands; and I have no hesitation in saying, that this can only be done in a complete, effectual, and convenient manner, by means of a wet-dock. The question therefore is, where can a wet-dock be most conveniently constructed?

If ground could be conveniently found on the City side of the Clyde, and out of the channel of the River, I would greatly prefer one being constructed on the solid ground, clear of the River, and out of the way of its floods; but unfortunately, the buildings on the City side are extended so far to the westward near to the River, and on high ground, that nothing can be done to advantage in this way, unless at a very heavy expense, or unless it is made so far down the River as to be inconvenient for the City.

. . .

On examining the ground with all the attention of which I was able, two situations only appeared to me suitable to the purpose of a wet-dock. The one is, cutting off a part of the present wharf at the Broomielaw, and making a wet-dock partly on this, and partly out of the present channel of the River. The other is that of Windmill Croft, on the south side of the River, where there is a piece of ground clear of houses, just large enough to admit of a convenient wet-dock, with suitable wharfs and warehouses.

The former being nearer to the City than the latter, in point of situation, has, no doubt, the preference, but in other respects, is inferior.

Reports on the Improvement and Management of the River Clyde and Harbour of Glasgow 1755–1853, ordered by the Clyde River Trustees (1854).

1807: The Wonderful Powers of Steam

Sir John Carr (1772–1832) was an English lawyer who for reasons of health did not practise: instead, he travelled and published accounts of his tours; these were widely read for what the *Dictionary of National Biography* calls his 'light, gossipy style'. In Spain he met Byron who begged 'not to be put down in black and white'. Here Carr views the various applications of steam in Glasgow's textile industry. John Duncan's factory was at 120 Argyle Street and Gillespie's calico printing works were in Anderston.

One of the most ingenious pieces of machinery which I saw is Mr. John Duncan's tambouring machine, which he has very recently brought to perfection, by which several needles (one which I saw contains sixty) are put in motion, and perform all the operations of tambouring by steam. This machine will perform as much as sixty women can, and will of course effect a very great reduction in the selling price of the article. The whole of the house in which these machines are is warmed by steam, at a very trifling expense. In mechanics, as applied to manufactures, Mr. J. Duncan has deservedly obtained very high celebrity. I saw also the process of weaving carried on by steam. It was curious enough to see the shuttle impelled backwards and forwards by mere vapour. I should scarcely have been more surprised to have seen a game at shuttlecock performed by similar agency. Simpson's muslin-manufactory is well worthy of notice, as are Thompson's machines for winding thread. At the houses where the singeing machines for burning off the superfluous threads of muslin are used, the traveller may see muslin of fine texture rolled rather slowly over a long and very thick bar of iron, red hot, with such care as not to take fire: formerly the price of singeing one piece, containing ten or twelve yards, was one shilling; it is now one penny. The singer indemnifies against burning. Cotton is the grand staple manufacture of Glasgow, which is carried on to an immense extent. I saw a very large building, intended for a cotton-manufactory, which will be warmed by steam, lighted by gas, and completely fire-proof. I had great pleasure in visiting the extensive calico-works of Richard Gillespie, Esq. In one of the apartments was an hydraulic engine, worked by compressed water, the powers of which were astonishing. Here again steam was the reigning agent: it set a washing and rinsing machine in motion; it printed and dried the calicoes, and warmed the different houses belonging to the manufactory.

Sir John Carr, *Caledonian Sketches, or a Tour through Scotland in 1807* (1809).

1812: Henry Bell and Steamboats

Henry Bell is usually credited with being the first to power a boat by steam. The engine was based on one designed by John Robertson for heating and circulating the water in the public baths at Helensburgh where Bell was manager. This account, written three years after the launch of the *Comet*, is by James Cleland, Superintendent of Public Works of Glasgow and indefatigable chronicler of the city in its formative years.

It was not till the beginning of 1812, that steam was successfully applied to vessels in Europe, as an article of trade. At that period, Mr. Henry Bell, an ingenious, untutored engineer, and Citizen of Glasgow, fitted up, or it may be said, without the hazard of impropriety, that he invented the steam-propelling system, and applied it to his boat, the Comet, for as yet he knew nothing of the principles which had been so successfully followed out by Mr. Fulton.

After various experiments, the Comet was at length propelled on the Clyde by an engine of three horse power, which was subsequently increased to six. Mr. Bell continued to encounter and overcome the various and indescribable difficulties incident to invention, till his ultimate success encouraged others to embark in similar undertakings, which has been done in a ratio only to be credited by the knowledge of the number of vessels which have been placed on the River. Owing to the the novelty and supposed danger of the passage in the Frith below Dumbarton, in vessels which had so small a hold of the water, the number of passengers at the outset were but small. The public, however, having gained confidence by degrees, in a navigation which became at once expeditious and pleasant, it was preferred to every other mode of conveyance; for the expedition of the voyage, and beauty of the scenery on the banks of the Clyde, are such as to attract alike the attention of the man of business and pleasure; and the watering-places all along the coast have been crowded with company beyond all former precedent, in consequence of steam conveyance. It has been calculated that, previous to the erection of Steam-Boats, not more than fifty persons passed and repassed from Glasgow to Greenock in one day; whereas it is now supposed that there are from four to five hundred passes and repasses in the same period. The passage between Glasgow and Greenock is about twenty-six miles, and is usually performed in three hours; and often, when the wind and tide are favourable, it is performed in less than two hours and one-half. The cabin and steerage are fitted up with every suitable convenience; the former is provided with interesting books, and the various periodical publications. Breakfasts, dinners, &c. are provided for those who may require them. The cabin fare is four shillings, and the steerage two shillings and sixpence.

Since the Comet began to ply on the River, it is very common to make the voyage of Campbeltown, Inverary, or the Kyles of Bute, and return to Glasgow on the following day. Steam-Boats have also been sent from the Clyde to Ireland, Liverpool, and London, some of whom weathered heavy gales of wind, and encountered high surfs.

James Cleland, *Annals of Glasgow* Vol. II (1816).

1818: Typhus Stalks the Wynds

In the ill-ventilated wynds and vennels of the old city typhus fever (here called 'Continued Fever') had established a grip since the 1740s when government troops returning from the Low Countries had brought it with them. The first major epidemic was in 1817, destined to be frequently repeated as fresh waves of immigrants fell victim. The author of this graphic description was Professor of Botany and a Physician to the Royal Infirmary, which was closed to typhus sufferers. He suggested building an isolated fever hospital, as well as trying to contain the disease by fumigating the houses of victims. In 1817 the death rate in Glasgow from typhus was about 7 per thousand over the whole population, but far higher in the wynds.

If any man wonders at the prevalence of continued fever, among the lower classes in Glasgow, or at its spreading from their habitations, let him take the walk which I did to-day with Mr. Angus, one of the district Surgeons. Let him pick his steps among every species of disgusting filth, through a long alley, from four to five feet wide, flanked by houses five floors high, with here and there an opening for a pool of water, from which there is no drain, and in which all the nuisances of the neighbourhood are deposited, in endless succession, to float, and putrify, and waste away in noxious gases. Let him look, as he goes along, into the cellars which open into this lane, and he will probably find lodged, in alternate habitations, which are no way distinguished in their exterior, and very little by the furniture which is within them, pigs, and cows, and human beings, which can scarcely be recognised till brought to the light, or, till the eyes of the visitant get accustomed to the smoke and gloom of the cellar in which they live. I have been to-day in several dens of this kind, where I did not see persons lying on the floor near me, till Mr. Angus, whom a previous visit had taught where to find them, inquired after their health. I was in one closet, measuring twelve feet by less than five, on the floor of which, he told me, six people had laid, affected with fever, within these few days, and where I saw the seventh inhabitant now confined. We found in one lodging-house, fifteen feet long, by nine feet from the front of the beds to the opposite wall, that fifteen people were sometimes accommodated; and when we expressed horror at the situation in which they were placed, the woman of the house, somewhat offended, and, I believe, a little alarmed lest we should cause some inquiry to be made by the Police, said, in support of the character of her establishment, that *each family* was provided with *a bed*, and that she very seldom had anybody lying on the floor. I shall only mention one other instance of misery. In a lodging-house, consisting of two rooms separated by boards, the first thirteen feet by eleven, the other fifteen by eight, twenty-three of the lowest class of Irish were lately lodged. To-day there are fourteen, of whom two are confined with fever, three are convalescent, and one only has hitherto escaped. There are only three beds in this house, (denominated, with that facetiousness which enables an Irishman to joke with his own misery, Flea Barracks), one of them in a press half-way up the wall, the others wooden frames, on which are laid some shavings of wood, scantily covered with dirty rags. Most of the patients were lying on the floor. A man, two sons, and an adult daughter, were lying side by side on the floor of the first room, their bedding of the same materials with the others, and the boys being destitute of shirts. Could imagination feign a combination of circumstances more horribly conducive to disease and immorality!

Dr Robert Graham, *Practical Observations on Continued Fever, especially that form at present existing as an Epidemic, with some Remarks on the most efficient plans for its suppression* (1818).

1819: Tenement Development in Bridgeton

Thomas Binnie (1792–1867) was a self-made man, typical of a host of jobbing builders who established themselves in the 1820s and '30s as the city expanded rapidly into what are now its inner suburbs. With little schooling, Binnie came to Glasgow to serve an apprenticeship, then set up in business on his own. With his own hands he built much of Monteith Row, beside the Green, where he also took up residence and became a burgess of the city. Despite short-term setbacks, as described here, Binnie became a rich man, building extensively in the East End, Laurieston and Hutchesontown, erecting ashlar tenements either as a contractor or speculatively on his own behalf. He often drew his own plans and, if this account is accurate, built with incredible speed. This account of his early years was written by his son.

At the time of his marriage my father had taken a lease of Westfield Quarry, near Rutherglen, and he continued to work that quarry for nearly twenty years. He had also, partly with borrowed money, erected a small property in Moore Street, the first he ever built on his own account. His mother and a sister removed into a house in that property, and continued to live there till the death of the former, a number of years later. After stocking his quarry and building this small property, my father had about £500 in his business and looked upon himself as a prosperous man. But misfortune was soon to overtake him. Early in the year 1819 he took a contract to build a tenement of four storeys in Main

Street, Bridgeton. As it was to be finished as quickly as possible, the contract for the whole work was given to him. He did the mason work himself, and for all the other departments he employed sub-contractors, who looked to him for payment. The building was begun about the middle of March, and so rapidly was the work done that the houses were occupied on the 28th May. Instalments of the price were paid as the building proceeded, but fully £400 remained due when the contract was completed, and before any of this was paid the proprietor failed. Some other losses followed, sweeping away the whole of my father's available money, and leaving him somewhat in debt. To add to his troubles, the unusual prosperity which had prevailed in the building trade for a number of years was for a time interrupted shortly after these losses were sustained. Toward the end of 1819 great distress prevailed among the working classes in the city, through want of employment, and the building trade seems to have suffered as much as any other. That winter my father had a large stock of stones in his quarry, and he had all his quarry plant, but he had no work to do, no ready money, and there were some creditors pressing for payment of their accounts. He had two apprentices serving the last year of their time, who lived with him, as the custom was in those days. Their wages were very small; they were good workmen—better than many journeymen—and my father offered them their discharge; but so little hope had they of obtaining work elsewhere that they refused to take it; they preferred to serve out their time. A few jobbings kept the wolf from the door, and also enabled my father to continue to pay his mother twelve shillings a week, a sum he had at the time of his marriage promised to give her as long as she lived. His own household had to be content with less, the family expenditure for food—including that provided for the apprentices—being often during that dreary winter less than ten shillings a week. Good porridge and milk, with a little bread and tea, for breakfast and supper; and potatoes and herrings for dinner, were the standing dishes. But even this economy in expenditure would not pay outstanding accounts when so little money was coming in. My father had in these circumstances to rely on the kindness of three friends who had occasionally lent him money, and probably discounted any small bill he might get in the course of business; for in those days there were no banking facilities for unknown tradespeople. The agent of one of the banks in the city had some time before actually refused to allow my father to open a deposit account. These friends deserve to be named: they were David Logan, Robert Thom, and James Young. My father in his trouble went to one of them and borrowed a sum of money sufficient to clear his most pressing liabilities, promising to repay it on a certain day two or three weeks later. When that day came he went to the second friend with a similar request; then to the third; and by always paying on the day agreed on, by varying the amount borrowed, and the time for which the money was retained, he managed to raise no suspicions of the straits to which he was reduced, and to keep all his creditors satisfied without sacrificing his property by a forced realisation.

T. Binnie, *Memoir of Thomas Binnie* (1882).

1819: Robert Southey cold and uncomfortable

Southey made his Scottish tour in a wet autumn, partly to see Telford's work in
constructing the Caledonian Canal. When he came to Glasgow one would have
expected the Poet Laureate to be introduced to Thomas Chalmers, the evangelical
preacher (see 1823), or other notables in the city. But there is no mention of any
Glasgow intelligentsia whatsoever. Nevertheless this is a lively (if unduly preju-
diced) account of his visit. In fact, the *Journal* was never published in his
lifetime.

We drove to the Buck's Head in Argyle Street. Large as this house is, they
had no room with a fire, when we arrived cold and hungry, at ten o'clock, on a
wet morning.

The Inns in large cities are generally detestable, and this does not appear to
form an exception from the common rule. But it afforded what I cannot but
notice as a curiosity in its kind unique, as far as my knowledge extends. In the
Commodité, which is certainly not more than six feet by four, there was a small
stove, which as I learned from certain inscriptions in pencil on the wall, is
regularly heated in the winter!

A City like Glasgow is a hateful place for a stranger, unless he is reconciled to
it by the comforts of hospitality and society. In any other case the best way is to
reconnoitre it, so as to know the outline and outside, and to be contented with
such other information as books can supply. Argyle Street is the finest part; it
has a mixture of old and new buildings, but is long enough and lofty enough to
be one of the best streets in Gt. Britain. The Cathedral is the only edifice of its
kind in Scotland which received no external injury at the Reformation. Two
places of worship have been neatly fitted up within. I observed, however, three
things deserving reprobation. The window in one of these kirks had been made
to imitate painted glass, by painting on the glass, and this of course had a paltry
and smeary appearance. The arches in those upper passages which at Westminster we used absurdly to call the nunneries, and of which I do not know the
name, are filled up with an imitation of windows: these are instances of the
worst possible taste. The other fault belongs to the unclean part of the national
character; for the seats are so closely packed that any person who could remain
there during the time of service in warm weather, must have an invincible nose.
I doubt even whether any incense could overcome so strong and concentrated
an odour of humanity.

I was much struck with the picturesque appearance of the monuments in the
Church yard—such large ones as we have in our churches, being here ranged
along the wall, so that even on the outside their irregular outline makes an
impressive feature in the scene. They were digging a grave near the entrance of
the Church; had it been in any other situation, I should not have learnt a
noticeable thing. A frame consisting of iron rods was fixed in the grave, the rods
being as long as the grave was deep. Within this frame the coffin was to be let
down and buried, and then an iron cover fitted on to the top of the rods, and

strongly locked. When there is no longer any apprehension of danger from the resurrection-men, the cover is unlocked and the frame drawn out: a month it seems is the regular term. This invention, which is not liable to the same legal objection as the iron coffins, is about two years old. The price paid for its use is a shilling per day.

Seeing some mountain-ash berries at a green-grocers, and others pickled and bottled in a little shop near, we asked at the shop for what they were intended. To my surprize, civilly as the question was asked, the woman seemed to consider it as implying some contempt, and insisted that they were only bottled with clear spring water—'just for curiosity'—mere things to be looked at. This was so impossible, that we asked the same question at the green-grocers, and there we were informed that they were preserved with sugar, as being good for sore throats.

Apples and pears are sold in Scotland by the pound.

The University has an ancient and respectable appearance. The Lion opposite the Unicorn on the steps leading up to what I suppose to be the Library, is the most comical Lion I ever beheld; more like a Toad, sitting erect in a grave attitude, than anything else. They have hackney vis-a-vis here drawn by one horse. And here I see that hearses in Scotland are ornamented with gilt death's-heads and cross-bones!

Robert Southey, *Journal of a Tour in Scotland in 1819* (1929).

1820: The Radical Rising from a non-Radical point of view

The Radical Rising, following on the heels of the Peterloo Massacre in 1819, caused great alarm to the civic authorities in Glasgow. On April 1st the 'Radical Committee for the Formation of a Provisional Government' posted proclamations calling on workers in the city to strike and take up arms. Within days an 'army' of around seven thousand men mustered near Paisley and a smaller force gathered in the Campsie Hills. Amongst the Strathaven Volunteers, who marched to Cathkin Braes and unfurled their banner (but did little else) was a 63-year old weaver, James Wilson. He was later apprehended, tried and, despite a plea of clemency, hanged and beheaded publicly in front of the Justiciary Buildings (the 'disgusting consequences' alluded to by Strang). In Sighthill Cemetery there is a monument to the leaders of the rising, Baird and Hardie. The attempt to take the city was effectively sabotaged by spies and informers, if not *agents provocateurs*. The Colonel Hunter referred to in this ironic account was Samuel Hunter, a fire-breathing editor of the *Glasgow Herald*. The author of this account of mobilising forces in defence of the city was John Strang (1795–1863) who later became City Chamberlain.

For many days previous to the famous *Wet Wednesday* was the town kept in hot water by the most threatening reports of approaching riot and rebellion; and, from Sunday morning, when the famous or rather infamous inflammatory placard was posted at the corner of the streets, all the public works and factories were closed, while the miners in and around Glasgow struck work, and wandered through the City in idle crowds, or collected in gloomy groups about the corners of the leading thoroughfares. As a safeguard and protection against lawless agression, troops were being called in from every quarter to meet the now imagined rising.

. . .

The proclamations of the Magistracy, too, ordering all the shops to be shut at six, and all the inhabitants to be indoors at seven, instead of tending to inspire courage created fear; while flying rumours, from the neighbouring manufacturing towns and villages, of mustering hordes of rebels, increased the general alarm.

Such was the precise state of matters when, on the morning of the 5th April 1820, as one of the Glasgow Sharpshooters, I leaped at five o'clock from my bed, at the reveillé sound of the bugle, and hastened to the rendezvous of the regiment. When I reached the square, it was evident, from the number of green-coated individuals pouring in from every side, that, as the danger increased, the determination to meet it was more decided. Before six o'clock, raw and murky though the morning was, I found myself among 800 bayonets, drawn up in a column of companies, ready to act at a moment's notice. For the honour of the corps, the muster-roll on being called showed few absentees, while several individuals answered to their names who were rarely seen on other more showy occasions. The gallant Colonel Hunter stood, as he said himself, 'on his own Galloway feet,' at the head of the column, having for some time dispensed with his Bucephalus, whose amblings under fire were rather calculated to dissolve the copartnery of horse and rider; and, after having with a stentorian voice called 'Attention,' commanded an instant examination to be made as to the contents of each soldier's cartouch-box, to discover whether it was that morning filled with the due number of ball-cartridges that had been formerly issued, and whether the flints of the rifles were fitted for producing immediate ignition. This duty over, the command to 'Fix bayonets' was next given; and when 'Shoulder arms' was added, there were in an instant as many bristling points thrown up as might have wooed down the fiercest thunderbolt from heaven without injury to mother earth! The corps never appeared in greater spirits, nor more ready to rush, if need be, against the whole Radical pikes that might muster; although it must in justice be added, that there was as yet no semblance of a single hostile pike to put that courage to the test. In silence and suspense the Sharpshooters thus stood, till at length a messenger arrived declaring that the London mail had reached the Cross, and that as yet all was quiet in England. The arms were instantly grounded, the bayonets unfixed and returned to their scabbards, and the order for dismissal was given, with a *caveat*, however, that the green *continuations* of the uniform should not be doffed, as was customary after the morning's parade, but should be worn during the whole day, to meet any sudden emergency that might arise. And

Heaven knows that not a few occurred on that eventful Wednesday, before the City clocks had chimed midnight.

With an appetite, which the cold sharp air of an April morning certainly did not appease, I hurried home, and sat down to a breakfast, to which, like another Dugald Dalgetty, I did ample justice, not knowing, in those ticklish times, when I might get another. During the breaking of eggs, the bolting of ham, and the swallowing of tea and toast, I was beset with a thousand queries as to the threatened dangers, which no doubt were considered to be imminent, especially when the *Glasgow Courier* was referred to, and which the evening before gravely put forth the following paragraph:—'that a general attack is intended to be made by the Radicals in this City on Wednesday is now beyond doubt. Cathkin braes is the site chosen for the encampment!' Notwithstanding this astounding announcement, I endeavoured to soothe all fears, on the ground of the strong military force of regulars in the City, and particularly on the determined attitude which had been taken by the Sharpshooters and the Yeomanry Cavalry to assist in maintaining order and suppressing riot.

On sallying forth to the streets which, during the forenoon, were filled with crowds of ill-conditioned individuals, it was plain that a crisis was approaching, and if an outbreak had begun, it seemed quite plain, from the inflammable materials which abounded on every hand, that it would not, under the most favourable circumstances, have been suppressed without bloodshed. The civic authorities, alarmed for the safety of the City, sat in solemn conclave during the whole day in the Buck's Head Hotel, while the military chiefs held their council of war within the same place. Pickets of dragoons rode out on all the roads leading to and from the town, to bring in every information they could collect, and especially to announce the approach of any body of Radicals that might be marching towards the City. One trooper after another arrived and departed, but still there was no cry heard of any coming combatants. At length, just as the clock struck three, a rumour flew like lightning through the town that thousands were on the road from Paisley, and would ere long enter the City. The very whisper of such intelligence created a universal panic. Shopkeepers at once put on their shutters, locked their shops, and hurried home. The principal streets presented the image of a siege. In a few minutes the Horse Artillery rattled along the causeway, and took up a position at each end of the bridge across the Clyde; while strong bodies of both Cavalry and Infantry hurried down at double quick pace to support this important position. The buglers of the Sharpshooters blew the assembly-call, and hundreds of the green-coated soldiers might be seen hastening to George-square. The whole day was gloomy and showery; but, at this moment, the windows of heaven opened and poured down such a torrent of rain as fairly cleared the streets of all loiterers, and left scarcely a soul thereon save the military, who, if they then encountered neither gun, pike, sabre, nor horsefly, met with as severe a ducking as ever fell to the lot of any one who ever wore a uniform. The watery Saint had, in fact, taken forcible possession of the skies, and seemed determined to use his powers as long as he could, and so effectually did he use them, that, by four o'clock, the redoubtable Falstaffian army of Paisley malcontents had dispersed into thin air, while the military had returned to quarters, and the Sharpshooters to their homes, without any immediate casualties being gazetted on either side, but, no doubt, with many *in futurum* from the cold and the rain to which they had been so mercilessly subjected.

Thinking that the day which had commenced so early and had been so bustling up to five o'clock might now 'cease its funning'—drenched with rain and not a little wearied—I hastened, like some of my campaigning brethren, to the shelter of my own fireside; while others, dreaming also that the day's military duties must now be over, retired to solace themselves with somewhat at *John Haggart's*, in Prince's-street, at that time the great rendezvous of bachelor Sharpshooters, in search either of a dinner at four or a rabbit at nine. On my arrival at my own house, where I found a group of anxious faces ready to welcome me, I soon doffed my dripping uniform, which I ordered to be placed before a blazing kitchen fire, and having donned my usual attire, sat down to a comfortable repast, in the hope of having nothing afterwards to do but go to bed, of which, from having caught a bad cold and sore throat, I was in some need. Under this comfortable belief, I scarcely allowed the City clocks to strike nine, before I consented to put my feet in hot water, swallow a gruel, and place my wearied limbs under the blankets. Forgetful of the past and of the future, I soon began to slumber, if not to sleep, when, just as I had arrived at a state of seeming unconsciousness, methought I heard the echo of a bugle call. Was it a dream or was it reality? It was impossible for some minutes to tell. But, alas! another fell blast resounded on my ear, and I at once woke to the certainty that I must, in spite of sore throat and all other ills, again leave my comfortable and health-restoring resting-place, and prepare for another threatening conflict. I rang instantly for a light, which was at once brought, and, on its arrival, I espied my dried regimentals gaping to receive the limbs of the already exhausted feather-bed soldier. I at once leaped into my Lincoln-green attire, buckled on my accoutrements, and seizing my rifle, which always stood by my bedside, sallied forth to the street, where, meeting a knot of those resident in the same locality, we fixed our bayonets, and hurried on, fearless of danger, towards the monument of the hero of Corunna.

The night, like the afternoon, was dark and dismal. The wind blew, and the rain rattled on the house-tops. The gutters rushed like rivulets, and scarce a lamp was able to withstand the extinguishing blast.

. . .

On reaching the square, which we had now done for the third time that day, we were told that, in order to save us from the pitiless pelting of the storm, the quarter-master had got the neighbouring church of St. George's open for our reception; and right glad were we to learn that we had so near a prospect of sacred shelter.

The scene which met the eye within this ecclesiastical edifice was perhaps one of the most striking that could well be imagined. Each pew was crowded with men fully equipped and ready for battle, each with his bayoneted rifle in his hand, eager to know and ready to execute his coming duty. A few glimmering candles, which had been hurriedly stuck up and down the church, tended to throw an air of gloomy grandeur over the silent and gaping corps.

. . .

And long and patiently they waited, listening for the coming foe, but hearing nothing except the pelting storm, which, however, of itself, was sufficient to have put the most enthusiastic Radical *hors de combat.* And this, indeed, it is believed it accomplished; for the night passed slowly and silently on, till, at length, the Colonel finding that his corps was not called upon to act, wisely decided upon sending all home, except a company, which, under the command of Captain William Smith, was marched to Queen-street to guard the Royal Bank from Radical spoliation, which they certainly succeeded in doing, without any loss, except that of being deprived of so early a breakfast as was enjoyed by their fellow-soldiers, and of allaying, by their presence at home, the deep anxiety which reigned in the bosoms of mothers, wives, and sisters!

Many curious stories have been told of the expedients resorted to by wives, mothers, and sisters, to retain the gallant Sharpshooters within doors on this critical night. One had his rifle hid; another could not find his uniform; and another, who had just been married, was urged to remain at home, on the very prudent plea that 'on such a night powder would not burn;' while others were very slyly told 'that they might fecht any nicht but this!' It is believed, however, that in spite of the best efforts used to retain many from the rendezvous, there was scarcely a single individual who did not answer to his name, and who did not that night parade within the hallowed precincts of St. George's Church; and once there, it may easily be conceived that none could well steal away, when it is recollected that our redoubted friend, Mr. William Black, then of Balgray, acted as sergeant of the door guard, with orders to let no one pass without due leave being granted.

Thus commenced and thus ended this famous day in Glasgow history—a day big with the threatenings of riot and rebellion—full of alarm and trepidation to many of her timid inhabitants—replete with the foolish fears of those who ought to have known better things—and marked by a military ardour on the part of the citizen soldiers, worthy of a better cause and a more dangerous enterprise; a day in which the elements conspired to cool excited imaginations, and to disperse the handful of miserable malcontents which nought but imbecility and madness could have roused to a threatening attitude; a day far more indebted to the outpourings of St. Swithin's bounty than to the grave counsels of the civil and military governors of the City; in short, a day which proved that rain and Radicalism cannot co-exist, and that, in the event of any similar turmoil being got up, as this certainly was most shamefully done, the fire-engine and a gravitation water-pipe would prove a far better means of quelling it than the six-pounder and the rifle! May we hope that we shall never again see another wet Radical Wednesday of the west; nor, what was worse, the shameless and disgusting consequences which followed in its wake?

John Strang, *Glasgow and Its Clubs* (1856).

1822: A Doctor's Incompetence

Born in Tradeston in 1818, Elizabeth Storie by her own account suffered most of her life physical agonies and mental anguish at the hands of certain doctors, lawyers and clergymen. She wrote out of 'a strong impression that injustice is often done to the poor, and more especially to the women of that class'. Her medical experiences make the most horrifying reading. She sued Dr Falconer and was awarded £1,000 and expenses, but he absconded. As a result of his treatment she had to undergo repeated operations on her jaw to enable her to eat. She bore all her misfortunes—lawsuits and excommunication included—with dignity, eking out an existence by dressmaking and millinery. She hoped her narrative might be a means of influence 'in favour of the oppressed against their oppressors'.

When four years and four months old, I was seized with a complaint common to childhood, called nettle-rush, a complaint which, when properly treated, is seldom known to be protracted over a period of more than a few days, and which is generally completely removed by the use of a little gentle medicine. But, alas for me! under it I fell a victim to the unskilful treatment practised upon me by one whom the Medical Faculty entitled to call himself Surgeon. My father, John Storie, was on intimate terms of friendship with Robert Falconer, weaver, who lived in the same street, and whose son, William, had lately become Surgeon. Dr Falconer, as this son was called, was in the habit of frequently visiting my father's house, and during this early illness of mine, he came in one day while my mother was in the act of giving me sulphur and senna. He asked my mother what was the matter with Elizabeth, (meaning me,) and what it was she was giving to me. She told him what she thought ailed me, and the remedy she was using, but he replied that that was no medicine for nettle-rush, but that he would send up a few powders that would do me good. Accordingly his brother Archibald brought some, two of which were given to me that day. I have a distinct recollection that they tasted like chalk.

. . .

On visiting me the next day, Dr Falconer ordered two more of the powders to be given to me, which was accordingly done. The day following he found me rather feverish, and took a bottle containing calomel out of his pocket, emptied some of it into a spoon, mixed it with water, and kept my hands down till I swallowed it. Like most children, I disliked medicine. The dose he gave to me tasted like the powders, and was of the same greyish white colour. I was ordered a warm bath and cold water to allay my thirst which was great. Dr F. called on the next day, still inquiring if there was any smell, and gave me another powder. On the fifth morning after his first visit he found me very feverish and restless. He gave me another spoonful from the bottle, and again ordered the hot bath. The same evening he called, and I was still more restless and uncomfortable. He did not make any change in his mode of treatment, though the prescriptions he had ordered seemed only to have increased the feverishness and restlessness of my complaint. He ordered two or three of the powders to be given to me daily—the hot baths to be continued—and cold water to drink as before. This treatment was continued for three weeks I think—I continuing in the feverish and restless condition I have described. The smell was by this time very bad, and my head began to swell to a great extent, and saliva to flow in large quantities from my mouth. Dr Falconer ordered me, while in this state, to be taken out of bed and carried round the house in the open air—the snow lying five feet deep on the ground at the time. The salivation continued—my mouth and gums began to mortify, and all my face to become black. My parents began to get seriously alarmed about me—and while they and some of the neighbours were one day standing round my bed and talking of my distressing condition, Dr Falconer came in. After looking at me he ordered me to be lifted out of bed, and asked for a basin. My sister took me on her knee. I did not know what he was going to do, but a sensation of great fear came over me.

. . .

While I was sitting on my sister's knee I saw the doctor pour a yellowish liquor from a bottle he had brought with him into a white basin. This was afterwards proved to be acquafortis. He then filled a syringe with this fluid. He asked John Campbell, a person who was in the house at the time, to assist him by holding my hands. He agreed to do so, and while doing this Dr Falconer discharged the contents of the syringe into my mouth. The agony I suffered from this cruel operation was so dreadful that I did not know what I was doing, and I believe I kicked the doctor in the face with such force as to cause him to fall backwards. He, however, in a few minutes afterwards repeated the operation. Part of my tongue fell off, all my teeth and part of my jaw-bone gave way. The pain I suffered was indescribable; but although I was in such agony, the doctor, irritated at some remarks from John Campbell about apparent neglect, went away in a passion and left me without prescribing anything to alleviate the intensity of the pain I was enduring. Some of the neighbours, more humane, ran to the Brewery, Buchan Street, Gorbals, and brought some porter barm which was made into a poultice with carrots and applied to my face. My mouth was soaked with barm sponge all night. I felt considerable relief from these applications. Dr Falconer called as usual next morning, and expressed surprise that I was alive. My father and mother were anxious to call in another medical man, but Dr Falconer would not hear of it. However they afterwards sent for Dr Smeal, who, as soon as he saw me, told them that I was 'ruined for life by the excessive use of mercury', and stated that the medical man who prescribed it must have known the effect of such treatment. My mother told him that I had got a great many powders, but she was not aware they contained mercury, otherwise her child would never have got them. He asked the name of the doctor who was attending me. My mother told him. He said, before going away, '*Your daughter may survive for two or three days, but not longer.*' My parents were deeply grieved to hear this, and anxious to see what further medical advice could do, they called in Dr Litster, who only confirmed Dr Smeal's opinion. Dr Litster called next day and examined the powders, and found that they contained two ordinary doses of mercury in each. He sent for Dr Falconer, and they held a consultation together, the result of which was that Dr Falconer said he would follow the same course of treatment to-morrow. Dr Litster told him he would be doing what he knew to be wrong. They then parted. Dr Falconer called again in the evening. He came up to me and said, 'Poor thing, she is far through; however there is a powder I would like to give to her, which is a certain cure;' but neither my father nor mother gave him any answer.

. . .

Next morning Dr Falconer sent up the powder by his brother, with directions how to give it. The powder was never given to me, though Dr Falconer was under the impression that I had got it. He called in the evening, and observing a jug standing by the fire, he lifted it and asked what it contained. My mother told him it was apple-tea. He said, 'Very good, give her as much of it as she likes to drink, but no other medicine. Poor thing, she will not survive long—there will be a change for the worse in the night, however; Dr Crawford and I will call in the morning.' Dr Crawford was Dr Falconer's partner. As my end was expected to be so near, many of the neighbours, as well as our own family, sat up with me that night. I grew no worse, though suffering almost unbearable agony. One of the neighbours, Mrs M'Arthur, occupied herself while sitting up in making what was intended to be my shroud. Mrs Angus crimped the border of the cap I was to have been attired in. Both these individuals were alive in 1851, and gave evidence then as to the truth of these statements. Morning came, and I was still in the land of the living, and the place of hope. The powder which was professedly to have done me so much good, having never been given to me, no change for the better or worse was perceptible. The doctor's inadvertent remark, 'there will be a change for the worse during the night,' seems rather to indicate that evil and not good was the expected result of the valuable powder he had sent to me. There was death in the powder, and he knew it. No wonder, then, at the astonishment of Dr Falconer and his companion in guilt, when they saw that life still animated the body they expected to find rigid in death. No wonder that they exclaimed, '*She is proof of shot,'* when the powder they intended for me was afterwards found to contain *as much arsenic as would have killed seven persons*!

Elizabeth Storie, *The Autobiography of Elizabeth Storie* (1859).

1823: Steamboats on the Forth and Clyde Canal

Pioneer steamboat travellers were inundated with guidebooks. By the early 1820s there were about a dozen regular sailings on the Forth and twice that number on the Clyde. In this guide a section deals with the Forth and Clyde Canal (completed 1790) and the Union Canal which had just been completed. Although the journey from Falkirk to Port Dundas took $5\frac{1}{2}$ hours, it was more comfortable than going by coach. Unfortunately the guide becomes increasingly unreliable, mis-spelling the Kelvin and shrinking the Maryhill aqueduct to about half-size. The journey begins at Grangemouth.

Here travellers for Glasgow land, and proceed by the *Forth and Clyde Canal,* which forms its junction at this place with the river Carron. A coach daily runs from Grangemouth to Loch 16, a distance of four miles, where the Track Boats commence their passage along the canal to *Glasgow;* and thence they set off, at stated hours, three times a-day. These vessels are fitted up solely for the conveyance of passengers, each having two roomy cabins, with every accommodation, including books, and other sources of amusement. Refreshments are also to be had; and the fares are considered moderate.

Along the course of the Canal, from the Forth to the Clyde, few objects of importance occur. In some places are still to be seen mouldering vestiges of the Roman Wall of Antoninus; as that barrier, formed to curb the fiery spirit of the Caledonians, ran nearly in the line of the canal. By this route, the excursion from Edinburgh to Glasgow is performed in a day; and being both economical and pleasant, is much resorted to by all classes of people.

From Grangemouth the canal passes near Carron, celebrated for the most extensive iron foundry in Europe, the villages of Kilsyth and Kirkintuloch, and at Port Dundas, in the vicinity of Glasgow, a basin is formed, where passengers for that city are landed. From this a small cut, called the *Monkland canal* is made, which runs some miles east, through a coal district, and by which Glasgow is supplied with this necessary article. The great canal is carried from Port Dundas westward, to join the Clyde; and three miles below the city is seen the most interesting object, perhaps, along its whole course, namely, the aqueduct bridge, which stretches over the beautiful valley and river of Kelvil. This bridge is a noble structure, consisting of four stately arches, 37 feet high, and 50 wide.

The Scottish Tourist (1823).

1823: Thomas Chalmers' Farewell

Thomas Chalmers (1780–1847), an Evangelical preacher and a prominent figure in the foundation of the Free Church of Scotland in 1843, was appointed minister of the Tron Church in 1815. Four years later he was transferred to St John's, a new parish in the East End, endowed by the Town Council. His aims, largely achieved during his eight years in Glasgow, were to reorganise the parochial system to provide better welfare for the destitute and better schooling. His first view of the city caused 'a desolation of heart', but he soon took up this challenge to practical Christianity. In 1823, worn out by his labours, he accepted the Chair of Moral Philosophy at St Andrews. This is a biographer's account of his farewell discourse at St John's.

Applications for admission had for several weeks been pouring in with distressing profusion upon those who had seats in that church. To many individuals of rank and consideration tickets were issued entitling them to a place on the pulpit stair or in the vacant area around the precentor's desk. As it was resolved that every possible effort should be made to secure admission to the regular seatholders or their friends, and to those to whom tickets had been thus appropriated, the elders and doorkeepers, assisted by a strong body of police, planted themselves, on Sabbath morning, at the main entrance to the church. At so early an hour as nine o'clock an ominous stream of foot-passengers began to turn into Macfarlane Street, and the roll of carriage wheels was heard sounding along the Gallowgate. Before the doors were opened, Macfarlane Street, Queen Street, and Campbell Street, were filled with excited groups waiting eagerly for admission. At last the main entrance was thrown open, the gathered crowd converged upon it, and the conflict commenced. For a brief season the efforts of the doorkeepers and their allies were successful; the assailants, however, multiplied so rapidly, and the mass accumulated behind drove on those before them with such impetuosity, that the well-guarded entrance was forced. When it was seen that success had crowned the efforts of the assailants, the crush through the passage became tremendous—a dense but still struggling mass of human beings compressed for a few moments into extreme compactness, and then expanding as the perilous passage at last was made and the interior of the church was gained—some to draw breath after the stifling squeeze—some to rearrange their dishevelled habiliments—some to turn an eager eye upon the scene of recent conflict. And now the tide of battle was for a moment turned as a party of the 73rd Regiment, summoned hastily from the adjacent barracks, forced their way through all impediments, and took up their position beside the entrance to the church. By their effective aid, and after much personal exertion, the elders and doorkeepers succeeded in obtaining access for a number of the congregation who otherwise would have been excluded. Still, however, even through the barrier of bayonets, the crowd continued to make way, till not a single spot of sitting or standing ground within was left unoccupied. Into a church seated for about 1700 nearly double that number was packed. 'The pew in which I sat'—one who was present has informed us—'contained fourteen sittings, but on that occasion twenty-six persons were crammed into it, some sitting, some standing on the floor, others standing on the seat.' The confusion grew within as the pressure somewhat abated from without; and it was no gentle or very Sabbath frame of spirit that prevailed. At length the preacher rose within that pulpit from which he was to address his hearers for the last time. In a moment the bustle ceased, and all the varied expressions of that great crowd of faces was turned into one uniform gaze of fixed and profound attention. After prayer and praise, the text, from Psalm cxxxvii. 5, 6, was twice distinctly read, and its general lessons having been unfolded and impressed, and the preacher coming at the close to speak to those from whom, as their minister, he was now to be finally dissevered,—'I will never forget,' he said, 'that it is your princely beneficence which has carried me forward in covering this parish with those institutions both of scholarship and piety that have done most to grace and to dignify the people of our beloved land. I will never forget the labours of that devoted band to whose union and perseverance I still look for even greater services than they have yet rendered to the cause of Christian philanthropy. I will never forget the unexcepted welcome and kindness of my parochial families, among whom the cause, that to the superficial eye looks unpopular and austere, hath now found its conclusive establishment. I never will forget the indulgence and the friendly regards of this congregation; and I beg to assure each and all of them, that if a cold and ungenial apathy, whether of look or of manner, was all the return that they ever could obtain for their demonstrations of Christian affection towards myself, it was not because I had not the conviction of that manifold good-will which was on every side of me, but that moving in a wide and busy sphere, and hurried in the course of a few moments from one act of intercourse to another with more than a thousand of my fellows, my jaded and overborne feelings could not keep pace with it. There are hundreds and hundreds more whom in person I could not overtake, but whom in the hours of cool and leisurely reflection I shall know how to appreciate. And when I gaze on that quarter—the richest to me of all the wide horizon in the treasures of cordiality and grateful remembrance—then sweeter than to the eye are those tints of loveliness which the western sun stretches in golden clouds above it will be the thought of all the worth and the tenderness and the noble generosity that are there. Oh! I never can forget the city of so many Christian and kind-hearted men.'

William Hanna, *Memoirs of Dr Chalmers* (1850).

1827: Audubon in Search of Subscriptions

Only Lizars the Edinburgh engraver was bold enough to take the initial risk of printing and colouring the life-size bird paintings of the American ornithologist John James Audubon (1785–1851). The project was taken over by Havell of London after Lizars's colourists went on strike, and between 1827 and 1838 about

175 sets of the 435 hand-coloured plates of *The Birds of America* were issued. Audubon expended a great deal of time and energy touting for subscriptions. This is the record of his disappointing trip to Glasgow. The one subscriber was the Hunterian Museum. There are two other sets at present in Glasgow, at the Royal College of Physicians and Surgeons and at the Mitchell Library.

> *Edinburgh, October 31,* . . . If I go to Glasgow and can only obtain names that in the course of a few months will be withdrawn, I am only increasing expenses and losing time, and of neither time nor money have I too great a portion; but when I know that Glasgow is a place of wealth, and has many persons of culture, I decide to go.
>
> . . .
>
> *Glasgow, November 4.* . . . I arrived here too late to see any portion of the town, for when the coach stopped at the Black Bull all was so dark that I could only see it was a fine, broad, long street.
>
> *November 8.* I am off to-morrow morning, and perhaps forever will say farewell to Glasgow. I have been here *four* days and have obtained *one* subscriber. One subscriber in a city of 150,000 souls, rich, handsome and with much learning. Think of 1400 pupils in one college! Glasgow is a fine city; the Clyde here is a small stream crossed by three bridges. The shipping consists of about a hundred brigs and schooners, but I counted eighteen steam vessels, black, ugly things as ever were built. One sees few carriages, but *thousands* of carts.

Maria R. Audubon, *Audubon and His Journals* (1898).

1829: Two Fires

In the early nineteenth century large buildings were particularly vulnerable to fire devastation because of the inefficiency of hand-pumped fire hoses. Theatres never lasted for very long. The first Theatre Royal was built in 1804 by public subscription and was reputedly a magnificent building. Its exterior columns can still be seen on the west side of Queen Street to the north of Royal Exchange Square. James Donaldson, cotton broker, moved his warehouse to South Hanover Street the following year.

> When living in this house, I witnessed the burning of the Queen Street Theatre, on the forenoon of Saturday, the 10th January 1829. While playing with some companions in the entrance of Gordon Lane, I suddenly felt myself in a darkness, if such a thing can be, that 'could be felt,' so that we were quite unable for the moment to discern each others faces. On the dense smoke that caused this darkness lifting off, my companions and myself made our way into Gordon Street. There we quickly learned the cause of the sudden eclipse.

Having so short a distance to go we were amongst the earliest on the scene, and posted ourselves in a doorway on the north side of St. Vincent Place, that, I think, of Mrs James Connell, No. 22. From this post of vantage we had an admirable and quite uninterrupted view of the conflagration in the back part or stage end of the theatre. As that, the west gable of the building, consisted of about five or six flats, and the flames were issuing from almost every window, the sight, even in daylight, was very grand. The one thing of it all that I was unable then to understand was the firemen throwing over the windows a number of ordinary bed-room mirrors, along with innumerable articles of dress, and of theatrical things in general. The heat of the fire was so great that the glass of my mother's front windows could hardly be touched without injury to the hand. The same effect happened to our back windows from the huge fire of Donaldson's store in Mitchell Street, corner of Mitchell Lane, which was burned down about November 1829. As considerable discussion regarding the true character of this store took place in the press after the publication of my few remarks upon the subject, I think it worth while to refer to this discussion here. The store was mainly a cotton one. Mr Donaldson was one of our great cotton brokers, and his store one of the largest in Glasgow. But on the occasion of this fire, according to the evidence of an entirely trustworthy witness, there was not only an immense quantity of cotton consumed, but large quantities of grain, and of butter also. My informant on this subject—for though I watched the fire from the back windows of my mother's house I cannot testify to this on my own authority—has been known intimately to me for over fifty years, and I have the utmost possible confidence in anything he vouches for as having happened under his direct observation. His statement is, that he witnessed the fire from the street and the removal of the cotton to the Flesher's Haugh, at the side of the river Clyde; that a spate in the river occurring at the time, washed large portions of the cotton, while still on fire, down the river; and that some of the cotton was carried down as far as Renfrew, and coming into contact with a cottage there, set it on fire. My friend also states, that large quantities of grain, much injured by water, was carted off and sold at a shilling a cart-load for distilling and brewing purposes. What I can recollect of this great fire, one of the greatest ever witnessed in Glasgow, is merely the display made by the fire itself on a dark winter night from a near and uninterrupted point of view, and the fact of the streets in the neighbourhood of the fire being laid for several weeks with the hose pipes employed to extinguish the still burning cotton.

Daniel Frazer, *The Story of the Making of Buchanan Street* (1885).

1830: Recollections of Bridgeton and Dalmarnock

This account gives a vivid picture of the East End when cotton spinning and weaving in the Clyde valley was still at its peak. A few years later Kirkman Finlay is complaining, before a Parliamentary Inquiry, that foreign competition has made the industry barely profitable. But mills still went on being built in Glasgow until well into the 1880s. William Guthrie here remembers his Bridgeton childhood when there were still 2,000 handloom weavers in the East End, giving the area its distinctive social and political character.

Bridgeton, from the time the first feu was taken, onwards to 1st January, 1847, was a suburb of Glasgow. It is well laid out, being almost a square from east to west and north to south. The two main thoroughfares are Main Street and New Dalmarnock Road—the first, about half a mile long from north to south, beginning at Barrowfield Toll and ending at Rutherglen Bridge; the latter, one mile long, from Barrowfield Toll to Dalmarnock Bridge, and the side streets run east and west. These two thoroughfares were under the Road Trustees, who kept them up in repair. There was what they called a Feuars' Court, composed of lairds of property. They elected a Provost from amongst themselves each year. Their duties were light, as they had only to look after the keeping of the pavements in repair, which got a lot of engine ash when necessary. There were no police and no lights on the streets except from the windows of a few shops and dwelling-houses, lighted with oil lamps or candles, as the most of the ground floors were occupied with weavers' shops, which had all outside shutters. The streets were very dark during winter. The weavers in those days had very long hours. They began work, some at six and some at seven o'clock in the morning, on till ten at night, and some longer. But the weaver shops were cheery. Most of the weavers could sing and talk and work at the same time. The weavers were politicians, and mostly all in favour of the Reform Bill of 1832, but few had a vote then; it was only lairds and those who had high-rented shops and places of business.

I will try to give you a description of what the place was like from 1830 and onwards. I will make my starting point at the south end of Dalmarnock Road, where there was at one time a ford across the Clyde. The water was very shallow. I remember when I was a boy of wading across the river just above where the bridge now stands. The first bridge was built by the Road Trustees. I cannot give you the date, as it was before my time. It was all built of wood on a sandy bottom. The piles in course of time began to give way, and the bridge became like a switchback. There was a rail track on each side for carts, and small footways between the rails and the parapet. The agreement with the Road Trustees was that they had power to levy tolls from carts, carriages, cattle, and foot passengers on condition that when the revenue exceeded the expenditure the bridge was to be free. About the end of the thirties it was found that the Trustees had been overpaid, and the public made a demand on them to free the bridge. They refused to do this, and, as the public were lukewarm in the matter, Peter Mackenzie, of the *Reformers' Gazette*, took the case in hand on his own responsibility, carried the case to Court, gained the plea, and the bridge became free. In a few years it became so dangerous that a new bridge had to be built at the east side of the old one. This bridge was on the same lines as the other one, and in course of time became another switchback. By an arrangement with the county authorities—the burghs of Rutherglen and Glasgow—there is now a handsome stone structure across the Clyde.

There was a large meadow on the river bank to the east of the bridge, which was let to cowfeeders for grazing their cows. It was free to the public, but, alas! the best part of it is now enclosed for a football club, and the rest filled up with rubbish. This meadow was very much abused by roughs from the town and Calton during the summer months. Every Monday they came in thousands and had prize fights either by men or dogs, and sometimes both; but this was put a stop to by the powers that be. There was a sand bank at the bend of the river, where the boys used to dig for cockadoos, as they were called. They were large mussels, about five inches long and two inches broad, and when found were empty. They must have belonged to a past age. It was said that pearls had been found in some of them, but I was never lucky enough to find any. There is still a rough footpath round this bank, but its beauty is destroyed.

William Guthrie, *Recollections of Bridgeton* (1905).

1831: The Opening of the Glasgow and Garnkirk Railway

Although the Monkland-Kirkintilloch mineral railway was the first line opened in Scotland, the Glasgow-Garnkirk railway—passing near Airdrie and Coatbridge—was the first passenger-carrying line (completed six years after the Stockton-Darlington railway). This painstaking account of the opening, written by a civil engineer, is from a volume of plates based on early photographs by D. O. Hill. The passengers are shown travelling in open carriages, impervious to the vapours issuing both from the locomotive and also from the nearby St Rollox chemical works (see 1858) whose owners, the Tennants, were the railway's chief sponsors. Return summer excursions were run from Townhead to Gartsherrie (north of Coatbridge). It was claimed that 'Genteel Parties will find the trip an agreeable and healthful mode of spending part of the day'.

The whole undertaking being now completed, the directors resolved to celebrate this occasion by a public opening of the railway and dinner, to which were invited, along with the proprietors and friends, the magistrates of Glasgow and other official persons, the professors of the university, and others. This took place on the 27th of September, 1831, and formed a very imposing spectacle; the two locomotive engines, which had been provided for the railway, traversing the line, and drawing behind them long trains of carriages and waggons, amid an immense concourse of spectators, assembled from the city and from all parts of the adjacent country, to witness so new and extraordinary a scene, lining the sides of the railway, and covering the bridges, and other prominent points, from which a view could be obtained. The one engine, the St Rollox, conveyed the directors and a number of ladies and gentlemen, to the amount in all of nearly 200; the other, the George Stephenson, drew a train of thirty-two waggons, loaded with coal, freestone, lime, grain, iron, and other articles of trade upon the line, to the amount of ninety tons, exclusive of the weight of the waggons, which must have increased the aggregate load to 120 tons; thus exhibiting, in a striking point of view, the advantages of the railway, both for the purposes of travelling, and for the transport of heavy goods. Under this prodigious load, which came to nearly twenty times its own weight, the latter engine yet advanced not only with perfect freedom, but with the speed of a stage-coach; while the former, with its two hundred passengers, darted along, in many parts, with twice the rapidity of the mail, and seemed evidently capable of acquiring any additional speed that might have been necessary or safe. In many parts, however, the trains advanced leisurely along, to give time for viewing the works of the line. The day was very favourable for the exhibition, and the scene altogether, particularly the operations of the engines, at one time advancing with their enormous trains slowly and majestically along, and at another flying past with such rapidity, amid the shouts of the assembled multitudes, was well calculated to excite the deepest interest, and to impress the beholder with a feeling of wonder and of exultation at the new and extraordinary powers which the triumphs of inventive genius had thus brought under the dominion of man.

. . .

The road for the railway is formed every where at least thirty feet wide, and on some of the embankments it is a little more. The middle part is occupied with the rails, which are laid in a double line all the way, for the carriages going in opposite directions. The rails are laid four and a half feet apart, and the two lines of rails are separated from each other also four and a half feet—making thirteen and a half feet between the extreme rails, and, including nine inches for space over each side, making in all fifteen feet in the centre of the road occupied with rails. The remaining seven and a half feet are neatly dressed off, and terminated along the cuts by water channels, and generally a low dry stone wall on each side. On all parts, excepting on moss, the rails rest at every three feet in their length on square pyramidal stone blocks, ten inches high, two feet by eighteen inches in the base, and tapered to eighteen inches by one foot at top, weighing at an average nearly three cwt. Over Robroyston and other mosses, the rails rest on a framework of timber, which is found to make a very substantial and firm foundation. After the moss had been brought to the requisite level, the whole breadth of the road was laid with branches of trees, on which were laid longitudinal beams of rough timber; on these, cross beams or sleepers were laid, in some parts three feet apart, and in others so near as six inches, according to circumstances; over these sleepers again were laid long-itudinal planks, forty feet long by nine inches broad, and four and a half thick, carefully half lapped at the joinings; on these the rails were laid, and from the extent of surface embraced by the longitudinal and cross beams, the weight of the rails and of the carriages is sustained with perfect effect; and owing to the elasticity of the moss below, the carriages are always found to move more smoothly and easily along here than on any other part of the way.

. . .

The work on the railway is performed almost entirely by locomotive engines. These have been made by Messrs Robert Stephenson and Co. of Newcastle, and have fully sustained the high character acquired for their engines on different railways by these eminent engineers. They are quite similar in their construction to those on the Liverpool and Manchester Railway, with all the improvements up to the date of their making. The first which arrived on the road was the St Rollox. The weight of this engine, without water in the boiler, is four and a half tons. The cylinders of the engines are not quite of the same dimensions; the one is ten inches diameter, and fourteen inches stroke; and, as the steam is applied at the pressure of fifty lbs. on the inch, the two engines together will be equal to one of twenty-six horse power. They lie horizontally under the boiler, and at the fore end of it, that is, directly under the chimney; while the piston rods, moving in fixed slides, act by connecting rods on two cranks formed on the axle of the hind wheels; and by the rotatory motion thus communicated to these, the progressive motion of the whole engine is effected. The wheels are of wood, hooped with malleable iron rims, four and a half feet diameter. The fore wheels are also of wood, and much smaller than the others, being only three feet three inches in diameter; the fore and hind wheels are not connected together, so that the adhesion of the one set only is available. The boiler is three feet diameter and six feet long. In the hinder end is a considerable projection all round the boiler, within which is the fireplace enclosed and surrounded with the water in the outer case projecting from the boiler, where much steam is found to be generated by the mere heat radiated from the highly ignited fuel. Between the back of the fireplace and the space below the chimney, a number of air tubes run horizontally through and through the boiler; along these the heated air passes in its way to the chimney, and by the large extent of surface which they together present to the water in the boiler with which they are all covered over, nearly the whole heat of the fire is communicated to the water instead of passing up the chimney, as it did in the old construction of engines with only one large heated air tube. In this manner an ample supply of steam is generated for the working of the engines, an object of the first importance.

George Buchanan, *Views of the Opening of the Glasgow and Garnkirk Railway with an account of the Lanarkshire Railways* (1832).

1831: Procession for William IV seen by Henry Cockburn

This gratifying account of a procession in honour of the new King William IV (who packed the House of Lords to ensure the passing of the Reform Bill) is by the

Edinburgh judge Henry Cockburn. As one of those who drafted the Scottish version, enfranchising £10 house-holders, he saw that the Parliamentary power of the landowners was hardly affected. In the 1833 election Glasgow, with a population of more than 200,000, had 7,000 registered voters and only two MPs.

On the 7th of September I went to visit in Renfrewshire, and on the 8th saw one of the great Glasgow processions, being one which took place on the occasion of the coronation of William IV, the reforming king. It was a magnificent and gratifying yet fearful spectacle. All the villages within many miles were in motion early in the morning, all pouring with devices and music into the Green, which was the great focus. I went to a window in the Court-house about eleven, and saw the platform erected for the managers, and all round it an ocean of heads and banners. I afterwards took the pains, through the police and Cleland, the Glasgow statist, and the chairman of the operatives, to ascertain the facts, and I don't believe that there were, including spectators, fewer than 100,000 persons on that field. An address was moved to the King, but I heard no articulate sound; and then the mass broke down into the portions that were to go in procession; and the rest streamed away to see the passing sight. I went with the local authorities to the Provost's house. He lived in St. Vincent Street, out of the intended line, but they deviated in order to testify their respect to him. Indeed it is one of the pleasing or (as it may happen) alarming features of these modern movements, that the people completely understand how much their force is increased by being orderly. All their plans were previously explained to the authorities, and whatever was objected to was changed. The procession took above two hours to pass, walking four abreast. Those engaged were about 12,000. They were divided into crafts, parishes, towns, mills, or otherwise, variously and irregularly, each portion bearing its emblems and music. The carters to the number of nearly 500 went first, mounted, their steeds decorated with ribbons. They were arranged according to the colour of their horses, and in honour of the administration the greys led. Then followed a long and imposing host in the most perfect order, all cheering the Provost as they passed, and all splendid with music and decorations. The banners were mostly of silk, and every trade carried specimens of its art, many of which were singularly beautiful, consisting of printing-presses, harpsi-chords, steam-engines, steam-vessels, looms and all sorts of machinery, all working, and generally with glass sides so that the working might be seen. The interest of these really exquisite models was not diminished by the countless efforts of grotesque wit with which each craft endeavoured to make its calling emblematic of the times and of the cause. Nothing surprised me so much as the music, even though I had been previously told that there was scarcely a mill or a village without its band. There could not be under fifty really good bands, generally consisting of about fifteen performers. King Crispin was to the eye fully as glorious as George IV when he entered Edinburgh. His retinue consisted of about 500 persons arrayed and arranged in mimic royalty, and all really splendid. No description of workmen was too high or too low for the occasion. The chimney-sweeps walked, and so did the opticians. Though there were groves of banners, we could only detect two tricolours, and these from their accompaniments were plainly not French in their principles. I did not observe any honour done to Hunt, and only once or twice to O'Connell. Beyond the disposition in favour of Reform, which was the object of the whole thing, there was nothing more popular than what might have been seen among the higher classes, and on any other occasion; almost every inscription or device was dedicated to Earl Grey, Lord Brougham, Joseph Hume, Lord John Russell, etc., and to reform, economy, peace, the king, and no burgh-mongers. Supposing (which was said to be the fact) that all Glasgow and its adjuncts had been idle for three days, it was computed that this exhibition had cost above £100,000. This is plainly extravagant, but its expense must have been very great. There was no soldier on duty, and no police officers except a few who were assisting, yet I never saw a populace in such order, or rather in such perfect good humour. Mrs. Cockburn and I walked with two children through the main streets with the utmost ease, and were even allowed on leaving the city to cut the line of the cavalcade by crossing it with a carriage, without a murmur. No excesses occurred during the whole day or night.

Journal of Henry Cockburn 1831–1854, Vol I (1874).

1832: A Female Felon in Anderston

By now police offices had been established at Bell Street (on the corner of the High Street), and in Gorbals and Anderston. In each the officer on duty kept a charge book, detailing the day's (and night's) events and taking statements; the vast majority of arrests were for drunk and disorderly conduct. Ann Finlayson is one of the few women lawbreakers recorded who was not a prostitute. A diligent constable noted that she was subsequently sentenced to six days' hard labour in the Bridewell, Duke Street. 'Main Street' is present-day Dumbarton Road.

Saturday the 14th Jany. 1832

Complains the Procurator Fiscal agt.
Ann Finlayson, Wife of David Niven, Labourer, residing in Partick, who was brought to the office this morning at a quarter to eight o'clock, charged with entering the dwelling house of Robert Nicol, residing in Kidston's land, Main Street, and while therein wickedly and feloniously breaking open a lockfast chest, and theftuously stealing and carrying away therefrom, about eight pound weight of Oat Meal, the property or in the lawful possession of the said Robert Nicol. She is also farther charged with having, on or about the seventh day of November last, feloniously entered the dwelling house of Robert Jaffray residing in Kirkwood's land, Main Street, and theftuously stealing and carrying away therefrom one blue and white printed Gown, one Cotton Damask Shawl, one black (?) Cloth Vest, one pair of Shoes, and other articles,

the property or in the lawful possession of the said Robert Jaffray. The Gown and Shawl were found on her person when apprehended.

Witnesses: Mrs Jaffray, Mrs Currie, Anderson Nicol, Sergt. McLean

Anderston Case Book 1810–32 (Strathclyde Regional Archives).

1832: William Cobbett's Impressions

The English radical William Cobbet (1763–1835) is best known for his *Rural Rides* round England (1830). It is perhaps not so well known that he followed this up with a tour of Scotland in 1832, being keen to visit that country—particularly Glasgow and the West—in the wake of the Reform Bill: 'The conduct of the Scotch with regard to . . . reform, has been . . . exemplary beyond description'. Reports of his tour were printed in his periodical, the *Weekly Political Register*, between September and November 1832. He was impressed by Glasgow—and by his reception there—and although an agriculturalist and anti-industrialist, he seemed awestruck by the Barrowfield textile dyeing and printing works of Henry Monteith (1765–1848). The Royal Exchange is now Stirling's Library.

And now what *am* I to say of this Glasgow, which is at once a city of the greatest beauty, a commercial town, and a place of manufactures also very great. It is Manchester and Liverpool in one (on a smaller scale) with regard to commerce and manufactures; but, besides this, here is the *City* of Glasgow, built in a style, and beautiful in all ways, very little short of the New Town of Edinburgh. The new Exchange is a most magnificent place; and, indeed, the whole of the city, compared to which the plastered-up Regent-street is beggarly, is as fine as anything that I ever saw, the New Town of Edinburgh excepted. The whole is built of beautiful white stone; and doors, windows, and everything, bespeak solid worth, without any taste for ostentation or show. The manufacturing part, with the tall chimneys and the smoke, is at the east end of the city, and somewhat separated from it; so that there is very little smoke in Glasgow. The river Clyde runs down through the city; and ships come up and lie by the wharfs for the better part of a mile. Goods are here taken out or shipped with the greatest convenience. Higher up than the point to which the ships come, there are three bridges, which cross the Clyde, for the convenience of going quickly from one side of the city to the other. By the side of the river, above the bridges, there is a place modestly called Glasgow Green, containing about a hundred English acres of land, which is in very fine green sward, and is at all times open for the citizens to go to for their recreation.

There is the finest, most convenient, and best conducted *cattle market* that I ever saw in my life. I do not like to see manufactories of any sort; but that of Mr.

Monteith, for the dyeing and printing of calicoes and shawls and handkerchiefs, and upon a scale of prodigious magnitude, I did go to see, and I saw it
with wonder that I cannot describe. First, there was a large room full of men,
engaged in drawing, upon paper, the flowers and other things which were to be
imprinted on their cotton; then there was another set to put these drawings
upon blocks of wood; then there was another to fasten on little pieces of copper
upon the wood; then there were others to engrave upon copper, in order to
print, pretty nearly as printing work is carried on; then came the men to mark
the copper with the blocks according to the drawings; and lastly came the
printers, who carry on their work by rollers, and effect their purposes in a
manner so wonderful, that it almost makes one's head swim but to think of it.
The buildings belonging to this dyeing and printing concern are as large as no
very inconsiderable country town.

Cobbett's Tour in Scotland (1833).

1832: Glasgow's Laudanum-Drinkers

Laudanum is an extract of opium dissolved in wine spirits and known medicinally
as a tincture. Opium's analgesic properties meant that both laudanum and opium
pills were widely used until Baeyer's discovery of aspirin at the turn of the century.
Rhubarb roots were used to make a strong laxative. Despite the addictive
characteristics of opiates they were socially acceptable; there was even a polite
fascination in the reveries produced by laudanum-drinking. Opium was also an
accepted treatment for the effects of cholera (see 1849). De Quincey, the best-
known literary opium-eater, stayed in Glasgow (see 1846) and had no difficulty in
obtaining supplies. Daniel Frazer was a partner in a family business of druggists
with premises at 113 Buchanan Street, later opening branches in Sauchiehall
Street and Kelvinbridge.

The butler or footman of a gentleman residing in St. Vincent Street—
somewhere about 1832–34—asked me early one morning, when my brothers
were at breakfast, for three ounces of laudanum. On my proceeding to label it,
he said there is no use in doing so as the vial has to be emptied into the medicine
chest bottle as soon as he got home—but I put the label on. In a quarter of an
hour or so the butler returned saying that he had made a mistake, that it was
tincture of rhubarb he was to have got. Had it not been labelled, the laudanum,
doubtless, would have been put into the tincture of rhubarb bottle, and the
person first requiring it, would have got the laudanum and been poisoned. The
little boy who had sold it would, doubtless, have got all the blame. This has led
me to be specially careful in keeping poisons, and to the distinctive labelling of
all dispensing bottle containing poisons, the last application of this principle
being the erection of the "Poison Room" in these new premises. As a set off

against this somewhat dismal story I here add one of a lighter character. Some forty years ago, when excessive drinking was much more common than now, and the drinking of soda water was largely resorted to as a restorative in the morning, a gentleman gave as his excuse for drinking soda water early in the day, that it was to quench the thirst he felt from having taken, on that special morning, too much salt to his egg.

The mentioning of the first of these incidents calls to my remembrance the laudanum drinking capacity exhibited by two of our early customers. The earliest of these was that of a then well-known glazier in Glasgow, who had for some years been a purchaser of laudanum through my brother when assistant in the Glasgow Apothecaries' Hall; when I knew him (about 1831) he was in the habit of drinking in our presence a full wine glassful (equal to four table spoonfuls), quite undiluted. He also regularly purchased about two pints at a time, supplied to him in metal flasks; these he was in the habit of carrying with him when travelling about the country in connection with his extensive business. The origin of this habit of laudanum drinking was the taking of it under medical advice for severe rheumatism in the head. The dose had gradually been increased till a wine glassful was substituted for the twenty or thirty drops taken at first. Anxious at times to wean himself from the habit of taking this huge dose, Mr——dropped a bit of putty into the bottom of the wine glass used for the laudanum. Succeeding with this, he gradually added more till the top of the glass was nearly reached, endeavouring by this method to get rid of the habit altogether; but just as this hope had, on several occasions, dawned upon him, a return of rheumatism or the recurrence of some domestic affliction induced a renewal of the craving, the putty was removed, and the full dose resumed. Mr——, quite a 'gash' old fashioned Scotchman, was in the habit of telling the number (which I won't venture to name) of *puncheons(!)* of laudanum that he had swallowed in his day.

Daniel Frazer, *The Story of the Making of Buchanan Street* (1885).

1834: Early Fire Regulations

The city's fire brigade, although allowed for in the 1800 Police Act, was not much in evidence until 1820 when it possessed six manual pumps and there were forty-eight firemen. At night they were roused to action by the watchmen alerting the Police Office and a big drum being beaten at the Fire Station ('Engine-house') in South Albion Street. Although there were fire plugs in the city's main streets, water-butts (each holding 160 gallons) were still needed at the scene of the fire, drawn there by horse and cart. In 1834 strict directions were issued to carters as to how to bring their horses to Albion Street, rates of pay and matters of conduct. Manual engines were used until 1870 when the first steam pumping engine was introduced.

Regular Carters: Sixteen carters who have good horses, and approved of by the Superintendent of Fire Engines, who reside near the Police Buildings, by entering their names and pledging themselves to attend when called upon, will be furnished with a signboard, on which will be painted their name and Fire Butt Carter, to be placed on their house or entry. The watchmen on the Beats where these Carters reside will be directed to call them immediately upon an alarm of fire. These Carters, and their servants, will be instructed in the mode of opening and closing of fire plugs; this is all the advantage that can be given to them, as, upon an alarm of fire, the first horses which arrive at the engine house, whether enrolled or not, if considered fit for the service, will be employed and their owners entitled to receive the following premiums and pay:-

First butt or engine   10s
Second ditto   7s 6d
Third ditto and others employed   5s
For every butt of water after the first, up to the sixth, 1s 6d—and for all above six, 1s.

Efficiency of horses: It being fully understood that the Superintendent is not bound to pay for any horses which he does not employ. Where none of the horses turned out are employed, the owners of the eight first arriving will be paid 2s 6d each;—if fewer than eight are employed, the rest, up to that number, will, in like manner, be entitled to 2s 6d each.— the horses in both cases being kept for half an hour at the Office, lest they may still be required. The Superintendent of the Fire Department, or whoever he may direct to act for him, is empowered to refuse any horse which he may consider unfit for service.

How to enter. to Engine-house, &c: The Carters must enter from Albion Street, and go out by Bell Street, each horse as he arrives being drawn across the lane on the north of the Office, from which position the Carters will be called in their order to receive their tickets. They must consider themselves, soon as they receive these, under the command of the Police, and in every way act in obedience to the orders of the Superintendent of the Fire Department, or whoever he may have placed in command; and must yoke his horse in butt or engine as directed. The attempt to break through any part of this rule, will infer the penalty of not receiving either premium or pay.

Care of engines &c: Carters must consider themselves as responsible for the carefully taking the engine or butt entrusted to their care to the fire, and bringing it back; if a butt, it must be returned to the Engine-house full of water; they will also be held accountable for the keys attached to the butt, and the service pipe.

Officer at the plugs: An Officer will be placed at each plug, to see that the

Carters take their turns and fill their butts properly, and make no unnecessary delay, that no injury is done to the plugs, and that the Carters are sober.

Regulations of the Fire Department of the Glasgow Police Establishment (1834).

1830s: Peever in Anderston

William Simpson (1823–99) was a lithographer turned artist who was born in Glasgow but travelled in Europe, America, India, Russia and even China, making rapid sketches (often in the thick of the fighting) which were published in magazines and newspapers. Before he left Glasgow in 1851 he made drawings of many city scenes which were later changed by railway and other developments. In the 1890s he made a series of paintings now in the People's Palace. In his autobiography (written around the same time) 'Crimean' Simpson clearly remembers the games children played in the streets of Anderston.

> Our games at that time were 'hide and seek,' 'robbers and rangers,' and 'high spy.' These were all games with running and hiding. 'Prisoner's base' came in, introduced, I think, from England. Other games were 'rounders' and 'housie,' which was rounders played without a bat. We threw the ball with the hand, and then ran round the 'dulls,' as we called the stones forming the stations. At the place where we struck the ball at rounders or threw it at housie there was a hole about a foot wide—this was the 'mug.' Three stones placed some fifty yards apart, forming a shape like a lozenge, were the 'dulls.' We also played cricket. 'Bools'—the Scottish word for marbles—implied a number of peculiar and ingenious games. We had marble 'bools,' and 'whinnies,' made from what was understood to be some kind of whinstone. But the common kind were only of baked clay. We had two games called 'muggie' and 'target,' in which the losers had to suffer the penalty of 'nags.' That was having a 'bool' projected against the knuckles. The gambling games were two. In one a 'mug' or hole, at the foot of a wall, was used. One boy took one or more 'bools' in his hand, and, according to the number, said to the other boy, 'Set us one,' or 'two,' or whatever was the number in his hand, the other boy placed an equal number, and the boy standing at the 'hail,' made a step forward, throwing all the bools into the mug. If they all went in he won, or if an even number chanced to remain in the mug, he won. But if an odd number remained, he lost. I still remember one boy who had a wonderful knack of throwing two marbles into a very small mug. This was important when there were only two, for if one came out the thrower lost.
>
> The great gambling game was called 'kep and smash.' A ring was marked about a foot from a wall, on a pavement; each boy placed in it a similar number of 'bools.' The burnt clay ones only were used in this game, except the 'plunker,' which was large, and made of the same clay as glazed jars. Each boy had his turn: he stood at the hail, and threw his plunker; if it knocked any of the

'bools' out of the ring they were his, but his principal object was to throw the plunker so that it first struck the pavement, then the wall, and thus rebounded, and he ran in, caught it, and then made a smash in the ring, knocking out as many of the 'bools' as he could, which became his. 'Kep and Smash' expresses the process of the game. 'Buttons' was another favourite game, and must have disappeared since from the change in costume. At that time brass buttons were worn on coats and waistcoats—a blue coat with brass buttons was the fashionable style. We boys called the coat buttons 'tosters,' as they were used for tossing, and the smaller ones on waistcoats were dubbed 'singlers.' Two singlers were valued as equal to one toster. Pitch-and-toss and simple tossing, 'head or tails,' were the two games at buttons.

. . .

'Pallall' or 'peevor' was the girls' game. Both these names were given to what is known in England as 'hopscotch.' The piece of flat stone, slate, or marble that was kicked from bed to bed marked on the ground was called 'peevor.' 'Pallall' and 'peevor' are other two words requiring the philologist to explain. A writer not long ago in a Glasgow paper announced a conclusion he had come to that the kicking of the peevor round the beds was in imitation of the course of the sun, and was a survival of the solar myth. The beds were numbered, and, in commencing, the girl stood in the semicircle outside, and threw the peevor into bed one. She then stood up, and lifting one foot began to hop from the semicircle; she had to hop and kick the peevor all round and into the semicircle. She next lifted the peevor and slid it along into bed number two. She then hopped from the semicircle into bed one, then to bed two, and pushed the peevor round as before. Next time she had to slide the peevor to bed three, and so on till she got to bed eight, and that was a game. If the peevor was kicked so that it stopped on any of the 'scores' or lines forming the beds, the girl was 'out.' I was an adept at this game, as well as at most of the lassies' games. The 'jumping-rope,' or skipping-rope, I was perfect at, and could do all the fancy movements with it, such as 'crossing' both forwards and backwards.

Autobiography of William Simpson, edited by G. Eyre-Todd (1905).

1834: The Glasgow Lying-In Hospital and Dispensary

The first institutional facilities for women giving birth in Glasgow date back to the 1790s when Dr James Towers opened a small lying-in hospital at his own expense (he became Glasgow's first Professor of Midwifery in 1815). In 1834 the Glasgow Lying-In Hospital and Dispensary was established with twenty-one directors drawn from the eminent men in the city's medical and professional circles. Its first premises were the Old Grammar School (on the second floor) in Greyfriars Wynd, then a house in St Andrew's Square, before moving in 1860 to Rottenrow where the present Glasgow Royal Maternity Hospital was built in 1908. These are some of the rules governing the running of the original hospital; in practice many illegitimate babies were delivered, although it had been feared that this might scare off philanthropic subscribers.

> 5. That this Institution may not in any degree tend to the encouragement of improvidence, none shall be admitted but those who are married and are really destitute, being unable to pay for medical attendance, and otherwise proper objects to be admitted to the benefit of this Asylum. These conditions shall be expressly vouched in the printed forms that shall be issued for the recommending of patients.
>
> 6. To poor women, who may wish to be attended in delivery at their own houses, that attendance shall be furnished to them upon leaving their addresses at the Hospital, along with a certificate from an Elder, District Surgeon, or other respectable person cognisant of the case, stating that the applicant is unable to pay for medical attendance.
>
> 7. At a stated hour, two days every week, Advice shall be given on Female Complaints, and the Diseases of Children, to all who may apply at the Hospital for that purpose, a part of economy which is expected to afford much relief to the applicants, & to contribute greatly to improvements in this very important part of Professional Knowledge.
>
> 9. The domestic arrangements of the Hospital, hiring servants, making markets, and similar duties, shall be under the management of a Matron chosen by the Directors, she being a person of unexceptionable character, qualified by education and practice as a Midwife. It shall be her duty also to superintend the ordinary cases of delivery in the Hospital, to call or summon the several classes of students entitled to be present at these cases, and to take care that every thing be done according to the rules of improved midwifery, and that rigid propriety and decorum be observed by every person in the Hospital. It would be proper that no more than four pupils should be at once in attendance on any ordinary case, and that after delivery the management of the case should devolve chiefly on the Matron, the students being admitted only at the ordinary hour of visiting along with the domestic Medical Superintendant.

Rules and Regulations of the Glasgow Lying-In Hospital and Dispensary (as agreed on by the Committee), October 6th 1834 (Glasgow University Archives).

1834: James Johnson's Description

Dr James Johnson was an insatiable traveller and a staunch patriot. This book's title page bears the explanation: 'being the Home Circuit versus Foreign Travel, a Tour of Health and Pleasure to the Highlands and Hebrides'. The doctor's previous visit must have been during the cholera outbreak of 1831–2. This time he took the steamer from London to Leith and did the Highland tour much as a

previous Dr Johnson had (see 1773), but in rather more comfort. On his way home
this dauntless pioneer travelled by steam-carriage on the road between Manchester and Liverpool, an ill-fated attempt to compete with the railway's expanding
network.

Glasgow appears to have been accidently built over one of Pluto's most
fashionable Divans—or of Vulcan's most extensive smitheries; for, at each
second of time, we see towering columns, or wreathing volumes of the densest
smoke, belched forth from a thousand infernal lungs, through pipes or tubes of
most gigantic altitudes and dimensions. The only place which can rival—or
perhaps excel—Glasgow, in this respect, is Bilston, near Birmingham, where
the inhabitants inhale more smoke and sulphur than if they lived in the crater of
Vesuvius during a smart eruption. The atmosphere of Glasgow is certainly
much less bright and exhilarating than that of Italy, or even of Edinburgh; and
no wonder, when we have so many tall and fuming pyramids, each of them
enceinte of a young volcano, threatening to illumine, but actually darkening the
gloom of even a Caledonian climate!

Although great part of the city of Glasgow is little inferior in architecture to
the New Town of Edinburgh, while it is infinitely more lively and animated, yet
there is something connected with the forges, the furnaces, the foundries, and
the factories—the steamers and the steam-engines—the tar and the hemp—the
cables and the anchors—the warehouses, casks, cotton bales, packing-cases,
rum-puncheons, tobacco hogsheads, and all the protean forms and denominations which manufactures and merchandise assume—that damped or annihi-
lated my romantic and picturesque ideas, and almost induced me to put a quill
behind my ear, and look as thoughtful as the crowds whom I met in the streets.

In every countenance that we contemplate in Glasgow, we see calculation—
in every feature some rule of arithmetic, (especially addition or multiplication,)
as legible as in the pages of Cocker. In Edinburgh, each physiognomy is
characterized by the lineaments of either law, physic, metaphysics, or divinity.
In Glasgow, there is also Mind in every face—but it is—'mind the main
chance.' At the time of my first visit to the Western capital, however, it is but
justice to say that there was an additional element of calculation in every
countenance—that of life and death. Choleraphobia intermingled its pale and
lurid hues with the tints of commercial anxiety and domestic affliction! The
inns and the theatres were deserted—man seemed cautious of associating with
his species, except in places of public devotion—funeral processions super-
seded the cheerful promenade—and the moral atmosphere was as sombre as
the physical!—In a subsequent visit, I found the streets as actively paced as
those of the Strand or Cheapside—the care of commerce, but no longer the
dread of pestilence, in every eye! In none of the principal streets did I see the
arm-in-arm lounging of the upper classes, or the snuff-taking, toddy-tippling
swarms of the lower orders, as in Auld Reekie.

We all draw imaginary portraits of what we do not see. I had pictured
Glasgow, in my own mind, as an immense town, with narrow streets, and

chiefly occupied by weavers, spinning-jennies, and operatives, of all descriptions, situated on the marshy banks of the Clyde. I was rather surprised and gratified to find the City of Glasgow constructed on the plan of the Houses in Edinburgh—namely, on Flats. Contrary to the order of rank in the intellectual city, however, I found the lower flats in Glasgow occupied by the best houses, and consequently the best tenants. The Clyde-flat, between St. George's Square and the river, may compete with most parts of the New Town of Edinburgh. Above George-street and Duke-street, rise various flats and gradations of habitations and inhabitants—till we come to the most surprising phenomenon which I ever witnessed on any part of the earth's surface—A Harbour on a Hill!! Looking up from one of the openings in Argyle-street, I saw, or fancied, a grove of masts far above the highest steeple in Glasgow! Well! thought I, if this be no spectral illusion, we need not wonder that 'Birnam wood should come to Dunsinane.' After half an hour's laborious ascent, scrambling from flat to flat, and from factory to factory, among cotton and carbon, sulphur and soda, I reached a lofty eminence that overlooked the great western metropolis, and found myself in—'Port Dundas!' This eccentric Port was crowded with shipping—not exactly equal in dimensions to those of the East India Docks, but fully as respectable, perhaps, as those which bore the eagled legions of Caesar to the shores of Britain, or the warriors of Woden to the banks of Loch Lomond.

Sauntering eastward from 'Port Dundas,' along the extended arms of this Harbour on the Hill, and surveying, with wonder and admiration, the singular scene that stretched down from this airy crest to the margin of the Clyde—this vast emporium of operatives—this city of the shuttle—this community of cotton-spinners—this world of weavers and unwashed artisans, living in an atmosphere of smoke and steam—I came, unexpectedly, to the foot of a colossal statue—not rivalling, certainly, in sculpture, the Farnese Hercules, or the Belvidere Apollo—but still the statue of a far better man, and a far greater hero than either of them—the Hero of the Reformation!

James Johnson, *The Recess or Autumn Relaxation in the Highlands and Lowlands* (1834).

1837: The Cotton Spinners' Trial

After the repeal of the Combination Acts in 1824 the cotton spinners attempted to get equal wages throughout the industry. Secrecy became essential since active membership of the Cotton Spinners' Association could mean being denied employment. A trade depression in 1837 led mill-owners to reduce wages. The spinners and other operatives came out on strike in April, and blackleg labour was subject to intimidation. In July John Smith was killed by a bullet that severed his spine; before he died he made this deposition in the Royal Infirmary. Evidence from Archibald Campbell helped to sentence five member of the strike committee to seven years in Botany Bay. A government Committee on Combinations of Workmen was set up after the trial, which took place in January 1838.

Appeared John Smith, who, being solemnly sworn, and warned by the sheriff to tell the truth, the whole truth, and nothing but the truth, as if in the prospect of death, depones, That he is forty years of age, is a native of Ireland, a cotton-spinner to trade, and for about the last four years has wrought to Messrs Henry Houldsworth & Sons, in their cotton-works, Cheapside Street of Anderston, near Glasgow. That, some time ago, the operative spinners in said cotton-mill struck work, and they have since continued idle: That the deponent, about three months ago, took work as a spinner, and got the wheels in said mill which had previously been wrought at by David Edwards, who stays somewhere in Cheapside Street: None of the old hands have since threatened to hurt the deponent, they they have passed him without speaking: That last night, he and his wife left home about ten o'clock, and went to a shop at the head of Clyde Street, where they got some tea; they then came down Clyde Street, and having bought some meal in the shop of one Bain, they were coming down the middle of the street, his wife being on his right hand, as he thinks, and when opposite Marshall's wood-yard, he was shot through the back, under the right shoulder, by some person behind him. At the instant of being struck, he called out he was shot, and he fell forward on the street, and became insensible of what was going on around him; he is unable to say who shot at him, and has no suspicion of who did so: That when he and his wife were passing the corner of Clyde Street, to go into the tea-shop at the top of that street, he saw Patrick Canovan, and Hugh M'Cafferty, and a third lad, with a white jacket and trowsers of moleskin, who were arguing together, but about what he could not learn; and, after leaving the tea-shop, the same persons were still at the corner, as he and his wife passed them and went down to Bain's. He did not observe whether they left the corner and followed him, nor did he hear any footsteps behind him, before being shot.

. . .

Archibald Campbell.—Is a cabinet-maker at Kirkintilloch. I lived there in July last. I live now in Calton of Glasgow. I remember coming to Calton from Kirkintilloch on Saturday evening. I travelled in the track-boat. I reached Glasgow between eight and nine, p.m. I walked from the track-boat in company of a man who had been in the boat with me. I walked from Port Dundas, and down the High Street. It was proposed to have some drink at King's in Stevenston Street, Calton. We went into a room; other persons, seven or eight were there. It was a private room, not a tap-room. By their dress they appeared to be spinners; but uncertain if they were so. I overheard a conversation among them. It was not said all at once. They were drinking. The first words I heard were—'Smith will be shot to-night.' This was about ten o'clock. On hearing this, I did nothing but looked at the party; the man who was with me was conversing to me at the time. I looked round, but could not say which of the party made the remark. A little after that, some one said—'It's a pity of poor Carmigan or Calligan. He's in Glasgow, but he is, or he'll be well hidden.' Uncertain which of the two names were used. I just turned round, and said— 'He'll be gey weel hidden if he's no gotten.' They just looked at me on this, *angry like*, at me speaking to them. The man who was with me was a man above thirty, or thereby. I have never seen him since. Next morning, (Sunday,) I heard that a man had been shot down about the Broomielaw on Saturday night.

The Trial of the Glasgow Cotton Spinners before the High Court of Justiciary at Edinburgh on charges of murder, hiring to commit assassinations, and committing and hiring to commit violence to persons and property, edited by James Marshall (1838).

1840: Death of a Climbing Boy

The most famous fictional treatment of 'climbing boys', as the apprentices of chimney sweeps were called, is Charles Kingsley's *The Water Babies* (1863); there is also Lamb's romanticised essay 'The Praise of Chimney-Sweepers'. Here is the chilling reality, in the evidence of witnesses in the enquiry into the death of an almost anonymous climbing boy, one 'John', aged about five or six. Despite the Chimney Sweeps Act of 1834 conditions in some places clearly did not improve much.

James Fleming, aged 16 years, an apprentice to William Forsyth builder, and the Declarant resides with his Mother Isobel Airds or Fleming in King Street of Calton near Glasgow. Declares That on Thursday the 23d. current the Declarant was desired by Mr Forsyth to. look over and superintend some Chimney Sweeps who had been employed to clear away the hardened lime which had accumulated in the Chimneys of a new tenement which he has lately erected near the Parkhouse Toll Bar on Paisley Road. That the Prisoner Francis Hughes was one of the Sweeps and the other was a little Boy named John. That the Boy was very ill clad having only a pair of trousers & a Shirt on, and he had no Jacket or Shoes. That the day was very cold & wet, and the Boy who did not appear to exceed five or six years of age, was very weakly. That there were forty two vents to be cleared out and the Boy went up one & down another till he had cleared out Thirty seven of the Vents. That the Declarant during this time was stationed at the top of the Chimney Stalk, and when the Boy was coming up the thirty Eighth Vent he delayed in it and Hughes who was at the top at the time called to him several times to come up and the Boy always said 'I'm coming'. That the boy was about twenty Minutes in the Vent when Hughes began to threaten him and say if he did not come up quickly he would take off his belt and thrash him. That it was about twenty Minutes past four when the Boy entered said Vent, and the Declarant is in the belief that he was ascending it & not descending said Vent when the Boy met with his death. That the Boy at the end of twenty Minutes or so, ceased to speak and Hughes & Declarant went away to look for a Rope to assist the Boy by putting it down from the top. That they could not find one, and when they returned to the Chimney top, they could get no answer from him when they spoke to the Boy. That Hughes put off his jacket & tried to descend the Chimney but it was too strait and he could only get down about two feet.

Robert Allan aged about 21, Journeyman Joiner in the employment of William Forsyth above designed, and the Declarant resides in North Cumberland Street of Calton near Glasgow Declares That the Declarant was at work in the New Building referred to in Precognition, and saw the two Chimney Sweeps referred to going about the premises. That about three in the afternoon the little Boy came down the Chimney of an apartment where Declarant was at work, and the Boy was complaining bitterly of cold and seemed to be very much exhausted & 'far through'. That his Clothes were in a wettish state, and the Boy on leaving said apartment went to the one immediately above, & as the flooring was not laid the Declarant could see betwixt the Joists. That Hughes the Prisoner was there and he was swearing at the Boy and threatening him. That after the Boy had got so far up said Chimney Hughes took a stick and put it up the Chimney & Kept thrusting away there, but whether he hit the Boy or not the Declarant cannot say, but at all events the Boy did not cry out as if hurt with the stick. That the Boy had been a good while in said Chimney, when the Declarant asked if the Boy was sticking and Hughes said he was but after the lapse of half an hour or so Hughes said he was moving on. That the Declarant wrought at the Building till half past four when he left it, at which time he had not heard of any thing having gone wrong. That the Declarant did not see Hughes strike the Boy, and altho he swore at him for his delay, he seemed kindly disposed to him in so far as he took him by the hand & led him across the Joists in case he might fall. And all this is truth.

Lord Advocate's Department Records: AD 14/40/242 (SRO).

1842: The Fearsome Cowlairs Incline

The Glasgow to Edinburgh railway was built by about 15,000 navvies at express speed, but in the teeth of opposition from the Forth and Clyde Canal Company. The railway engineers' intention was to bring the line into the city at a high-level station near Port Dundas, but the Canal Company refused to allow the construction of a viaduct. So the line had to make an impossible descent of 1 in 42 into the very heart of the city to what is now Queen Street station (the present one dates mainly from the 1870s). Nothing deterred, the engineers devised a steam-driven continuous rope for hauling trains up the incline and for slowing the descending trains. Some excursion trains had as many as forty carriages and on these occasions the upward rope sometimes broke, leaving passengers to find their own way out.

Immediately on passing the Station at Bishop-Briggs, we proceed on an embankment as far as the road from Glasgow to Kirkintilloch, on crossing through below which we at the same time enter the Barony parish, and a deep excavation through sandstone and other alternating rocks. This cutting, which is nearly a mile in length, and of an average depth of little less than fifty feet, is another work of gigantic dimensions, and one which was likewise carried on under great difficulties; but, like all the other portions of the undertaking, bearing ample testimony to the great skill and fearless enterprize which have guided to a safe conclusion all the operations of this Herculean task. At the entrance to the excavation, a short distance to the left, stands Huntershill, once the residence, as it should have been the property of Thomas Muir, Esq. younger of Huntershill, well known as having been condemned to exile for the expression of his political opinions. The passage through this narrow and deep fissure is very interesting, the face of the rocky walls being richly diversified by the most brilliant and intense display of metallic colours washed down by the oozing moisture filtered through their indurated sides; and the streaky tinges of the varying mineral beds are striking and peculiar. After emerging from the impending precipices of this enormous gallery, we sweep along an embankment commanding a delightful view of the level and fertile vale through which the Kelvin steals in shaded beauty to the Clyde. Towards the left hand, or rather almost directly in front, the eye is met by the huge towering chimney of St Rollox, a stupendous work, as yet only in progress, but sufficiently extensive to command the wondering gaze of every passer by. It is to be four hundred and twenty feet in height, and is fifty feet in diameter at the base. This being the first symbol of the productive power of Glasgow, the effect is such as cannot fail to impress upon the stranger a tolerable idea of the grand scale on which the works of the manufacturing metropolis of Scotland are conducted. A little further on, we arrive at the wooden platform for collecting the tickets from the passengers, directly opposite to the Railway Company's Workshops at Cowlairs. These are on a very extensive scale, occupying not less than three hundred and sixty-nine feet in front, being one hundred feet wide, and two storeys in height. At this point the locomotive-engines are detached from the trains, which are made fast to the endless rope for conducting them down the inclined plane. The rope is worked by two fixed engines of thirty horse-power each; the engine-house being surmounted by a handsome chimney-stalk upwards of ninety feet in height, has a fine effect upon the brow of the steep bank. The train being set in motion, proceeds with great rapidity down the Tunnel through Bell's Hill, upwards of three quarters of a mile in length, cut almost exclusively through rock, yet arched over, and brilliantly lighted with gas throughout its whole extent. On emerging from the subterrannean recesses of the tunnel, the astonished traveller finds himself transported into an almost fairy palace; this is the Passengers' Shed at the Glasgow terminus. This spacious and splendid erection, which is elegant as well as commodious, is furnished with a beautiful passengers' parade on each side, covered in by a roof supported on forty-eight columns arranged in double rows, besides the principal roof between them, a light and elegant fabric of the great span of sixty-four feet. The shed is upwards of two hundred and thirty feet in length, and, including the promenades on each side for the passengers, it is not less than eighty-five feet in width. There is also a splendid Booking-office, with access to waiting rooms, and every other convenience for the accommodation of travellers.

Guide to the Edinburgh and Glasgow Railway (1842).

1843: Prostitution

'The intense and unresting labours of years spent in contact with the most degraded classes, with malignant types of disease and loathsome forms of vice, told upon his constitution.' So wrote a contemporary of the city missionary William Logan (1813–1879). A former colleague of John Bright's in Rochdale, he worked for social as well as moral reform—indeed he regarded the two as inseparable, whether with regard to child abuse, temperance, sanitary conditions, education, or, as here, prostitution. A tireless visitor in the slums, he was watchful and compassionate, a friend to all; and published his observations in volumes of *Moral Statistics.* In the early 1840s the problem of prostitution was causing particular concern in both Edinburgh and Glasgow. The capital was alleged to harbour 800 full-time girls while Logan numbered the Glasgow girls at 3,000, although his fellow campaigner Ralph Wardlaw (see 1853) estimated 1,800. Even allowing for (perhaps understandable) exaggeration, Logan's statistics are horrifying enough. Not surprisingly his pamphlet sold out (7,000 copies) in a short space of time.

Number of houses of ill-fame	450
Average number of prostitutes (four in each house)	1800
Number of bullies or 'fancy men'	1350
Number of mistresses of said houses	450
Total living on prostitution	3600
Number of visits of men to each house weekly	80
Making weekly visits to the 450 houses	36000
The girls receive, on an average, from each visitor 1/- making the sum weekly, of	£1800
Robberies (2/6 from each visitor is a low average)	4500
Average sum spent on drink, 2/- by each visitor	3600
Total for prostitution weekly	£9900
Do. do. annually	£5148000

Number of girls who die annually (six years being their average life-time) three hundred!

. . .

Mistresses are all old harlots—seldom make money—and are, in general, very ignorant. Several who keep first-class houses in Glasgow cannot sign their names. In each of the houses they claim half of what the girls receive in *presents* and charge high for board: £1 weekly in first-class houses; and 14s in second houses. The girls have also to pay for the loan of dresses, &c., and when they have money, which is seldom, it is spent on drink, fruit, trinkets, shows, low musicians, &c. In first-class brothels it is quite common for the girls to receive from £1 to £5 from visiters.

I have stated that 2s are spent on drink on an average by each visitor, but the fact is, only *one-half* of that sum is spent while he is present. The mistress receives the money, and pretends to go or send out for the intoxicating liquor, (except where public-houses are regular brothels,) and it is an understood law, that she retains one-half of the sum for what they call in England 'wack brass,' and in Scotland 'the good-will of the house.' Drinking is also very common in first and second-class houses. Some mistresses send out for it, and others sell it in the house at a great profit; but regular visiters are aware of this, and generally cause it to be brought in. It is not long since several *gentlemen* drove up to a first-class house in my district, in a carriage and four horses; they had along with them a basket filled with bottles.

William Logan, *An Exposure, from personal observation, of Female Prostitution* (1843).

1844: Gartnavel Asylum Opens

The first half of the nineteenth century was a period of 'humane reform' in the treatment of the insane, with a generally more positive and constructive approach than previously (although it was not until 1857 that comprehensive lunacy legislation in Scotland was enacted, with district Lunacy Boards). The Directors of the new Asylum at Gartnavel (replacing the 1810 building on Parliamentary Road, which was considered now too near the heart of the city) claimed that it was the first erected on the principles of using no mechanical restraints in treatment and of having 'distinct buildings for . . . Patients of different ranks, divested of all gloom or appearance of confinement'. Certainly this song, by one of the inmates, paints an idyllic picture of the Asylum as a kind of prototype Holiday Camp, with every kind of occupational therapy available.

SONG

Composed for the occasion, and sung at the grand entertainment given on opening the New Asylum, Gartnavel.

AIR—'*A landlady in France.*'
Good bye, old house! good bye!
Thro' the new one let us pry,
On this hill called Gartnavel it is standing, O;

'Tis the finest house you'll find,
Throughout Europe, of the kind;
The view from it is pretty and commanding, O.

. . .

There's a Billiard Table, too,
If you handle well the Cue,
And like to knock the Balls about the Table, O;
A Back-Gammon-Board and Chess,
With the Baggatelle no less;
Play at any, or them all, if you are able, O.

. . .

For working, there's the ground,
Sev'nty acres all around,
If you like to take a spade and try the lev'ling, O;
We've to dig a Curling Lake,
And a Bowling Green to make,
Which ought to be without the slightest bev'ling, O;

. . .

While Attendants one and all,
Into this New System fall,
Now in buckles, belts, and muffs, there's no dependence, O;
'Tis the pleasing word and kind
Soothes the agitated mind—
A humane, but firm and uniform attendance, O.

J.R. Adam, *The Gartnavel Minstrel* (1845).

1844: Messiah at the City Hall

Victorian Glaswegians regularly packed the City Hall (and later the St Andrew's
Halls) in their passion for concerts and recitals. This particular performance was
no ordinary one. The formation in 1844 of the Philharmonic Society to give what
was the first complete performance in Scotland of Handel's *Messiah* inaugurated
the great tradition of choral singing in Glasgow—exemplified for many in Sir
Hugh Roberton's Glasgow Orpheus Choir (1901-51)—but continued today by the
Scottish National Orchestra Chorus. This chorus is the direct descendant of the
Philharmonic Society (founding along the way the orchestra that was to become
the SNO), is still amateur (though its standards are professional), and still features
Messiah in its repertoire. This particular performance was to raise money for The
Royal Infirmary.

The society instituted for the purpose of bringing out the 'Messiah' of
Handel on a scale proportioned to the greatness of the work, and consistent

with the elements which could be gathered together for a chorus in Glasgow, and to test whether Glasgow was prepared to give countenance to such music, fixed on the evening of Tuesday, the 2nd April, for the working of their experiment, and we rejoice to be able to say that it has had a most successful issue. Every thing turned out favourably; and the ladies and gentlemen of the society composing the chorus, who had been in training for some months previously, assembled in high spirits. At seven o'clock the platform was filled with the performers, 220 in number, each one seemingly anxious that the Oratorio should be done full justice to—so that the people of Glasgow might have an opportunity of proving whether this performance should be the solitary attempt, or the first of a series. All eager to follow the slightest suggestion which might contribute to the desired end—trusting to the skill of Mr. M'Farlane, their conductor, they waited but the lifting of his baton to burst out into the mighty chorus. The choristers, amateurs belonging to Glasgow, were placed on the platform erected at the west end of the City Hall, in two compact phalanxes, tier above tier, with the instrumental corps, a number of whom were amateurs, also inhabitants of Glasgow, led by Mr. Dewar of Edinburgh, in the centre. One moment's pause, up went the baton of the conductor, and the overture was heard, grave and potent, fore-shadowing the coming tide of music,—not one jarring note—not a quaver out of place; and the thousands of auditors were hushed as though a spell had begun to operate.

. . .

The performance of the 'Pastoral Symphony' was not exactly to our taste; there was much twaddle and no simplicity. Here and amongst the instruments we thought we could detect sundry ambitious attempts at adorning the chaste movement by the introduction of the trickery of dexterous manipulation, which with some people is meant to pass current for high art, but which, in such circumstances, in our opinion, is not far removed from impertinent quackery; these fantastic gambollings, which seem to form part of the fashionable taste of the time, only interrupt the even flow of Handel's music, and detract from the solemnity of its movements. While speaking of the instrumental part of this performance, we may as well state here, that in the accompaniment to all the songs of the Oratorio, the instruments were by far too prominent, in some cases they were so loud as almost to drown the voice of the singer.

. . .

The choruses were executed in a manner which proves satisfactorily that there is taste and knowledge sufficient amongst the amateurs of Glasgow to maintain an efficient choral society. There were few among the auditors who could fail of being struck with the grandeur of these masterpieces, and the more fastidious and severe critics must have been delighted with the strictness of time, and attention that was paid to propriety of accent and expression. In the

'Hallelujah,'—all was done for that most wonderful chorus that could be done by the number,—we wish that there had been five hundred voices equally well trained, rather than only the one hundred and seventy. 'His yoke is easy,' the tenor was undecided and heavy. 'Behold the Lamb of God' was well sung; would it not have been an improvement to have sung it in slower time—the solemn dignity of its transitions is more apparent when sung in the slowest adagio; the words of the chorus, 'Behold the Lamb of God that taketh away the sins of the world,' dare not be irreverently uttered, and Handel has in this part of his work done as much as can be accomplished in the way of making music a commentary upon, and exposition of, the words of Divine truth.

The performance of the 'Messiah' has established the right of Glasgow to the title of one of the music loving cities of Britain, and has proven that the noblest works in musical science only require to be brought forward in like manner, to meet the liberal support and encouragement of the people.

The British Minstrel, Vol. II (1844).

1846: De Quincey looks down on the City

De Quincey, the English Opium-Eater, lived in Glasgow on a number of occasions during the 1840s—mainly to escape his Edinburgh creditors. He stayed with J. P. Nichol, Professor of Astronomy at the University, whose house formed part of the new observatory built at Dowanhill to avoid the worst of the atmospheric pollution. Glasgow's population at this time time was 365,000.

What makes the Glasgow Observatory so peculiarly interesting is its position, connected with and overlooking so vast a city, having as many thousands of inhabitants as there are days in a year (I so state the population, in order to assist the reader's memory), and nearly all children of toil; and a city, too, which, from the necessities of its circumstances, draws so deeply upon that fountain of misery and guilt which some ordinance, as ancient as 'our father Jacob,' with his patriarchal well for Samaria, has bequeathed preferentially to manufacturing towns—to Ninevehs, to Babylons, to Tyres. How tarnished with eternal canopies of smoke, and of sorrow; how dark with agitations of many orders, is the mighty town below! How serene, how quiet, how lifted above the confusion, and the roar, and the strifes of earth, is the solemn observatory that crowns the heights overhead! And duly, at night, just when the toil of overwrought Glasgow is mercifully relaxing, then comes the summons to the labouring astronomer. Everywhere the astronomer speaks not of the night, but of the day and the flaunting daylight, as the hours 'in which no man can work.' And the least reflecting of men must be impressed by the idea, that at wide intervals, but intervals scattered over Europe, whilst 'all that mighty heart' is, by sleep, resting from its labours, secret eyes are lifted up to heaven in astronomical watch-towers; eyes that keep watch and ward over spaces that make us dizzy to remember, that register the promises of comets, and disentangle the labyrinths of worlds.

Thomas De Quincey, 'The System of the Heavens', from *Speculative and Theological Essays.*

1847: Napier's Foundries

Although iron ships were first built in the 1830s, it was the Govan yard of Robert Napier and Sons which started production of large passenger ships in iron. They made their initial reputation with marine engines, but in the 1840s they started equipping Government warships and building ships for the Cunard Steamship Company which carried the transatlantic mail. Napier had come a long way since setting up as a blacksmith in Greyfriars Wynd near Glasgow Cross. The *Examiner* reporter here evidently feels he is in the presence of one of the wonders of the machine age, words failing him at one point in the welter of technical details.

The Vulcan and Lancefield Foundries

Our notices of the Cunard steamers and of the Government frigate Dauntless which are being furnished with engines at the above-named foundries, may excite some curiosity regarding the foundries themselves. As far as we can learn, no other foundries in the world are able to compete with these named either for the magnitude or perfection of the work they produce. At all events a brief account of the works which, along with the building-yard at Govan, furnish constant employment to some 14,000 or 15,000 of our working men, cannot but be generally interesting. The works are situated in Anderston, on the banks of the Clyde. The Vulcan Foundry is situated between Washington-street and McAlpine-street, and is about a hundred yards from Broomielaw-street, and the Lancefield Foundry is a little further west, and lies on the north bank of the Clyde. The enterprising proprietor, Mr Robert Napier, does the whole fitting up vessels, both wood and iron, and consequently his works are very extensive. The wright shops of Lancefield foundry are between the Clyde and the Broomielaw-street, and the foundries, etc., are on the other side of that street, and cover an area, we should suppose of several acres. The first process we notice is that of casting or smelting the metal and running it into moulds. On the west side of the work, in connexion with a large building, there are three smelting furnaces, which can throw off respectively at one casting eight, six, and five tons, and also an air furnace, which holds from 35 to 40 tons. When very large castings are done, the smelted metal is put into the air furnace till a sufficient quantity is produced. A number of moulders are at work in this department, laying down moulds and preparing them for the metal. The heavy castings are moved with cranes and other similar apparatus. The floor of this building is sand, and some large castings require a pit dug of the size of a small house! There are also two air furnaces for brass, which can throw off respectively two tons and four tons each. The brass is smelted in portable crucibles, which are lifted out of the furnace, and the melted brass is poured directly from them into the mould. To give some idea of the extent of the brass castings, we may state that the steam pistons of the Cunard steamers are of brass, and each weighs about four tons, being ninety inches in diameter, and of proportional thickness.

Another building is one of the smith's shops, where there are above twenty forges, all blown by air fanners, from which pipes communicate with the furnaces. In the front row of the buildings is the finishing shop, where a number of men are at work, polishing and otherwise finishing different parts of steam engines. The jointing and polishing is done with extreme accuracy, and, minute as is the work, very rarely a mistake occurs. On the east side of the works the most important and complex part of the work is carried on. There an engine of forty horse power is keeping in constant motion various turning and planeing machines. Some of our readers will hardly deem it credible that pieces of metal weighing ten tons can be put in a lathe and turned with as much ease as a penny bobbin. The lathes are all driven with belts, but in order to give slowness and power, two, three, and even four sets of wheels and pinions are introduced. Some of these wheels are of great size and strength, weighing several tons, and two of the lathes weigh nearly 40 tons. On Thursday we saw a cylinder cross-head of four tons weight attached to a perpendicular wheel of a lathe and turned round as if it had not weighed an ounce. An instrument was applied to its centre, and a hole some six or eight inches in diameter scooped out. Cutting tools were then applied, and as its extremities slowly turned round, these shaved off the metal as easily as if it had been soft wood. The power required to drive it when the tools were cutting some four feet from the centre may be more easily conceived than described. In some cases, however, the metal being operated on is fixed and the instrument revolves. In boring cylinders, for instance, they are screwed to the boring machine, and the instrument which cuts them slowly revolves. The borer is a wheel on the spindle of the lathe, in which turning irons are fixed, and the spindle moves forward self-acting into the cylinder as it cuts its way. The heavy machinery shakes as some of these huge bores is being made . . . .

The works are admirably conducted. The machines are of the first-rate quality, and many of them were constructed within the works, and of a description to be found nowhere else. They are kept in first-rate order, and every one about the extensive work seems perfectly master of his department. The only noise is that of the machines and hammers, not an idle, much less an improper, word is heard. The men are happy among each other, and respectful of strangers, and all being at their work. Many of them have high wages, and probably we are not over-estimating the fact, when we say that the 1400 men employed have each, at an average, three depending on him, which would be, in all, 5200 persons deriving their subsistence directly from the works.

The capital laid out is incalculable, and the works we consider one of the most splendid triumphs of talent and of enterprise of which our city, or any other, can boast.

The Glasgow Examiner, 16th October 1847.

1848: The Bread Riots

The 1840s were a decade of depression and hunger and consequent demand for political reform. 1848 was the Year of Revolution in Europe; the *Communist Manifesto* was issued in February, and in April the Chartists petitioned Parliament in London. This eye-witness account of the Glasgow riot of 6 March is by the poet and essayist Alexander Smith (1829-67), at that time employed as a muslin pattern designer. His later political conservatism may be traced to the impact on him of this 'hideous dream'.

During the commercial distress of 1848–49, and the agitation consequent on the flight of Louis Philippe and the establishment of the French Republic, Glasgow had the bad eminence of going further in deeds of lawlessness and riot than any other city in the empire. The 'Glasgow operative' is, while trade is good and wages high, the quietest and most inoffensive of creatures. He cares comparatively little for the affairs of the nation. He is industrious and contented. Each six months he holds a saturnalia—one on New-year's day, the other at the Fair, (occurring in July,) and his excesses at these points keep him poor during the intervals. During periods of commercial depression, however, when wages are low, and he works three-quarter time, he has a fine nose to scent political iniquities. He begins to suspect that all is not right with the British constitution. These unhappy times, too, produce impudent dema-gogues, whose power of lungs and floods of flashy rhetoric work incredible mischief. To these he seriously inclines his ear. He is hungry and excited. He is more anxious to reform Parliament than to reform himself. He cries out against tyranny of class-legislation, forgetting the far harder tyranny of the gin-palace and the pawn-shop. He thinks there should be a division of property. Nay, it is known that some have in times like these marked out the very houses they are to possess when the goods of the world are segregated and appropriated anew. What a dark sea of ignorance and blind wrath is ever weltering beneath the fair fabric of English prosperity! This dangerous state of feeling had been reached in the year spoken of. Hungry, tumultuous meetings were held on the Green. The ignorant people were maddened by the harangues of orators—fellows who were willing to burn the house of the nation about the ears of all of us, if so be *their* private pig could be roasted thereby. 'The rich have food,' said they, 'you have none. You cannot die of hunger. Take food by the strong hand wherever you can get it.' This advice was acted upon. The black human sea poured along London Street, and then split—one wave rushed up the High Street, another along the Trongate—each wasting as it went. The present writer, then a mere lad, was in the streets at the time. The whole thing going on before his eyes seemed strange, incredible, too monstrous to be real—a hideous dream which he fought with and strove to thrust away. For an hour or so all order was lost. All that had been gained by a thousand years of strife and effort—all that had been wrested from nature—all the civilities and amenities of life—seemed drowned in a wild sea of scoundrelism. The world was turned topsy-turvy. Impossibility became matter of fact. Madness ruled the hour. Gun-shops were broken open, and wretched-looking men, who hardly knew the muzzle from the stock, were running about with muskets over their shoulders. In Buchanan Street a meal cart was stopped, overturned, the sacks ripped open with knives, and women were seen hurrying home to their famishing broods with aprons full; some of the more greedy with a cheese under each arm. In Queen Street a pastry cook's was attacked, the windows broken, and the delicacies they contained greedily devoured. A large glass-case, filled with coloured lozenges, arranged in diamond patterns, stood serene for a while amid universal ruin. A scoundrel smashed it with a stick; down rushed a deluge of lozenges, and a dozen rioters were immediately sprawling over each other on the ground to secure a share of the spoil. By this time alarm had spread. Shops were shutting in all directions, some of the more ingenious traders, it is said, pasting 'A Shop to Let' upon their premises—that they might thereby escape the rage or the cupidity of the rioters. At last, weary with spoliation, the mob, armed with guns, pistols, and what other weapons they had secured, came marching along the Trongate, a tall begrimed collier, with a rifle over his shoulder, in front. This worthy, more than two-thirds drunk, kept shouting at intervals, 'Vive la Republic! We'll hae Vive la Republic, an' naething *but* Vive la Republic!' to which intelligible political principle his followers responded with vociferous cheers. At last they reached the Cross. Here a barricade was in process of erection. Carts were stopped and thrown down, and London Street behind was crowded with men, many of them provided with muskets. On a sudden the cry arose, 'The sogers, the sogers!' terrible to the heart of a British mob. Hoofs were heard clattering along the Trongate, and the next moment an officer of Carabineers leaped his horse over the barricade, followed by his men, perhaps a dozen in all. The effect was instantaneous. In five minutes not a rioter was to be seen. When evening fell the Trongate wore an unwonted appearance. Troops stacked their bayonets, lighted their fires and bivouacked under the piazzas of the Tontine. Sentinels paced up and down the pavements and dragoons patrolled the streets. Next day the disturbance came to a crisis. A riot occurred in Calton or Bridgeton. The pensioners were sent to quell it there. While marching down one of the principal streets, they were assailed by volleys of stones, the crowd meanwhile falling back sullenly from the bayonet points. The order was given to fire, and the veterans, whose patience was completely exhausted, sent their shot right into the mass of people. Several were wounded, and one or more killed. When the pensioners were gone, a corpse was placed on boards, carried through the streets shoulder-high by persons who, by that means, hoped to madden and rouse the citizens; a large crowd attending, every window crammed with heads as the ghastly procession passed. As they approached the centre of the city, a file of soldiers was drawn across the street up which they were marching. When the crowd fell back, the bearers of the dead were confronted by the ominous glitter of steel. The procession paused, stopped, wavered, and finally beat a retreat, and thus the riots closed. That evening people went to look at the spot where the unhappy collision had taken place. Groups of workmen were standing about, talking in tones of excitement. The wall of one of the houses was chipped in places by bullets, and the gutter, into which a man had reeled, smashed by the death-shot, had yet a ruddy stain. Next day tranquillity was in a great measure restored. Masses of special constables had by this time been organised, and marched through the city in force. Although they did not come into contact with the rioters, the bravery they displayed in cudgelling what unfortunate females, and *keelies* of tender years, fell into their hands gave one a lively idea of the prowess they would have exhibited had they met foes worthy of the batons they bore.

Alexander Smith, *A Summer in Skye* (1865).

1849: Cholera and the City Centre

Dr Sutherland's description of the old city centre demonstrates in sickening detail why cholera spread so quickly after the outbreaks in 1832 and 1848. Opium was the standard treatment for the diarrhoea symptoms, but there was no effective remedy for the dehydration which made cholera so painful and deadly.

It is in those frightful abodes of human wretchedness which lay along the High Street, Saltmarket, and Briggate, and constitute the bulk of that district known as the 'Wynds and Closes of Glasgow,' that all sanitary evils exist in perfection. They consist of ranges of narrow closes, only some four or five feet in width, and of great length. The houses are so lofty that the direct light of the sky never reaches a large proportion of the dwellings. The ordinary atmospheric ventilation is impossible. The cleansing, until lately, was most inefficient, and, from structural causes, will always, under existing arrangements, be difficult and expensive. There are large square midden-steads, some of them actually under the houses, and all of them in the immediate vicinity of the windows and doors of human dwellings. These receptacles hold the entire filth and offal of large masses of people and households, until country farmers can be bargained with for their removal. There is no drainage in these neighbourhoods, except in a few cases; and from the want of any means of flushing, the sewers, where they do exist, are extended cesspools polluting the air. So little is house drainage in use, that on one occasion I saw the entire surface of a back yard covered for several inches with green putrid water, although there was a sewer in the close within a few feet into which it might have been drained away.

The water-supply is also very defective; such a thing as a household supply is unknown, and I have been informed that, from the state of the law, the water companies find it impossible to recover rates, and that, had the cholera not appeared, it was in contemplation to have cut off the entire supply from this class of property.

The interior of the houses is in perfect keeping with their exterior. The approaches are generally in a state of filthiness beyond belief. The common stairs and passages are often the receptacles of the most disgusting nuisances. The houses themselves are dark, and without the means of ventilation. The walls dilapidated and filthy, and in many cases ruinous. There are no domestic conveniences even in the loftiest tenements, where they are most needed, except a kind of wooden sink placed outside some stair window, and communicating by a square wooden pipe with the surface of the close or court beneath. Down this contrivance, where it does exist, is poured the entire filth of the household or flat to which it belongs, and the solid refuse not unfrequently takes the same direction till the tube becomes obstructed.

Dr Sutherland, *Report on the Measures Adopted for the Relief of Cholera in Glasgow during the Epidemic of 1848-49 (Appendix A).*

1850: The pros and cons of Glasgow Fair

Two contrasting pictures of Glasgow's annual holiday. The Fair (instituted c. 1190) was an eight-day holiday until the 1860s when the present arrangement of a fortnight at the end of July was adopted. The extracts from the *Guide* give an impression of some of the attractions on offer in the late 1840s; there would also have been a mass of stalls, sideshows and penny theatricals ('geggies') in Jail Square near the Green. The puritanical writer in the *Scottish Temperance Review* has a different idea of holiday enjoyment (although it is not clear what that is). Declaring his disinclination to describe the 'horrors' of the Fair, he then proceeds, in the tradition of moral reformers, to do just that.

Queen's Theatre

Lately erected in Green Dyke Street, by Mr Calvert, but for a short period will be under the management of Mr Glover of the Prince's. During the Holidays an interesting panorama of the overland route to India, from Southampton to Calcutta, representing views on Sea and Land of 3,000 miles, is each day exhibited. The views include all the distinguished and remarkable objects which arrest the eye of the traveller during the excursion, from the period of leaving the shores of old England to the arrival in India.

The artistes, Messrs S. Bough, J. M'Donald, and Mr Glover who assisted them, deserve great credit for their masterly delineations. The whole is described by a gentleman in a most instructive manner, and it is pleasing to observe the marked attention paid to his discursive statements. In addition to the above we are also treated to a sight of the wonderful performances of Mons. Lupriol, the gymnastic professor, and the astonishing feats of the great American slack rope dancer, Henry Walker, also a dioramic painting of the ruins of the Temple of Mars, Modern Italy, painted by Samuel Bough Esq., for the Queen's private Theatricals. The Prices of admission are Boxes, 6d.—Side and upper do. 4d.—Pit 2d.—Open the entire day.

The Patent Hydro-Incubator

For hatching eggs. This is a most novel and interesting exhibition, and cannot fail to excite and enlist the reflective faculties of every beholder. Chicken-hatching by steam! Who could have believed that such a mysterious triumph would be added to the other wonderful achievements of this subtile element. Watt could never have dreamt of such a result, when experimenting on its power in the construction of the steam engine. But true it is, and of verity, the frisking little creatures come forth from their limey envelope, the shell, to the light of day, with no other maternal superintendence than the friendly aid of a small sheet of warm water. The Incubator is a wooden box with a glass covering, below which the eggs are ranged, and acted on by heated water, regulated by a thermometer. The heat is supplied by a charcoal stove, which keeps up a continuous warmth. As soon as the little stranger has freed himself from his encumbrance, and had sufficient rest, he is placed in a warm bed of straw, and afterwards handed to the care of the hydro-mother, who soon inspires him with sufficient energy and life to get on for himself in the world. In he goes to the little court-yard provided for his use, and mixes with his mates, of whom there is always a goodly number, frisks about, picks his food, apparently as happy as if he came in the legitimate way of generation. The admission is only One Penny, and cannot fail to interest every body.

Music Saloons

These establishments form a sort of intermediate link between the theatre and the tavern, and partake partly of the character of both, affording, however, a much more rational and intellectual resort than the latter. They are conducted with great regularity, and particular care is taken to secure professionals of respectability as well as of talent. The entertainments being nearly restricted to vaudeville, a constant succession of engagements is necessary to keep up sufficient attraction, and the public has thus always an opportunity of hearing the newest musical productions of the day. During the Holidays, the Saloons are open every day from 12 o'clock; and, collectively present an amount of diversified talent that affords ample means for the gratification of every taste, from the pure and heart-touching simplicity of Scottish melody, to the irresistible ludicrousness of national humour—the broad jokes of the Negro representative and the keen point of Irish wit and English repartee;—from the deafening castanet accompaniment of the African break-downs, to the light and graceful motion of the accomplished danseuse.

The majority of the Music Saloons are situated in Saltmarket, and are consequently near the very centre of attraction. There is no charge for admission, and the refreshments, which are generally of a good quality, are sold at a moderate price. The following short glance at the several establishments will give an idea of their relative merits.

The *'Shakespeare,'* 36 *Saltmarket; Proprietor, Mr. Lowden.*—This Saloon and the Bowling-Alley in connection with it, are the favourite lounges of 'Young Glasgow,' and in respect to musical talent—vocal and instrumental— and accommodation, is the leading house of the kind in the city. The best feature in the present company is two comic duet singers, who sustain their parts with great dramatic effect and happy individuality of character. The sentimental and comic departments are also well supported.

The *'Odd-Fellows',*' 31 *Saltmarket; Proprietor, Mr. S. Sloan.*—The entertainments here are well supported by popular and clever professionals, in comic, sentimental and characteristic singing, including Mr. John M'Gregor, the old Scottish comedian, whose thorough appreciation of the national character enables him to give happy effect to the quaint songs and stories in which he appears. Mr. Baylis, (one of the artists of Professor Anderson's Balmoral Castle,) is also engaged here, and exhibits his very ingenious Automata.

The *'Jupiter,'* 46 *Saltmarket; Proprietor, Mr. W. Crawford.*—This popular Saloon is supported by Miss Coutts, whose characteristic songs are very piquant, Mr. C. Sharpe, Mr. Thomson, Mr. Cooke, a skilful performer on the banjo, and Mr. Alister M'Lean, a Highland piper and dancer, who appears in both capacities at the same time, with an effect which it is not easy to describe.

The *'Sir Walter Scott,'* *Saltmarket; Proprietor, Mrs. Baxter.*—The attractions at this Saloon are not inferior to those of the others, and amongst the novelties comprise a *rara columba* in the person of a female Ethiopian Serenader whose performances are worth witnessing, as much from their intrinsic merit as their novelty.

Panoramas, Caravans, Etc.
In addition to the foregoing list there are about a dozen of these places strewed about the Fair; such as Views of the Pope's return to Rome, Nineveh, the Frozen regions, Pekin, Glasgow, and the Wreck of the Orion; and several portable halfpenny Peepshows. We have a Wizard in kilts, in a scurvy looking shop at the foot of the Saltmarket, showing off his magical feats for a halfpenny; and close by, the Jack Sheppard drama in Mumford's toll booth, performed for the same price.

Further on, and we have Giants and Giantesses nearly eight feet high, and crocodiles and serpents in the same exhibitions; with dwarfs, of both sexes, scarcely reaching on tiptoe to the top of the giant's boot. There is, likewise, a variety of Wax Figures,—kings, queens, and notorious malefactors, misers, and other oddities. From all of the exhibitions of this latter fry there is an incessant yelling and vociferation, deepened by the noise of gongs, speaking-trumpets, &c., to arrest the attention of the onlookers to the incredible wonders they have to show for a penny.

. . .

We believe, then, that one of the most direct and manifest tendencies of these exhibitions and entertainments is, to encourage and extend the hideous and already prevalent enough vice of prostitution. We believe, and we take the responsibility of announcing it as a fact, that in the brothels additions are made to the regular staff, by reinforcements from Edinburgh (and perhaps other towns), to meet the extra demand of the time. And we believe, though we cannot take the responsibility we have taken in the former case, that in the manager of one of the most respectable 'affairs,' and one eminently attractive during the Fair, the first-class prostitutes of the city find an active friend and patron, and that they are either admitted *free* on presenting themselves, or have tickets sent round to their various establishments! To such an extent has their presence been perceptible, that letters have been written to the public papers regarding it; and 'respectable' men have declared that they could not attend if it were continued.

One of the most saddening reflections in regard to the Fair is that it *necessitates*, in the case of a large number, that they shall be degraded far below the level of humanity. Such is the case, we humbly think, with many of the actors and performers—the *furnishers* of our most popular entertainments. *Can a 'clown' be religious?—can* he even have self-respect? And, to go no farther, are *any* of the characters who take part in the disgusting exhibitions *outside*, in a position to do their duty either to God or man? And in countenancing practices which necessitate this state of things, are not we verily most guilty?

Hitherto our remarks chiefly apply to the celebration of our Fair *within* the town. 'At all events,' some of our *Fair* friends will say, 'you must be pleased with the thousands who betake themselves to the steamer and railway.' But we are not. We want that when our people get holidays, seldom as it is, they should at least be able to *enjoy* them. We humbly submit that, as things are managed at present, this is impossible. Twenty thousand, it is estimated by the *Herald,* went down the river on Saturday. With even the immense accommodation which we have in the number of steamers plying, is it possible that 20,000 human beings could 'enjoy' themselves in them? Assuredly no. And we know that, crowded as they were, the supply of passengers was far from being exhausted; and many, rather than go on board in such crowds, condemned themselves to 'the shows' and all their horrors. This brings us to submit to our readers another department of the horrors of the Fair. First comes the drunkenness on board these crowded steamers. This we are assured, by parties who went in various directions, was very prevalent. We can also bear witness to its extent ourselves, having been for sometime on board one not so crowded as some of the others. One of our friends told us of a party of eight or ten, who, before they got to Rothesay, had 'three bottles of whisky and a fight' amongst them; the three bottles being well nigh finished before the fight began. But the evil of the 'crowds' does not end when they leave the steamer. Not only is our city, during the Fair, a horrible nucleus of immorality and wickedness; it sends our multitudes to pollute and demoralise the country. It is stated on the most unquestionable authority, that hundreds of men and women lay in the woods and fields about Rothesay on the nights of Saturday and Sunday of the fair-week. Lodgings were not to be had even at a high price; and some of the places that were made available, revealed scenes such as we have of late so often heard of, as peculiar to metropolitan lodging-houses. In one attic of which we heard, *fifteen*, male and female, were accommodated! In a bed-closet, in which only *two* could *stand* out of the bed, *six* were 'accommodated'—two men and four women!

Reader, what think you of the Fair? It's a fine old custom. Beautiful to read in the papers about its 'fun,' and its 'frolic,' and its 'laughter-loving citizens!' In our opinion, it is a horrible and most wicked custom.

What's to be done? Some evils are simple, some complicate, some *a puzzle*. This one and its remedy are simple. Every one must see that 'the crowd' is the Fair. The magistrates, we understand, have withdrawn *their* sanction from the Fair; why should not all employers do the same? Why should they not each consult his own convenience (during the proper season,) and give his workers their needed holidays at a time and in a way in which enjoyment and profit are possible? Take away the crowd and you take away the show, the theatre, the circus, and all unhealthy stimulus to all other wickedness which these afford.

Guide to Glasgow Fair (c. 1850) and *Scottish Temperance Review* (August 1850).

1851: Death Toll of Under-Fives

The 1850s was a decade of epidemics. Cholera haunted the city until the coming of fresh water from Loch Katrine and the closure of contaminated drinking wells. Smallpox vaccine had been available since Jenner's discoveries of the 1790s but no mass programme was undertaken until the Vaccination Act of 1864 which required children of six months to be immunised. In poorer areas people still left corpses in charnel houses rather than burying them, further assisting the spread of disease.

It appears that in 1851 the deaths under five years are more in proportion to the whole mortality than in any one of the three previous years, a result that prominently marks the existence of an element of destruction to which the infant population of our City is exposed. It is from this element of destruction among children, that the high figure of annual mortality chiefly arises in Glasgow, and other manufacturing towns; for if we reduce the deaths under five in these towns, to the average percentage which the deaths at these ages bear to the living in other places, the remaining deaths to the remaining population will be throughout but little dissimilar.

That Glasgow should have lost by death, during the last four years, 14,371 children, under two years of age, or 32.14 per cent. of the gross annual mortality, is fearful to contemplate, and loudly calls for something being effectually done for the preservation of the infants of the poor, among whom this high mortality exists. The want of care on the part of the mother, called to toil beyond her home, which is left filthy and neglected,—the want thereby of nature's nutriment to her child, who, when crying to others for food, is too often only soothed by opiates, or when assailed by disease, is permitted to die without the aid of medical skill or nutritious appliances, are all elements in this frightful waste of life. Can nothing be suggested to meet this cruel calamity?

John Strang, *Report on the Mortality Bills of the City of Glasgow and Suburbs for 1851.*

1851: The Nuisance Arising from Smoke

The 1827 legislation requiring factory owners to control emissions of smoke if complaints were made by five adjoining householders contained laughable penalties. Not until the Public Health Act of 1875 were industrial (but not domestic) chimneys brought under some sort of control. The principle of complete combustion of soot-containing gases—by mixing them with oxygen within the furnace—was well known but not much put into practice. The author of this *Report* was a merchant living near Calton Place, then a fairly smoky vicinity downwind from Dixon's Blazes. A thousand copies were printed by the Police Committee and circulated among the major factory owners.

I calculated, from the number of establishments (300) named in the returns furnished to me, that this general inspection would take from a month to six weeks, a large portion of each day being occupied in entering in a journal the particulars connected with each visit. While carrying on this general inspection, it appeared a desirable thing, if possible, to have by the end of it, some additional examples of improvement effected by dint of persuasion and entreaty, so that, when ready to prosecute such parties as might be selected for prosecution, I would be able to state from experience how much good was likely to result from a continuance of the exercise of remonstrance and entreaty. It was desirable to be able to point to examples, both territorial and personal; and the locality most suitable, as a territorial example, seemed to be Buchanan Street, as much damage to the valuable property, and annoyance to the inhabitants, in that quarter, is caused by the smoke emitted from the works in that neighbourhood. These works are, in number, six, viz., three calenders, two foundries, and one place for roasting malt. It cannot be said that Buchanan Street is the smokiest part of the city, but a little smoke there, is, in consequence of the value of the property exposed to its influence, a greater nuisance than a greater quantity would be in many other parts. That locality possesses the advantage of being central, and easy to visit by parties desirous to see the means used, and from the small number of the works, any improvement would have been at once discernible. As personal examples, a small number of the leading houses in various branches of trade were selected, upon whom I waited, and represented to them the duty they owe to the public, on account of the prominent position they occupy, and that proceedings against the owners of small establishments could not be adopted so long as no improvement was made in theirs. The success has been very indifferent. In Mitchell Street, one of the foundaries has adopted a plan by which the nuisance is mitigated, and the malt-roasting place will be removed at or before Whitsunday, but the three calenders and the other foundry are in the same condition as before. The attempt to obtain a territorial example may therefore be said to have failed; and the same fate has overtaken the attempt to obtain personal examples, only one firm having been prevailed upon to adopt Juckes' Patent. I have visited nearly 500 establishments. The greater number of furnaces are in connection with steam boilers; but there are many employed for other purposes in chemical works, dye-works, foundries, steam-engine manufactories, distilleries, &c. &c.

. . .

Generally speaking, I have been received by the parties more favourably than a commercial traveller in quest of orders would have been. In a great many cases, I was welcomed as a friend. In a very few, not over three or four, did the parties show decided incivility; and, in one case only, was language used unfit for publication. The whole body of smoke producers may be comprised under one or other of two classes: first, those who are willing to adopt really effective means, and, second, those who are unwilling. There are degrees of willingness, descending from those who are really anxious to prevent nuisance, to those who are willing to do as others do; and there are degrees of unwillingness, rising from apathy, or a desire not to be annoyed with whatever can be avoided, to those who refuse point blank to stir a hand, or expend a sixpence, and who do not hesitate to say, that smoke cannot be, and never will be consumed; that it is not hurtful either to health or comfort; that the whole agitation is a piece of humbug, and should be put down; that Glasgow was made by smoke, and that without smoke its prosperity would cease.

G. W. Muir, *Report on the State of Engine and Other Furnaces used in Manufacturing and other Establishments in Glasgow; and on the Means to Prevent Nuisance Arising from Smoke* (1851).

1851–52: Macdonald's Rambles

Open countryside and nearby village life were a surprising feature of the mid-Victorian city. Among those who found the energy and leisure to escape to it was the writer and naturalist Hugh Macdonald (1817–60), a friend of Alexander Smith (*see 1848*). Born in Bridgeton, Macdonald was apprenticed as a block-engraver at the Barrowfield calico-printing works founded by the Monteith brothers (*see 1832*). His literary gifts were appreciated by James Hedderwick, founder of the *Citizen*, who offered him a job on the paper. It was here that the famous *Rambles Round Glasgow* first appeared, encouraging artisans to enjoy rusticating in the independent burghs of Rutherglen and Pollokshaws. Regarding the sanctity of the Green, Macdonald could not foresee that five years later the 'enlightened and public-spirited' Town Council were seriously tempted to lease out part of it for coalmining.

Few towns can boast such a spacious and beautiful public park as the Green of Glasgow, with its widespreading lawns, its picturesque groups of trees, its farwinding walks, its numerous delicious springs, and, above all, its rich command of scenery. The 'lungs of London' may exceed it in extent of surface and in artificial adornment, but in beauty of situation and variety of prospect our own Green certainly surpasses any of the street-girt metropolitan breathing-places. The Green of Glasgow lies to the south-east of the City, on the north bank of the Clyde, which, in a fine bold sweep, forms its southern boundary. It embraces in all about 140 imperial acres, and is surrounded by a carriage-drive two and a-half miles in length, besides being intersected in every direction by gravelled walks, overhung, in some instances, by the foliage of stately trees, which forms a pleasant screen from the noonday sun or the pelting shower; while every here and there seats have been erected for the convenience of the weary lounger.

. . .

From the period of the Revolution until the present time, a succession of improvements on the Green have been effectively carried out. The landward boundary is protected by walls and railings—banks have been formed to restrain the incursions of the river—moist places have been drained—the Molendinar and Camlachie burns have been arched over, and are now conveyed by invisible channels to the Clyde—hollows have been filled up—inequalities have been levelled—trees have been planted—and enclosures have been formed; while the general aspect has been greatly ameliorated and beautified; Among the more prominent benefactors of the Green in time past, were Provosts Peter and George Murdoch; the latter of whom formed the fine serpentine walks, bordered with shrubbery, which are still remembered by the old inhabitants, but which were removed in consequence of certain abuses to which they were occasionally liable. In our own day, the late Dr. Cleland distinguished himself by his attention to the amenities of the Green; under his auspices the splendid carriage-drive was formed, and many other improvements effected. More recently, Councillor Moir has deservedly gained golden opinions by his exertions in the same field; and when his projected ameliorations are completed, the Green will undoubtedly present an appearance vastly superior to what has hitherto been witnessed, and which will challenge comparison with that of any public park in the empire.

. . .

The welcome sunshine, penetrating even into wynds and vennels with its golden invitation from on high, has called forth their wan and filthy inhabitants in swarms. In the vicinity of the Saltmarket, where we have made our *entrée*, the Green is all alive with squalid groups, the children of misery and vice. Beguiled by the radiance of the summer noon, they have sneaked forth, for a brief interval, from their reeky and noisome haunts, to breathe for a time the comparatively 'caller air.' Unfortunate females, with faces of triple brass hiding hearts of unutterable woe—sleeping girls, who might be mistaken for lifeless bundles of rags—down-looking scoundrels, with felony stamped on every feature—owlish-looking knaves, minions of the moon, skulking, half-ashamed at their own appearance in the eye of day; and, alas! poor little tattered and hungry-looking children, with precocious lines of care upon their old-mannish features, tumbling about on the brown and sapless herbage. The veriest dregs of Glasgow society, indeed, seem congregated here. At one place a band of juvenile pick-pockets are absorbed in a game at pitch-and-toss; at a short distance, a motley crew are engaged putting the stone, or endeavouring to outstrip each other in a leaping bout, while oaths and idiot laughter mark the progress of their play.

You must not confound these parties with what are called the lower orders of our City. There is a deep within a deep in the social scale; to compare even the humblest working-man with such wretches would be in truth a wicked libel. The industrious poor are now at their various useful, and therefore honourable occupations, and the heterogeneous crowd before you are the idle, the vicious, and the miserable—the very vermin, in short, of our civilisation. Poor wretches! let us not grudge them the limited portion of the Green where they invariably herd—let us not take from misery its few hours of sunshine.

. . .

Leaving the City then by Rutherglen-loan, on the south side of the river, this sweet morning in the 'leafy month of June,' we proceed cheerily on our route. It is some time, however, before we get completely beyond the region of smoke. If fashionable Glasgow is progressing towards the setting sun, her manufacturing industry is moving at an equally rapid rate in an opposite direction. If crescents, squares, terraces, and villas, of every imaginable order and disorder of architecture, are rising at the west-end, mills, printworks, and foundries are almost as profusely springing up by way of counter-balance towards its eastern extremity. In the direction in which we are now proceeding, where a few years since there were nothing to be seen but gardens and fields of waving grain, there is now a large community of factories and work-shops, and a perfect forest of tall chimneys. The sight of such a vast extension of our manufacturing capabilities is doubtless highly gratifying to our local pride, yet, while muttering something about the flourishing of Glasgow, we are fain to hasten on our way, as we feel but a limited degree of pleasure in lingering, where our lungs are necessarily made to perform the rather disagreeable functions of a smoke-consuming apparatus.

. . .

Rutherglen consists principally of one street, which lies in a direction nearly east and west, and is about half a mile in length. This thoroughfare, which is broad and well paved, has a number of wynds or narrow streets branching off to the north and south. Like most old towns it has been built without any fixed plan, and has consequently somewhat of an irregular and straggling appearance. The houses have but little pretension to architectural elegance. They are mostly plain two-storied buildings, with a considerable sprinkling of low thatched cottages, which give it a somewhat old-fashioned and primitive aspect.

. . .

We find ourselves in the immense Bakery of Crossmyloof, inspecting with interest the manufacture of quartern loaves. This extensive establishment, perhaps the largest of the kind in the Queen's dominions, is the property of Mr. Thomson of Camphill, by whom it was erected in 1847, for the purpose of supplying the City of Glasgow with bread similar in quality to that used in London. Commencing operations on a small scale, the increasing demand has gradually necessitated an extension of the premises, until at the present time operations are carried on in four large bakehouses, fitted up with every requisite convenience for securing cleanliness and expedition. There are no less than twenty-six ovens generally at work, attended by from forty-five to sixty bakers, as the demand increases or diminishes. A number of other hands also are constantly employed in subsidiary operations, such as preparing the yeast, which is done on the premises, removing and packing the bread, &c., while no fewer than six large vans are constantly engaged carrying the loaves as they are prepared to the insatiate City, and distributing them amongst the various agencies. Some idea may be formed of the extent of this monster baking manufactory when we mention, that it requires not less than five hundred sacks of flour on the average weekly, out of which it turns from 40,000 to 43,000 quartern loaves. Mr. Dalgetty, the active and intelligent manager, obligingly conducted us over the establishment, explaining the various processes through which the flour must pass ere its final transformation into the wholesome 'staff of life.' Cleanliness, order, and neatness, pervade every department; and we must admit that we have seldom seen a more curious or cheerful sight than we witness in one of these lengthened and spacious bakehouses, where thirty well-powdered operatives are busily engaged thumping, pelting, turning, cutting, weighing, and kneading immense masses of plastic dough, which, in their experienced hands, rapidly assumes the requisite form and consistency.

Taking leave of our friend Mr. Dalgetty, we now leave Crossmyloof, and wend our way towards Pollokshaws, which is situated about a mile to the southward. At this point the road diverges, one branch leading to Kilmarnock, by Mearns; the other to Barrhead and Neilston, by Pollokshaws. The country in the vicinity is beautiful in the extreme, and within the past year or two a number of fine villas have been erected in the neighbourhood. The majority of these have gardens and elegant flower-plots attached to them, and altogether the locality has a highly pleasing and attractive appearance. The walk from Crossmyloof to Pollokshaws is of the most pleasant description. On either hand are wide-spreading and fertile fields, relieved at intervals with patches and belts of planting, farm-houses, and gentlemen's seats. About half the distance it is uphill, but afterwards it gradually declines towards the hollow in which, on the banks of the Cart, here a considerable stream, the town is situated.

Pollokshaws is a tidy and thriving little town, somewhat irregular in appearance, and containing a population of about 5,000 individuals. An air of bustle and life about its streets furnishes a perfect contrast to the dulness and languor which generally prevails in towns of similar extent in the rural districts. There are a number of extensive establishments for spinning, weaving, and dyeing within its precincts, which furnish employment for the greater portion of its inhabitants, the residue being principally hand-loom weavers, miners, and agricultural labourers. Calico-printing was also at one period carried on here to a considerable extent; but of late years, we understand, this department of trade has been, in a great measure, if not altogether, discontinued. The inhabitants have the usual characteristics of a manufacturing population. There is the common preponderance of pale faces and emaciated forms, accompanied with the sharpness of intellect which manifests itself in diversity of religious and political opinion. Every shade of political principle indeed finds here its own little knot of adherents; while the fact that there are not fewer than nine separate places of worship, great and small, sufficiently indicates the variety of points from which the great question is contemplated. The precise number of schools which are in the town we have not learned, but we understand that this important department of social improvement has not been by any means neglected, while an extensive public library furnishes the necessary intellectual pabulum for the studious portion of the adult population.

· · ·

The village of Maryhill is in the immediate vicinity of the bridge, from which it is seen in its most favourable aspect. Being nearly if not altogether of modern erection, the village has a clean and tidy appearance, and is arranged with considerable regularity. There is a number of public works, such as printfields and establishments for bleaching, in its vicinity, in which the population (a large proportion of whom are of Irish origin) are principally employed. The village itself presents few attractions to the rambler, but the country in its neighbourhood, especially along the valley of the Kelvin, is characterised by a more than ordinary degree of beauty.

Hugh Macdonald, *Rambles Round Glasgow* (1854).

1853: Harriet Beecher Stowe in the Cathedral

Harriet Beecher Stowe (1811–1896) toured Europe in the wake of the success of *Uncle Tom's Cabin* (1852). She was especially welcome in Glasgow which, despite its dependance on cotton, had strong anti-slavery sympathies, exemplified in the Glasgow Emancipation Society, one of whose leading lights was the Congregationalist minister Dr Ralph Wardlaw (1779–1853). A doctor had to be called in to relieve the effects of Mrs Stowe's first day in Glasgow but she rallied the following evening, as she 'had engaged to drink tea with two thousand people'. During this bunfight in her honour she reflected whimsically on the size of the teapot 'whether old mother Scotland had put two thousand teaspoonfuls of tea for the company, and one for the teapot, as is our good Yankee custom.' She is wrong on one point: in Glasgow the Provost was elected every three years.

As we came towards Glasgow, we saw, upon a high hill, what we supposed to be a castle on fire—great volumes of smoke rolling up, and fire looking out of arched windows.

'Dear me, what a conflagration!' we all exclaimed. We had not gone very far before we saw another, and then, on the opposite side of the car, another still.

. . .

As we drew near to Glasgow these illuminations increased, till the whole air was red with the glare of them.

'What can they be?'

'Dear me!' said Mr. S., in a tone of sudden recollection, 'it's the iron-works! Don't you know Glasgow is celebrated for its iron-works?'

Dimly, by the flickering light of these furnaces, we see the approach to the old city of Glasgow. There, we are arrived! Friends are waiting in the station-house. Earnest, eager, friendly faces, ever so many. Warm greetings, kindly words. A crowd parting in the middle, through which we were conducted into a carriage, and loud cheers of welcome, sent a throb, as the voice of living Scotland.

I looked out of the carriage, as we drove on, and saw, by the light of a lantern, Argyll Street. It was past twelve o'clock when I found myself in a warm, cozy parlour, with friends, whom I have ever since been glad to remember. In a little time we were all safely housed in our hospitable apartments, and sleep fell on me for the first time in Scotland.

. . .

The next morning I awoke worn and weary, and scarce could the charms of the social Scotch breakfast restore me. I say Scotch, for we had many viands peculiarly national. The smoking porridge, or parritch, of oatmeal, which is the great staple dish throughout Scotland. Then there was the bannock, a thin, wafer-like cake of the same material. My friend laughingly said when he passed it, 'You are in the 'land o' cakes,' remember.' There was also some herring, as nice a Scottish fish as ever wore scales, besides dainties innumerable which were not national.

Our friend and host was Mr. Bailie Paton. I believe that it is to his suggestion in a public meeting, that we owe the invitation which brought us to Scotland.

By-the-by, I should say that 'bailie' seems to correspond to what we call a member of the city council. Mr. Paton told us, that they had expected us earlier, and that the day before quite a party of friends met at his house to see us, among whom was good old Dr. Wardlaw.

After breakfast the visiting began. First, a friend of the family, with three beautiful children, the youngest of whom was the bearer of a handsomely-bound album, containing a pressed collection of the sea-mosses of the Scottish coast, very vivid and beautiful.

If the bloom of English children appeared to me wonderful, I seemed to find the same thing intensified, if possible, in Scotland. The children are brilliant as pomegranate blossoms, and their vivid beauty called forth unceasing admiration. Nor is it merely the children of the rich, or of the higher classes, that are thus gifted. I have seen many a group of ragged urchins in the streets and closes with all the high colouring of Rubens, and all his fulness of outline. Why is it that we admire ragged children on canvas so much more than the same in nature?

. . .

In the afternoon I rode out with the lord provost to see the cathedral. The lord provost answers to the lord mayor in England. His title and office in both countries continue only a year, except in cases of re-election.

As I saw the way to the cathedral blocked up by a throng of people, who had come out to see me, I could not help saying, 'What went ye out for to see? a reed shaken with the wind?' In fact, I was so worn out, that I could hardly walk through the building.

It is in this cathedral that part of the scene of Rob Roy is laid. This was my first experience in cathedrals. It was a new thing to me altogether, and as I walked along under the old buttresses and battlements without, and looked into the bewildering labyrinths of architecture within, I saw that, with silence and solitude to help the impression, the old building might become a strong part of one's inner life. A grave-yard crowded with flat stones lies all around it. A deep ravine separates it from another cemetery on an opposite eminence, rustling with dark pines. A little brook murmurs with its slender voice between.

I was disappointed in one thing: the painted glass, if there has ever been any, is almost all gone, and the glare of light through the immense windows is altogether too great, revealing many defects and rudenesses in the architecture, which would have quite another appearance in the coloured rays through painted windows—an emblem, perhaps, of the cold, definite, intellectual rationalism, which has taken the place of the many-coloured, gorgeous mysticism of former times.

After having been over the church, we requested, out of respect to Bailie Nicol Jarvie's memory, to be driven through the Saut Market. I, however, was so thoroughly tired that I cannot remember anything about it.

I will say, by-the-way, that I have found out since, that nothing is so utterly hazardous to a person's strength as looking at cathedrals. The strain upon the head and eyes in looking up through these immense arches, and then the sepulchral chill which abides from generation to generation in them, their great extent, and the variety which tempts you to fatigue which you are not at all aware of, have overcome, as I was told, many before me.

Harriet Beecher Stowe, *Sunny Memories of Foreign Lands* (1854).

1854: Opening of Victoria Bridge

Replacing a fifteenth-century bridge, James Walker's Victoria Bridge took three years to complete. To carry the enormous increase in horse-drawn traffic, it was built as wide as Telford's Jamaica Bridge (largely rebuilt in 1899) and its four massive piers were sunk extra deep to allow for dredging operations in the river. Built of white sandstone faced with Irish granite, it was the largest urban bridge of its time. Although the Caithness paving took three months to arrive, the Victoria was opened on the day specified in the contract. This account gives an idea of the ceremony involved in opening the oldest of the Clyde bridges on a freezing day. Linking Stockwell Street with Gorbals, it still carries more than 20,000 vehicles per day.

On Monday forenoon, this magnificent structure was formally opened by the Lord Provost and Magistrates, and other members of the Bridge Trust, in the presence of an immense concourse of spectators . . . . The weather was bitterly cold, and the Clyde was frozen over, but still it was delightful for the season; and the ceremony formed a very excellent introduction to the enjoyments of the

New-Year holiday. At eleven o'clock the Magistrates, Bridge Trustees, and other authorities assembled in the Council Chambers, where carriages had been previously drawn up for their accommodation. The procession . . . filed off in the following order:-

Advanced Guard of Police
The Band of the 77th Regiment
Lieutenants of Police
Assistant Superintendents of Police
Superintendent of Police
The Council Officer
The Town's Officers
The Lord Provost and Magistrates
The Bridge Trustees, including the County Representatives
The Engineer of the Bridge
The Sheriffs
The River Trustees and City Officials
The American and French Consuls
The Principal of The University
Officers of The Regiment, and Private Gentlemen
Rear Guard of Police

The procession, which was headed by the Lord Provost in his carriage and four, proceeded down Hutcheson Street, along Trongate and Argyll Streets, down Jamaica Street, along Glasgow Bridge and Carlton Place, to the south side of Victoria Bridge. The band of the 77th Regiment played inspiring airs on the route, and the streets were crammed, whilst the windows of the houses, to the uppermost flat, were filled with spectators. The procession was repeatedly cheered by the multitudes. On the Lord Provost's carriage arriving at the bridge, the barriers were removed, and the procession moved along, every one loud in admiration of the completion of a structure which is calculated for ages to redound to the honour of the civic authorities who projected, the architectural genius of Dr. Walker who designed, and the workmanship of Mr. York who produced it. On arriving at the north side, the Lord Provost alighted from his carriage, and proclaimed the bridge open to the public in terms of act of Parliament. The fine band of the 77th then struck up the National Anthem, the crowd cheered, and as the procession went on by Stockwell Street, and the police guarding each end of the bridge followed in the wake of the carriages, the spectators rushed pell-mell across the newly opened thoroughfare, cab drivers drove their vehicles with like eager rivalry, for a first place; and the crowd, which was not so large as might have been expected, gradually dispersed. The ceremony occupied only a few minutes. The conduct of the populace was most orderly and exemplary.

Glasgow Herald, Friday 6 January 1854.

1855: Wylie & Lochhead's Store

This is how one of Glasgow's early commercial empires (and a household name to rival Marks and Spencer) appeared in its magnificent prime. Wylie & Lochhead set up shop in 1827 mainly as a coaching business, but also as undertakers. This side of the business boomed in 1832 with the outbreak of cholera. The firm's subsequent success in retailing led to the building of the six-storey Buchanan Street 'warehouse' or department store. Unfortunately the core of this fine building, copied in their Princes Street shop, was destroyed by fire thirty years later. But it was speedily rebuilt just as it had been before. Now, although Wylie and Lochhead buildings still survive, they have passed into other hands (the Buchanan Street shop is part of Fraser's) and the firm has returned to its original undertakings—hired transport and funerals.

This strikingly handsome and commanding edifice rises from the street to an elevation of seventy feet, comprising six lofty and commodious floors, and possessing a splendid façade that is simply one huge window, so admirable has been the consideration devoted to securing a perfect light for the interior. The fine frontage on Buchanan Street is sixty-six feet in extent, and the building runs back in the rear to a depth of nearly 210 feet. The structure is composed of brick, with richly ornate terra-cotta facings and decorations, and its entire architectural design is at once chaste, tasteful, and eminently well suited to a warehouse of this character. The interior, in every detail of arrangement and construction, can only be described as an embodiment of the best modern principles of structural science.

. . .

Every feature of arrangement and 'laying-out' in this warehouse is a study in the achievement of the greatest possible commodiousness combined with the finest obtainable effect in general appearance; and the result in its entirety leaves absolutely nothing to be desired. Each showroom is a picture, and the whole establishment is a complete exemplification of every industrial branch undertaken and developed by the house. The system upon which the interior of the warehouse has been constructed is that of several successive tiers of immense galleries running round the entire edifice, one above another, and leaving in the centre a space entirely unoccupied, from the ground floor to the immense ellipsis of glass and ironwork that roofs the whole. Thus on the very dullest day any light that exists in the street without, or in the air above, is available to its fullest extent within this establishment. The principal departments here represented, with their several locations in the building, are as follows:- On the ground floor: curtains, table covers, bedding, upholstery, carriage furnishing, blankets, and naperies, cabinet furniture and upholstered goods, ironmongery, and ship furnishing, the latter being mentionable as a special feature of much importance. In the first gallery: carpets, rugs, mattings, floorcloths, linoleums, crumb-cloths, &c. In the second gallery: paper-hang-ings, mural decorations, iron and brass bedsteads, and furniture. In the third and upper galleries: hall, library, office, and parlour, dining, drawing, bed, and smoking-room furniture of every description. The stock held is enormous, both in point of extent and of variety, and a perfect reconciliation has been effected by the firm between the highest of quality and the most moderate of prices. To stand in any part of this warehouse and survey all that is visible from any one point of view of the magnificent display of superior goods it contains is simply a privilege, an artistic treat, which should certainly enhance the pleasure of making a purchase in an establishment where the convenience and satisfaction of customers constitute at all times considerations of paramount importance. Messrs. Wylie & Lochhead are noted for the perfection to which they have brought every branch and department of their business and industry; and it would savour strongly of invidiousness to single out from the midst of so much conspicuous excellence any individual feature of the stock for special mention. Bedding, furniture, paper-hangings, decorations, carpets, rugs, iron and metal ware, floor coverings, upholstery, and general furnishing of every description—all these are distinct specialties in themselves, and all illustrate the best achievements of modern times in their several lines.

The firm's principal works are at Mitchell Street, where upholstery and polishing are done; Kent Road, where cabinet making, gilding, glass silvering, and bedding are carried on; Whiteinch, where paper-hangings in all the different classes are manufactured; and Berkeley Street stables, where there are over 300 horses and a magnificent stud of Belgian horses, all employed in cab and carriage hiring, and funeral undertaking, this branch of their business being the largest in Scotland. The storing and removing of household effects are largely undertaken, for which a large staff of workmen are employed and gigantic pantechnicon vans. The trade controlled is enormous in magnitude, and world-wide in scope; the connection maintained is of the most valuable, distinguished, and extensive character; and so thoroughly has the house identified itself with Glasgow, and become one of the features of that great western metropolis, that visitors to the 'City of the Clyde' are in very truth not considered to have properly 'done' the place until their tour of inspection has included a survey of Messrs. Wylie & Lochhead's magnificent premises. The honours attendant upon commercial success rarely extend beyond such notoriety and celebrity as this.

Glasgow of Today (1888).

1855: The Goldocracy of Glasgow

The Glasgow habit of imputing the worst possible motive to any action and the brusque Glasgow demeanour are gently derided in this 'story of Glasgow life' by Frederick Arnold, the first novel to be set entirely in Glasgow: a romantic tale set

against the background of student life. In the preface Arnold writes that such cities
as Glasgow, Edinburgh, Liverpool, and Manchester 'possess many features
of society peculiar to themselves that would richly repay the labours of the novelist'.

The people of Glasgow, that is to say, the Goldocracy, have a peculiarly
pleasant and amiable code of their own. They charitably presume every man to
be a blackguard till he proves himself to be a gentleman. If a man has adorned
his captivating person with peculiar care, they think him a swell—if he happens
to be in the rough, they pronounce him a snob—if he wears moustaches, they
think him a swindler or a foreigner, generally, indeed; they consider the terms
synonomous. If you talk much you are a bore—if you talk little, you are a
simpleton—if two young people innocently chat and walk together, there is an
improper flirtation—if you play one of the beautiful ancient sacred tunes, or on
Sunday, in meditative mood, stray into the quiet country lanes, as Isaac was
wont to do at eventide, you are that worst of sinners, a Sabbath-breaking
sinner—if in a steamboat or railway you speak to a gentleman, you are an
intruder—if to a lady, you are an impertinent scoundrel, or a base, designing
villain. As to such small courtesies as offering a seat, proffering a newspaper,
returning a civil answer to a civil question, these useless little amenities are
never thought of. In considering if you shall admit a man to your friendship, or
to be the suitor of your daughter, such trifling little items as birth, connection,
principles, amiability, habits, knowledge, are never taken into consideration.
They may receive a passing notice; but the grand question, the question that
swallows up all other questions, is, how much is he worth—twenty, fifty,
eighty, one hundred thousand, two hundred thousand pounds? Assuredly the
worship of the golden image is as much set up in Glasgow as ever it was upon
the plain of Dura.

. . .

It is between four and five o'clock in the evening. The watery beams of the
setting winter sun are lost in the glare of the lit lamps. A steady crowd is pouring
eastward along Argyle Street, and westward along Sauchichall Street. Carriages are rolling away from Buchanan Street, and omnibuses to Partick and the
Crescents are filled to the very doors; inside them little boys are ejected from
their seats, and gentlemen chivalrously stand up to allow ladies to sit. Hundreds
of young girls are pouring down Queen Street and Miller Street from
M'Donald's manufactory, not without insult from well-dressed blackguards.
The gas is turned off in Stirling's Library, and the tired officials are dismissing
the young juveniles, for whose accommodation the place seems specially
provided, from their well-thumbed novels. The courts of the College are
utterly deserted; the professors are reposing on their laurels, sofas, and arm-
chairs, and Scotch students are betaking themselves to the national abomination of a tea-dinner. The air is clogged with heavy, unwholesome vapour. The

mud, horrible as of Cocytus, is penetrating your Wellingtons, and the perpetual missling, drizzling rain is blinding your eyes. The angry glow fades from the murky sky, and the great shadows of the night deepen on the city.

Frederick Arnold, *Alfred Leslie* (1855).

1856: Madeleine Smith at Rhu

To polite Victorian society the Madeleine Smith trial of 1857 was sensational beyond bounds. In newspaper reports details emerged daily (through a very frank two-year correspondence) of the liaison between the attractive daughter of a successful Glasgow architect and a penniless packing clerk called Pierre Emile L'Angelier. This letter was written to L'Angelier's landlady, an elderly spinster who encouraged the affair. It gives an idea of how the female Smiths spent the summer months at Rhu.

> Dearest Mary,—What a length of time since I have written you! But Emile told me you were at Gourock.
>
> . . .
>
> My sister and I were at Arrochar last week. I had never been there, and I was quite delighted with the wild highland scenery. We were on Loch Lomond—it is indeed the Queen of Scottish Lakes. The water was like a sheet of glass—the sky so blue and clear—in fact it was more like a picture than reality. Nothing I enjoy so much as fine scenery, and next to the scenery itself comes a fine picture of the same subject. I have been too busy for sometime, so have not had so much reading as I should like. Mama has not been well, and that has occupied a good part of my time; but next week I shall begin again, as by that time I think she shall be quite convalescent. Since I last wrote you I have read 'Sidney Smith's Life,' and I like it very much. I have also read 'Life of Lord Cockburn,' which I did not much like. The characters mentioned are all too old for me to remember, so I could not take the same interest in it an older person would. I am now at the life of 'Sir R. Peel,' but there is so much regarding Politics in it, that I find it rather dry sort of reading; but papa asked me to read it, so I shall do it.
>
> I have got two dogs now to make pets of, 'Pedro' and 'Sambo,' both of them terriers. They are most affectionate. Their great delight is killing rats, and I assure you I gratify them in their desire. I fear I shall not have the pleasure of seeing you yet this summer, as I know of nothing that shall call me to Glasgow, till I come for the winter. I do long to be acquainted with you, and I don't see how it can be managed. I think I must just have patience, and wait for a little time yet. All things may yet end well, but I rather fear dear Emile and I shall

have annoyances yet. But we must hope for the best. Adieu for the present. With kind love, I am, dear Mary, your affectly.,

Mimi.

Friday afternoon.

Trial of Madeleine Smith, ed. F. Tennyson Jesse (1927).

1857: Poor School Attendance

Robert Somers was a campaigning Victorian journalist. In 1847 he had visited the parts of the Highlands worst affected by the potato blight and the Clearances. His conscience was stirred by the sight of evicted families camping on Glasgow Green. Ten years later (and once again for the *North British Daily Mail*) he turned his attention to the chaotic condition of Glasgow's elementary schooling, in particular to the Private Adventure Schools run by barely literate teachers usually in unhealthy surroundings. Not until 1866 (*qv*) was an exhaustive survey of the city's schools produced, leading to the Scottish Education Act five years later.

> In 1857 we find only 1 in 14 at school in Glasgow, being only one-half of the average school attendance of all parts, and immeasurably less than that of the best educated parts, of Scotland. Is it possible that any of us can rest under a knowledge of this fact with any ease or satisfaction of mind? The comparison stands equally bad between us and almost any country of Europe, with the exception perhaps of Spain and Russia. In France there is 1 in 8 at school, in Holland there is also 1 in 8, in Prussia and many parts of Germany there is 1 in 6, and in Switzerland there is 1 in 5. Glasgow thus to be left behind by every honourable community, and sunk in education to the level or below the level of the abject and superstitious dregs of Europe! There is more than a point of honour here, though that alone should prick us to the quick. The low state of education in this city should fill us all not more with shame than with dismay, for this is the source of that coarseness of mind, that drunkenness, blackguardism, crime and pauperism, which degrade so many of our population, and which in the nature of things must tend more and more to accumulate. This is a prospect to which no sane and no good man can quietly compose himself. A great extension of education, therefore, and with extension of great improvement of the quality of our school instruction, of our school buildings and apparatus, and of the whole spirit and scope of our educational system, we take to be a work in which this great community will apply itself with all but unanimous conviction, by whatever means it is to be accomplished.

Robert Somers, *Results of the Enquiry into the State of Schools and Education in Glasgow* (1857).

1857: Nathaniel Hawthorne in the High Street

The old College in the High Street dated from the 1630s, but was demolished by the City of Glasgow Union Railway Company who took over the buildings for offices when the new university was built at Gilmorehill (see 1868). This wry account comes from a tour made by Hawthorne when he was American consul at Liverpool. It includes a description of the Lion and Unicorn staircase which was saved and preserved at the west end of the new university. The Principal was Dr Duncan Macfarlan who was appointed in 1823.

> . . . my wife and I walked out, and saw something of the newer portion of Glasgow; and really I am inclined to think it the stateliest city I every beheld. The Exchange, and other public buildings, and the shops, especially in Buchanan-street, are very magnificent; the latter, especially, excelling those of London. There is, however, a pervading sternness and grimness, resulting from the dark gray granite, which is the universal building material both of the old and new edifices. Later in the forenoon, we again walked out, and went along Argyle-street, and through the Trongate and the Saltmarket. The two latter were formerly the principal business-streets, and, with the High-street, the abode of the rich merchants and other great people of the town. The High street, and still more the Saltmarket, now swarm with the lower orders, to a degree which I never witnessed elsewhere; so that it is difficult to make one's way among the sallow and unclean crowd, and not at all pleasant to breathe in the noisomeness of the atmosphere. The children seem to have been unwashed from birth, and perhaps they go on gathering a thicker and thicker coating of dirt till their dying days. Some of the gray houses appear to have been stately and handsome in their day, and have their high gable-ends notched at the edges, like a flight of stairs. We saw the Tron-steeple, and the Statue of King William Third, and searched for the old Tolbooth; but are not quite certain whether we found the remains of it or no. On the authority of an old man, whom my wife questioned, we suppose that a tall, antique tower (called, I think, the market-cross) standing near the end of the High-street, appertained to the Tolbooth. The sidewalk, along which we went, passes right through this tower.
>
> Wandering up the High-street, we turned once more into the quadrangle of the University, and ascended a broad stone-staircase, which ascends, square, and with right angular turns, on one corner, on the outside of the edifice. It is very striking in appearance, being ornamented with a balustrade, on which are large globes of stone, and a great lion and unicorn, curiously sculptured, on the opposite sides. While we waited here, staring about us, a man approached, and offered to show us the interior. He seemed to be in charge of the college-edifices. We accepted his offer, and were led first up this stone-staircase, and into a large and stately hall, panelled high towards the cieling [*sic*] with dark oak, and adorned with elaborately carved cornices and other wood-work. There was a long reading-table, towards one end of the hall, on which were laid pamphlets and periodicals; and a venerable old gentleman, with white head and

bowed shoulders, sat there reading a newspaper. This was the Principal of the University; and as he looked towards us, graciously, yet as if expecting some explanation of our entrance, I approached and apologized for intruding, on the plea of our being strangers and anxious to see the college. He made a courteous response, though in exceedingly decayed and broken accents, being now eighty-six years old, and gave us free leave to inspect everything that was to be seen. This hall was erected two years after the Restoration of Charles II, and has been the scene, doubtless, of many ceremonials and high banquettings, since that period; and among other illustrious personages, Queen Victoria has honored it with her presence. Thence we went into several recitation or lecture-rooms, in various parts of the college-buildings; but they were all of an extreme plainness, very unlike the rich old Gothic libraries, and chapels, and halls, which we saw in Oxford. Indeed, the contrast between this Scotch severity and that noble luxuriance and antique majesty, and rich and sweet repose, of Oxford, is very remarkable, both within the college-edifices and without. But we saw one or two curious things; for instance, a chair of mahogany, elaborately carved with the arms of Scotland and other devices, and having a piece of the kingly stone of Scone inlaid into its seat. This chair is used by the Principal on certain high occasions; and we ourselves, of course, sat down in it. Our guide assigned to it a date preposterously earlier than could have been the true one, judging either by the character of the carving, or by the fact that mahogany has not been known or used much more than a century and a half...

There is a Museum belonging to the University but this, for some reason or other, could not be shown to us just at this time and there was little else to show. We just looked into the college-gardens; but, though of large extent, they are so meagre and bare—so unlike that lovely shade of the Oxford gardens—that we did not care to make further acquaintance with them.

Then we went back to our Hotel; and, if there were not already more than enough of description, both past and to come, I should describe George's Square, on one side of which the Hotel is situated. A tall column rises in the grassy centre of it, lifting far into the upper air a fine statue of Sir Walter Scott, whom we saw to great advantage, last night, relieved against the sunset-sky, and there are statues of Sir John Moore, a native of Glasgow, and of James Watt, at corners of the square. Glasgow is certainly a noble city.

Nathaniel Hawthorne, *The English Notebooks* (1941).

1858: Tennant's works and Campbell's warehouse

James Dawson Burn visited Glasgow to look for outstanding examples of the benefits of free enterprise. He was struck by the great range of manufacturing industries and the growing number of retailers. He looked around the rapidly spreading city centre and found that it was good—compelling evidence of the 'mental energy' and 'strict application' upon which successful enterprises were built. Particular notice was given to J. & W. Campbell's monster warehouse in Ingram Street. In these two extracts Burn visits the famous St Rollox chemical works founded by Charles Tennant to manufacture an effective bleaching powder from chlorinated lime and praises the growth of the new 'shopocracy' from the bazaar-like establishments of earlier in the century.

Mr. Tennant patented his new method in 1798, when the torch of civil war was fiercely burning in Ireland. Since that time St. Rollox has been pre-eminent for the manufacture of bleaching powder. Sulphuric acid, the vitriol of commerce, is made in these works in really fabulous quantities. The generality of people look upon vitriol as a very unimportant article, and therefore have no idea of its real value as an agent to the well-being of society. There is nothing strange in this, when we consider that the most learned only see things in part; and although many of the secrets of nature have lately been unfolded to the astonished gaze of man, there are still numerous agents whose wonders are yet in store for us. Without vitriol, neither bleaching powder, soap, nor soda could be made. Electro-plating could not be carried on, our dye-works and electro telegraphs would instantly be brought to a stand. The fact is, sulphuric acid may be looked upon as the very life's blood of many of the arts, and without it, chemistry, the great humanizer of mankind, could neither live, move, or have its being.

When we trace large rivers to their source and follow them in their windings to the ocean, we find they gradually expand; and we can scarcely believe them to be the offspring of the tiny rivulets we once beheld them. Those who can remember Mr. Charles Tennant's works at St. Rollox between fifty and sixty years ago must have observed it, like the rivulet, gradually swelling into a huge establishment. For sometime after this business was commenced, it is said that the whole produce of the work was sent down to Glasgow daily upon a hand-barrow!! It must be remembered, however, that such is the altered state of manufactures since then, that one house now in Glasgow will consume more chemical produce than the whole of the manufacturing houses on the banks of the Clyde did sixty years ago. This brings to our mind a statement we heard related of the Messrs. James & William Campbell. It is said (and we believe truly), that these gentlemen have more counter-fittings in their three ware-houses than there was in all Glasgow when they commenced business in 1817!

The interior of St. Rollox works is certainly the most extraordinary labyrinth ever man put his foot in. We have no idea of the number of furnaces in operation for making the three principal articles—soda, soda-ash, and chloride of lime—but there must be some hundreds. The soap department is itself a large manufactory. In this place sixty tons are produced upon an average weekly. When the soap has undergone the process of making, the material, while in a liquid state, is put into iron-frame moulds five feet deep by fifteen inches. When the soap becomes solidified it is cut into long blocks by a fine piece of wire, these again are cut into wedges of a certain weight and built up into large stalks. A stranger in going into this warehouse would conceive he was being introduced into the society of an immense quantity of bricks of various colours.

The most extraordinary part of the works is that in which the sulphuric acid is made. In going into this place we pass between two mountains of sulphur, each of which contain 5,000 tons. We then enter a devil's den, with an immense row of glowing furnaces on each side of us and huge lead tubes above our heads and around us. After we have been half roasted and our lungs struggling with the atmosphere, loaded with sulphuric gas, our good Mentor takes us up a flight of narrow wooden steps until we ascend some hundred feet above the surrounding buildings. It would be utterly impossible to describe the surprising scene that meets the view. Immediately beneath us there are fifty-eight lead chambers for receiving the sulphurous gas, and converting it into vitriol; each of these immense aereal reservoirs hold 21,000 cubic feet of gas. These chambers are approached by many miles of wooden stages, from which, down to the south and west, the huge city forms a most glorious picture with the cathedral in the foreground, with the impress of 700 years.

Turning our eyes to the north-east, we are confronted with the mammoth stalk, whose altitude is 450 feet, with a base of 50 feet, and 9 feet 6 inches over the top. This huge monster is continually pouring his sooty treasures into the region of the clouds.

We are once more on the solid earth, and much of it is melting in our presence. Men are moving about like spirits in the fitful glare of the fiery furnaces; some are breaking up the mountains of crystalized soda, others again are bearing immense loads of salt into furnaces. We may mention that this material is the basis of all the leading articles manufactured in the work, with the exception of vitriol.

. . .

Less than forty years ago, the first-class retail shops in Glasgow, were lighted by narrow projecting bow-windows. The manner in which some of these places were fitted up internally, was generally characterised by plainness and simplicity; in fact, some of them were homely with the fellowship of dirt! Many of the shopkeepers of those days kept a little of everything, and if age was any advantage to their wares, their customers were sure to be well suited.

The modern commercial philosophy of 'small profits and quick returns', was too abstruse a question in social economy to be understood so far back in the infancy of trade. The warehouse of Messrs. James & William Campbell, stood alone in its glory for many years. About twenty years ago, a perceptible change was creeping over the business part of the town—the old shop fronts were being acted upon. A window was amputated in one place, and a gouty hanging storey in another. Where surgical operations could not be made available to benefit the health and appearance, the destroyer stepped in, and a modern building was erected by men with modern notions, on the old site. The new tariff of the late Sir Robert Peel did more for the improvement and decoration of places of business in Glasgow, than it is possible for us to describe. Instead of the retail shops being small, ill-ventilated dark, and dirty, with stupid, stolid-looking fellows behind their counters, the town is now full of commercial palaces, in which there is no expense spared, either in the internal or external arrangements; while the attendants are not only *au fait* to their business, but what is of equal importance, they have learned the art and practice of civility. Of late years, the sale of *cabbage* and *courtesy* have been found to be compatible.

The material prosperity of a town is the result of private enterprise, well-directed industry, and the prudent application of capital to manufacturing or commercial pursuits. From what have been stated in these pages, some idea may be formed of what reproductive labour has done for Glasgow. Had her people been merely dealers and consumers instead of producers, the river Clyde would yet be overflowing her banks, and the mineral treasures that lie beneath the soil would have been allowed to have remained undisturbed in the dark caverns of the earth.

The gulph stream of commercial prosperity, that has carried the population onward with extraordinary rapidity during the last twenty-five years, has produced many changes in the social habits of the people. Men cannot live among riches without being influenced by them, either directly or indirectly. We know no town in the United Kingdom, where the trading community have undergone such a signal change in their manners and habits as that body has done in Glasgow. A love of finery, and an assumption of gentility, pervades a large portion of society. People who have large sums of money passing through their hands in the way of business frequently forget the liabilities of their position. One year's success in trade—nay, a single transaction, may completely change a man's position in society. Under such circumstances we know how apt the majority of men are to forget the past, and look forward to the future with a blind confidence. We believe it to be a fact, that there is no place in the world where there is a greater struggle among the trading community to rise on the social scale than what exists in Glasgow at the present time.

James D. Burn, *Commercial Enterprise and Social Progress* (1858).

1859: Up Townsend's Chimney

Until 1859 the famous 'Tennant's Stalk' had been the tallest chimney in Europe (*see 1858*). It was now surpassed by the chimney of Joseph Townsend's glue works (said by J. D. Burn to have effected 'a chemical necromancy'). This structure had been damaged by a high wind shortly after construction, and it was to allay fears of its unsafeness that the public were invited to climb the repaired stack. Between the 7th and 11th of October nearly 3,000 people ascended for the view—a novel experience, as this account vividly describes.

In the year 1857 the foundation brick was laid of the tall and comely chimney which now towers from Crawford Street Chemical Works above all its smoky compeers, and excites the admiration of every sweep practising within 50 miles of its portly base. To the general public, too, the colossal structure forms an object of uncommon interest, indicating as it unmistakeably does, that the vile gases which live and move and have their being in the works for which the chimney has been erected, will for the future leave the place of their birth at an elevation much too high to be within offensive range of even the most aspiring noses in the community, not excepting that of the Smoke Inspèctor, the olfactory powers of which are of the most extensive and discriminating character. High above all other chimneys will the gases and smoke from the works be discharged; and pleasant is it to contemplate that the former cannot return to *terra firma*, except in a perfectly purified state; and that the latter, instead of smutting our faces and shirts, will fall among far distant clodhoppers, whose washing bills are small. The chimney which is to effect this desirable end, with regard to the smoke and gases from Mr Townsend's works, is 468 feet high from the foundation, or 454 feet from the surface of the yard in which it stands so conspicuous an object; so that it will be seen by the uncalculating reader that its foundation extends to 14 feet under ground. This foundation, which, like the chimney itself, is of brick, and of circular shape, is 47 feet in external diameter; and the base of the chimney, at the level of the ground, is 32 feet wide. The inner diameter, at the base is about 20 feet, being a space considerably greater than that occupied by many an humble citizen's drawing-room; and the wall, at the same portion of the structure, is 5 feet 3 inches thick, exclusive of a coating of fire-brick one foot and a half deep, which reaches up about 50 feet on the inside. This coating of fire-brick is necessary to protect the main wall from the ravages of the tremendous blast of flame which will be discharged into the chimney from flues leading from the several stoves and furnaces of the works; for such is the force of the blast and the heat of the flame carried from the various furnaces that, thick as the brickwork of the wall is, it would soon fall a prey to their destructive influence, by mouldering away or cracking—either of which casualties would cause the mighty and massive fumiduct itself to end in smoke. To build the chimney no fewer than a million and a half of bricks were required, each of which is capable of sustaining a pressure equivalent to 90 tons per square foot, while the utmost pressure which they may ever be expected to be exposed to, and this only during the most violent storm, is 15 tons, or about one-sixth of their strength. The weight of these sturdy and undoubted bricks is 8,000 tons; and the cost of putting them in anything but a 'thin red line' over each other, is estimated at about £8,000. Having given the reader the foregoing details respecting its construction, we shall now ask him to accompany us up the chimney. Having got through a narrow aperture in the thick wall at the base of the structure, we are placed in a cage raised with a rope and guide rods, similar to that used at a coal mine, and hoisted by a steam pulley into darkness at the rate of 70 yards a minute. Our first sensation on leaving the 'warm precincts of the cheerful day' is not that we are going up a chimney, but down a shaft at the Antipodes to be chucked out on this side of the globe. By the time we have abandoned that idea, and made sure of our too daring and adventurous hats, we find ourselves on a platform some eight or ten feet wide, and within three feet of the coping stone of the great stalk. The prospect upon all sides from the top repays the self-preservative anxiety of the ascent. The lower part of Lochlomond is visible; Dumbarton and Green-ock, and the windings of the (German)-silvery Clyde are not too remote to be distinctly seen; Bute and the lofty peaks of Arran can be caught a glimpse of; and the aristocratic Edinburgh cannot keep out of view. Looking nearer home, Glasgow lies beneath: all the ramifications and circumbendibuses of its streets and suburbs, forming a bird's-eye map, and its tall spires, and chimneys less pretentious than this one, hiding their diminished heads under the begrimmed hood of smoke and steam which hangs over the city, many feet below the top of the new stalk. To the east, nearly 20 feet below the spectator, stands the St. Rollox Stalk, puffing in a self-sufficient manner, as much as to indicate that its rival, though very tall for a two-year-old, has not yet learned to smoke like it, but at the same time doing its duty with commendable assiduity. At night, the view from the top of the chimney is really grand; owing to the purity of the atmosphere, the stars appear with a brilliancy not visible to gazers from the grovelling earth: the hundred furnaces of the city vomit forth flames on every side: the course of the streets is clearly traceable by the lamps, which appear like narrow twinkling chains of fire; and looking farther off, one sees the lurid light of the numerous furnaces which are at work for many miles around.

North British Daily Mail, 10 October 1859.

1860: Water from Loch Katrine

Queen Victoria set the Loch Katrine water flowing in October 1859, but only as far as Mugdock Reservoir near Milngavie. It was another five months before the reservoir was full enough to carry a barely adequate maximum of 25 million gallons per day to the north of the city. As this account shows, there were some hitches in connecting Glasgow with the Trossachs, mainly because of the high pressures involved—a great advantage for the Fire Brigade who could now dispense with the water-butts (*see 1834*). The engineer of the Loch Katrine pipeline, John Frederic Bateman, also invented a self-closing valve activated by the increasing velocity of the water. Whether it was effective in this instance (which took place near Canniesburn Toll) is not related.

Considerable excitement was occasioned in Maryhill on Tuesday evening by the bursting of one of the large pipes by which the water from Loch Katrine is conveyed to Glasgow. The pipe burst in Main Street, nearly opposite the branch office of the Union Bank. The water for some time discharged itself into the air to a height of about 20 feet, causing great destruction of property and danger of life. In a short time every corner around for a considerable distance was entirely flooded, and so strong was the current running towards the Kelvin through Gairbraid farm steading, that in the court-yard it was impossible to pass through it. The whole of the out-houses in connection with the farm were completely flooded, particularly a byre, in which were about 40 cows, and which had a beautiful stream of water running down its centre. The private house of Mr Renwick, the occupier of the farm, also suffered very much; indeed in several rooms the water stood two feet deep. Mr Renwick had a beautiful garden lying to the south side of the house, which has been completely destroyed. The water took this way on its course to the Kelvin, cutting up the garden fearfully—in some cases the channels thus formed were three or four feet deep—and carrying the greater part of the surface of the garden a considerable distance, as far, indeed, as the avenue leading to Beechbank Cottage, the residence of J. L. Ewing Esq. The soil thus removed from the garden choked up the avenue to the height of from three or four feet, so that to get out of his own house Mr Ewing had to go by a round about way and climb over his garden wall.

Several other families in the neighbourhood suffered severely, being forced to leave their houses; and the horses in some stables had to be removed to another resting-place for the night. The scene about half past ten was indeed pitiful and alarming. Right and left might be seen poor families labouring away with bucket and broom, doing all they could to bale out the water from their houses. The man stationed at Maryhill to take charge of the works was immediately on the spot to turn off the water. The Water Company's local engineer was prompt in his attendance. An hour, however, elapsed before the water subsided, and when it did so it left a large hole in the centre of the street where the disruption had taken place. A great many people were, of course, walking about the spot, eager to see what damage had been done; and among the rest were some females. One who was walking carelessly along went right into the hole, up to the neck in water; and had it not been for the timeous assistance of some gentlemen, it is quite possible that the poor girl might have been drowned, as the hole was about five feet deep, with an insecure bottom; at all events, she could not have had much relish for her cold bath on such an evening.

Glasgow Sentinel, 3 March 1860.

1862: Constable Campbell Gives Evidence

This is part of the testimony of Colin Campbell, a 22-year-old 'rookie' who was unfortunate enough to be patrolling along Sandyford Place the night that Jessie

McPherson was killed with a meat cleaver. During his duty, from 8 pm to 6 am on a pleasant summer night, he didn't notice anything was amiss. But then Constable Campbell had been told to keep his eyes peeled for prostitutes and vagrants who frequented the waste ground adjoining the back lane, affronting the respectable householders of Sandyford Place. This case was the first investigation undertaken by the Glasgow Police instead of by the Procurator Fiscal with sheriff's officers. Not for the last time they arrested the wrong person, in this case Jessie McLachlan, a Servant.

I have been in the Glasgow police force since 10th December last, and since about the 20th June my beat has been Sandyford Place and neighbourhood. In the summer when families go to the coast they report the fact at the police office, and their houses are put under charge of the constable on the beat. In the beginning of July last, No. 18 Sandyford Place was so circumstanced. Between half-past eight and a quarter to nine o'clock on the night of Saturday, 5th July, I was standing at the door of 18 Sandyford Place, with the handle of the door in my hand, trying it if secure, and at that time the door of 17 opened, and two women came out. I saw no man. One of the women pulled to the door, but did not shut it. They stood on the door step speaking, but I did not hear anything they said—not a word; they were speaking low. They so spoke for about five minutes, and one of them went back to the house and shut the door, and the other went eastwards, along Sauchiehall Street. I followed the latter as far as the corner of Elderslie Street, where my beat stops; she continued eastwards along Sauchiehall Street, and I paid no more attention to her, and can't say where she went. I do not know either of these women. I am sure Jessie M'Intosh or M'Lachlan is not one of them. I did not know the deceased Jessie M'Pherson. The woman that went along Sauchiehall Street was a low-set, stout woman, red, fat face, white straw bonnet with blue ribbons, dark grey cloak. I can't describe the gown, and she would be about twenty or twenty-two years of age, and had a decent, servant-like appearance, and seemed quite sober. The other woman had a white mutch on—no bonnet, a light-coloured gown, white apron, not very tall—a little taller than her companion; thin, dark hair, about twenty-nine years of age, and also sober. I saw no more of these women. I was often back to 18 that night, but I saw no person at No. 17, and everything seemed quiet within. I went off duty at six on the following morning.

I heard of the murder about eight o'clock on the following Monday night, before going on duty, and I was taken before detectives and asked if I heard any noise about 17 Sandyford Place during the night of Friday or morning of Saturday. I had heard no noise, and had seen no person go in or come out of that house that night or morning, and I said so. I did not at that time remember the circumstances of the two women. I remembered it, however, between nine and ten that Monday night, when examining door No. 18, and I told Captain M'Call about it about eleven o'clock.

I am able to fix Saturday as above, because I wrote a letter about five o'clock that afternoon in my lodgings, to my father Donald Campbell, ploughman to a farmer, whose name I forget. I mind now, it is John M'Kenzie, at Keppoch, near Oban. After writing that letter I put it in my pocket to post when I should go on duty, and when at the corner of Elderslie Street, as before mentioned, I happened to put my hand in my pocket, and I found I had not posted my letter, and I turned and posted it at the Receiving House at Sandyford Toll, which is short way beyond my beat. My beat ends at Kelvingrove Street, and Kelvingrove Street runs into Dumbarton Road, near Sandyford Toll.

I wrote the letter on the kitchen table in my lodgings, and my landlady, Mrs. M'Kay, was going back and forwards all the time.

Trial of Jessie McLachlan, edited by William Roughead (1911).

1863: Cuthbert Bede in Tartan-Land

The facetious tones of the novelist and *Punch* artist Edward Bradley ('Cuthbert Bede', 1827–89) make a pleasant diversion among the observations of literary visitors to Glasgow. He noted that the visitor 'has this advantage over the resident: he comes to a place, and sees it, whereas the other lives in it without seeing it; and because he can set eyes on such and such a spot at any time, very often never sees it at all. With the visitor it is very different. He feels that his hours are numbered; and that, unless he pokes up all the lions without loss of time, their roaring will very probably never be heard by him'. He is also not loath to tell a tale against himself.

A little before nine o'clock in the morning, we saw Trafalgar Square, London, and at half-past ten at night we are in Glasgow, and under the tutelary care of St. Mungo.

Thankfully we gather together our luggage, amid a storm of supplications from porters and cab-drivers. We have been recommended to go to the George Hotel, in George Square; and we incautiously ask the question, how far it may be to that locality.

'George Square, Sir? oh, ever such a way, Sir!' replies a cannie Scotch porter, in a dialect that I feel myself quite unable to put down on paper, and which I therefore translate into the Anglo-Saxon tongue.

'But how far?' I ask, as his answer, though charmingly indefinite, is not satisfactory.

'Oh, iver such a way! quite in another part,' is the reply. 'But here's a grand hotel close by—ye'll see it here, Sir; where the lights are shining—the Queen's Hotel—the grandest in the ceetee—and I'll carry all yer things there—and ye won't have the expense of the cab-hire.'

So, touched by this *argumentum ad pocketum*—which, after all, is frequently the most effective of arguments—and, being tired and desirous of getting into comfortable rooms with as little loss of time as possible, we yield to his persuasive powers. With the aid of a porter's knot, he, and a companion

Goliath, sling our portmanteaus and other *impedimenta* over their shoulders; we form ourselves into a procession of four, and, closely following up our new edition of Porter's Progress we take a few steps out of the station yard, and, in a few more seconds, are within the swinging doors of the Queen's Hotel. A minute or so has decided the fact that the porter's recommendation had proceeded from very satisfactory premises, and had conducted us to premises equally satisfactory. Perhaps he received a *douceur* for every traveller brought under his convoy to the hotel doors, and, by the aid of this refresher, could plead with fervid energy in this particular hotel's favour; but, however this may be, the cause he advocated was a good cause. The hotel was everything that could be desired; and right glad were we to avail ourselves of its manifold comforts.

While we were having tea, I said to the waiter, 'How far is the George from here?'

'A very few yards, Sir; just on the other side of the Square.'

'Then is this Hotel in George Square?' I asked.

'Yessir,' said the waiter.

But my opinions regarding the porter I reserved until the waiter had left the room. Doubtless, that porter went to bed happy at having proved too cannie for the Southron. I trust that his slumbers were equally as sound as were mine, on that my first night in my tour in Tartan-land.

. . .

What is known as 'the Highland costume' is, of course, not to be met with in the Glasgow streets, unless we encounter a stray professional piper and beggar who has donned the kilt and its etceteras as a matter of trade; for, as is well known, the artistic representations of the street of a Scotch city, dotted over with variegated figures in the picturesque 'garb of old Gaul,' is nothing better than an artistic license. Neither in Glasgow nor in Edinburgh, during a considerable stay, did I see the Highland costume, except on some dressed dolls in the toy-shop windows. Nevertheless, there are imaginative people in the world who think that a Glasgow man ought to be clad after the Scotch fashion. In a German play, for example, that was produced at the chief theatre in Vienna, the hero was a Glasgow banker who had settled in St. Petersburgh as a money-dealer of the Empress Catherine. Despite the severity of the Russian winter, this gentleman appeared upon the stage in what was believed to be the usual costume of a Glasgow banker, viz., a kilt, a pair of jackboots, and a cocked hat with a plume of feathers. This banker also preserved his nationality by feasting upon the Glasgow dish of 'hot-a-meale pour-ridges and patatas with mutton-rosbif,'

. . .

Even when seen, as I first saw them, on a bright summer's morning, the Saltmarket, and the High Street, and their purlieus, with all their materials for novelty and quaint picturesqueness, evidence so much that is sickening both to the moral and physical senses, that one leaves their precincts depressed and sad at heart, and thankful to escape to purer air and scenes.

But I had afterwards an opportunity to visit these places on a Saturday night. It is then that all their peculiarities are brought most clearly upon the surface. The gaslight falls on a dense crowd of human beings surging like the swarm of an anthill, amid scents as numerous and diversified as those discovered by Coleridge at Cologne. All the peddling and huckstering life of the lowest grade of shops is to be found here in full force; and, of all the shops, those for the sale of whiskey are the most numerous. The disproportion that they bear to the shops for the sale of meat and tea is most suggestive. What in London would be gin-palaces, are here 'cellars' and 'stores.' Next in importance, in point of number, to these places, are the shops for the sale of tobacco; and, on a Saturday night in the Saltmarket, all these places are doing a roaring trade. The smoke of 'vile tobacco,' grown chiefly in convenient cabbage gardens, and mixed with the refuse of the true Virginian weed, hangs heavily upon the air, without purifying it. While the nose is assailed with countless stinks, the ear is stormed by a babel of bastard Scotch and bad English, mixed with fragments of genuine Gaelic, and the rolling periods and rough brogue that mark the Irish Celt. There are old clothes' shops and brokers' shops in abundance, where your presence is fervently solicited, and where you may purchase for next to nothing garments and furniture that will last you for next to no time—the dirt being given in *gratis*. A short, thickset gentleman with a red face, and redder hair, beseeches you to expend a bawbee on his 'harrins,' which are cheap and filling at the price. Another gentleman, also very hairy and red, forces upon you the beauties of his 'soft goods,' which comprise cotton, calico, handkerchiefs, and such like. A 'souter,' or shoemaker, proffers you the chance of treading in the shoes of another man, whose character, if it was as large and solid as his cast-off boots, you would despair of emulating. A 'carlin,' or fat old lady, with a brick-dust head of hair glimmering in the gaslight, offers you the refreshment of bannocks, and sowens, and crowdie at her stall, where you may have an *al fresco* entertainment at a small charge, in the presence of a knot of bare-legged callants, whose mouths water at the unattainable delicacies. At every step there is an inducement held out to you 'jest to wet yer thrapple;' until a fight between two drunken women drives you from the scene, and you crush your way through the wriggling mass, wondering how often the girls get their naked toes trod upon on a Saturday night in the Saltmarket.

Cuthbert Bede, *A Tour in Tartan-Land* (1863).

1864: Murder in the Cowcaddens

The Cowcaddens, which grew early in the century as Port Dundas developed into an important transport and storage centre, has always been one of the most densely populated areas of Glasgow. Even in 1945 it still contained more than 500 people per acre—a figure only equalled by Gorbals-Hutchesontown. In the 1860s the remedy for intolerable conditions was usually strong drink, and in Maitland Street no less than seven of its forty houses contained licensed premises. A map of the time shows how industry was freely mixed in with housing: nearby were soap, dye and asphalt works and further pollution came from the Phoenix Foundry. Maitland Street today is overshadowed by the Cowcaddens high-rise flats to the north of the Theatre Royal.

A Shocking Tragedy

At a late hour on Tuesday night an atrocious murder was perpetrated in Maitland Street, Cowcaddens. The victim is a woman about thirty years of age, named Jessie Gordon, and the person by whose hands the unfortunate creature has been bereft of life is Peter Blair, a joiner by trade, residing at 544 Dobbie's Loan. It would appear that the parties had lived together for a number of years as man and wife; about a month ago, however, they separated for some cause which remains as yet unexplained. Shortly before 11 o'clock on Tuesday night they appeared together in the public-house of Mr Alex. Ferguson, in Maitland Street, where they were supplied with two glasses of whisky and a glass of ale. After they had been in the place a short time, a quarrel arose between them, and presently their voices were heard in loud altercation. In the heat of the dispute, the woman was seen by some parties in the shop to throw a bottle at her companion, and Blair was subsequently heard to threaten that 'he would do for her.' Almost immediately afterwards, Blair left the shop, and proceeded down Maitland Street towards Dobbie's Loan. The woman followed him out, and took the same direction along the street. No one seems to have taken any particular notice of them at this time; but a minute or two afterwards the attention of the persons in Mr Ferguson's shop, and of every one else within ear-shot, was arrested by a loud cry of murder proceeding from the quarter towards which they had gone. A girl, named Catherine Lyon or Nelson, who happened to be in Ferguson's, at once ran down the street, in the direction of the cries, and about forty yards from the shop door she found the woman Gordon standing on the pavement, with blood spouting from a wound in her neck. Nelson lost no time in giving information of what had occurred at the Cowcaddens Police Station, and a constable was presently on the spot. By this time the unfortunate woman was surrounded by a crowd of people, to whom she intimated that she had been stabbed by the man in whose company she had been seen. By this time she had lost a great deal of blood, but she was still able with a little assistance to walk to the Police Office. When she got inside the Office, she was beginning to stagger, and her face was assuming that ghastly whiteness which results from profuse haemorrhage. Within a few minutes after the alarm had been raised, Dr Renfrew was in attendance. He administered the usual restorative resorted to in such cases, but without success, for the patient gradually sank, and expired about 25 minutes after his arrival. When the body was examined, it was discovered that two wounds had been inflicted.

E

. . .

Judging from the appearance of the wounds, one would infer that they were probably inflicted with a small pocket-knife. More than once, while on her way to the Police Station, she attributed the deed to Blair. On being taken into the Office, she said—'I'm done for,' and, when asked who had stabbed her, she stated that it was 'her husband'—meaning, as was understood, the person with whom she had cohabited. As for Blair, it seems that about ten minutes after the fatal occurrence he was seen standing at the corner of Maitland Street and Cowcaddens. A young man there went up to him and informed him that the police were in search of him, whereupon he at once decamped.

Apprehension of the Murderer

Notwithstanding that a large number of the police were engaged all Tuesday night in searching for Blair, and acquaintances of the accused along with constables were placed at all the railway stations and at the steam-boat quay, they did not succeed in the object of their pursuit. At nine o'clock on Wednesday morning, however, the apprehension of Blair was accomplished in the simplest manner possible. At that hour he entered the spirit shop of Alex Ferguson, Maitland Street, which he had left with the deceased the night before a few minutes before the commission of the murder, and said he would like a glass, as he felt 'very bad.' Mr Ferguson gave him the glass, and after it had been drunk, he passed round the counter and seized him, saying he was a prisoner. Blair, who looked stupid and dazed, like a drunken person experiencing the effects of a debauch, asked with a surprised air why he was used in that manner. Mr Ferguson thereupon told him that his wife, who had been stabbed the night before, had died; that he was accused of the murder, and that the police were in search of him. Blair, on hearing this, trembled violently, yet denied that he had committed the murder. A policeman was sent for, and to his custody Blair was consigned. At the Northern Police Office, however, he seemed quite cool and collected when informed that he was in custody on the charge of murder. He repeated that he had not committed the crime, adding that when he left Ferguson's public-house the night before he did not see the deceased, but had gone straight to a friend's house in Sauchiehall Street, where he had passed the night. He stated that he had done this, because in his own house at Dobbie's Loan there was no bedding or furniture, the deceased having for the purpose of getting drink sold or pawned all the household goods he had. On examining his clothes numerous spots of blood were found on the right sleeve and breast of his vest; and from one of his pockets there was taken a knife, which appeared to have been newly sharpened, oiled, and polished. The blade of the knife is fully 2 inches in length, about a quarter of an inch in breadth, and will, we are afraid, be proved to be such an instrument as that with which the foul deed has been done. In his pocket also was found a small piece of sand paper, which appeared to have been recently used in polishing some hard substance. His description, as recorded in the police books, is as follows: 'William Blair, joiner, 40 years of age, 5 feet eleven inches in height, and a native of Largs.' He says that he has been working at his trade with Mr Denham. While giving all these particulars he maintained the same indifference, looking, indeed, as if the police had committed a blunder in apprehending him. When, however, he was soon thereafter placed at the bar of the Northern Police Court and formally remitted by Bailie Mirrlees to the Sheriff on the charge of murder, he abandoned his careless manner, and manifesting tokens of great fear, seemed to realise the seriousness of his position. He was shortly after removed in a cab to the County Buildings, for examination by one of the Sheriff-Substitutes. The news of the murder having spread rapidly in the Cowcaddens district, a large number of persons had assembled to see him placed in the cab in which he was removed.

Glasgow Sentinel, 27 February 1864.

1866: Ticketed Houses

The city's first Medical Officer of Health, W. T. Gairdner, was appointed in 1863. His immediate concern was to reduce the spread of infectious disease through overcrowding. In a densely packed population approaching 450,000 'overcrowding' was not easy to define, but smaller houses or flats with subdivided rooms seemed to be the main problem area. The Glasgow Police Act of 1866 (coinciding with the City Improvement Act which began the demolition of large areas of sub-standard housing) introduced the system of Ticketing. A brass plate was fixed to the front door by an inspector, stating the total cubic capacity of the house and the maximum number of people (to the nearest half) who could sleep there. It was then up to the police, and later health inspectors, to make night-time checks on the occupants

Any person appointed by the Board from time to time may enter any dwelling-house which consists of not more than three apartments, for the purpose of measuring in cubic feet the space contained therein (exclusive of lobbies, closets and presses, and of recesses not exceeding four feet in depth and not having a separate window therein, and not perfectly clear from floor to ceiling and from wall to wall, and exclusive also of recesses in which there is any fixture whatever), and to mark on or over the outside of the door of any such dwelling-house if the cubic contents thereof do not exceed two thousand feet, or to affix thereto a ticket, on which are marked, in such position and style as the Board see fit, the number of such cubic feet, and the number of persons exceeding the age of eight years who, without a breach of the provision next hereinafter contained, may sleep therein; and any person who obliterates, defaces, removes or alters such marking or ticket shall be liable to a penalty not exceeding ten shillings.

If any dwelling-house which consists of not more than three apartments is used for the purpose of sleeping in by a greater number of persons than in the proportion of one person of the age of eight years or upwards for every three hundred cubic feet of space, or of one person of an age less than eight years for every one hundred and fifty cubic feet of space contained therein, (exclusive of lobbies, closets and presses, and of recesses not exceeding four feet in depth and not having a separate window therein, and not perfectly clear from floor to ceiling and from wall to wall, and exclusive also of recesses in which there is any fixture whatever), or by a greater number of persons than is marked thereon in pursuance of the provisions hereinbefore contained, every person so using or suffering it to be used shall be liable to a penalty not exceeding five shillings for every day or part of a day during which it is so used or suffered to be used; and any persons authorised by the Board may, from time to time, enter such dwelling-houses if they believe that these provisions are being contravened.

City of Glasgow Police Act 29 & 30 Victoriae, cap 273.

1866: The Tobacco Children

This passage formed part of an exhaustive survey into the state of education in Glasgow before the passing of the Scottish Education Act of 1872. This set up local School Boards, financed by central government, and made attendance compulsory for nearly 87,000 Glasgow children aged from five to thirteen. Before that, public education was to be had at Sessional Schools, equivalent to Parish Schools in country districts, where the master lived off the fees charged. There were also charitable Mission Schools in the poorest areas, referred to here as Day-Schools. Private Adventure Schools were usually set up by factory owners to free more women for work. It appears that teachers and premises were not always ideal. The tobacco children came mainly 'from houses near the river and the authors estimate that more than a third could not read, write or 'cipher'.

In the course of the report of this district, we have mentioned 'tobacco-boys' more than once. You may perhaps be interested to know something about them. The Clyde district is the centre of the tobacco trade in Glasgow. There are about thirty manufacturers in all employing the labour of very young children. The number of 'tables' maintained by these thirty firms is nearly 250, and at each table three children are engaged, or in all 750. This is a somewhat larger number than were apparently engaged in 1864, according to the evidence given in the 'Children's Employment' Commission. Each journeyman has a table, and requires three children. One child strips the tobacco leaf, one keeps the journeyman supplied with the stripped leaf, and one turns the spinning-wheel. They are called strippers, pointers, and spinners. In some works girls are employed along with boys. Each boy and girl is searched on leaving the workshop; the boys by a man, the girls by a young woman. The children are of the lowest grade. They are to be found at work as young as seven years, but the greater number are older than this,—nine, ten and eleven, with a few above twelve.

. . .

The parents are of the class that do not in the least care to have their children at school. Besides, many of the children have no parents. Those who have charge of them can hardly be persuaded to send them to the evening school. They will often in preference send them out to beg, to sell matches or blacking or evening newspapers, or, it may be, to pilfer and steal. In a word, scarcely any of the parents of tobacco children care a rush for schools or education. The wages earned are from 1s. to 3s. 6d. a week. They are paid, we believe, by the journeymen. Their work is pretty easy and regular, from six in the morning till six at night, with two hours for meals. The day-schools in the district are seriously affected by the tobacco-works. It is no uncommon thing, on a Monday morning especially, for the children on their way to school, as they pass by the tobacco-shops, to ask if any boys are wanted by the journeymen. If there is a demand the supply is at once forthcoming, and for weeks or months the children are absent from school. If there is no demand they pass on their way, to make the same inquiry next Monday morning.

James Greig and Thomas Harvey, *Report on the State of Education in Glasgow* (1866).

1868: The First Football Match

Football has been played in Glasgow since at least 1590, when one John Neill was asked by the Council to furnish annually 'sex guid and sufficient fut ballis'. Organised football began with Queen's Park who were formed in July 1867. A year later their secretary arranged the first known match between Scottish sides with Thistle (not Partick Thistle).

Dear Sir,
I duly received your letter dated 25th inst. on Monday Afternoon, but as we had a Committee Meeting called for this evening at which time it was submitted, I could not reply to it earlier. I have now been requested by the Committee, on behalf of our Club, to accept of the Challenge you kindly sent, for which we have to thank you, to play us a friendly Match at Football on our Ground, Queen's Park, at the hour you mentioned, on Saturday, first proximo, with Twenty players on each side. We consider, however, that Two-hours is quite long enough to play in weather such as the present, and hope this will be quite satisfactory to you. We would also suggest that if no Goals be got by either side within the first hour, that Goals be then exchanged, the ball, of course, to be kicked of from the centre of the field by the side who had the original Kick-

off, so that both parties may have the same chance of wind and ground, this we think very fare and can be arranged on the field before beginning the Match. Would you also be good enough to bring your ball with you in case of any break down, and thus prevent interruption. Hoping the weather will favour the Thistle and Queen's.

I remain,
Yours very truly,
(Sgd.) Robt. Gardner
Secy.

Kevin McCarra, *Scottish Football: A Pictorial History* (1984).

1868: The University Moves to Gilmorehill

Plans to move the University to a totally new site were first mooted in 1859. The Senate bought land adjoining the West End (Kelvingrove) Park for £65,000 and commissioned Sir George Gilbert Scott, a leading spirit of the Gothic Revival, to design a building to grace Gilmorehill. Construction started in 1867 and the building was still incomplete when occupied three years later. An early strike by trade unions resulted in most of the labour force coming from the North of England. Much of the sandstone was dug from the immediate vicinity and from Giffnock Quarry; seams of coal were also discovered in the grounds. The foundation stone was laid in 1868 by the Prince (later to become Edward VII) and Princess of Wales, a visit attended with due pomp and ceremony.

Argyll Street and the Trongate were thronged from end to end with all sorts of vehicles and by innumerable foot passengers. The omnibuses were positively packed on the top with sightseers, while open carriages, cabs, waggons, dog-carts, and even donkey-carts, were moving in both directions with their living loads. I came in contact with a waggon load of fish-wives going westward; and in front sat one of them, evidently a leader, and she was a tearer. She was dressed in a mutch scarcely so white as snow; she was awfully fat, not very fair, and considerably more than forty—if I may be allowed to estimate a lady's age. She was apparently in excellent spirits, however, and as the waggon rolled along the fishy amazon cheered and waved a dirty pocket handkerchief, to the astonishment and delight of the pedestrians. After this came a trades' procession, but it was not of great length, and besides it was too straggled to be effective. Then came a 'lifeboat,' mounted on a carriage, filled with sailors, and drawn by a couple of horses. It was a temperance concern, and was followed by the 'sons of temperance' in marching order, but the family was not very large. Then came the red-coated engineers, followed by other corps of riflemen, by three pieces of artillery, &c., &c., and all were bound for Gilmorehill or the West End Park.

By this time it was getting near twelve o'clock, and I made tracks for George

Square with the view of taking up my stance, but I was rather late. Every street converging on the Square was blocked up with omnibuses, carriages, cabs, lorries, and other vehicles, and every one of them was turned into a stand for the time-being. I tried to get upon a lorry, but the attempt was a failure, and then I bored my way into Ingram Street and succeeded in getting in between the barricades and two lines of Volunteers. Here I was assailed by a policeman, but I gave him a look of defiance and marched along triumphantly until I turned into North Albion Street, when I began to get a little uneasy about my position. I saw that the streets were being cleared, and the worst of the matter was that there was no way of getting out. The barricades were backed by a solid mass of men and women; the end of every street was blocked up in the manner above described, and as I was devising some means of escaping a second policeman came across my path and ordered me to go back. I appealed to the sergeant in charge of the party, and was passed along to the front of the old College, where I took my stand on the pavement, which was clear of the crowd.

A few minutes afterwards three or four horsemen made their appearance in College Street, and the cry was 'There they come!'—The horsemen came, certainly, but, like Royal Charlie, the rest of the procession was 'lang a-coming,' and it came in a very questionable shape. After waiting some time longer, the College half of the procession made its appearance and disappeared down the High Street. Then there was a long break, leaving the whole of College Street clear; and just at this moment a large brown dog came tearing along at full speed, pursued by two or three policemen. After the dog came the first of the Municipal dignitaries, and then more of the same, and then we had another serious break in the procession. I was beginning to think that the Provost and the Prince had given us the slip by taking the nearest cut to the City Hall, when the carriage of Sheriff Bell appeared, escorted by the Head Constable and the Inspector of Cabs, and followed by a police orderly, armed with a green silk umbrella! The Sheriff's carriage turned into the High Street, and then the Provost's appeared at the Fire Engine Station. Captain Smart then abandoned the Sheriff and returned to escort the Chief Magistrate of the city, and then we had another break and a clearance of College Street. At length the helmets of the Yeomanry Cavalry appeared, and the cheers of the crowd rang along the street, and the waving of handkerchiefs from the windows began, and I knew by these signs that the Royal party were in sight.

. . .

I shall now jump from the old College in the High Street to the New College on Gilmorehill, where the great ceremony is about to take place. Being furnished with an open sesame by the kindness of my good friend the Chief Constable, I crossed the new bridge over the Kelvin, and walked up the winding roadway between two stationary lines of Volunteers, escorted by a stout and able superintendent of police. Then I entered the quadrangle of the College, and was amazed by the circular sea of faces which burst upon my sight in a moment. The whole space, in fact, was packed with human beings, to the number, it is said, of 20,000, all in holiday attire; while the tops of the walls, the scaffold poles the trees inside, and even the building cranes, were crowded as thickly as men and boys could sit or stand.

We waited patiently for some time and then the big-wigs began to appear. Several Town Councillors, who had wandered out of their way in the West End Park, found their seats occupied when they came, and they had just to put up with a good squeeze like ordinary men. After this the College Professors emerged from old Gilmorehill House, and walked down the crimson-covered gangway to the platform. The Professors were followed by the Bailies, six or eight in number, wearing cocked hats, swallow-tailed coats, knee breeches, ruffled shirts, bright fretted buttons, and glittering swords! My conscience! Was it not a pity that so many worthy men were compelled to make such 'Guys' of themselves for duty and for fashion's sake? The Lord Provost in all his glory followed the Bailies; and then came the Marquis of Bute on the run, followed by the trumpeters, the Prince and Princess of Wales, and the rest of the Royal party. Then arose a cheer from that gathering of 20,000 which sounded sublime, after which we had the National Anthem from the Choral Union, and then the ceremony began. There was an address to the Prince of Wales read by Principal Barclay, and a reply from the Prince, and a prayer from Dr Caird, and then his Royal Highness spread the mortar, and the signal was given to lower the all-important stone. The steam was put on, but unfortunately the handle had been turned the wrong way, for the stone, attached to a wire rope, rose into the air and began to whirl round, to the intense amusement of the spectators and the amazement of the men in charge. The motion was soon reversed, however, and the work was completed to the satisfaction of everybody present. Then the Princess stepped forward, trowel in hand, to lay the other stone, and at this stage of the proceedings the enthusiasm of the vast assemblage rose to its highest pitch. The men folks cheered and waved their hats and the ladies made a free use of their handkerchiefs, while the young and beautiful mason, with a witching smile upon her face, laid the stone in famous style. Then the Choral Union struck up the 'Doxology,' which they kept up and continued long after a man on the platform had given them several frantic signals to stop, but stop they would not until the music was drowned by the cheers of the audience, when the Royal party rose to leave the platform.

This concluded the ceremony and after it was over I made my way outside, and from the eastern slope of Gilmorehill I looked towards the West End Park, and the prospect was magnificent. People were dotted over its whole surface, and in some parts they were packed as thickly as they could stand, while from the top of Gilmorehill to the eastern end of the Park there stretched the long serpentine double line of Volunteers, on the route to be taken by the returning carriages. Passing over the Kelvin I got into the Park, where I got on board a milk cart, and drove to the residence of the Lord Provost in Bath Street, where I was almost squeezed to a sandwich before I was rescued by a friendly policeman. At length the Royal party came, and an old wifie standing beside me on seeing the Princess, held up her hands and exclaimed—'Oh! there she is sitting just like a swan!' Getting out of the crowd when all was over, I came upon a street ballad-singer, who was entertaining a numerous circle by a song made for the occasion, of which the following lines may be taken as a specimen:-

> 'The Prince with pleasure was received,
> And the people seemed to be all pleased,
> For some had got their throats well greased
> Welcoming the Prince that morning.
> They saw him off safe in the train,
> And good luck attend on land and main,
> They a visit soon may pay again,
> To Glasgow in the morning.'

It would be the height of presumption or sheer madness for me to prolong my narrative after giving this outburst of song. I shall therefore conclude my long yarn, in case I should weary out the patience of my ever indulgent readers.

Glasgow Herald, 9 October 1868.

1868: The Dark Places of Glasgow

The title of David Pae's novel tells it all: *The Factory Girl; or The Dark Places of Glasgow: showing evil over-ruled for good, iniquity punished, and virtue rewarded*. A headlong Victorian melodrama, mixing romance and high moral tone with sensational accounts of underworld life, it featured a novelist searching for 'colour' ('I intend to write a tale of Glasgow life, and I want to make it as true as possible'). Here we have a glimpse of factory life. The previous year the real-life Factory Girl, Ellen Johnston, had published her autobiography and poems although her ending was not so happy—the Barony poorhouse and an early death. Pae was the editor of *People's Friend*.

To an observant spectator, who stood at the moment in the centre of the Green, it could not fail to be singularly impressive and suggestive. The heat and glare of noontide had gradually lessened as the afternoon wore on, and along with the decrease of heat from above, a gentle but most refreshing breeze came down the river, and was wafted over the open Green, to be inhaled by the crowds who lounged or rambled upon it with grateful avidity. To the north and west lay the city in dense compactness—houses, chimneys, and pointed gables standing in thick array against the clear western sky, which was already taking on the deep, golden hues of sunset. Above the houses hung the sun with chastened and broadening disc, and round about him were a few fleecy clouds, whose edges he was gilding, and whom he would, ere long, cover with the most effulgent glory. Between the tops of the houses and the sun and the clouds lay a haze produced by the smoke which was ascending from the thousands of dwellings, and thickening and increasing as the evening fires were lighted to effect the preparation of the evening meal.

Across, on the south side of the river, and far down by its eastern bank, and away verging to the north, were tall chimneys and long blocks of high square buildings, with many rows of windows, which flashed back the beams of the sinking orb of day. From those many buildings came puffing jets of smoke—and the rush, rush of the engine, like great heart beats, and the clanking noise of the machinery, which uttered its voice in its iron-labour-song, harsh and uncouth as its own hard self. From every one of the buildings came these various noises, and they hit upon the ear of a wanderer on the Green with individual distinctness, for the distance was not great enough to cause them to blend together, but only to mingle in quick confusion, and to give a strong idea of bustle and earnest activity.

These were the cotton factories and other large works which give such character and importance to Glasgow. From the south-west to the north-east they spread themselves with the Clyde flowing between, ready to bear away their productions to other and far-off lands. There within their brick walls the spirit of commerce and manufacture is rampant; there does nature and man labour together to produce what is useful and ornamental, that the wants of the world may be supplied, and that thousands, nay, millions, of its population may live.

Encircled by these noisy factories was the Green and the river—the former dotted in one direction with trees, and covered everywhere by groups of laughing, romping ramblers, and the latter bearing on its clear bosom pleasure boats with their happy occupants, who sang and and played on musical instruments as the rowers took them up or down the stream.

. . .

At six o'clock was heard the ringing of many bells, and presently the workers poured out, and the beating of the engines were silenced, and the light steam jets blurted out no longer from the small pipes. The day's toil was done, and the realeased operatives walked out rejoicing to refresh themselves with food and rest, and so prepare for the labour of the coming day.

One only of the factories continued to send forth its many noises. From its tall chimney the smoke rose black and dense; the motion of its engine was distinctly heard; and the whirring sound of machinery, deadened by the walls and the distance, travelled forth on the gathering stillness of the evening air.

Let us turn in the direction of the factory, for we shall find within it some in whom we expect to make the reader interested.

We leave the lodge, and passing up the archway, lofty and not ill-lighted, we reach a door to the left, and opening it find ourselves in one of the immense floors of the mill. What a sight meets our view! The monster apartment contains some five hundred power-looms all going, each tended by a young girl just at or approaching the age when lovers are in their thoughts, when their eyes reveal the feelings of their hearts, and send out soft killing glances from beneath silken eyelashes.

There was just such a room in Dexter's factory, and, in the summer evening we have tried to describe, it afforded a spectacle of busy bustle and activity. The iron shuttles flew to and fro, carrying the fine threads along, and weaving them into the woof, while the web of beautiful fabric grew behind it so close and even. Behind every loom was a girl, watching it with quick, careful eye, ready to unite any broken thread, and to supply it with proper food. There were girls of all sorts in that room, some of them pretty, others more commonplace, but all neatly dressed in clean short-gowns and skirts which left foot and ankle free. They looked quite brisk and happy, though day after day they had to keep watch by their looms in the midst of the deafening roar of machinery, while the sun shone without, and the flowers bloomed in the woods—and fields without the city glistened fresh and green under the summer sky.

All this these busy factory girls knew little of, yet did they not seem sad or languid. Some of them were, indeed, pale and sickly; but others wore the rosy hue of health on their cheeks, and had laughing lips and sparkling eyes.

David Pae, *The Factory Girl* (1868).

III

The Cancer of Empire (1870–1945)

Introduction

'Four fine parks ... , innumerable factories, engineering, chemical, cotton, shipbuilding &c; 200 churches and chapels; 100,000 dwelling houses; a population upwards of half a million ... ' These were the city's principal features according to *Tweed's Guide to Glasgow* in 1872. Explosive population growth was to continue during the last quarter of the century, more by enlarging the city's boundaries than by immigration. With the annexation of the last of the suburban burghs in 1912 (Partick, Pollokshaws and Govan) Glasgow's population topped the million mark, making it the Second City of the Empire. By the end of World War II, after further expansion in the 1920s and 1930s, the city housed 1$\frac{1}{4}$ million. Some of these would be temporary munitions workers, others would be refugees from eastern Europe who stayed.

During this period almost all the notable buildings in the present-day city centre were built—a process described by one historian as Glasgow's 'monumental orgasm'—plus a fair number of others since replaced. The list begins with the St Andrew's Halls (destroyed by fire in 1962) and probably ends with the Beresford Hotel (now the Baird Hall of Residence) near Charing Cross, built for the Empire Exhibition of 1938. Most of the large department stores, the station hotels, the head offices of commerce and industry all belong to this period, not to mention the unmistakable productions of Charles Rennie Mackintosh.

Yet the city never sprawled. Space was at a premium and the tenement was the new kind of housing. The older areas around Glasgow Cross were now a source of pestilence and in the 1870s the City Improvement Trust began clearing and rebuilding; the shortage of land meant that they were forced to charge rents that were too high. Fifty years later a London journalist was still horrified by Glasgow's housing problem, coining a new title for the city (see 1924).

With the dawning of this century, through better medical treatment and sewage disposal, major epidemic diseases were brought under control; but in 1945 there was still a marked difference between the health of young children in Glasgow and in Edinburgh. Among adults respiratory diseases and alcoholism were far more prevalent than elsewhere in Britain.

Glasgow Corporation began building its first 'scheme' after World War I and by 1945 the city's housing stock comprised 281,000 houses. In the inner city, however, people still lived at densities of 500 to the acre. Inexorably the Corporation (as it became in 1895) extended its influence into the lives of its citizens, providing electric power, parks, sanatoria, an art gallery, trams and sewage farms; for a few years there was even a municipal telephone system. It was, and remains, a major employer whose political master for more than fifty years has been the Labour Party.

The first International Exhibition in 1888 brought crowds of visitors from the south, mainly by the new railway system. In the Edwardian era the better-off supported the arts, particularly music and painting, whilst for the less serious-minded there were music halls, roller-skating rinks, football and, in the 1920s, cinemas. At the weekends there were the Clyde steamers, listening to the soap-box orators on the Green, or escaping to the nearby hills.

With the decline in textiles and the growth in heavy engineering and shipbuilding there was an increased demand for steel; this was to come from steelworks linked by rail with the Lanarkshire coalfields. In the heart of the city, as international trade boomed, new docks were being built further and further downstream. A new labour militancy grew up during World War I. In 1922 Glasgow returned ten Socialist M.P.s and The Red Clyde was a phrase in common usage.

The 1930s marked a low point in the city's fortunes as factories and yards shed labour. Certain neighbourhoods were terrorised by street gangs, and the police found themselves dealing with civic corruption as well. In 1933 work stopped on the new Cunarder at John Brown's; both Beardmore's forge and Fairfields yard were on the point of collapse when rearmament began. Glasgow had a good war: the Clyde was extensively used by troopships and the merchant fleet, the city's economy was reinvigorated by providing supplies and munitions, and it was nearby Clydebank that received the worst of the German bombs. But with the return of peace the old problems still remained, and further new ones would have to be met.

1870: Shebeens

In 1870 the *North British Daily Mail* (in 1901 to become the *Daily Record*) was one of three daily newspapers published in the city. A number of articles under the series title 'The Dark Side of Glasgow' exposed the vice and degradation that was commonplace in the wynds around the Gallowgate. Many of the properties mentioned were owned by the City Improvement Trust prior to demolition. This extract describes the different kind of shebeens that existed for out-of-hours drinking; here whisky of a sort could be procured at 3 pence per pint. Clearly the *Mail's* correspondent must have accompanied the police on raids.

The effect of the shebeens has been to keep the streets in their neighbourhood in a continual turmoil; drouthy and disreputable characters and thieves turn night into day, prowl about till four or five in the morning, every now and then refreshing themselves at the shebeens until they become drunk and disorderly and are carried off to the Police Office, making night hideous with their yells and imprecations. On these occasions the Cross of Glasgow is a veritable Pandemonium, and the rogues and vagabonds, when they have no innocents to fleece, wrangle and quarrel amongst themselves like a pack of hungry curs. At these times it is dangerous for any respectable citizen to pass through the streets in the Central District, as they stand a good chance of being plundered and maltreated. Fights are frequently got up for the purpose of collecting a crowd, in the midst of which pockets are picked and watches snatched. Once the thief has secured the plunder, he generally makes for some of the labyrinthine closes in the Trongate or Saltmarket, whence by means of one or other of these numerous outlets he contrives to escape, or a confederate is ready in waiting who relieves him of the stolen property; so that even if he be caught nothing is found upon him. These are the classes who bring most grist to the mill of the shebeener. They cannot keep up their nightly orgies without his aid, and he not only supplies them with drink for themselves, but his house, is in many cases a convenient rendezvous to which they lead their unsuspecting victims, whom they ply with adulterated drink until they are in a condition to be easily fleeced.

Many young men are led astray through these shebeens, where, coming in contact with thieves and loose women, they become the victims of intemperance or licentiousness, and going from bad to worse frequently take to embezzlement or thieving. They cannot indulge in these stolen drinks except in the society of the very lowest description, and by this contact their sense of right and wrong becomes rapidly blunted, and the result is that many of them go to swell the list of our criminal population. Servant girls, too, who are out for their Sunday evenings are frequently taken into these shebeens by their so-called sweethearts, and the effect upon them cannot but be most demoralising.

'Respectable' Shebeens

There are various kinds of shebeens, some being very much worse than others. Some of the proprietors are honest enough, except in so far as they cheat the revenue; but their customers in all cases are at the best of a questionable character. A shebeener will sell drink to any man or woman who may come for it, and one of the most respectable of them said to us, 'I'd sell it to Satan himself if he had the money to pay for it.' Beyond the unlicensed sale of liquor, however, they do not go, and for their own safety they try to keep their customers as orderly as possible whilst in their premises. In this class of shebeen may be found working men and tradesmen's assistants, who, being driven out of the public-houses before their convivality has reached the culminating point, finish their evening's tipple with the shebeener, frequently landing in the street in a state of inebriation, an easy prey to the thief, &c.—or fit subjects for the police office, where 'sorrow returns with the dawning of morn,' and 'a sair head and a dry thrapple' awaken him to a sense of the drawbacks of shebeening. The larger shebeens affect the main thoroughfares, such as Trongate, London Street, The Saltmarket, and the Gallowgate. They generally have one large room, capable of accommodating at a pinch from 30 to 40 people. Then a smaller room for select customers, and when these are full, the family kitchen takes in the rest. Under their least unfavourable aspect, however, they are by no means inviting quarters. Shebeening is attended with much inconvenience and discomfort, both to the frequenters and the keepers, and it has often puzzled us what pleasure can possibly be found in sitting for hours amidst a conglomeration of fish-bones and fragments of sodden pastry, in crowded low-roofed rooms, filled with clouds of bad tobacco smoke, and reeking with the tainted breaths and perspiration of a most unprepossessing company, not to speak of the danger incurred of an arrest and a fine of 40s, which the law imposes, or a lodging in the comfortless cells of the police office. As for the proprietors, the profits to them are great, and they can easily afford to pay an occasional fine of £10. Indeed they laugh at the penalty, and regard it merely in the light of a species of black mail, which they willingly pay in the hope of a short period of impunity. Still, theirs is not a very attractive occupation. They cannot call their homes their own. The very privacy of their sleeping room is invaded by their drunken, debauched patrons, to whose foul talk their wives and their children—frequently in bed where the men are drinking—are compelled to listen, fortunate if indeed they escape being made the subjects of their coarse and hideous jokes. Truly the money they earn is very filthy lucre.

Disreputable Shebeens

Another class of shebeeners frequent the wynds, and their houses are the rendezvous of thieves and loose women. One apartment with a bed in it serves their customers, who never sit very long at a time, but tumble out and in all night. In these fights and thefts are constantly occurring, and especially on Saturday nights. Up till four or five on Sunday morning they are the scenes of riotous and unholy revelry. These constitute the second act in the evening's amusement of shebeen frequenters, who, already 'pretty well on' with the supplies taken in at the larger houses, are led into these dens by midnight prowlers, who ply them with stupefying drink until they are turned out into the streets in a helpless condition and robbed. Should they show any resistance very short work is made of them, and broken heads and crushed ribs are the result.

Another class of shebeens are what are called the 'wee shebeens,' where 'drouthy neebors neebors meet'—not with their legs under the mahogany (or what does duty for it) of their hosts, but on the stair head, where a drunken old hag in a greasy 'mutch,' with trembling hand, pours out from her black bottle a compound of whisky and methylated spirits, a glass of which being swigged off in the dark and the money paid, the recipient staggers down the stairs, and out again to the streets. Against this class of shebeener it is almost impossible to obtain a conviction. The next and worst description are the houses of ill-fame, where shebeening is also carried on, and where every kind of debauchery, in its worst and most loathsome form, flourishes in rank luxuriance. Here men and women crowd promiscuously together, and drink and fight, and steal and curse, and swear, and spend the evening. Here the student of human nature may behold a picture of infamy, brutality, and filth, utterly divested of any redeeming trait, and without one single ray of light to modify the dark picture.

North British Daily Mail, 27 December 1870.

1870s: A Childhood in Langside

This account of a prosperous middle-class Victorian family is by the portrait painter Harrington Mann (1864–1937). He was one of seven children whose father

John Mann was the founder of an eminent firm of accountants at West Regent Street. Langside was a new district of villas and high-quality tenements built mainly for the professional men who started work later than their counterparts in trade or industry. This picture of a childhood spent amongst domestic servants, overshadowed by a stern and distant patriarch, is from an unpublished autobiography.

The shadow still remains of a very early period of many days and weeks in bed, of cod liver oil, sponge cake and grapes, of Doctor Duncan presenting me with a book inscribed on the front page with the words 'To my most patient of patients'. Many a visit he paid in his one-horse brougham. He wore a well-trimmed beard of red, and his stethoscope of antiquated type (in cylindrical form) fitted exactly into his top hat and remained there, when not in use. Was the stethoscope made to fit the hat, or the hat to fit the stethoscope? I cannot tell.

At other times we had the terrible experience of being locked in the bathroom with Bessie the nurse, who burnt a stick of yellow sulphur on a metal tray. The bathroom had been turned into a torture chamber, as we choked and gasped for breath. I do not know what ailment this barbarous treatment was supposed to cure. It remains a horrible memory to this day.

Bessie was our nurse during all my early years, and when time came for her to marry and set up a house of her own, it seemed like a great black cloud over the horizon when I was told she was going to leave us.

Katie, the cook, was tolerably good in her kitchen, especially with her daily morning porridge, without which a Scottish breakfast cannot be imagined . . . . One day we found some enormous footprints all over our child gardens. We took Katie out and showed them to her, and asked her if she knew anything about it. She was noncommittal and tried to stave off our implied accusation. All she said, however, was:

'It must hae been some flat-footed buddy'.

Her description of an owl was very good when we asked her what sort of a bird it was.

'It's yin-o-they-kin-a-nicht hawks'.

Poor dear, she left my mother's service after many years, and started a small sweet shop in one of the poorer districts of Glasgow. It was a terrible failure, and she had to come back to us. Domestic service was a much easier life, with no worries.

Childhood songs are never quite forgotten. 'Grannie Frazer'—the old monthly nurse who always made her appearance when a new baby was about to be born—used to sing, 'Here we go looby loo, here we go looby light', or 'There was a lad was born in Kyle, rantin' rovin' Robin'. Besides many Scottish songs, my Aunt Helen used to sing American Negro melodies, very popular in those days, perhaps because it was not long after the American Civil War, and the abolition of slavery. There was 'Dandy Jim from Caroline', and 'Buffalo girls won't you come out tonight', and 'Gwine to run all night, gwine to run all day, I bet my money on the bobtailed nag, somebody bet on the bay'.

'Old James' wore the greasiest coat to be remembered or imagined. Although he could neither read or write, he called for the orders every morning from the local butcher, and never made a mistake during the large round of calls he had to make.

. . .

Methodical to a degree, my Father was a great collector of coins, stamps, odd pieces of string and old newspapers. There were cupboards full of the files of the 'Glasgow Herald', and when the mass grew to an excessive bulk, my Mother would surreptitiously remove a few bundles which were never missed. He possessed an extensive library and was a great reader. His collection of coins was of considerable value.

I do not want to say it in an unkindly way, for it was more of a joke than otherwise, that when one of us had recovered from some childish ailment and a bottle of medicine remained unfinished, my Father had been known to drink the remainder so that it would not be wasted.

From the Harrington Mann MSS in Kelvingrove Art Galleries.

1872: The New Tramway System

The Glasgow Tramways and Omnibus Company (a public company) was given a 23-year lease by the Corporation to run horse-drawn trams in the city. The fares were a penny per mile. Initially the enterprise did not make money, but under general manager John Duncan handsome profits accrued to the shareholders— and also to the Corporation's sinking fund. The network was soon extended westwards to Kelvinside and Whiteinch, eastwards to Dennistoun and Bridgeton, and south as far as Queen's Park. Cars ran every four minutes from early morning to midnight, but drivers and conductors had to work long hours to maintain this level of service. Here is an account of the official opening of the first $2\frac{1}{2}$-mile stretch of rail.

Yesterday forenoon the system of tramway travelling was inaugurated in Glasgow. That portion of the tramway from St George's Cross to Port Eglinton being completed, the directors decided on opening at once; and for that purpose had the lines inspected by Colonel Hutchison for the Board of Trade, who reported as to their substantiality and authorised their being opened for public traffic.

Yesterday forenoon, by invitation of the directors, the Lord Provost, Magistrates and Town Council and a large number of gentlemen assembled at

St George's Cross (junction of St George's Road and New City Road) in order to formally open the line. Seven cars were brought from the depot in Cambridge Street and ranged along the Great Western Road—two or three being drawn by three horses abreast and one in front with postilions in uniform while the others were drawn by two horses abreast and one in front with postilion. The crowd assembled to witness the ceremony was very large; and various comments were made as the cars, drawn by splendid horses, and under the guidance of smart, neatly-dressed postilions, ran past the Cross to their station on the Great Western Road. The first car was reserved for the Lord Provost and Magistrates and Town Council, and it moved off at five minutes to 12 o'clock amid the cheers of the multitude. The car passed smoothly along the rails, the streets in the route being lined with spectators, all anxious to see the first public trial of a new method of conveyance which, in a short time, will monopolise the traffic and run the present omnibuses off the street. Special interest was manifested as to how the cars would take the sharp curve when leaving Cambridge Street, and passing into Sauchiehall Street. The car slowed a little but kept the rail easily, and there is little doubt that when both men and horses become better acquainted with cars, and the road becomes smoother, the curves will be taken quickly and easily. It requires a good deal of vigilance on the part of the police to keep the line clear—more especially at Argyle Street and Jamaica Bridge where there is such an amount of traffic; but although this new method of travelling nearly revolutionises all the former rules of the road, a little practice and a little care will go a great way in remedying any evils that might be found to exist. The run to the head of Eglinton Street was done slowly, and some gentlemen were heard to say that they were disappointed at the rate of speed; but the return journey, from the head of Eglinton Street to the depot in Cambridge Street,—a couple of miles—was accomplished in 13 minutes. This speed might even be increased, and doubtless it will be so in a short time.

Glasgow Herald, 20 August 1872.

1874: The Western Infirmary

This account of the funding and construction of the original Western Infirmary gives an idea of Victorian farsightedness and philanthropy at work. For a city of more than half a million people the Royal Infirmary (founded 1792) was clearly insufficient, inconveniently situated and also beginning to show its age. The new infirmary was near to the engineering and shipbuilding yards where the most serious accidents often occurred, as well as being next to the resited University. It was opened in the autumn of 1874, designed by John Burnet (1814–1901), also responsible for the Stock Exchange and the St Vincent Place Clydesdale Bank building. With the addition of a new 264-bed building on Dumbarton Road in 1974, Burnet's block is now used for storage and some laboratory work.

Independent altogether of its usefulness as a clinical school for the *alumni* of Glasgow University, the Western Infirmary, being reared at Donaldson's Hill, when completed, will confer a great boon on the inhabitants of the West End of the city, and of Partick, Govan, &c. These districts have risen within the last dozen years or so into considerable importance, and the want of an hospital in their midst has for a long time been much felt. The idea of erecting an institution of the kind in another part of the city than that in which the Royal Infirmary is situated was first mooted by the University authorities, and the project of the new hospital, in its earlier stages, was conducted mainly in connection with the scheme for the removal of the University. A site was secured in the neighbourhood of the new college buildings, and plans for the building were prepared by Mr. John Burnet. It became apparent, however, towards the end of the year 1870, that it would be advisable to solicit separate assistance from the inhabitants for the hospital, and with this end in view a public meeting was held on 18th January, 1871. With the grant from the University Building Fund and the subscriptions which were obtained from the general public, the scheme went on apace. The building has been designed for 350 beds, the cost of which, including the sum expended in the purchase of the site, would have been £93, 000. On account, however, of the enormous outlay required, it was resolved only to proceed with a part of the structure, which will afford accommodation for 185 beds. Building operations were commenced on 17th March, 1871, and on the 10th of August following the foundation-stone was laid with masonic honours. The edifice is being constructed on the block principle, and has been described by the architect in the following terms:'The whole length of the main building when complete, extending from east to west, is 400 feet. The extent of the portions running north and south is 260 feet. It may be considered as consisting of nine ward blocks, together with a centre one, containing the theatre for surgical operations and lectures. The blocks intersect one another at three places, in each of which are placed the stairs, hoists, and shoots. The medical clinical theatre is situated in a low building to the west, the washing department in a similar one to the north. The wards vary somewhat in size. The larger wards, of which there are seventeen, contain from 14 to 18 beds, each having windows on either side. Other wards of smaller size make up the complement. The wards are 15 feet high and 26 feet wide, and are otherwise of such dimensions as to afford from 105 to 110 square feet of floor space, and 1,575 cubic feet for each bed. In general, the two upper floors only are appropriated to wards, but in the western wing, where the ground falls considerably, part of the third floor also contains wards. The dispensary for out-door patients is in this wing. Ample accommodation is provided for stores, linen, &c., for the apothecary department, for the consultation of the physicians and surgeons, for the rooms of the superintendent and matron, the physicians' and surgeons' assistants, the nurses and other servants, and for several convalescent airing-rooms. In designing the hospital for 350 beds, it is intended that the number of patients should be limited to 300, so that different parts of the house may periodically be vacated in succession and undergo suitable purification. The heating is effected both by open fire-places and by the circulation of hot water. Ample means of ventilation have been provided for, and all the sanitary arrangements are upon the most approved principles. When the building is complete the in-door patients will be admitted on the east side of the central court, the out-door or dispensary department being on the opposite side of the court; but for the present provision for their separate entrance at the western side is made.'

Glasgow News, 22 January 1874.

1874: Pollution of the Clyde

By mid-century the river in the centre of Glasgow was largely raw sewage. The author of *Tweed's Guide to Glasgow* (1872) was commendably honest about this: 'Its colour is inky, its composition muddy and its effluvia at times, when the steamers are churning up its hidden ugliness, beastly'. A report by the Town Council in 1866 proposed pumping Glasgow's sewage along a pipeline to the coast at Troon. An alternative method was to use it as manure on surrounding arable land. Neither idea was followed up, and it was not until 1876 that a sewage purification scheme was implemented. This official report by the Sanitary Inspector shows that it was not before time.

Main sewers and natural streams within the City boundary—all now used for drainage purposes—measuring together very nearly one hundred miles, receive and convey in their ramifications through the City the sewage from 101,368 dwelling-houses, and from sale-shops, warehouses, manufactories, and workshops, numbering in the aggregate 16,218; including 31,927 water-closets, 71,291 sinks, 3,865 fixed basins, and the urine from 121 urinals, 5,288 ashpits, 935 privies, 2,304 stables, and 311 cow-houses, and discharge the same direct into the Clyde from 42 outlets, of which 33 are situated below the Weir, 18 on its north bank, and 15 on its south bank, with two manufactory outflows by private drains, the one a chemical work and the other a distillery, and 9 above the Weir, 4 on its north bank, and 5 on its south bank.

In addition to the latter, and in the same part of the River, 20 manufactories discharge their waste outflow by private drains direct into the Clyde—12 on the north and 8 on the south bank—consisting of 7 dye-works, 1 confection manufactory, 5 cotton mills, 1 paper mill, 5 weaving factories, and 1 spinning mill; 12 of these outflow water and steam only, and 8 manufacture waste, making in all 64 points of discharge, 35 of which are below and 29 above the weir. 480 of the manufactories included in the foregoing aggregate number contribute to the sewage as follows:- 120 manufacture waste outflow, 262 water at various degrees of heat, 89 steam and water, and 9 blow steam only into the sewers.

The estimated volume of the whole discharge into the River daily, as near as can be calculated from Messrs Bateman and Bazalgette's Report, after making allowance for increase of population and manufactories since date thereof, is 400,000,000 gallons, or at the rate of 70 gallons per head of the population, exclusive of rainfall.

Memorial and Report on the Pollution of the River Clyde for the Health Committee of the Police Board (1874).

1876: John Lavery's early experiences

Orphaned at the age of three, John Lavery (1856–1941) left County Antrim to stay with a pawnbroker uncle in Saltcoats in his early teens. He first ran away from school for a week to live rough, sleeping on Glasgow Green and contracting smallpox. His second visit ended in a Gallowgate doss-house. But the lure of Glasgow proved strong: he arrived again at the age of seventeen and stayed intermittently until 1890, when a one-man show established his reputation in London. Despite his sister's suicide and the death of his first wife after childbirth, Lavery seems to have kept a strong affinity for the city and willingly added his name to the Glasgow Group of painters.

I painted my first picture in 1876, when I was twenty. A woodcut of the 'Death of Chatterton' appeared in a magazine about that time. It affected me very much and was the cause of my very first attempt at a picture. I was helped by the brother of my landlady, who was a copper-plate engraver and knew a little about drawing, showing me how to square it off on a larger scale. I spent many months stippling it in water-colour and when finished I thought it good enough to offer for sale. The difficulty, of course, was to find a buyer; but a raffle was suggested and tickets were issued at half a crown each. After the frame and the drinks all round had been paid for, I realized eight or nine pounds. Before the final draw the picture was on view in the bar parlour of a friendly publican, a patron of the Arts, which included boxing.

. . .

In the School of Art I made the acquaintance of a fellow-student whose father had a furniture shop on the island of Islay. McTaggart, the great Scottish painter, when he was young held exhibitions there, and my picture was included in one of these. Then at long last for the first time I saw my name in print in the two-page catalogue. When the exhibition opened I bought the local newspaper, the *Glasgow Herald*, the *Scotsman*, and others, expecting to read long articles on the exhibition, more especially on the discovery of a young genius, myself. Armed with half a dozen papers I could not wait until I got home to my lodgings, and yet was ashamed to be seen reading them in public because I felt sure that everyone would know who I was and what I was looking for. I found a quiet corner in a backyard and went through every page, even the advertisements, without finding any mention of the show. To-day to be ignored is not so painful as it then was.

. . .

After my three years' apprenticeship as a miniature painter over photographs on ivory was up, I took a small flat in a tenement house in the west end of Glasgow with a brass plate on the door, JOHN LAVERY, ARTIST, at the same time taking another engagement with another photographer at £100 a year. At the end of that time he desired to renew the engagement at £200. I thanked him but did not accept. He was not pleased and his parting shot was, 'Well, ma man, ye may want to come back before lang, but mebbe I'll no want ye.'

. . .

In those days in Glasgow the existence of the artist's model was made known by advertisements in the *Herald*, which brought forth all kinds of applicants for the post. One morning I found sitting at the studio door a ragged, barefooted child of about seven or eight. 'Would you be wanting a model, sir?' 'Have you been sitting?' 'A wus sitting to Rattray.' Her reply indicated a familiarity with the profession that was surprising. Mr. Rattray was a stained-glass painter and I inquired what she had been posing for. 'A wus posing for an angel, and he gave me saxpence an oor in ma claes and ninepence in ma skin.'

She compared favourably to the girl who came to pose as Marguerite for a picture of the garden scene in *Faust*. She was terribly upset when Faust got a bit familiar in the greenhouse that was being used as a dressing-room. She rushed out and refused to let him near her. Faust was a hussar that I had got from the barracks close by. She was very refined in her appearance and genteel in her choice of language. She would not pose again, saying to her friends, 'I would not have went if I had knew.'

Sitting at dinner one afternoon in the house of a friend, we heard a loud knock on the front door and a strange voice in the hall wanting to know if Lavery were there. A burly Highland policeman entered the dining-room, looked hard at me and said, 'Are you Lavery?' 'Yes,' I answered with some anxiety. 'Weel, ye're gutted.' It was his delicate way of breaking the news that my studio had been burnt to the ground and my first masterpiece, 'Tis better to have loved and list,' had gone with the rest of my belongings.

I cannot remember ever feeling so happy. I was insured for £300. At the moment I could not pay my rent long overdue, and my present sitter, a busy city man, had got tired of sitting for his portrait. On the morrow he was giving me my last sitting, and I was in a terrible mess as I knew I could not possibly finish it. I had pawned everything I could get money on, literally my shirt, for food. I met with much sympathy, even from people who did not like me, and it was difficult to hide my joy at the though of getting £300, a larger sum than I had ever had before.

Sir John Lavery, *The Life of a Painter* (1940).

1870s: J.J. Bell at the Coast

John Joy Bell (1871-1934)—best known for his portrait of irresistible juvenile mischief, *Wee MacGreegor*—in the last years of his life turned to writing reminiscences of Victorian Glasgow. He was brought up in Bank Street (Great Kelvin Terrace), the son of a factory-owner, and the Clyde coast was therefore the mandatory destination for family holidays. The S.S. *Benmore* was built in 1876 for Robert Campbell and held a maximum of 934 passengers. Carrick Castle pier, at the mouth of Loch Goil, is used only occasionally, although a recent holiday development promises to bring back some of the popularity it had in its Victorian heyday.

The Glasgow summer holiday was then essentially a family affair. Even when the children were grown up, they did not go their different ways. I remember a family of thirteen holidaying together. I knew a family of eighteen, though I was never in their holiday house. Possibly there would not have been room for one more. It may seem funny, absurd, but there it was.

We were not seven then—only four; but there were an infant and a granny who required much attention, and a West Highland maid who sat down and wept copiously at frequent intervals, because the granny reminded her of her own granny, who had departed this life fourteen years earlier. Fortunately there was also a nursemaid, a Glasgow girl, a young person who never got ruffled, and who, when things went awry, sang 'My Grandfather's Clock', 'Tommy, Make Room for Your Uncle', and other ditties of the day, at the top of her voice—otherwise I do not see how my mother could ever have got the packing done. I have no idea of what went into all the trunks and hampers; I only know that when the hour came they filled a spring-van.

Luggage apart, it would have been an awkward business to change from train to steamer at Greenock, and the usual method for families like ours was to 'sail all the way', either from the Broomielaw or from Partick Pier, the latter being for us the more convenient point of embarkation. So thither on a fine Friday, about noon, we were rattled over the stony streets in a couple of cabs.

Our ultimate destination was a farmhouse at Carrick Castle, on Loch Goil. My mother had had no opportunity of viewing it in advance, but the place had been warmly recommended to my father by a friend, as one unspoiled by man—or words to that effect.

We arrived at Partick Pier far too early. The sun shone hotly; the tide was low; and it was before the days of the Clyde's purification. Not to be squeamish about it, the Clyde at Glasgow was then a big sewer. We and other families waited and waited. In the heat babies began to 'girn'; small children grew peevish; little girls complained or looked pathetically patient. For boys there was always the entertainment of the shipping—liners, channel and river steamers, cargo vessels, barques, barquentines, brigs and schooners, dredgers, hoppers, ferries.

At last the white funnelled *Benmore* came chunking cannily down the river, already with a fair complement of passengers, for it was the first of the month. She was almost new, the first river steamer to have a 'half-deck' saloon. For some forty years thereafter she led a steady, useful existence, once distinguishing herself—about 1912, I think—by striking, one foggy morning, a sunken rock off Innellan, and lying there for a week or so, submerged to her bridge.

She came alongside; the families were shepherded on board, to find seats where they could, and the luggage was added to the existing mountains. Luggage went free then. Years later, I witnessed the indignation of a family at being charged a trifle for their piano's conveyance. The *Benmore* resumed her journey, still cannily, for every now and then appeared on the banks boards bearing the words 'Dead Slow', the warning necessary in order that the wash from steamers should break lightly against the shores of the shipyards or the dredgers at work.

And now the warm air was full of the clangour of shipbuilding. Skeleton frameworks, one after another, and hulls nearing completion rose high above the banks. One could see the riveters, like pigmies, perched aloft, and the glimmer of their fires. 'What an awful noise.' said the ladies, while the men complacently surveyed the tremendous scene of industry—and prosperity. What would not all of us give to hear that hammering again? How merry to our ears it would sound today!

On the other side of the river we called at Govan—where the *Orient*, of the line of that name, almost completed, lay moored, testing her propeller, churning the murky water into brownish foam—and Renfrew, where another family or two joined us.

Soon after that it was plainer sailing. Clydebank, as a shipbuilding town, was not there; the river began to widen between green fields, and the increased speed meant a current of air, grateful to every passenger. Lunch baskets and parcels were produced, and the children fed. I dare say every mother there could have done nicely with a cup of tea, but there was no tea-room on board—nor was there then such a thing, as we know it, in all Glasgow.

You would have seen comparatively few fathers on board—impossible, had declared the majority, to get away from business so early; and, anyway, fathers were not expected to be of much assistance on such an occasion. Some of those present took advantage of the lull caused by hunger among their progeny, and went 'down to see the engines'. The others contented themselves with pipes or cigars—I doubt whether you would have found a cigarette if you had searched the ship. Nor would you have seen a banana among the children.

It was a peaceful enough passage—with a pause at Bowling, and maybe also at Dumbarton, with its amazingly long pier reaching out from the Rock over the shallows—to Greenock's Custom House Quay.

There was no space on the deck for 'steering laddies' to run about and get into mischief, so the mothers were free, more or less, to relax. Some of them may have dozed after the struggles of the morning. But all, as you might have heard, at one time or another, gave thanks for the mercy of fine weather. You might have heard also heartrending reminiscences of family journeys to the coast when 'it rained all the time, and the boat was even more crowded than this one'.

J. J. Bell, *I Remember* (1932).

1881: A City of Small Houses

James Burn Russell (*see also* 1885) was Glasgow's Medical Officer of Health during the 1870s and 1880s, an early practitioner of environmental health. He had studied at the Royal Infirmary under Lister and later was Medical Supervisor of the fever hospital in Parliamentary Road. In a crusade to improve living conditions in the city he collected an exceptional amount of data about Glasgow's housing. Unfortunately his recommendations were not always sympathetically received. In this public lecture he considered the connections between poor housing and ill-health. At this time the average life expectancy was 44 years for women and 31 years for men.

Glasgow is pre-eminently a city of small houses. There are, in round numbers, 107,000 occupied houses within the municipality. Of these, 30 per cent. consist of but 1 apartment, 44 per cent. of 2 apartments, 15 per cent. of 3 apartments, 6 per cent. of 4 apartments, and the remainder, or only 5 per cent., consist of 5 apartments and upwards. The average number of rooms in each house is $2\frac{1}{3}$ (2.34), and of persons inhabiting each house nearly $4\frac{3}{4}$ (4.738); so that, including every house in Glasgow, from the humblest to the most luxurious and capacious, there are rather more than 2 persons (2.054) to each apartment: and the average rent of each house is £11 6s. 9d. These figures represent the average judgment of the householders of Glasgow on the question presented to each individually, and decided by each independently, and according to the best of his intelligence: What accommodation do I require, and how much ought I to set aside out of my income to pay for it?

It is the occupants of small houses whose ear I wish to gain.

There are certain common broad conditions of health for the provision and maintenance of which the authorities are responsible. These are—clean soil upon which to stand; pure water and pure air, with all the subsidiary arrangements for drainage, cleansing, and scavenging. It is especially necessary in the interest of the small householder that the local authorities should do their duty in these regards. Even he, however, is a ratepayer, and can make his voice heard through his representatives, and give them moral support and stimulation in their contests, on his behalf, against the vested interests of property. Glasgow is well off in regard to all these general conditions of health except one—the quality of the air. Our water is the purest, our air the most impure in the three kingdoms. This is distinctly remediable, by improvement in the general arrangement of streets and buildings, and by the enforcement of the Smoke Act, and the more rational use of coal. As things are, the greatest obstacle to domestic ventilation is the offensive quality of the outer air. Our housewives find that the best thing they can do is to shut it out with all its smuts and smells. This is a matter worth the attention of Ward Committees and other associations of ratepayers.

In the choice of a house, every householder may assist in a general reform and improvement of the character of the city. The buyer makes the market. So long as there are tenants for unhealthy houses, there will be unhealthy houses to be had. But you may justly say: when we go into the market to buy our food we are protected by the laws of the country from the risk of buying adulterated or injurious articles; why should we not also be protected from the more serious risk of having a house which is not 'of the nature or quality demanded?' I can only reply that you ought to be so protected, and that you have only to say it must be, and it shall be. Every house ought to be inspected, and tested, and certified to be in its general structure and arrangements habitable before it can be offered for habitation. As things are the introduction of inhabitants is the test applied.

Public Health Administration in Glasgow, edited by A. K. Chalmers (1905).

1883: Fenian Explosions

The incidents described here took place late on a Saturday night, shattering the customary tranquillity of a Victorian sabbath. There were, of course, no Sunday newspapers, so rumours would have abounded until the Monday morning when the *Herald* carried the full facts. Similar outrages had occurred in Liverpool and a connection was made with the Glasgow Ribbon Society which held Fenian meetings in Jail Square. The police were tipped off by a fruit-hawker who had agreed to keep vitriol in his stable for the Society. In September there were ten arrests: these prototype urban guerillas all received long sentences of penal servitude. Lilybank Road is now Kilbirnie Street.

On Saturday evening, shortly after ten o'clock, the inhabitants of Pollokshields and its neighbourhood were started by an explosion the nature of which could not at the moment be surmised, although the impression instantaneously conveyed to the mind was that some terrible calamity had occurred. The air was first disturbed by a profound, concentrated shock, succeeded by a rumbling noise which continued for a second or two, and affected the nerves not less painfully. 'What has happened?' was the question which rose to every lip. People ran to their windows and looked out into the night. Glancing northward in the direction of the city, it seemed as if a fire were raging in the neighbourhood of the harbour: scanning the sky to the east, the upward glow was seen to be much more vivid to that quarter, and with a sickening dread the mind reverted to Tradeston Gas-works. The possibilities attaching to any disaster there were such that people shrank from accepting this as an explanation of what had occurred; but when the gas in dwelling-houses became perceptibly lower, and for a little time appeared likely to go out altogether, there was no longer any doubt as to the source of the disturbance. What had happened was extremely alarming; what might still happen no one could tell. An explosion had taken place in connection with one of the gasometers, attended with injury to the person and damage to property, yet it is a matter of thankfulness that the results were not much more serious. How the explosion occurred need not be referred to at this point in our narrative; all that need be said is that it was limited in character, and that its effects were restricted within a comparatively small area. What is chiefly to be regretted is the suffering entailed to the members of several families whose dwelling-house were situated immediately outside the works. In all, eleven persons were injured, one of them seriously, while the damage to neighbouring tenements was pretty much confined to the breaking of windows.

The principal portion of the Tradeston Gas-works is situated on the north side of Lilybank Road, but the large gas holder, to which the disaster occurred, was erected on a piece of ground to the south of that road, and therefore entirely detached from the main works. On the east side of this ground is a large foundry; to the north is Lilybank Road; to the west is Muirhouse Lane, in which there are a number of old single-storey dwelling-houses, and behind these are a carpet-beating establishment and a ropery, reached by a gateway off Lilybank Road; while to the south is a vacant portion of ground bounded by Maxwell Road. So far as can be ascertained the holder was in good working condition, and no danger of any kind was anticipated. In accordance with the usual custom, this portion of the works closed at six o'clock, and after that hour no one was allowed to enter the place except the watchman and the man whose duty it was to test the gas in the holder. Up till ten o'clock on Saturday night there was nothing to arouse the slightest suspicion, and John M. Gibson, the tester, made his usual examination. He had only, however, completed his duty and entered the 'governor' house when he was startled by a loud explosion which shook the building to its foundations. Beyond the shock he sustained no injury.

The sound of the explosion was heard for miles around, while the houses for nearly a mile in circuit were more or less affected by the shock. Those who observed the occurrence at the very outset state that suddenly, and without any warning, a volume of fire leapt high into the air, immediately followed by a sound resembling the simultaneous discharge of artillery. A hissing sound succeeded, and then there was a second explosion, but of less intensity that that which preceded it. As a consequence, the large holder suddenly collapsed and the gas in the street lamps and houses around as suddenly fell and would have gone out but for the action of Mr Kay, the manager of the works, who, seeing the state of matters, at once turned on a supply to Crosshill and Pollokshields from another holder. Information of the occurrence was immediately conveyed to the police and to the fire brigade, and detachments of each body were soon on the spot, the former under the charge of Superintendent Donald, and the latter under Mr Bryson. The explosion, which was toward the south-west—the direction from which a slight wind was blowing—set fire to the carpet-beating factory and to the ropery, but these were speedily extinguished by the fire brigade. Had it stopped there the damage would have been comparatively slight. But so strong was the force set free that that the fire passed right through the houses in Muirhouse Lane, forcing open doors, breaking windows, smashing the crockery, and sorching the inmates. In one home the fire made a hole at the foot of the bed and passed right through the front windows and the door, cracking the walls, bringing down the whole of the plaster of the roof, and leaving the house in a state of wreckage. In an adjoining house a woman, who was sitting with a baby in her arms, jumped through the window in her alarm. After the effects of the shock had passed away it was discovered that with the exception of a portion of her hair being singed she was all right, and that her child had also providentially escaped. The principal force of the explosion seems to have struck the house occupied by a family named Butler, for, besides the damage done to the building and its contents, all the members of the family were more or less injured—two of them, the father and a young boy 11 years of age, very severely. Fortunately Drs James and Robert Chalmers, the district surgeons, were in prompt attendance, and dressed the wounds of the sufferers. They also sent for the ambulance waggon, and, with the exception of two children, had all the injured conveyed to the Infirmary.

Glasgow Herald, 22 January 1883.

1883: The Central Station Hotel

As the railway war hotted up again in the 1870s, the various companies vied with each other to provide imposing stations and luxurious hotels in the main city centres. In 1880 the Glasgow and SW Railway Co. opened the St Enoch Hotel, with a staff of eighty and 200 bedrooms, setting a high standard in luxurious accommodation. But three years later the Caledonian Railway Co. had completed building work on the Central Station Hotel, although it was not to be officially open until 1885. The delay was partly caused by converting the building from its original purpose—an office block for administrative personnel. When more platforms were added to Central Station in 1901–6 the hotel was extended along Hope Street.

This new grand hotel, in connection with the Caledonian Railway, was opened last month, under the management of Mr. Charles Lord, formerly of the Cannon-street Hotel in London. It is of vast size, as there are no fewer than 550 apartments within the building, giving accommodation for over 420 guests, in addition to 170 servants and officials. The main entrance is situated at the corner of Hope-street and Gordon-street. It leads into the entrance-hall, which is laid with marble mosaic flooring. One end of the hall is fitted up with settees and desks for writing; another portion with an office for telegrams, letters, and parcels, hairdressers' shop, hoists, and lifts. On the same level with the entrance-hall, opening to Hope-street and to the station, are the public smoking-room and dining-room for gentlemen in the city. These are handsome apartments, the former measuring 50 ft. by 40, and the latter 66 by 36. On this floor is a dining room for the upper servants of the hotel, and the servants of visitors. Ascending by the marble staircase, situated in the tower, the first floor is reached, on which are the principal public rooms. The table d'hôte room, or grand dining-hall, is at the south end of the Hope-street corridor. Its interior, designed in the old baronial style, has a rich and imposing appearance. Its dimensions are 90 ft. in length by 40 in width and 29 in height. In the centre are two arches supported on columns of dove-coloured marble, while the walls are lined with richly-grained oak for about 18 ft. high—the upper portion being decorated with embossed canvas, coloured with maroon and gold. Adjoining the dining-hall are the ladies' coffee-room and the general coffee-room, which is decorated in woods of American walnut, ebony, and mahogany. On this landing are the drawing-room, 38½ ft. by 18 ft.; the music-room, reading-room, two writing-rooms, smoking-room and billiard-room, 54 ft. by 30 ft. The other floors contain suites of rooms comprising sitting, dressing, bed, and bath rooms, all opening off each other. The furniture in the public rooms is of mahogany, oak, and ebony woods, handsomely upholstered; and in the bed-rooms American walnut and oak. In the carpeting of the establishment 1000 yards of Axminster have been used for the staircase and corridors, 800 yards of Wilton for the public and sitting rooms, and 5400 yards of Brussels for the bed-rooms. From the various parts of the house 1200 electric bells communicate with 600 indicators; the speaking-tubes extend to fully 5000 feet, weighing 4½ tons, and the wires in connection with the bells measure 29 miles and weigh 2½ tons. The culinary department is on the basement floor, with ample store-rooms, wine-cellars, and plate-rooms, engines for the hoists, the electric light, and ventilating apparatus, and for the extinction of fire.

Illustrated London News, 14 July 1883.

1884: Recommendations for Tourists

No-one visiting Glasgow to see the city's Victorian splendours could afford to be without Kirkwood's indispensable *vade mecum*. It revealed which theatres one could safely visit without fear of impropriety, the addresses of the main Temperance Societies, or where to find a city porter (and what to pay him). This is very much a bourgeois view of Glasgow's services and entertainments. But in the 1880s respectability was a strong force, and people went to great lengths to achieve it. Being a respectable tourist was certainly hard work—to visit all Kirkwood's recommendations would have taken at least a week.

Great Western Road is a continuation of the eastern portion of the New City Road, and passes in a direct line westwards, through Hillhead and Kelvinside West, to Anniesland Toll, where it merges into the Scotstoun Road. It is one of the longest, straightest, and most elegant streets in Glasgow. The eastern part, within the boundaries of the city proper is the least attractive, the open space at Burnbank (the drill-ground of the 1st L.R.V.) breaking the line of building, and giving it an unfinished appearance. Immediately opposite the drill-ground is St. Mary's Episcopal Church, or Western Cathedral, a fine building in the early English style of architecture; the spire is not yet finished, but the congregation have in contemplation its completion at an early date. A little further west, on the left, is Woodside Established Church; and on the right is Lansdowne U.P. Church, having one of the handsomest spires in the city. Crossing the Kelvin by a bridge, built partly of stone and partly of iron, the Great Western Road enters Hillhead, and is lined on both sides by substantial buildings containing shops in the first portion, and at the top of the slight incline by handsome terraces of large houses. Passing over the incline, and directly opposite the Kelvinside Free Church, are the gates of the Botanic Gardens and Kibble Palace. From this point westwards, the road runs between beautiful terraces, principally of modern architecture, having grass plots and shrubs in front. On the south side of the road, from the skating-pond westwards to Anniesland Toll, is the equestrian pad, which is greatly taken advantage of. Southwards from the skating-pond, on an eminence, are the extensive buildings and the tastefully laid-out grounds of the Royal Gartnavel Asylum for Lunatics. The Kelvinside and St. Vincent Place tramway cars traverse the whole length of the road as far west as Hyndland Drive.

. . .

Nuisances.—The following is a list of the principal abuses and offences constituting nuisances, which will be at once suppressed on their being brought under the attention of the authorities. Riotous or indecent behaviour, keeping disorderly houses, exposing for sale unsound meat or adulterated food, the sale or exhibition of indecent publications, gambling and baiting of animals, foul drains, public games and shows (under certain circumstances), begging or importuning, beating carpets or mats before 8 a.m., obstructing the thoroughfares or footpaths, furious driving, keeping over thirteen pounds of explosives in an unlicensed place, storing substances injurious to health, discharging fireworks on the public streets, posting bills without permission, keeping vicious animals, dangerous excavations or unguarded areas, overcrowding houses or letting those which are filthy or infected, smoke, noxious vapours, and noisome smells. Why the city authorities should object either to indecency or noisome smells, and yet be guilty of having a public urinal in such a leading thoroughfare as Renfield Street, we do not profess to be able to explain.

. . .

Pollokshields is a pleasant suburb, composed principally of detached villas, with one or two terraces, lying about two miles south-west from the Royal Exchange. The houses are substantially built, and the streets are spacious and well planned. From the facility with which it can be reached from the city, it is a favourite residence with many business men. The best routes are by the Shawlands cars, which pass near it on the east, in addition to which omnibuses run to and from Glasgow several times a day; or by train either from St. Enoch to Strathbungo and Pollokshields Stations, or from the Central to Shields Road.

. . .

Streets.—Glasgow is probably the best-paved city in the world, the roadways being, in nearly every instance, composed of granite blocks, and the pavements of asphalte, or Caithness flags, the chief exception being the principal part of Buchanan St., where wooden blocks are used instead of granite. There are about 150 miles of streets and lanes in the city, which are kept in repair at an annual cost to the ratepayers of over £30,000. To give directions for the guidance of foot-passengers might seem superfluous, were it not that these would appear to be necessary. In riding or driving, the rule of the road is strictly enforced by the police; but in walking, the usual rule of keeping to the right is, in nearly every instance, dispensed with. Each for himself is the motto acted upon. Those who are merely loitering should, of course, be careful to keep out of the way of others evidently intent upon business; for nothing is more annoying to one in a hurry than to be suddenly stopped by another crossing or standing in their path. Another frequent source of annoyance is from the manner in which some ladies and gentlemen swing about their umbrellas and walking-sticks, or carry them protruding from under their arm, to the danger and hurt of any who may approach them. Houses under repair, or in course of erection, should be avoided, as materials or tools are easily dropped, and may cause serious injury. Workmen are, as a rule, careful not to soil the clothes of others by jostling against them; but, at the same time, it will be well to be on one's guard. In regard to the crossing of streets, the only points to be considered are where and when to cross. Few places in town are really dangerous to one with his wits about him; but no one who is at all timid should attempt to cross diagonally at a point where four streets meet, as the conflicting lines of traffic render much more caution and wariness necessary. Policemen are stationed at the more dangerous points, and will willingly assist the nervous.

F

Sunday.—The Scottish Sunday is proverbially not a pleasant day for strangers. The shops and places of amusement are shut; all business and travelling are at a standstill, and only the churches and parks are open. A few trains run on some of the main lines, but these do not allow of excursions for the day. One or two of the river steamers formerly ran to the coast; but since the liquor licenses were withdrawn, they have ceased doing so. The hotels, indeed, are open; but no liquors are supplied unless to those living in the house, or to *bona-fide* travellers, who must sign their name; and if they make a false representation, they render themselves liable to prosecution. If the weather permit, the parks, however, will repay a visit, as they always present an animated appearance, and every opportunity is given for enjoying a quiet stroll. There are many pleasant drives in and around the city, and at any of the carriage-hiring establishments conveyances may be hired.

. . .

Telephone.—The first telephone was placed in Glasgow towards the end of 1879; but so rapid has been the development of this means of communication, that already there are over 800 exchange and 300 private lines. Until quite recently, there were two companies; but these have now been amalgamated, and are controlled by the National Telephone Company (limited), having its principal office at 13 Royal Exchange Square. Subscribers may have either private wires connecting any two or more points, or wires connecting with the exchanges of the company, and thus affording direct communication with all other subscribers. In the case of a private wire, the renter has it under his own control, and can use it at all times without the intervention of the company's servants. The charge for a private wire is at a fixed annual rent, varying with the situation and the distance between the two points connected. The exchange system is worked as follows: Each subscriber has a wire, bearing a number, running from his own office or residence to the company's nearest exchange or operating room. On wishing to speak with another, he rings up the exchange to which he himself belongs; and, on being answered by one of the operators, he gives his own number and the number of the firm he wants, and is at once put in communication with the other subscriber with whom he desires to communicate. On each ringing his bell, the signal that conversation has ceased, the two lines are immediately disconnected, so that either may be connected afresh at once with another line. The exchange of the company is open day and night, Sundays included; and in addition to an exchange in Hillhead, ten call-boxes for the use of subscribers have lately been opened. Subscriptions vary, according to the distance of members' houses or places of business from the Exchange.

C. Kirkwood, *Dictionary of Glasgow* (1884).

1885: The Children of the City

In this lecture, given before an Edinburgh audience, J.B. Russell's humanitarian principles are self-evident. His thesis is that children deprived of opportunities for play and exercise will grow up to be poor physical and moral specimens of adulthood. His descriptions of 'the disadvantages of child-life' incidentally demonstrate how young children amused themselves in the 1880s. Russell's solutions are indeed far-sighted: peripheral housing schemes and inner-city renewal took another eighty years to become reality (*see also* 1881).

In this aspect of play consider the position of our city children. They are impelled by a restless, ceaseless instinct, and not by the Devil, as the landlords and the police seem to think. Pent up in common stairs and in back courts, without a bit of space which they can call their own, their play inevitably becomes in great part mischief. What can a poor boy do but pull bricks out of the walls of the ashpit to build houses with, or climb upon its roof and tear the slates off to make traps for the city sparrows? If they fly kites the policeman cuts the string: if they dig holes in the court to play at marbles, the factor denounces them to the police: if they play ball against the wall, the policeman grabs the ball: if they make slides on the pavement, he puts salt upon them: if they try to swim in the river, they are almost poisoned by the sewage, and when they come out it is to find the man in blue waiting for them beside their clothes: if they pitch a wicket on an empty building site, the birl of the well-known whistle stops the game before they have completed their innings. The girls are no better off. As you feel your way along the dark lobbies, blinded by the light you have just left behind you, you stumble over them playing at houses. As you ascend the stairs you have to pick your way through their assortment of broken dishes and odds and ends with which they are reproducing their meagre experiences of house-keeping and shopping.

. . .

'What can we do for them?' First, let me say, you can do much for yourselves. Every facility for locomotion—the tram, and suburban train—makes it less a sacrifice of personal convenience for the toiling fathers to choose a house as far afield as possible. I advise working-men to live as far from the heart of the city as they can, but I wish specially to speak of what can be done by public effort after you have done your best to help yourselves. Here the philanthropist is met by his familiar bewildering difficulty. Life is fleeting. There are human beings *now* undergoing hardships, suffering from abuses. Can nothing be done to ameliorate on the one hand, while on the other the radical cure is being patiently worked out? This question must be put with peculiar urgency in reference to everything which affects the welfare of children. Their childhood is passing rapidly away. Every year it ends for some of them. But there are some things which can be done at once. We can in various

ways bring the children to the country, and do some little bits of good work in
the town. The larger task of bringing the country in such measure as is possible
into the town involves the revolutionizing of the prevailing principles of laying
out and building cities, and the carrying out of improvements in the course of
years.

Public Health Administration in Glasgow, edited by A.K. Chalmers (1905).

1880s: The Glasgow School of Painters

The Glasgow School of painters (known more colloquially as The Glasgow Boys)
flourished from the late 1870s to the end of the century. Disdained by the Scottish
artistic establishment, they received invitations for group exhibitions in major
American and European art galleries. The 'father' of the School was W.Y.
MacGregor (1855–1923) who painted landscapes from his studio in Bath Street.
Other Boys, like Hornel and Lavery (*see* 1876) had only short stays in Glasgow,
while most derived their inspiration from the countryside in Galloway and
Berwickshire. Practically no-one used the city as subject matter. Harrington
Mann studied at the Slade, then travelled on a scholarship to Paris and Italy before
returning to Glasgow in 1889. Like his friend Lavery, he later left for London to
make a living from painting portraits.

At this time [1860s] most of the painters devoted their talent and energy to
landscape or 'subject' pictures. They had a ready sale for their work. There
must have been a phenomenal wave of general prosperity in those years. Every
drawing-room and dining-room in the city of Glasgow was plastered from dado
to cornice with some sort of painting in oil, framed in a magnificently vulgar
way. The fashion was to show not even an inch of empty space between the
frames. The pictures seemed to jostle with each other for the best places. It was
easy to see what a harvest existed for those earlier painters. As a boy I knew
several of them. They were jolly, amiable fellows. Their canvases were snatched
up by eager buyers before the paint was dry. They had a roaring time.

. . .

Tom MacEwan painted cottage interiors, generally with an old woman
reading a bible, a cat asleep by the fireside. Duncan MacKellar painted
Jacobites in their kilts and plaids. They all had stories to tell. But with the
coming of the new school, their popularity began to wane. The climax came
when one of their number, Davidson, produced a canvas of a small child in tears
over a broken doll, while her grandfather looked on. The title ran: 'I think it'll
need the glue pot'. This was too much for E.A. Walton. He immediately
christened them the 'Glue Pot School', and the title stuck to them. The

anecdote picture, which had enjoyed a long and glorious life in Glasgow, was at last dead, although it may have survived elsewhere.

Before setting out on my two year's visit to Italy with the Legros scholarship, I had been foolish enough to get rid of my Glasgow studio, looking forward to an absence which seemed long at the time, but when it was over, how short it had been. John Lavery had taken over the studio when I left, and on my return, his remark was very naturally, 'Why did you give up the lease instead of sub-letting it to me?' which I had not thought of doing, but he promised that when he migrated to London, as he did a year later, I should have it again. It was by far the best studio in the town. R.W. Allan, Wellwood Rattray and James Guthrie in turn had painted there, and I was glad to be in possession once more.

Now began a momentous period of my life. I had worked for five years in London, one year in Paris and two years in Italy, while here actually in my native city, where the sun is loth to shine and where a drizzling rain is the usual order of the day, I was to learn more about painting than in all those former years. Here was a group of young painters making a great name for themselves. The 'Glasgow School' was already becoming world famous. These young men were struggling along with an unerring instinct for the most modern art problems of the day. They knew more about the true principles of art than all the students I had met in London or abroad. It was a most stimulating atmosphere to breathe.

Colour was their one thought; they painted in colour, they thought in colour. All beauty to them could be translated into colour. Form was to them but a clothes line, on which to display their colour impressions. Even skill in the handling of paint, or the management of a masterly stroke of a brush, counted for less than the capacity to see colour everywhere and in everything, and to record it. Draughtsmanship, with them, counted for too little.

Colour training had been sadly neglected in the time of Legros. Drawing, drawing, form, form was drummed into one at the Slade, and paint, like chalk or charcoal, was used solely to express form and design.

As I have said, the Glasgow painters had a very sound idea as to what constituted 'good colour' and 'bad colour'. W.Y. MacGregor used to say he always ate mince pies when he could get them. He said they improved his colour sense, and he was a brilliant colourist. He modestly put it down to mince pies. It is all the same worth trying, Heaven knows with some of our painter friends it would do no harm, beyond possibly an attack of indigestion.

From the Harrington Mann MSS in Kelvingrove Art Galleries.

1885: Lipton's Giant Cheeses

If he did not already in himself epitomise the self-made tycoon, the Tommy Lipton legend would have had to be invented. The son of Irish parents from County Monaghan, Lipton (1850–1931) was born in Crown Street, Gorbals, and his first job was as a stationer's assistant at the age of ten. After a spell in America he set up a small ham and egg shop in Stobcross Street, working all hours and sleeping behind the counter. From one came many: Lipton became a millionaire, the host of princes, with a taste for beautiful yachts. Only one of a number of successful grocery chains established in the 1870s, Lipton's became the biggest through using advertising to increase demand. The giant cheeses were one promotional stunt, described here by a correspondent of *The American Dairyman*.

Mr Thomas J. Lipton of Glasgow is recognised as the largest retail provision dealer in the world. His principal stores are in Liverpool and Glasgow, but Mr Lipton has no less than *thirty* other stores in the chief cities of Great Britain. For several years it has been the custom to provide gigantic cheeses for the more important of these establishments, to be cut at Christmas time. They have at times been charged with gold and silver coins in order to add to their attraction to buyers, while the price has been no higher than that of other first-class American cheese.

The excitement attending the cutting of one of these cheeses, which had been for weeks exhibited in one of the great windows of the market, can hardly be imagined. We have, however, had an engraving prepared from a photograph taken on Christmas Eve of last year, showing the rush at one of the Lipton markets. A friend who was present gives a graphic description of the occasion and a vivid idea of the surging crowd and of the almost frantic efforts of men and women to secure a slice of the great Yankee cheese. Of course, now and then, a woman faints and has to be cared for; hats are crushed and coats accidentally torn in the ever goodnatured struggle. Many of the buyers, having no patience to wait until they get home, tear open their booty on the outskirts of the crowd, and the lucky ones announce with shouts their good fortune when they clutch the shining guinea and make a rush for another five pounds of the cheese . . .

Within one may see the counters, shelves and slabs of solid white marble, glistening in their cleanliness, while upon them are piled tons of the choicest dairy produce upon one side and of the best 'hog products', ham, bacon, lard etc, upon the other, while the salesmen and attendants, clad in immaculate white linen caps, frocks and aprons, wait upon the changing throng of customers. The scales, weights, guard-rails are of solid burnished brass.

It is needless to say that the most scrupulous cleanliness and order everywhere prevail, in fact dominate each establishment.

Northern Sports and Pastimes, December 1885.

1886: Fire in Parkhead

David Willox (1845–1927) kept a diary from 1872 until 1886; the first six years chart his family life and work (and stoppages of work) at Beardmore's Parkhead

Forge where his high moral standards brought him into conflict with management and workmates alike. Isaac Beardmore, who took over after his brother William's death in 1877, Willox describes as 'a tyrant of the deepest die'. Willox was eventually dismissed in 1878 (the reason given, that he had been there 'long enough') and set up a chemical work on his own account. He went on to become a much respected local councillor. This is his heart-breaking account of a tragic fire in his own home near Parkhead Cross.

On Monday morning, November 6th, 1882, I asked Janet my wife, to make a little furniture polish for me in the house, as I had not time to do so myself. Ever willing to assist me, she readily agreed to do so, and, for that purpose, got the different articles from me—chiefly turpentine and beeswax. I was busy in the work at the time, and paid no further attention, until some one shouted—'O! Davie, your house is on fire!' Our house at that time was adjoining my work, up one stair, at 46 Burgher Street. I at once rushed round to the house, and, on entering, saw the pot in which Janet had been making the polish, standing about a yard from the kitchen door blazing, and the house nearly full of smoke. I leaped over the burning pot, and made towards the window where the water was, for the purpose of lifting the window to let the smoke clear away; but a chopin can lying in the jawbox full of water caught my eye, and, lifting it, I dashed the water on the floor where some of the burning liquid had been spilt and was still burning.

At that moment Robert Watson, who had been assisting Mr. Stewart to build a shed for me in the work, came rushing in the lobby, and, seeing the great blaze at the door, leaped upon it for the purpose, I presume, of extinguishing the flame. The result was like a flash of lightning. 'My God! Robert, you have done it now!' I exclaimed, and I instantly dashed open the window. The house was instantly filled with flame and smoke, the flame rushing out of the window in a solid sheet.

My wife and some of my children had come running to me on my first entering, and at that time there was not one of them burned, so far as I could see; but when the pot was spilt it was impossible to escape being burned; in fact, I wonder still how one of us escaped with our lives. The doorway, so far as I could see, was barred by a solid sheet of flame. What was I to do? Not one second did I lose to consider. I instantly seized my wife, and, lifting her, dropped her over the window, her fall being partially broken by the neighbours. I then dropped over another three of my family, but in the smoke and confusion I can hardly say who they were. I afterwards learned they were Jeanie, Charles, and Alex.

During this time, I was suffering terribly, so much so that I was compelled to get outside.

I entreated some one to go in and hand out the rest of my family, as I felt certain there were some in yet, but the flame and smoke were so dense that they could not get in. Seeing this, I rushed up the ladder again and into the house, keeping low, as I saw the flame inclined to the roof. I called amidst the smoke—'Weans, are there any o' ye there,' and David and James came running to me. I immediately put them over the window, and followed them myself. On reaching the ground, I asked my wife if all the children were out, and she thought they were. I asked 'Where is the Wee Man?'—meaning Alex. She could not tell me. Fearing he was still in the house, I again went into the house by the window, and, keeping on my hands and knees to save me from being suffocated by the smoke, I crawled through the house, to feel if I could find any one. I think by this time the liquid had burned itself out, but the gas-pipe near the meter had taken fire as well as the door and other woodwork near, which were extinguished by some of the neighbours.

I shall never forget the horrors of that morning. I need not mention my bodily sufferings; my mental torture was extreme. My family were all conveyed to the Royal Infirmary, except Charles, who I afterwards learned had not been so severely burned as the others. My 'Wee Man' and I were taken in the same cab, and I remember when I put my hand to my head in the agony of pain, he said—'O! Father, don't do that.' The dear little thing seemed to forget his own pain in his sympathy for me. If ever a child was attached to a parent, it was Alex. to me. Methinks I see him still; and well I remember him sitting on my knee, which he did for two full hours on the night preceding the accident.

I cannot speak too highly of the kindness and consideration shown us at the Infirmary, one portion of a Ward being set apart exclusively for the use of my family; but all the kindness and skill of that glorious Institution could not save my 'Wee Man's' life. He died that night, and the Nurses, in their kindness, brought his dead body to me that I might look upon it for the last time. I had requested this indulgence, as I myself was in a different Ward. I verily thought my heart would burst while I held him to my bosom, and kissed his already cold lips. How reluctantly I handed him back to the Nurses I need not tell.

Diary of David Willox (unpublished typescript in the Mitchell Library).

1887: Inside a Photographer's Studio

James Whyte (1848-1915) advertised himself in the early 1900s as 'The Popular Photographer', and allowing for the exaggeration of *The Mercantile Age's* puff, within four years of setting up he had already earned the soubriquet. He began in business in 1871 as a coal merchant and agent for the Westminster Fire Insurance Company and on taking up photography professionally still ran the earlier concerns in tandem for a couple of years until sure of the new one 'taking'. Photography, in particular the *carte-de-visite* branch, was booming—in 1887 in Glasgow there were over sixty photographers—and Mr Whyte exploited pretty well every aspect of it in a highly efficient way: offering subscription terms, supplying 'portraits' in oils (i.e. painted-over photographs), and paying attention to economy in production. In the 1870s he lived in the Gorbals area; in 1890 he moved to Pollokshields. He operated from two large premises in Jamaica Street.

Here there are two well-appointed dressing-rooms, two artists' rooms, a dark-room, finishing-room, and three studios—one having a north, the other a north-east light, and a centre for copying; a framing and finishing department, a toning and fixing department, and a large printing department. Whilst in the studio our eyes were attracted hither and thither by the very beautiful examples of photographic art, including in-door and out-door work, especially one set of photographs of the Sailors' home and Queen's Dock Dining Rooms, which groups of exterior and interior have certainly been most successful.

. . .

From our inspection of the framing and finishing room it became apparent to us that a very large subscription or club trade was being conducted by Mr. Whyte. This branch of the business is gradually developing, and we are glad to know of it, for the reason that at a slight cost individuals or families can obtain well-executed cartes-de-visite, and portraits done in water or oil to adorn their albums or walls, who otherwise would not be able to afford them. After examining the beautiful printing department, &c., we left to inspect the new premises at 75 Jamaica Street. These premises are just opened, and are trading under the title of the Glasgow Photographic Company to save confusion, although Mr. James Whyte is the sole partner. Four flats of this property have been acquired, and decorated and fitted in the most artistic style. The first floor is occupied by the counting-house and finishing-room, the other rooms being retained for a private residence. Whilst passing out of the counting house our attention was directed to a very beautiful life-size portrait in oil of Sir Michael Connal. Upon the second floor we found ladies' and gentlemen's dressing-rooms, neatly papered and painted in oak, floor covered with linoleum, and furnished with Austrian bent wood furniture; the laboratory, where all the chemicals, papers, &c., are submitted to tests, so as to avoid imperfection in after operations; an enlarging-room, where negatives can be enlarged from cartes-de-visite up to life-size, is also appointed in the most approved manner; and a show-room, where many beautiful example of photographic work are displayed.

From here we are conducted to studio No. 1, which possesses a north-eastern light, fitted with beautiful rustic and art furniture; backgrounds from the brushes of the most celebrated artists; also cameras with the newest patents, instantaneous shutters, and the hundred-and-one little things so necessary to a perfectly-appointed studio have received attention. At the end of the studio there is a dark-room, fitted with heavy double curtains to effectually exclude the light whilst the operations of developing and fixing are being conducted.

On the flat above is studio No. 2, which is spacious and excellently appointed for groups, and No. 3, which is fitted especially for midget or signature portraits. We ascend again to the floor above, where the printing principally is conducted. The extent of the printing department may be pretty well understood when we state that the day we visited this establishment the finishing-room had completed seven hundred cartes-de-visite, besides cabinets—that being only an ordinary day's work for the house. Everywhere great economy is manifest. Mr. Whyte understanding the chemistry of his trade, is successful in recovering a very great quantity of his silver. We witnessed the operation of washing and recovering, and we were altogether taken by surprise at the percentage of the chloride of silver recovered. All these points are watched, so that Mr. Whyte, by economical work, can produce exquisite portraits at the cheapest possible rates. Everywhere John Ruskin's doctrine about light and consequent beauty and sweetness has been attentively considered, for Mr. Whyte knows that without a flood of regulated light his colours, tones, and, in a great measure, his labours are lost.

The Mercantile Age, 16 May 1887 ('Half-Hours in Art-Rooms').

1887: Harry Lauder at the Scotia

The Scotia Variety Theatre (116 Stockwell Street) was originally built in 1862 by James Baylis. When he died in 1870 his widow Christina took it over—a formidable lady by all accounts but one who paid her artists well. It burned down in 1875 only to be replaced by a bigger and better theatre. Mrs Baylis retired in 1892, but the Scotia carried on, later renamed the Metropole, until destroyed by fire in October 1961. Throughout the Baylis regime it was run as a temperance music hall—the 'turns' provided spirits enough. It was here that the Scots singer and comedian Harry Lauder (1870-1950) made his first public appearance in the city—his previous engagements had been at 'Glesca bursts', evening entertainments with limitless tea and pastry for a shilling a head where the audience burst paper bags as a sign of disapproval. In this extract from his autobiography he appears to have confused a later episode with the time of his first Scotia appearance—still, the 'Boer war' amateur makes a good story, and helps to put over the music-hall atmosphere.

There was a famous old music-hall in Glasgow at this time called the Scotia. It was run by a most competent woman, Mrs. Baylis. She believed in giving local talent a chance. One evening a week several trial 'turns' were put on. This was easily the most popular night of the week at the Scotia—the patrons got free rein for their criticisms and for a peculiarly mordaunt [sic] type of humour which I have never come across anywhere else in the world. If a newcomer could 'get it across' with the Scotia audiences on a trial night he had the right stuff in him. Several reputations were made in the Scotia on such nights; thousands were blasted irretrievably. Taking advantage of a half-holiday I went up to Glasgow and asked Mrs. Baylis for a trial turn. She looked me up and down and said 'What are ye?' 'I'm a comic,' I replied. 'Well, all I can say is that you don't look like one,' was her only comment. Then she turned to her desk and went on working. 'I'm really no bad, Mrs. Baylis,' I pleaded. 'Gie me a

chance an' I'll mak' them laugh!' Probably the doleful expression in my words
and on my face moved dear old Mrs. Baylis to a reconsideration of my request.
At all events she turned around smilingly and remarked, 'Laddie, you're
making' me laugh already; come up a fortnight to-night and I'll let ye loose
among them for a minute or two. Ye'll maybe be sorry ye were sae persistent!'

When the time came for me to go on the stage at the Scotia I was shaking in
every limb. The trial turns preceding mine had all got short shrift. Most of
them were 'off' in less than half a minute, and those that didn't willingly retire
of their own accord were promptly hauled off by the stage manager by the aid of
a long crooked stick which he unceremoniously hooked round their necks. The
oaths and blasphemy employed by some of the disappointed would-be stars in
the wings were only equalled by the riotous mirth of the audience in front. The
Boer war was in progress at the time and one of the amateurs, who had had a
particularly villainous reception, stopped after the first line of his song, spat
three times right into the auditorium, right, centre, and left, and yelled out, 'I
hope the bloody Boers win.' With that he stalked into the safety of the wings,
muttering and cursing and gnashing his teeth. As it happened, I 'got over'
pretty well, being allowed to sing two songs with a minimum of interruption
and caustic comment. This was really a triumph for any trial run at the Scotia.
Before I left, Mrs. Baylis came round and congratulated me. 'Gang hame and
practise, Harry,' she said. 'I'll gie ye a week's engagement when the winter
comes round'. I took Mrs. Baylis's advice.

Sir Harry Lauder, *Roamin' in the Gloamin'* (1928).

1888: The International Exhibition

Queen Victoria's most splendid visit to Glasgow was in August 1888 to visit the
International Exhibition in Kelvingrove Park. The main pavilion, situated where
the bowling green and tennis courts are now, was in the form of a huge, domed
mosque. The much-admired Machinery Hall was on the site of the Art Galleries,
built subsequently from the proceeds of the Exhibition. $5\frac{3}{4}$ million people visited
the many attractions which included a shooting gallery, a switchback railway,
floodlit rugby, a reconstructed Bishop's Castle and the Bachelors' Cafe. The only
relic of the Exhibition is the Doulton Fountain, now on Glasgow Green. Before
going to Kelvingrove, Queen Victoria was presented with a golden casket in
George Square. On this occasion Glasgow pulled out all the stops.

The city of Glasgow, the greatest in population of the provincial cities of the
United Kingdom, and one of the greatest in trade and industry, was honoured
by her Majesty the Queen, on Wednesday, Aug. 22, with a gracious visit which
was performed under the most gratifying conditions, favoured by fine summer
weather, and attended with the customary tokens of a public festive welcome
sustained by the cordial enthusiasm of a loyal Scottish population. The Queen,
who had not been at Glasgow since 1849, when she was accompanied by her

lamented husband, the Prince Consort, had now two special purposes in view there; namely, first to perform the ceremony of opening the new Municipal Buildings lately erected in George-square for the City Corporation; and secondly, to inspect the Great International Exhibition of this year, held in the grounds adjacent to Kelvingrove Park, at the west end of the city. The President of this Exhibition. Sir Archibald Campbell, Bart, M.P., of Blythswood, which mansion is at Renfrew, about eight miles from Glasgow, was the host of her Majesty during the two or three days of her sojourn in the neighbourhood, and conducted the official reception of her Majesty at the Exhibition. The Lord Provost of Glasgow, Sir James King, at the head of the Magistrates and Council of that city and 'Royal Burgh,' did the honours of the Municipal Corporation. These gentlemen, with all the official persons, managers of the Exhibition, citizens, and members of the Scottish nobility and gentry, who bore part in the proceedings, and with the people of Glasgow and of the neighbouring town may be congratulated on the success of the arrangements, and on the agreeable impression produced by the Queen's visit.

. . .

St. Enoch Station was reached at ten minutes past four o'clock. Here elaborate preparations had been made for the reception. The station is the terminus of the Glasgow and South-Western Railway, and the spacious interior and also the extensive square readily lend themselves to the art of the decorator. The immense arch of the station was draped with flowing curtains and enlivened with wreaths of evergreens and flowers. The ornate fronts of the station and hotel were brilliant with colour. Around and over the entrance to the latter, palms and shrubs were massed in great abundance. From the first and third floors draperies of crimson and yellow were hung. Along the whole length of the second floor, where the ornamentation was orange edged with red, trophies and shields were disposed at intervals, and all the balconies were bright with foliage. Flags waved from the dormer windows on the roof, and the Royal standard was hoisted on the staff of the tower surmounting the whole building.

The Royal party then walked across the platform, which was laid with crimson cloth, to the carriages in waiting at the south-west corner of the station. Headed by an escort of the 15th Hussars, the Royal pageant departed from the station, and proceeded amidst the hearty cheers of the people to the new Municipal Buildings, going by way of St. Enoch's-square, up Buchanan-street, along St. Vincent-place, to the front entrance of the Municipal Buildings in George-square.

On this part of the route the decorations were very fine. The opening from St. Enoch's-square into Argyle-street was spanned by the first triumphal arch, shaped and painted so as to imitate a structure of freestone. It was surmounted by a Royal crown. The somewhat sombre appearance of the arch itself was relieved by flowing draperies of rich crimson, looped with orange. Looking up

Buchanan-street, the eye was almost dazzled by the profusion of gorgeous colours. Flowing stripes of variegated material, and flags of almost every nationality, hung down the fronts of the handsome buildings or waved across the fashionable and busy thoroughfare. The east end of Sauchiehall-street was conspicuous also by the richness and the taste of its display. A long avenue of Venetian masts, rising from tufts of foliage, led up to the triumphal arch, which stood at the highest point of the street, near the Corporation Galleries. Along the line wreaths and streamers filled the spaces between the masts, while strings of artificial roses stretched from side to side, presenting from a distance the appearance of a light roof of pink and white. The triumphal arch was most elegant; its piers were shaped into niches, lined with crimson and filled with palms and towering shrubs. The arch itself was of trellis-work, filled out with verdure, and relieved by masses of flowers. Beyond this the decorations were continued to Kelvingrove Park.

At the entrance to George-square another triumphal arch, similar to the first in general effect, had been erected. The square itself, which had been kept clear, presented a very effective scene. Three sides of it were lined with gold-tipped Venetian masts, adorned with flags and wreaths. The frontages of all the buildings on these three sides were decked with coloured hangings, while in striking contrast the new Municipal buildings were unadorned, save by the Royal Standard, which waved over the porch. The bright green square of lawn, with the beds of bright fresh flowers, came as a pleasant relief to the eye. The Municipal Buildings, the foundation-stone of which was laid five years ago, had been completed externally for some time. They were constructed from the designs of Mr. W. Young, architect, London, and standing on one of the finest sites in the city, are in every way worthy of their position. They occupy the entire eastern side of the square. Within the square, the equestrian statues of the Queen and Prince Albert were effectively decorated. The tops of the pedestals were trimmed with heather, and at the corners were shields bearing the arms of England, Ireland, Wales, and Scotland. Surrounding the bases were banks of flowers and rare plants. As the Royal procession drove through the square the greatest enthusiasm prevailed among the spectators who had the pleasure of witnessing the procession both going and returning.

Illustrated London News, 1 September 1888.

1888: Overcrowded Housing

The results of the 1881 Census produced some startling statistics regarding the overcrowded inner city. Here the Medical Officer of Health at the time examines the effects of population density: on average each Glaswegian in the 1880s lived just 8 yards from his neighbour. But in reality some areas were far more overcrowded, with a density as high as 348 people per acre (children under 8 counting as only half). Clearly the 'ticketing' policy (*see* 1866) had not been very successful in the face of a rising population.

The point of time to which my statements refer is the 4th of April, 1881, when the census was taken, and nothing capable of expression in figures as to the condition of the population was left to surmise. The inhabitants of Glasgow numbered 511,520 souls. The area of the earth's surface on which they lived extends from E. to W. 5 miles, and from N. to S. fully 3 miles, and contains 6111 acres or fully 9½ square miles. These data enable us to work out the most important physical fact in the condition of men in the aggregate, viz. the surface on which they live. A man may learn to exist without air for several minutes if he wishes so to distinguish himself; a man may live for several days without food: and clothing is not at all essential to life, but *space* to live on and in is an absolute necessity. I do not wish to be led into a discussion of 'the rights of man' as a citizen, but it is well now-a-days to remember this at anyrate, that if man has any rights at all, one of them certainly is—the right to enough of the area of the earth's surface to afford him standing room, and enough of the cubic space of air thereon at least to crouch in. You may call it a luxury to give him room to lie down in, and space to stretch himself in, but to deny him standing and crouching room is to say in the laconic language of Aytoun's ballad, 'You shall not exist for another day more!' In the phraseology of vital statistics the proportion of population to the earth's surface is called the density of that population. In Glasgow the density is 84 persons per acre. The exact meaning of this statement is, that if the whole population were distributed equally over 6111 acres there would be on each acre 84 persons; or if each person were assigned his own share of this acre it would of course be the 84th part of an acre, or about 58 square yards. The significance of this fact can be brought home to your minds only by comparison with other cities. There is only one city in Great Britain which exceeds Glasgow in density, and that is Liverpool, where there are 106 persons to the acre. The only city which approaches Glasgow in density is Manchester, where there are about 80 persons to the acre. The density of London is only 51, and of Edinburgh only 55. Excepting Greenock and Edinburgh no other town in Scotland exceeds half the density of Glasgow; most are far below that figure.

I am anxious to emphasize this difference by the accumulation of facts which can be expressed in cold figures. Figures are beyond the reach of sentiment, and, if they are sensational, it is only because of their terrible, undisguised truthfulness. You must not think of the inmates of those small houses as families in the ordinary sense of the term. No less than 14 per cent. of the one-roomed houses and 27 per cent. of the two-roomed contain lodgers—strange men and women mixed up with husbands and wives and children, within the four walls of small rooms. Nor must I permit you in noting down the tame average of fully 3 inmates in each of these one-apartment houses to remain ignorant of the fact that there are thousands of these houses which contain 5, 6, and 7 inmates, and hundreds which are inhabited by from 8 up even to 13!

Public Health Administration in Glasgow, edited by A. K. Chalmers (1905).

1890: Patients at the Victoria

Following the example of the Western Infirmary (*see* 1874), the Victoria Infirmary (affectionately known as 'The Vickie') was opened in 1890 to serve the South Side. It had 84 beds, two visiting surgeons, two visiting physicians, two Assistant Medical Officers, Matron and Superintendent. Like the Western it expanded as needs arose and funds allowed: by 1936 it had 555 beds and had purchased land at Philipshill, Busby, for an auxiliary infirmary. These rules for patients help to give some idea of life in a Victorian hospital.

2. On admission they must hand over all valuables or money in their possession to the Porter or Nurse, who will deliver the same to the Superintendent.

. . .

4. They shall, unless incapacitated from doing so, take all their meals at the Ward tables, and must stricly confine themselves to the diet prescribed. They must not receive any article of diet from friends who visit them. Any person bringing food or liquor to a Patient shall immediately be dismissed from the House, and shall not be permitted to revisit it.

. . .

6. All Patients shall be silent when the Medical Attendants or Strangers visit the Ward.

7. They must conceal no disease, and no circumstances relating to it, and must take their Medicines regularly, and in the manner prescribed.

. . .

9. Patients shall get up out of bed only when adjudged fit to do so by the Medical Officers, and remain up only so long as they shall be allowed. Unless compelled by disease no Patient shall be out of bed after 8 o'clock p.m. in winter, and 9 o'clock p.m. in summer.

10. No Patient shall disturb the Ward by talking loud, quarrelling, or swearing, nor by smoking tobacco; neither shall they enter any Ward except their own.

11. All Patients who are able shall wash themselves every morning before breakfast, in the basins provided for the purpose; and in all other respects they shall pay the strictest attention to cleanliness.

12. They shall assist their fellow Patients when they are able, and when the Nurse desires them. They shall do any kind of work not inconsistent with their recovery, as certified by the Medical Attendants, and under the direction of the Superintendent or Matron.

13. They shall be particularly careful of everything belonging to the Infirmary, such as Bed-clothes, Utensils, Bottles, Phials, &c.; and Drugs not used must be carefully returned to the Nurse or the person from whom they were received. No Patient shall conceal or put away anything among the bedding.

14. Friends shall be allowed to visit the Patients on the afternoons of Tuesdays and Fridays, from 3 to 4 o'clock, and on Sunday forenoons, from 11 to 12 o'clock.

. . .

16. No reward or gratuity is to be given by the Patients to any Medical Officer, Nurse, or Servant on any account whatever.

17. Patients transgressing any of the Rules of the House, or acting rudely to the Officials or Nurses, may be summarily dismissed by the Superintendent.

Constitution of the Victoria Infirmary of Glasgow with Rules and Regulations (1889).

1892: Women Students

In 1883 Queen Margaret College for women moved into a large mansion near the Kelvin, originally built for an art collector (now occupied by the BBC). Here courses in the arts and humanities were given, often by university teachers, and in 1890 a medical school was also opened. Two years later the University Senate agreed to incorporate the College, and begin offering degrees to women, if an endowment fund of £20,000 could be provided. More than half of this was raised by the students themselves who put on a 'monster bazaar' at the St Andrew's Halls.

Ever since going into residence at Kelvinside the College has flourished greatly. Its students have averaged two hundred, and have distinguished themselves by taking many honours. From henceforth, of course, all University degrees will be open to them, but hitherto the chief honours attainable in Arts and Science have been the Higher Certificate, the Certificate in Degree Subjects of the Glasgow University and the St. Andrews' title of L.L.A., besides any English or Irish degrees they chose to work for. Many, however, have been students who have studied a few special subects from pure love of culture, and without any hope of obtaining any distinction.

. . .

One bright morning last summer I was allowed a peep into the sacred precincts—for, well as I knew the rest of the College, this portion was to me quite a *terra incognita*. It was a Saturday, and all classes were over for the week; but in the large, cool-looking physiological laboratory I found an enthusiastic student hard at work, preparing and mounting microscopic specimens of tissues for the collection which each student is taught to make for herself. Busy as she was, she did not seem to mind my interruption, but showed me all manner of wonderful things—slices of the nerves of frogs and of the lungs of kittens—with the most charming courtesy. Watching her pretty animated face as she tried to explain things to my ignorance, and noticing how neat and smart was her gown, and how dainty the arrangement of her dark wavy hair, I thought that merely looking at her was a sufficient refutation to the theorists who hold that women who go in for such pursuits must of necessity be either masculine viragos or unattractive frumps. Presently, leaving her to her work, I ascended to the chemical laboratory, a large, bright room, where the students practise, besides chemistry proper, the whole art of compounding, from the first preparation of the drugs from their elementary form, up to the mixing and blending of the most elaborate prescription. This room is fitted up in the most modern manner, with a glass balance room, for protecting the various fine powders from the least current of air, and another glass cupboard for evil-smelling compounds, the fumes of which pass off at once by a special ventilator.

Then I was taken to inspect the anatomical laboratory, the only jealously guarded spot in the whole College. I had never seen a dissecting-room, and all sorts of gruesome tales awoke in my memory as I somewhat shrinkingly followed my guide. But I was most agreeably disappointed. Everything was the acme of scrupulous neatness and order, and the spotless floor, the well-scrubbed dissecting-tables, and the bright windows told of the most exacting care and cleanliness. It was one of the few really hot days of last summer, with the thermometer somewhere over eighty in the shade; yet, although the carefully covered-up bundles on the tables told that there were subjects for dissection in the room, the air was as absolutely pure and taintless as any I have every breathed. This, I was told, is due to a special compound which is used in the preparation of the subjects. Off the laboratory is a dressing-room, as all the students are obliged to wear a special dress here, which must be changed before they return to other parts of the College. But no medical school, however well equipped, can hope for success unless able to offer its students clinical instruction. This has been secured at the Royal Infirmary, where, by the kindness of its managers, 110 beds have been reserved for the exclusive teaching of women, who can also study in the large out-patient department, and can take special cliniques for ear, throat, eye, &c. The Glasgow Maternity Hospital and the Sick Children's Hospital are also available for the students. For the benefit of those who may think of adopting medicine as a profession, I may add that the class and hospital fees, including all the regular subjects of a four or five years' course, amount altogether to only about £80.

But now to turn to the subject of the present bazaar. It was worked and toiled for for nearly two years past, and so it has but repaid the care lavished upon it now that it has been successful in gaining the coveted £10,000 necessary for completion of the endowment fund, besides clearing all expenses. The scheme of decoration employed was decidedly a very happy one, being most appropriate to the occasion. The Grand Hall was fitted up in imitation of Princess Ida's College, immortalised by Tennyson, and all the pretty stall-holders wore College, or Portia, caps and gowns, varying in colours at the different stalls. Nearly all the ample suite of halls in St. Andrew's Hall were utilised, there being no fewer than two variety entertainment rooms, besides the regular theatre, refreshment-rooms, cloak-rooms, &c. The various stalls which surrounded the Grand Hall were simply crowded with exquisite goods of all kinds, an enumeration of which would only prove wearisome to those who were not present.

The Lady, 8 December 1892.

1890s: Washday Regime

These formidable instructions are taken from the standard manual for young Victorian housewives. With large families the need for instruction in household management and cookery was indeed great and by the time of the author's death *Household Cookery* had sold around 200,000 copies. Margaret MacKirdy Black (1830–1903) started the West End School of Cookery in 1878 beside the McLellan Galleries. This was merged with the larger Glasgow School in 1908 to create the first so-called College of Domestic Science (the 'Dough' school) in Britain, although it is antedated by Schools of Cookery in London and Edinburgh. For most Glasgow households the 'boiler' would have been situated in the back court wash-house, and every family would have a turn once a week.

Washing—If possible, 1 or 2 hours ought to be added to the day at the beginning of the washing day, to prevent the wheels of the household machinery getting out of gear before the day is over, and prevent the breadwinners from feeling unnecessary discomfort.

First light the boiler fire and fill the boiler; then make and take a cup of tea, which is the best and a necessary refreshment before starting hard work at an early hour. By this time the water is warm. If the day be dry, it is best to wash the flannels first, as they must be dried quickly, and are best dried in the open air.

To Wash Flannel —Prepare two tubs, into which put warm or tepid, but *not hot*, water. Add to this, in the first water, a large table-spoonful of melted soap and a dessert-spoonful of ammonia; but only add the ammonia when you are quite ready to begin to use the water. Into the second tub put less soap, and if the flannels are not dirty, do not add ammonia.

Ammonia is an alkali which helps quickly to remove grease and dirt, and does not leave the flannel hard as it evaporates.

Having had your flannel well shaken out, put one article at a time into the first water, and wash it quickly. It must not be rubbed with soap or with the hand, but dumped up and down and moved about under the hands, as rubbing makes the fibres and wool of the flannel go into a hard thick mass and shrink. The only parts that should be rubbed are any cotton bands or button-holes; these may require to be rubbed with soap and with the hands also.

When the first washing is finished, put the same garment into the second water, wash quickly, and wring out. A wringer is of great benefit to flannels, as twisting the flannel in the process of wringing has been found to make it shrink. A wringer is, therefore, a valuable utensil in the laundry. If the flannel be clean and nice, shake out very well, fold and clap, and leave in the fold for 5, but not more than 10, minutes. If not quite clean, put through a third tepid water with scarcely any soap and no ammonia. Repeat this process, putting only one article into the water at a time.

Flannels should be hung out in warm sunshine or at least on a bright day, and dried very quickly. If such an atmosphere is not to be had, then hang up near a good fire and dry quickly. It makes flannels thick and hard to leave them long damp.

. . .

Paraffin Washing—This method of washing has been much spoken against, and has a few disadvantages, but it has also many advantages, both to the clothes and in saving labour in families where there is much work. The only clothes that can be washed in this way are white cotton or linen, as it would spoil the colour of prints.

Fill an ordinary boiler rather less than half-full—say about 2 gallons of water; put in a quarter of a pound of a yellow soap cut up into thin shavings, and 1 large table-spoonful of paraffin. Let them boil up. Then shake out the clothes and put them in dry, pushing them down with a stick. When as many are in as can conveniently be covered by the water, let all boil for half-an-hour, pressing the clothes at intervals down with the stick. Take them out into a tub with cold water; wash through this, then through another water; rinse, blue, and finish in the usual way.

Put coarser articles into the boiler, to which add more soap and paraffin.

The precautions necessary are, that the water in the boiler must be really boiling before the clothes go in; and it must be kept in ebullition, as paraffin is an oil and floats on the top, and will be apt to discolour the clothes. Also, care must be taken when putting it in, for if it gets into the fire it will blaze dangerously. Finally, plenty of water must be used to rinse, so that the smell be removed.

Paraffin soap is now made, and serves much the same purpose as a cleansing agent, and of course is not in danger of blazing by contact with the fire; but it seems to have no other advantage.

Margaret Black, *Household Cookery and Laundry Work* (n.d.).

1896: The Underground Breaks Down

It took five dangerous years to build the Glasgow Underground. In its 6½ mile
circuit it passed twice under the Clyde and once under the Kelvin; initial
objections were made to the project in case the Clyde required further deepening.
The carriages were pulled by a steam-driven cable until 1935 when electrical
traction was introduced. The two accidents described here closed the District
Subway (as it came to be known) for five weeks. When completely new rolling
stock was eventually introduced and the stations refurbished (1977–79), the re-
opening was dogged by similar embarrassing teething troubles. In its heyday in
the 1950s the Underground carried more than 34 million passengers a year;
nowadays it can manage only 12½ million.

The Glasgow District Subway . . . was opened for public traffic yesterday.
For weeks previously private trials of the cars had been made with thoroughly
satisfactory results. The first train yesterday left Govan Cross at five o'clock in
the morning, running by way of Partick, a second leaving Copeland Road and
running by way of Kinning Park. The early cars were largely taken advantage of
by workmen, and from eight to ten o'clock there was a great rush of all classes,
the various outlying stations especially being fairly besieged. Despite this fact,
the cars, capable of holding each about 50 passengers, ran with almost perfect
regularity, and the officials were beginning to congratulate themselves on the
success of the inauguration. Unfortunately, however, there was a complete
breakdown on the outer circle between three and four o'clock in the afternoon.
Where the cars stopped in the tunnels a good deal of inconvenience was caused
to passengers who had to get out and walk along the line to the nearest station.
Fortunately, so far as can be ascertained, no one sustained any injury. With
only the trains in the inner circle running, the traffic became congested. The
cars, already full, were besieged and, despite the utmost efforts of the officials,
there were some ugly rushes. The cars in consequence were run with great
irregularity, and at times it took about half an hour to go from Govan Cross to
West Street. Up to eight o'clock crowds continued around the entrances to the
stations, and latterly the officials had to close the doors. Until the hour of
closing—eleven o'clock—various platforms presented a busy aspect, and rather
than be disappointed many persons waited for hours in order that they might
have their first run over the subway. For reasons which will not be obvious to
the public, who naturally take an interest in the matter, the management
decline to give any specific information as to the cause of the breakdown, and
even decline to state approximately when the outer line will again be open for
public traffic.

. . .

About eleven o'clock at night an accident of a most alarming character
occurred on the subway immediately to the south of St Enoch Station. From

the somewhat meagre information which could be gathered owing to the lateness of the hour, it seems that a car was standing on the line at a point underneath the Clyde waiting for the signal to advance to the platform at St Enoch. This car was run into with considerable violence by another one which came up behind. The latter vehicle was crowded with passengers, and the force of the impact was sufficient to knock them with great severity about the compartment. A great deal of the glass of the carriages was broken. Naturally the passengers were all greatly agitated, and it was with considerable difficulty that their fears of a further mishap could be allayed.

Glasgow Herald, 15 December 1896.

1897: The SCWS Building in Morrison Street

The original Co-operative stores, whereby profits were returned to customers in the form of dividends, go back to the 1830s when a Glasgow Co-operative Bazaar was set up by Alexander Campbell. By 1869, when the Scottish Co-operative Wholesale Society (SCWS) was formed, there was an obvious demand for manufactured goods. Shirts and boots were some of the first items to be produced from Co-op factories. By 1887 the SCWS had started building a 12-acre factory-village at Shieldhall. Ten years later the opulent new Headquarters building in Morrison Street was complete. The following account of the inaugural procession to Morrison Street shows the wide diversity of manufacturing carried out by Societies in the West of Scotland.

In the procession somewhere about 350 vehicles were brought into requisition, and about 200 of them were those used by the various societies in the conduct of business. Many of the lorries were fitted up with awnings carried on four posts, and seats provided for the members of the societies being conveyed through the city, while the horses were gaily decked with many-coloured ribbons and artificial flowers.

The productive and the city societies, owing to their greater facilities, had much larger contingents than those coming from a distance, but the general appearance and the fine quality of the horses were the subject of much comment among the thousands of people who lined the streets along the route of the procession. Shortly after ten o'clock some of the country representatives began to arrive, and, on account of the excellent organisation of Mr Caldwell and his assistants, who were mounted on horseback, in conjunction with the aid rendered by the police, a start was made from the Green very shortly after the time set down on the programme.

The Scottish Farming Association had six pair of horses, with riders, as if starting for a day's work in the fields, and a milk cart, over which was a model plough with the motto, 'We are jolly good fellows who follow the plough.' The Scottish Wholesale had fifty-six vehicles drawn by sixty-five horses, and being the first Society in the procession proper, their leading lorry was drawn by six horses with outriders, and on the front of the draping was a portrait of Robert Owen, the pioneer of the Co-operative movement. Figures detailing the trade done by the various departments were displayed prominently, and among them were the sales for 1896, amounting to £3,449,465, profits and interest to £176,154, while the number of employees was put down at 4,635. This division clearly indicated the employees at Shieldhall had not been idle. The Cabinet Factory had models of the various articles of furniture made by them, in addition to a circular saw cutting a log of wood, while the upholstery showed a crocodile from which they obtain skins to cover suites, etc. The Shirt Department had a representation of a hovel, in which sat an old woman in squalid surrounding making shirts, over the top of which was the well-known couplet from Tom Hood's 'Song of the Shirt.' Immediately following this were a number of neatly dressed young ladies making these garments with the appliances used in modern factories. The Printers had machines at work throwing off Co-operative literature, which was being spread broadcast among the spectators; and, among other things, a chapel, with the old man and the inevitable 'devil.' The Hosiery Department also gave an object-lesson by contrast. In the foreground of the lorry was a girl in ancient costume, knitting with her ordinary needles, while behind was the modern hosiery machine in operation. The Boot and Shoe Factory had tanners, etc., at work, and displayed the facts that 12,000 skins, valued at £30,000, were tanned annually, and a million pairs of boots were sold in a year. The Tobacco, Tinware, Preserves, Clothing, and other departments, all did their part in making a splendid exhibition, and the Shieldhall Fire Brigade on a hose carriage made a good finish.

The United Baking Society had an excellent turnout, there being some sixty vehicles between vans and other conveyances. A magnificent brides-cake standing on a base of green velvet was a source of admiration specially among the young ladies who lined the route. Among other outstanding features was a case with corn and flour surmounted by two large loaves. Among the mottoes here were some which were very appropriate, *e.g.*, 'We knead the staff of life,' 'Fewer millionaires, fewer paupers,' 'We check the growth of large fortunes.' The directors of this society also put the windows of the tearooms at the Glasgow Cross at the disposal of a large company, who got an excellent view of the procession as it passed the corner, and arranged for the drivers and all those who had helped in their arrangements for the day returning to M'Neil Street, where a substantial tea was prepared for them.

Co-operative News, 9 January 1897.

1898: Scotland v. England at Celtic Park

Under the heading 'The Greatest Match Ever Played' this understandably anonymous reporter colourfully depicts both the supporters and the players at an early Home International between Scotland and England (the first was in 1872).

The *Observer* was a weekly Catholic paper. *Greatest* was clearly not intended to describe the standard of play but rather the size of the crowd. In 1896, 60,000 had been allowed in and the crowd spilled onto the pitch to get a better view—they were persuaded back to the stand by missiles from supporters at the back. The mixture of horse-power and horseflesh must surely have posed parking problems. It is clear that Glaswegians were already taking to celluloid roll-film cameras, a novelty of the 1890s. Short films had been shown in the city's variety theatres since 1896, proving a great draw, so the presence of a cine camera is understandable.

Since the palmy days of Neronic Rome, when surging thousands thronged the Flavian Amphitheatre to witness the games in the arena, the world has seen no such muster of sport-seeking humans as weekly sallies forth to watch the big football matches in the great centres of the game. Undoubtedly football is a mammoth boom. From a small and unauspicious beginning, the game has been slowly but steadily forcing its claims upon the sight-seeing public. The climax of its popularity, so far, was reached on Saturday when

A Colossal Assemblage

Of 50,000 persons turned out to watch the great International struggle between the chosen representatives of the Thistle and the Rose. All Scotland was agog over the affair. The streets of Glasgow on Saturday presented a unique spectacle. From early morn, a stream of enthusiasts poured eastward to the scene of battle, eager to secure coigns of vantage at the field. From noon an unbroken procession of vehicles followed, the types ranging through the whole gamut of conveyances from the snorting, crowd-dispersing motor-car to the harmless necessary growler. Lumbering char-a-bancs, ancient 'buses, festive four-in-hands, decayed broughams, resurrected shays, natty hansoms, and flag-bedizened brakes moved and mixed in the tortuous vehicular current the whole forming a pageant that only Epsom roads on Derby Day could equal. At Celtic Park—the Mecca of this caravan of football pilgrims—the scene was stupendous—imposing. An army of police and soldiers marshalled and distributed the crowd: strong railings, stout fences, and impassable barricades kept the enormous masses fairly stationary, and prevented the

Wild Surges and Frenzied Crushing

That, two years ago, culminated in the tidal wave of mad humanity leaping the barriers and sweeping in wild tumult across the field. The oval stretch of turf was rimmed with an expectant crowd, the rows rising tier above tier, forming living walls to a vast amphitheatre that irresistibly suggested the Roman Coliseum. The scarlet tunics and floating plaids of the military, the blare of the brazen trumpets, the measured pace of the patrolling cordon, lent to the ensemble something of the pomp and circumstance of war. A battalion of pressmen, many kodak-fiends and a cinematographist were on the spot, prepared to record and perpetuate the incidents of the great struggle for the benefit of that huge slice of footballdom unable to be present in the flesh.

Indeed the mere spectacle of the crowd was a sight to see; a sight eclipsing the muster at Thames' side at Boat-Race Day or at Carson City during the big fight. 'Cock o' the North' the pipes shrilled forth, and to these inspiriting strains the players emerged from the pavilion and spanked after the ball across the field. A great cheer arose when it was seen that Scotland had won the toss and had the aid of a stiff breeze. Amid a perfect fever of excitement

The Fateful Struggle Commenced

From the very outset it was seen that the Scots were overmatched and outclassed. They lacked speed, resource, skill, and the pretty finesse that wears down the stoutest opposition. The Southrons revealed a brilliancy of form at once delightful and effective. At times their passing was so accurate, so beautifully judged, and so machine-like as to approximate to the delicate strokes of a billiard player. From foot to foot, from head to head, the ball sped with puzzling swiftness, the men wriggling out and in among their opponents with sinuous, sudden swerves. And then, the speed of the wingers! the arrowy rushes of Athersmith; the lightning spurts of Spikesley! Wheldon's sureness, Bloomer's slippery tricks, and Smith's unselfish distribution, simply broke the hearts of the Scottish defenders and compelled the unwilling admiration of the multitude. With masterful ease the Englishmen bore down on the Scotch citadel and scored. Soon they repeated the feat, and, as a match, the function was as good as over. The home lot was, with one exception, more than disappointing. They were simply a useless feckless jumble of

Colossal Frosts

Slow, turgid, nervous, blundering, they made an awful mess of their mission and their name. Cowan, the mighty man from the Midlands, began well, but soon fell away, and finished the utterest failure that ever stepped on a football field. Anderson should have saved both goals. Drummond was helpless against the speed and dodgery of Fred Spikesley. Gibson played like a girl. Robertson, game to the heels strove nobly, but in vain, to checkmate the wily Bloomer. In front, the men wandered and blundered like spavined gee-gees. Our own Campbell was the worst man in the worst vanguard that ever carried Scottish colours to disaster and defeat. Bell made a gross mistake in trying to rush and bustle Williams. Maxwell was never once seen in the game. Indeed, the selectors who chose and placed the Scottish forwards clearly proved their inability to fulfil the weighty task entrusted to them. The second half opened brightly. With the madness of desperation the Scotsmen flung themselves headlong at their adversaries and succeeded in forcing a goal. But their madness lacked method. The Sassenach came again and Bloomer drove home the third and final nail in the Scots' coffin. The thing became

An Inglorious Fizzle

Thousands hurried from the field disgusted. The home players grew worse and worse, and became the butt for the coarse humour of their whilom admirers.

Nobody was sorry to hear the closing whistle, which left England victor by 3 goals to 1.

We find considerable gratification in the fact that the one player on the Scots' side who remained unbeaten throughout and grandly stemmed the Saxon onslaught, was an Irishman. Dan Doyle was the mainstay and saviour of the Thistle. His generalship was superb. He made no mistake. He held Athersmith safe all through, and his heading, punting and accurate place-kicking almost redeemed his side. Well done, Dan!

Taken on their merits, the teams were much further apart than the score would indicate. The onus of defeat lies, not so much with the players, who doubtless strove their best, but rather with the selectors, who made a disgraceful jumble of their task, and turned out a team that couldn't beat decent third-raters.

Glasgow Observer, 8 April 1898.

1898: The Opening of the People's Palace

With money from various trust funds the Town Council set aside a budget for building a museum and gallery to act as a cultural centre for the East End. From the start the People's Palace was seen as a branch of the new galleries at Kelvingrove (not completed until 1901), with the top floor designed as a picture gallery for housing temporary exhibitions of the Corporation's extensive art collection. Only the first floor was intended to be a local museum; on the ground floor were a reading room and recreation room. Behind were the Winter Gardens 'for the display of flowers and sub-tropical plants or for popular musical entertainments'. Furious controversy greeted the original plan to open for three hours on a Sunday. However, there were half a million visitors within five months of the opening. G.W. Ord, the first curator, describes the busy scene.

The enormous crush of visitors in the months of January and February was no doubt largely due to curiosity, the place having been very well advertised by the Sunday opening agitation, but this is not a sufficient explanation of the great popularity the institution still enjoys. When the sale of the catalogue was stopped at the end of May, owing to changes in the exhibits, we were still selling an average of 800 a week, and we can yet see in the hands of visitors well-thumbed yellow-covered catalogues, such as we were selling in the beginning of February. The true secret of this popularity lies, I think, not so much in the exhibits, as in the general appearance and arrangement of the building, partly also in its supplying a meeting-place—clean, pleasant, and well-lighted—for the people of the east-end of the city, not the least of the wants of that locality. Of all the departments, the picture galleries were unquestionably the most popular, and during the first three months special arrangements had to be made in the evenings to prevent overcrowding in that part of the building. As might have been expected, the picture with a story was the great draw, landscape, unless containing figures of animals, being usually passed over with but slight attention. Round such paintings as E. Radford's 'Weary,' J. Hamilton's 'Massacre of Glencoe', Hugh Cameron's 'Funeral of a little Girl on the Riviera,' Robert Herdman's 'Abdication of Mary, Queen of Scots,' and others of a like nature, the people always massed, and considerable difficulty was experienced in keeping them moving round. A number of pictures of Old Glasgow, notably Sam Bough's 'Garngadhill' and John Knox's 'Trongate,' aroused great interest, especially in the older section of the visitors. Of the arts and crafts exhibits, wood-carvings, books, and metal-work appeared to appeal more to the people than pottery, glass, or textiles, but even these cannot be said to have received the same minute and careful inspection as the few mechanical models in the artisan section. It is, however, very difficult to say what kind of exhibit is likely to interest any given class of visitor. Between the members of the 'black squad' and Irish laces and embroideries there would seem to be very little in common, and yet a crowd of riveters stood round the case containing these exhibits for a full half-hour on one occasion discussing the comparative 'niceness' of each, and the amount of work that each had entailed. Taking all things into consideration, the visitors were exceedingly well conducted, and beyond the taking away of a few tickets and labels no damage has been done. At first, the spitting habit, so characteristic of an east-end multitude, gave us a good deal of trouble; but the posting of a few bills and a little firmness on the part of the attendants soon produced a good effect, and it is now, as far as we are concerned, almost completely eradicated. A tendency to shouting among the younger part of the visitors had also to be put down, but, with very few exceptions, the admonitions of the attendants were taken in good part, and we have found that the stretching of a piece of string across any portion of the rooms is quite sufficient to keep the people out of the part marked off.

Museums Association Annual Report (1898).

1899: The Opening of the Glasgow School of Art

Not many accounts of the opening of the new School of Art building exist. The architect, Charles Rennie Mackintosh, an ex-student who had caught the eye of the director Francis Newbery, was a young draughtsman with Honeyman and Keppie. This was his first submission for a major competition. Due to the School's lack of funds the building had to be done in two stages, being completed in 1909. Mackintosh's designs were undoubtedly controversial—note the muted criticism of 'primarily utilitarian'—and could not have been more different from Scott's Gothic University buildings at Gilmorehill. Many had perhaps expected a neo-classical building, a style Mackintosh described as 'cold and lifeless as the cheek of a dead Chinaman'.

The new School of Art, opened yesterday by Sir James King, is a building eminently suited for the purpose for which it is intended. Externally it is, as everyone with an appreciation of artistic simplicity and fine design is bound to confess, a structure which will long remain as a monument to the strong originality and artistic conception of Glasgow designers. The opinions passed by the guests at yesterday's function were varied, but all expressive of admiration. Already the walls, in corridor and studio, are hung with samples of students' work; along the narrow green and white lined passages stand statues, while upstairs are antique tapestries and cases of art curios, every one with a definite use of its own; for, as one of the speakers pointed out, both in building and furnishings the School is primarily utilitarian. Special notice may be given to the specimens of work chosen for the Paris Exhibition.

The cloak-rooms, in common with the woodwork throughout the building, have the walls of an artistic shade of green, and are lined from floor to ceiling with little cupboards for the use of students. The upper parts of the other rooms and corridors are in pure white. The principal class-rooms, of course, face the north, but for the dark days of winter a fine electric light system has been fitted up, the wires being arranged so that the student may fix the light exactly over his head wherever he be sitting. Altogether this building is one worthy the object for which it is intended, and in keeping with the high reputation already gained by disciples of the Glasgow School of Artists.

Evening Times, 21 December 1899.

1901: The International Exhibition

The International Exhibition of 1901 was even more of a success than the 1888 Exhibition. Between May and November, under almost cloudless skies, $11\frac{1}{2}$ million visitors arrived, including Tsar Nicholas II. A surplus of £40,000 was made, mainly due to the popularity of the water-chute on the Kelvin. As well as James Miller's Spanish Renaissance-style exhibition halls, visitors could inspect the almost completed municipal Art Galleries. Owing to the Queen's death in January, the opening celebrations were rather toned down, as this fashion article clearly demonstrates. Some ladies, however, still contrived to glitter. Amongst the wives and daughters of the financiers and industrialists who had backed the Exhibition Frances Macdonald (wife of C.R.M.) seems to have been the sole artistic representative.

Gowns and Gossip

Our first gathering in our splendid Art Galleries, inaugurated only yesterday by the King's eldest daughter, must needs be a memorable one. The long corridors, in a blaze of light, the great halls of statuary were to be seen under the happiest of auspices, with music playing and a gay crowd of citizens in uniform and brightly coloured gowns moving among the palms and statues and making the scene brilliant and picturesque. The walls were, it must be confessed, only of interest to the passing eye, and the treasures they displayed were for the time being glanced at casually with good intentions of learning to know them another day. The scene from the windows that looked on the lively grounds of the Exhibition was for the moment more to our taste at the end of an important and exciting day when our great venture had been so happily launched.

Without perhaps any intention of retaining mourning except in cases of domestic bereavement, the majority of the ladies were in black. One or two notable gowns there were of scarlet, others of rose and many shades of pink, some of blue, and many of heliotrope and white, but certainly the greater number of the guests did not wear colours. The ladies who received were in black, Mrs Macfarlane wearing a brocade gown trimmed with chiffon, and having a cluster of yellow roses on one shoulder; while Mrs Crawford had a handsome toilette of black satin relieved with white and chiffon. Miss Crawford was gowned in pale heliotrope, with the decolletage trimmed with white chiffon and tiny white chiffon ruches on the skirt, and Miss Macfarlane had a striking gown of black net over scarlet. A beautiful gown worn by Mrs Robert Glen of black transparent stuff was richly pailetted with a gleam of steel among the black, and a handsome design of white lace applique on the skirt. Mrs Wilson's dress was of net and jet, and had white lace sleeves and an attractive trimming of white lace applique on the skirt. Mrs Henderson was in black silk with velvet and chiffon. Mrs King, also in black, wore brocade with a jetted bodice and pink roses, and Mrs Adamson had a distinguished toilette of black velvet and rose point, her daughter accompanying her in the dainty muslin frock she wore a couple of days ago as her sister's bridesmaid. Mrs Gilmore was in black and jet. Mrs Spiers wore black over purple, and Mrs Thomson was in black relieved by a lace fichu. One of the handsomest gowns was worn by Mrs Mason, and this also was black satin, with the skirt cut in vandykes over white, and the corsage of white silk veiled with black, the combination of black with white chiffon having a charming effect. Mrs Robert Anderson had a charming gown of cerise with a jetted overskirt and long transparent sleeves sewn with jet. Miss Cuthbertson came in white with a lace overskirt and chiffon craped and edged with fringo. Miss Blackie and Miss Clara Blackie wore black, and Miss Marion had a silver grey striped gown. A striking gown of white silk and chiffon was worn by Miss Macdonald, the clever Glasgow artist.

Evening News, 3 May 1901.

1901: The Glasgow Man

J.H. Muir was the pseudonym of three young Glaswegians who together recorded their observations of the city at the dawn of the Edwardian era. They were James Bone, later to become a Fleet Street editor, A.H. Charteris, a lawyer, and Muirhead Bone, later famous as an artist. The book was written to satisfy the curiosity of visitors to the International Exhibition of 1901 as to the qualities of Glasgow and her citizens. This passage describes the chief characteristics of the industrialist—'the man who counts'.

The man in the square hat has been described as the typical Glasgow man, because it is he that is seen most often in the business parts of the city. But we do not forget that he is not the cause, but the product, of her greatness. To a superficial eye he would seem to be a parasite buying and selling what other men produce, and yet he renders services to his fellows which justify his existence. Still it is not he who makes Glasgow a centre of industry and a home of manufactures. That is a man of quite another kind, who is rarely seen on the streets, and, save to his own circle, is hardly known even by head-mark. He is to be found in the engine shops of Springburn or Govan, in the shipyards by the river, in the factories of the South Side and East End. We would gladly describe him, but we know him only by name. He controls a great enterprise of manufactures, and since that succeeds we assume that he has brains and inventive power, and a skill inherited or acquired. But what manner of man he is we cannot tell you. He does not live in the public eye, does not enter the Town Council (the haven under the hill for the square in hat), does not often rise to knighthood. The papers, indeed, mention his name from time to time, now as sitting as a man of skill on a Royal Commission, now as presenting pictures to the Corporation Galleries, now as being a leader in musical affairs, and always as a subscriber to the Lord Provost's charitable funds. And yet, for all the popular ignorance of him, he is the important man in Glasgow. For it is he and his kind that, by an ability far rarer and more specialised than the middleman's trick of selling and buying, keeps Glasgow in her place among the towns of industry. His are the original brains, which devise or adopt new ways to do old things, or invent processes to do old things and keep the industries vigorously alive. Glasgow depends on him for bread and butter, and this may be his recompense for obscurity. For, were the furnaces to be shut down, or the shipyards paid off, or the factories closed, destitution would march from Parkhead to Maryhill, and would teach the merchant that the producer is more necessary to a community than a middleman.

J.H. Muir, *Glasgow in 1901* (1901).

1903: Erchie and Edward VII

In May 1903 King Edward VII visited Scotland, coming to Glasgow for one day to see the Art Galleries, the University (*see* 1868) and the newly-built Royal Technical College in George Street, the first to be instituted in Britain. The Royal Tech was a direct descendant of the Andersonian Institute, which offered free instruction in mechanics and chemistry after the example of Professor John Anderson, and was to become the University of Strathclyde in 1964. The following account owes its inspiration to the surprising fact that the Royal party left from Maryhill station on their return journey to Dalkeith Palace. Scott Gibson was a socialist councillor, notorious for long and disruptive speeches, who had just defeated Lord Provost Chisholm to gain a Council seat (see also 1905). From the series of Erchie and Jinnet pieces that Neil Munro wrote for the *Evening News* under the heading of 'The Looker-On'.

Erchie Sees the King

'I saw him and her on Thursday,' said Erchie, 'as nate's ye like, and it didna cost me mair nor havin' ma hair cut. They gaed past oor kirk, and the session put up a stand and chairges ten shillin's a sate. "Not for Joe," says I; "I'd sooner buy mysel' a new pair o' buits"; and I went to Duffy and says I, "Duffy, are ye no' gaun to ha'e oot yer bonny wee lorry at the heid o' Gairbraid Street and ask the wife and Jinnet and me to stand on't?" "Right," says Duffy, "bring you Jinnet and I'll tak' my wife, and we'll ha'e a rale pant." So there was the four o' us standin' five mortal oors on Duffy's coal lorry. I was that gled when it was a' bye. But I'll wager there was naebody gledder nor the King himsel', puir sowl! Frae the time he cam' into Gleska at Queen Street Station till the time he left Maryhill he lifted his hat three million seven hundred and sixty-eight thousand and sixty-three times. Allooin' that he lifted it six inches every twist that means that His Majesty was graciously pleased to lift his hand aboot the height o' Ben Lomond, and exercise energy equivalent to lifting four ton o' Duffy's coal up two stairs every half-oor. Talk aboot it bein' a fine job bein' a King! I can tell ye the money's gey hard earned. Afore he starts oot to see his beloved people, he has to practise for a week wi' the dumb-bells, and feed himsel' up on Force, Grape-nuts, Plasmon, and a' thae strengthenin' diets that Sunny Jim eats.

. . .

And Jinnet

I thocht first Jinnet maybe wadna gang, her bein' in the Co-operative Store and no' awfu' taken up wi' Royalty, but, dod! she jumped at the chance. "The Queen's a rale nice buddy," she says: "no' that I'm personally acquainted wi' her, but I hear them sayin'. And she used to mak' a' her ain claes afore she married the King." So Jinnet and me were oot on Duffy's lorry sittin' on auld copies o' 'Reynold's News', and hurrayin' awa' like Jinnet saw was a woman wi' a wean and it's face no' richt washed. "Fancy her bringin' oot her wean to see the King wi' a face like that," says Jinnet, and gies the puir wee smout a sweetie. Frae that till it was time for us to gang hame Jinnet saw naething but weans, and her and Duffy's wife talked aboot weans even on. Ye wad think it was a baby show we were at and no' a King's procession. Duffy sat wi' a Tontine face on him maist o' the time, but every noo and then gaun up the street at the back o' us to buy himsel' a bottle o' broon robin, for he couldna get near a pub, and I sat tryin' as hard's I could to think hoo I wad like to be a King, and what kind o' waistcoats I wad wear if I had the job. On every hand the flags were wavin', and the folk were eatin' Abernaithy biscuits.

. . .

The Royal Progress

At aboot twelve o'clock cannons begood to bang. "Oh, my! I hope there's nae weans near thae cannons or they micht get hurt," says Jinnet. Little did she think that at that parteecular meenute the King was comin' doon the tunnel frae Cowlairs, and tellin' Her Majesty no' to be frichted. When the King set foot in the Queen Street Station, he gied the wan look roond him, and says he, "Is this Gleska can ony o' ye tell me?" "It is that, wi' Your Majesty's gracious permission," says the porter; "sees a hand o' yer bag." "I mind fine o' bein' here yince afore," says the King, and gangs oot into George Square. "Whitna graveyaird's this?" he asks, lookin' at the statues. "It's no' a graveyaird; it's a square and that's the Municeepal Buildin'," somebody tells him. "That'll be the place where they keep the Scott Gibson," says the King; "man, it's a rale divert thon. I wonder if I'll see't." "He's no' lowse the day," he was tell't, and looked rale chawed when he heard it. His Majesty then laid a foundation stone as smert's ye like wi' his least wee bit touch, and then went into the Municeepal Buildin's and had a snack. He cam' oot feelin' fine. "The Second City of the Empire!" he says. "I can weel believ't. If it wasna for my business bein' in London I wad ha'e a hoose here. Whit am I to dae next?" They took His Majesty doon Buchanan Street. "No' bad!" says he. Then he cam' to Argyle Street, and gaed west past the Hielan'man's cross at the heid o' Jamaica Street. He sees a lot o' chaps there wi' the heather stickin' oot o' their ears and a tartan brogue that thick it nearly spiled the procession. "The Hielan'man's Cross," says he; "man aye! I've heard o't. Kamerhashendoo. If I had thocht o't I wad ha'e brocht my kilts and my pibroch and a' that." '

Evening News, 18 May 1903.

1905: An American in Glasgow

In 1905 an enquiring American was doing the rounds of major European cities; he was a Professor in Civic Administration named Frederic Clemson Howe. What he saw in Glasgow impressed and puzzled him. A manufacturing city's municipal administration, comprising almost entirely confirmed capitalists, were able to provide all the basic services for rich and poor from the public purse. The reason, he discovered, was that most of these services were extremely profitable. The chemical purification plant at Dalmuir, which had just been completed, was naturally part of his itinerary.

I went out to the sewage disposal works at Dalmuir. An old employee took me in tow. He explained how the sewage was collected; how it was separated by chemical treatment, how the water was purified before being poured into the River Clyde. It was so pure, he said, that it was fit to drink. He offered me a glassful, but I told him I wasn't feeling thirsty at that moment. So he drank it himself. He told me how much the city received from the sale of the sludge as fertilizer. He explained the process as a gardener might describe the cultivation of some rare flower he had given his life to producing. The man had been in the city employ a long time. There was little dignity, and less pay, about his position. But he was a citizen of no mean city, and he was proud of his job. He was loath to let me leave him and his cesspool. It was all so important to him, he felt it must be equally important to the rest of the world.

Enthusiasm and interest, devotion and pride—these are the characteristics of Glasgow citizenship. I have talked with the heads of the city departments, with a score of town councillors, with police and fire officials, with clerks, bathhouse custodians, and conductors on the tram-cars—with all sorts of men, Tories and Liberals, Radicals and Socialists, from the Lord Provost down to the cab-driver. And this is the only citizenship I have been able to find.

Graft? Yes, I found some talk of graft. The Glaswegian doesn't call it that. He doesn't know the word. But here and there a man would shake his head and say: 'The council isn't what it used to be.' 'It rather amazes me,' said a newspaper editor, 'to read what you Americans are always saying about us. Of course though, I am a pessimist, but I cannot help feeling that the outlook here isn't very good. The make-up of the council is changing. No, I have no personal knowledge of corruption, but there are men who have. I'll give you a note to a former councilman,' mentioning a prominent business man; 'he knows all about the way things are going down in the council chamber.'

It was true, then, this that I had so often heard in America—that no city could go in for such extensive business as Glasgow had undertaken without corruption; that public ownership was bound to demoralize a city. And here it was. Had even Glasgow nothing to teach America? For that was what I was looking for, lessons in city administration.

I called on one of Glasgow's most distinguished citizens. He had been in the council fifteen years, and had but recently retired. He, too, was inclined to send me away with the indefinite remark that the council was not what it once was; that there were two or three aldermen who had no visible means of support; mere adventurers, he called them, who were making use of their positions in questionable ways.

'Let me see,' I inquired, remembering Chicago, Philadelphia, and St. Louis. 'You have no street-railway, gas, or electricity franchises to give away; no contracts to light the streets, for you do all these things yourselves. You have abolished the contractor, and do all of your own work. You have no franchises, grants, or privileges, have you?'

'Oh, nothing of that kind, if that's what you mean by graft,' he promptly replied.

This was mystifying. Here was corruption, but corruption without cause, for there was no one to tempt the official. And men do not bribe themselves. When pressed to be more definite, he said: 'Well, there's Bailie so and so,' mentioning a member of the Council. 'He was sitting in license court some years ago, and one evening he found on his desk an envelope containing fifty pounds. It was from a public-house keeper who wanted a license.' 'That was bad,' I suggested. 'Was the magistrate prosecuted?' 'Of course not,' came the indignant protest. 'He didn't keep the money. He made the matter known at once, and the applicant was arrested. And, of course, he didn't get his license.'

I professed the proper amount of horror, and asked, 'Any other instances of graft?' 'Well, that was a number of years ago. There was another case of the same kind, but it wasn't so bad as that, and we couldn't prove anything. But,' he continued, 'the trade is very active in politics. The liquor interests are said to have backed one or two men for the council, men who have no business or profession, and who simply live by their wits.'

Undoubtedly 'the trade' is active in politics. The council names fourteen of its members as magistrates in the police court. They determine what licenses shall be granted, and what refused. There is evidence that the trade has organized for protection. It is certain that it aided in defeating Sir Samuel Chisholm, one of the most distinguished councilman the city ever had. He had made himself obnoxious by a crusade against the traffic. Sir Samuel is a prominent wholesale merchant. After having been in the town council for half a generation, he became Lord Provost, the highest distinction in the community. As Lord Provost, he urged the clearing of some disreputable slums and the erection of model dwelling-houses for the poor. This would have involved an increase in the tax-rate. The more parsimonious among the taxpayers combined with the trade and put up a clever young man (an evangelistic street speaker) and returned him to the council against Sir Samuel. They now speak of their representative as an 'adventurer,' a socialist. Yet they concede that he never neglects his duties, and is a dangerous antagonist. And all admit his cleverness and power.

That's as far as graft goes in Glasgow. The city is not menaced by any special privileges. It is a government of the taxpayers, by the taxpayers. For only taxpayers vote. I never knew a city that hated taxes as much as does Glasgow, and talked so everlastingly about the rates. Any measure involving taxation, even for the relief of the poor, and the poor of Glasgow are terribly poor, indeed, has to pass a jealous scrutiny. Away back in the sixties, the ratepayers defeated Lord-Provost Blackie, who had promoted the splendid clearance schemes for the destruction of the city's worst slums. Glasgow is a taxpayers' administration. I fancy it was these same taxpayers who took over the various undertakings of which the city is so proud. With Scotch thrift, they hated to see the profits go into private pockets.

But I was not through with graft. I had read in the London *Times* that the increasing army of municipal employees was a menace to British institutions. I knew something of the spoils system in America; knew that most people who feared municipal ownership, feared it because of this fact. And here in Glasgow there are 15,000 men in the city's employ. One-tenth of all the voters are on the

G

pay-rolls. Here was the only possible source of corruption. For nobody even suggested that the city had been sold out to the trade or that the so-called 'adventurers' in the council had ever sacrificed the city for their own advantage. I had been told by a prominent citizen that the employees in the gas department had once organized and threatened to put the city in darkness if their wages were not raised. Here was something real, something I could verify. This was something ominous, for all of our cities are adding to their activities and taking on new burdens which involve an increasing number of employees. I went to Mr. James Dalrymple the manager of the tramways, which the Glasgow people say are the best in the world. The department employs 4,400 men. I asked Mr. Dalrymple if his men were in politics; if their unions had ever endeavoured to influence the council, or had tried to coerce the city. 'Never within my knowledge,' he said. 'The city is the best union they can have for the city pays good wages, better than the private company did. The city gives the men a nine-hour day; it provides them with free uniforms; they have five days' holiday a year on pay, and get sick benefits when off duty. They do not need any union, although the city would not mind if they did organize. There were one or two instances of protest over piece-work, but we told the men they could work as they pleased. There has never been a strike, and never since the department was opened in 1894, have they attempted to influence the election of a councilman.'

. . .

Glasgow says it would be just as absurd for the owner of a sky-scraper to permit a private elevator company to collect fares from his tenants, or for an outside plumber to own the fixtures and collect for light and heat, as it is for a city to turn over its streets to private tramways, gas and electric lighting companies. Glasgow prefers to do its own plumbing and run its own elevators.

These are the big things Glasgow does. They are the spectacular exhibits. But it does other things. A mere enumeration of its enterprises makes a long catalogue. It runs several farms upon which it uses the street refuse as fertilizer. It has brought them to a high state of fertility, and produces provisions for its departments. Even from this source it has a net income of $3,000 a year. It has a wonderful system of sewage disposal which is nearing completion. The River Clyde has always been a foul-smelling stream, but the city is expending millions to purify it through the destruction of its sewage and the use of the sludge as fertilizer. The city fire department has a big workshop at the central station where it builds all of its own aparatus, just as the tramway department erects its own cars. Glasgow seems bent on being rid of the private contractor. The alderman smiles when charged with socialism, and says it is good business for the city to erect its own cars, to make its own fire apparatus, and employ its own men. And now the council is after the big contractors who build and sewer the streets. It recently asked for tenders for the construction of a sewer. The lowest bid received was $600,000. The city suspected a combine, and proceeded to build the sewer itself at a cost of only $375,000. Now it receives estimates from its own engineer on all jobs, and is rapidly becoming its own contractor. It pockets the profits which formerly went to the middleman, just as it pockets the dividends which formerly went to the tramway company.

Thus Glasgow looks after her people. She is as frugal as a Scotch parent. I fancy the parable of the talents rather than that of the prodigal son finds most favor in the Scotch soul. There is no waste here. In her thriftiness, Glasgow takes profit from her people. Possibly they love her the better for her thrift. But it looks like usury to the outsider, her enterprises earn so much.

But the council does not use these earnings to relieve the taxpayer, as is frequently asserted. Not a penny of it goes to such a purpose. It is all returned to the undertaking—used to pay bonds, improve the system, and reduce the cost to the consumer.

The same thrift characterizes little things. For Glasgow neglects nothing. Her motto is 'Let Glasgow flourish.' Interpreted by the aldermen this means municipal dividends. The city makes money on its slum-clearance schemes, upon which model dwellings have been erected, and which are now paying their way in rentals at a rate which in time will leave them free from debt. Glasgow undertook this project back in 1866. It cost a lot of money, but it checked disease and brought down the death-rate. The undertaking showed a deficit for a number of years, but is now justifying itself financially as well as otherwise.

But Glasgow has few deficits. A council committee hates a shortage in an undertaking just as a proud banker suffers from a bad loan. Some years ago the city conceived the idea of Saturday afternoon concerts in the public halls. At first they were of a rather frivolous sort. They now offer the best of entertainments, and during the winter months fine oratorios and splendid choral work is presented to weekly audiences of 30,000 people. The admission fee is but two cents, but even this pays. Not much, it is true, for profit is not the object, but the joy of it all is heightened by the fact that it pays its way. Even the sewage collected at the sewage disposal works realizes a handsome sum, when sold as a fertilizer, as does the cleansing department, which has the care of the streets.

The city scorns not the pennies of the laboring man who halts in the evening for a game of bowls on the municipal greens. It gathers in the coppers from the millions who frequent the twelve public bath-houses which have been erected in various parts of the city, as well as the pennies of the poor who make use of the public laundries which are connected with them. We are going in for such things all over America, but I doubt if any of our cities even attempt to make them pay.

But it is not unlovely—this thrift. It is probably the height of wisdom. A people values that which costs them effort. They value the lodging-houses provided for men and women alike, where a bed can be had for a few cents. They value the widower's home, where the working man with children can leave his infants under proper care. And they value all the more the baths, the concerts, the game of bowls on the green, because they have paid their full worth, and paid it to themselves. And during the long winter months the council invites the people to lectures in its own halls, of which there are thirteen, where it tells them all about these things. The lectures are free to all and the chairmen of the committees and the managers of the undertakings go all over the city discussing such subjects as 'The Health of the Community,' 'The Corporation Tramways,' 'The Glasgow Police Force,' and 'The Public Parks.' No wonder the man on the trams was wise—wiser even than the average American alderman. He had been taken into the confidence of his city. It is this reciprocal relationship that accounts for Glasgow's fine citizenship. The city cares for the people, and the people in turn are jealous for the city.

F.C. Howe, 'Glasgow', *Scribner's Magazine* (1906).

1907: The High Street Exposed

Here is a picture of High Street that seems to reflect Thomas Annan's photographs of closes and streets taken thirty years previously before the City Improvement Trust began its work. This report on 'The City of St Mungo' is from a kind of investigative travelogue 'addressed to the intelligent and inquisitive stranger', in which institutions, education, religion, art, literature, humour, food, drink, etc., are 'described and criticised' in an 'honest and fearless attempt to set down the truth as it appeared to the writers'.

As you pass under the arch of the Cross steeple—all that remains of the stately Tolbooth, once 'the admiration of strangers and travellers'—any symptoms of luxury or wealth that may have greeted your eyes in the now deteriorated Trongate, formerly the business centre of the city, cease to be discernible. Though much has been done by rebuilding to cleanse this, not so long ago one of the worst plague spots in the city, you quickly recognise that you are now within a portion of the kind of region which has struck certain colonial visitors to the city with amazement and horror. No splendid warehouses or gaudy shops here attract your notice. While the old rookeries have been cleared out on the east side of the street, their place has been taken mainly by a dead wall, hemming in railway goods offices and stations. Alas! along with the rookeries have also been cleared out the old University buildings. Surely, you say, they might have been preserved in some form or other. Or were these railway stations an absolute necessity to the well-being of this portion of the city? No! they were not. It was merely a question of cash. The railway company were prepared to pay a fancy price for the site; and the Gothic pile on the distant Gilmore Hill rose out of the ashes of the Old College in the High Street.

The west side of the street has not been interfered with. It has simply fallen into low estate, through the gradual and inevitable development of the city westwards. The character of its frequenters, the character of the neighbourhood is reflected in the character of the shops and places of refreshment. Since public-houses in the side streets and lanes would not be under sufficient surveillance, it is the public-house centre of the neighbourhood; and in the public-houses we have the only indication that in the now decayed neighbourhood there was once a University. Above one you read the legend 'University Bar,' above another 'Old College Bar,' and in the window of a third, the 'Old College Dining Rooms,' a scrawled document informs you that you can have within the best 4d. dinner—of three courses!—in the kingdom—which announcement 'dings' the London Soho 'a' to sticks'! Pawnshops also abound. Here the 'publics' could hardly flourish without them, nor they without the 'publics'! Evil-smelling fish shops, doubtful-looking oyster cellars, poverty-stricken eating-houses, and dirty Italian ice-cream shops are the other favourite social haunts of the street. A few of the shops make a brave attempt to assume an alluring appearance, but the majority are not pretentious or inviting: miscellaneous provision stores, small tobacco and newspaper shops, shops which display choice portions of stringy beef and greasy pork at rockbottom prices, and shops whose windows are filled with miscellaneous fruit and vegetables that once were green. If the day be fine a portion of the High Street and the adjoining streets have a display of bunting, in the shape of towels and miscellaneous underclothing, which dangle from the windows to dry in the murky and foetid air.

In the High Street the hatted male or the bonneted female ceases to 'bear the gree.' A miscellaneous assortment of clerks, commercial gents, shop girls, shopping ladies and country visitors no longer mingles, as in Argyle Street and the Trongate, with the crowd of slovenly and untidy passers-by. A large proportion of the occupants of the High Street are women and they are nearly all slatternly. Most of them are comparatively young—even of those that look hopelessly middle-aged. As a rule they are bare-headed, except when their head is covered with a dirty shawl; and if it be summer, and even when it is not summer, some are bare-legged. A few coquettishly sport a fringe. They saunter mostly in twos or threes, or stand gossiping aimlessly in small groups. When the shawl—as often as not of faded tartan—is not made use of as a head-dress, it is thrown around the shoulders, and, more often than not, from the edge of the shawl emerges the dull, dirty, sickly, unsmiling face of a puny infant. On few of the faces of those shawled maidens or madams are there any traces of beauty. Most of them have long parted with gracefulness and even smartness—if they ever possessed them. Some are depraved. Many are quite respectable. The faces of a few are sodden, or rosy and pimpled, with drink. The majority show the discoloured pallor conferred by the crowded slum. Their voices have usually a rusty and raucous tone, whether the accent be touched with the Irish brogue, or the Highland lilt, or the tinker twang of slum-bred Glasgow; and their talk is occasionally spiced with mild womanly oaths. Some of the men have a hooligan aspect. They are mostly young, and the majority are either street loafers, or mechanics, mill workers or porters out of work. Nearly all wear greasy black caps and dim, discoloured jackets, with napkins, that once were gaudy, round their necks. They loll at street corners, or in front of the public-houses, or stroll listlessly about, or gaze into the unattractive shop windows;

and as you pass them highly spiced oaths are wafted to you on the muddy
atmosphere.

T.F. Henderson and Francis Watt, *Scotland of Today* (1907).

1909: *The Glasgow Herald*

This piece of puffing was not too far from the truth, written when the *Herald's*
influence (and readership) was large and wide-ranging. From its modest beginnings as the Glasgow *Herald* & *Advertiser*, hand-printed every week at the rate of
100 copies per hour, it established itself among dozens of other city periodicals as
reliable and comprehensive in its coverage of local and international affairs and
of special service to commerce. With the introduction of steam presses in the 1840s
mass production became possible (1500 copies per hour) and the railway system
gave overnight distribution throughout Scotland. F. Harcourt Kitchin was the
Herald's editor at this time, and the legendary but unlikeable Robert Bruce its
parliamentary correspondent. These were the paper's golden days when it had no
rivals of much substance. An edition was even run simultaneously every night in
Edinburgh.

The 'Glasgow Herald' may fairly claim to be one of the most representative,
and therefore most notable, of Glasgow institutions. In commercial matters—
which include finance, trade and manufacture in all their branches, labour
questions, and, especially, shipping and shipbuilding—it is the recognised
authority in all Scotland, the North of England, and the North of Ireland. In
the matter of Foreign News it enjoys equal facilities with the best of the London
dailies; a special service from New York keeps it in close touch with the public
life of the American Continent; and it is the only Scottish newspaper connected
with its London Office by day and night by private wire. It commands the
services not only of its own large reporting staff, and of all the Press Agencies,
but of a huge retinue of special correspondents all over Great Britain and
Ireland, and is thus in instant possession of all the details of every event of any
significance; its Scottish news is a special feature, and not a Scotsman from
Maidenkirk to John o' Groats can open his 'Herald' without finding in it
something of local interest. Though it is published in a commercial centre, its
agricultural columns challenge comparison with those of any other paper in the
kingdom; and it contains the fullest and latest information on football, cricket,
golf, racing, billiards, and every other form of sport. On what is called the
literary side—a happy description, for literature is the adjusted mirror of life—
it is easily the first among newspapers published out of London, and has
nothing to learn from the best Metropolitan journals. Unlike some of these,
indeed, it has devoted increasing attention to its leading articles, which contain
the well-weighed and carefully expressed judgments of competent authorities
on home and foreign politics, education, literature, and every other question of

public interest. Its musical and dramatic criticisms are of the highest possible quality, and its special articles add to the other functions of the paper that of a first-class magazine. Its broad and liberal views and independent outlook may be regarded, indeed, as the daily expression of all that is best and worthiest in a city that has always been remarkable for the union in its citizens of industrial activity with intellectual and social earnestness—a city whose progress in culture and civic government is all the more inspiring since it has owed nothing to the adventitious advantages of pleasure, climate or metropolitanism.

Advertisements

As a result of its ever-increasing efficiency as a newspaper, the 'Herald' has acquired an almost unique position as an advertising medium. It is long now since it has had the right to style itself the largest and leading advertising medium out of London, and at certain times of the year the 'Herald' would be entitled to withdraw the Metropolitan exception. As a matter of fact, it comes next to the London 'Daily Telegraph' in advertisements. Naturally, this reacts favourably upon the circulation. Apart from any desire for news, the ordinary needs of life compel every Scotsman, and nearly every Briton, to buy a 'Herald' now and again. To an imaginative or speculative mind, the 'Herald' advertisements make splendid reading; and in certain moods of ennui, such as those induced by a wet day at the coast or a prolonged railway journey, they form an invaluable solace—in many cases to the benefit of an advertiser.

Glasgow Today (1909).

1910: Old Easterhouse

As well as being an Art Gallery Department official, Thomas Brotchie was an amateur artist, dedicated open-air enthusiast and local antiquarian. He wrote a number of rambler's guides, with pen and ink illustrations, which described the countryside beyond the boundaries of the Edwardian city. In many cases walks began at the terminus points of the tramway system. This one (entitled *Old Monkland and Bishop's Loch*) begins at Easterhouse station on the 'underground' (i.e. low-level) line from Queen Street and includes a picturesque description of the Monkland canal, now under the M8 motorway.

It would be difficult for the lover of nature, the archaeologist, or the artist to find a more instructive walk than that which may be enjoyed within the boundaries of Old Monkland, in close proximity to the city of Glasgow. The unpretentious little district now to be described is within easy reach of all city dwellers, yet it glories in the possession of sylvan beauties, difficult to excel, or even to equal. A brief twenty minutes per the underground from Queen Street Station and we are at the starting point, Easterhouse. Standing at an altitude of 220 feet, the villagers enjoy an abundant supply of fresh bracing air, combined with the privilege of a magnificent panoramic view of the hills and broad acres of Lanarkshire. Essentially modern in its principal features, it, however, still has in its midst the original 'theekit' clachan, picturesque in detail, but condemned by modern sanitarians, and shortly to be razed to the ground. In spite of that fact, a hardy race was reared beneath its thatch. A native to whom we spoke informed us that her forebears for four generations back had been born, lived, and died in the old cottages, the two last to pass away having, notwithstanding obsolete household sanitary equipment, reached the ripe ages of 80 and 82 respectively.

T. C. F. Brotchie, *Some Sylvan Scenes near Glasgow* (1910).

1912: Bridie in the Slums

The plays of the Glasgow doctor Osborne H. Mavor (1888–1951), better known as James Bridie, have sometimes been criticised for not addressing, as Shaw's did, contemporary life or social problems; but, in Ivor Brown's telling phrase, he was capable of 'seeing beyond the flesh and pharmacy'. As this extract from his autobiography shows, as a doctor he had ample first-hand experience of 'life'. Bridie later was a leading light in the founding of the Citizens' Theatre in 1943.

Among the silt into which Matthew White and I dived and delved was a house near the Municipal Buildings and back to back with a fire station. It had been a noble house in its time but was now farmed out. There was no light on the rotten staircase, and we had to pick our way over and among drunken men laying among their gastric contents. The passage was not too difficult, for it was a broad and well-designed staircase. The corridor at the end of which our patient lived also contained its hazards and was not supplied with light. Among the rags and filth of the little Irish home the patient and her mother were having a first-class row. The Virgin and the Saints were being invoked to the accompaniment of words from a rather less exalted vocabulary. The baby was just about to be born. I had to conduct the confinement by myself. I was protected by a cold in the head from the atmosphere in the room, but Matthew White had to retire to the street and be ill. Before the *accouchement* I am sorry to say we had to lift our hands to a woman not in the way of kindness. We threw the grandmother downstairs and didn't see her again. It was a fine, healthy boy. The young howdie waits with a good deal of trepidation for the baby's first comment on the world into which it is born. This little purple Celt gave tongue grandly, I remember.

In the morning I looked out of the disreputable window and saw the firemen's wives cleaning up before breakfast on the verandahs of their tidy little flats. The sun was shining—not, indeed, into the room where I stood, but the mother was very pleased with her child and with us. She thought her husband would be very pleased too when he got back from his three days' scatter.

Cleanliness and honour and filth and dishonour were pretty evenly mixed in the 'district.' Among other things I found that the caste system, which provides such engaging little comedies among the well to do, was held here with a desperate passion. The respectable poor saw their children walking on rotten planks. At any moment they might fall into the cesspool and be drowned. The badge of rank was cleanliness, and cleanliness was preserved in bug-infested houses with one tap in a kitchen sink as its only instrument. The children went out to school like new pins, and there was a patch of clean air in the foetid fog.

James Bridie, *One Way of Living* (1939).

1914: Mrs Pankhurst at St Andrew's Halls

At 8 pm on March 9th 1914 Mrs Pankhurst was due to address a large crowd at the St Andrew's Halls. As she began, the platform was charged by 120 Glasgow police who had a warrant for her arrest and return to Holloway Prison under the 'Cat and Mouse' Act. The Glasgow Suffragettes, who had strong support from members of the Independent Labour Party among others, had barricaded the platform and armed themselves with Indian clubs. Witnesses stated that they and Mrs Pankhurst were brutally treated by the police, and there was a demonstration outside the St Andrew's Square police headquarters later the same evening. Press reports were also unfavourable to the Glasgow Police, and the Chief Constable was required to give an account of the proceedings to the Scottish Office. (The same Chief Constable was again accused of heavy-handedness in dealing with the 40-hour-week strikers in George Square five years later.) These extracts from a file in the Scottish Record Office present the same scene from the differing viewpoints of two witnesses, Inspector Walker and a member of the audience in the balcony above the platform.

Inspector Walker
'About 8.5 p.m. I . . . rushed up the stair followed by sergeants and constables . . . I was the first to enter the Hall in uniform in front of the platform . . . we were immediately assailed with chairs, flower pots, water bottles, and other missiles thrown from the platform by men and women who fought like tigers. The platform was well fortified with strands of barbed wire run along in front of it, covered with flags and tissue paper which prevented the progress of the police . . . I drew my baton for the purpose of protecting myself, but I did not strike anyone with it. A number of constables drew their batons but I could not say I saw any person struck by a constable. The ladies were all well armed with clubs.'

Mr Leonard Gow
'I had an uninterrupted view of the scene, a scene which must have made the blood of every true man present boil with indignation and shame. I went to the

meeting a non-militant, and not being conversant with Suffragette politics was unaware that Mrs Pankhurst was liable to arrest, my object being to learn the Suffragists standpoint from one of their Leaders . . . The audience consisted of over three, probably four thousand people, men and women, and among these present were representatives of our most respected families in the City . . . . After Mrs Pankhurst had been speaking for a very few minutes, the platform, which please mark, was occupied solely by women, old and young, was rushed by detectives and policemen with drawn batons who laid out in all directions, hitting and felling women whose only offence was that they crowded around their leader evidently trying to protect her from violence.'

Scottish Record Office, File HH 55/336, 'The Arrest of Mrs Pankhurst in Glasgow'.

1914–15: Women and Children Do War Work

The Clyde experienced an economic boost during the First World War that rejuvenated shipbuilding and engineering. Standard designs for for the mass production of warships became acceptable: more than 400 were launched during the last year of the war. By 1918 nearly half the munitions workers were women, attracted by relatively high wages. In 1915 there was government control of rents to prevent house factors evicting families not involved in war production so that they could charge higher rents.

While many of the characteristics of life between 1914 and 1918 were the same all over the country, there were differences. The latter were perhaps mainly of two kinds. On the one side the south and east coasts of Britain were within closer reach of the immediate area of hostilities, and were subject to air-raids. In the West of Scotland no reports of guns, fired in anger, were heard. It may have been for this reason, it may have been through national temperament, that fluctuations of opinion concerning the course of the war were much less extreme than in some other districts. There were never the abrupt alternations between optimism and pessimism to which London was subject. Then on the other side there was a difference between a district such as this, which was in the thick of war production, and other places whose resources did not admit of such activities to a similar extent. Thus within the general picture of life during the war there are variations as between different localities.

The shock of the declaration of war brought the inevitable disorganization of the life of the district. Not only was there mobilization with its strain, but there were the business arrangements to be made during the service of masters and men who were mobilized in their territorial units. Then there was the preliminary uncertainty and lack of confidence concerning business of all kinds under the new and unknown conditions. The state of Glasgow harbour in the first week of war was typical of the great upheaval. It was jammed with shipping, so that not only were all berths occupied but the centre of the river was congested, sometimes three vessels being moored abreast in mid-stream. Some were German boats detained or brought in by the Navy, while many others were British and neutrals which were held back from sailing by the owners. The effect of the shock and of the consequent disorganization of the Foreign Exchanges was to make trade dull; there was unemployment and a number of people felt some anxiety about supplies of food being maintained. Before the end of 1914, or at least early in 1915, there came the beginnings of a change. There was the general movement towards 'business as usual', supplemented, in the case of the Clyde, by the demands of the Admiralty on the shipyards and extending from these to all the related industries. The river during the war was a remarkable sight. The shipyards were working as they had never worked before. Warship building and repairing was being pressed on. Later, new slips were laid down when the demand for mercantile tonnage became intense. The yards were a scene of ceaseless activity. In some places the ships were shrouded with canvas where new types of war-vessels were under construction.

At first, apart from the general personal anxiety concerning the war, there was little change in the social life and habits of the people. There was something of a 'dour' pride in the feeling that, apart from private grief and private anxieties, the enemy should not be allowed to disturb the usual life of the people. Changes, however, there were. Naturally many kinds of enjoyment were suspended, though later some reappeared in a modified form as organized entertainments for the members of the forces. Perhaps the first sign of the strain on social conditions by war emergencies was the threatened rent strike in Partick and Govan in September 1915. These districts were largely inhabited by shipyard workers, and the pressure on the shipyards had caused a demand for houses which was difficult to satisfy.

The joint effect of increased recruiting and the development of the production of munitions brought the first great changes in the social life of the district. Already, as recruiting developed, there had been upheavals in many houses. Now the women became industrial workers to a vastly increased degree. Not only so, but there was a great transference of women's work, taking the general form of a movement from other occupations to various forms of munition and related work. The working of the tramway system affords an illustration of the latter. The Glasgow system is an extensive one and some of the lines run far into the country. The total track is about 198 miles, and in 1918–19 464 million passengers were carried. The total staff numbered well over 6,000. In September 1914 the Corporation decided to raise and equip two battalions in the New Army, and within twenty-four hours 1,100 names had been given in by men in the Tramway Department, and by the end of the year 1,756 men had enlisted from that Department. At first there was some disorganization of the service during the training of women, but later it was carried on with remarkable regularity, considering the circumstances. The largest number of women employed was 2,388, of whom 306 were drivers. The replacement of men by women was thought out to minute details. Thus a comparatively picturesque costume was designed for women conductors in which the celebrated green-and-black tartan of the Black Watch was utilized. The social consequences of the increased employment of women were of almost infinite variety. It is only possible to indicate some of the most important. Partly through the combination of separation allowances and munition earnings, possibly to some extent owing to the restricted liquor conditions, children were both better fed and better clothed. While there was a considerable influx of female labour, much was drawn from the district. But in many cases it was not possible to provide housing accomodation where the labour was employed (as for instance in a new National Factory such as Georgetown) and the workers had to travel by train. Where there were children to be cared for, this added to domestic difficulties, and these became intensified when rationing came into force. To some extent this problem partly solved itself in so far as an urgent demand arose for boy and girl labour; which, though undesirable in several respects, had at least the effect of keeping young boys and girls out of mischief into which under war-time conditions they might otherwise have fallen. This effect was necessarily temporary; the absence of the fathers and the increased employment of the mothers in factories resulted in a serious relaxation of parental control, while the high scale of juvenile earnings fostered a sense of independence which has since manifested itself in several undesirable ways. The increase of crime in 1920-1 is to some extent attributable to this relaxation of parental control and constitutes an almost inevitable result of the exigencies of the pressure of war industry. The range of juvenile employment in Glasgow and the surrounding district was very remarkable. It was one of the social portents of war conditions to see the small scraps of humanity that were entrusted with comparatively responsible work, both in factories and in services outside them.

W. R. Scott and J. Cunnison, *The Industries of the Clyde Valley During the War* (1924).

1915-16: *Forward* against the War

Although the Clydeside group of MPs, led by the charismatic James Maxton, were to have their moment of glory (see 1922), it was shortlived. Of more long-lasting influence was the Socialist newspaper *Forward* (1906-1960). Described by Colm Brogan as 'not the last word in balanced judgment and mature wisdom', it nonetheless sold up to 40,000 copies a week during the 1920s when it was edited by Tom Johnston. During the War it was suppressed (allegedly for incitement to disaffection) for a few weeks after reporting Lloyd George's hostile reception by Clydeside munitions workers. These extracts give something of the paper's anti-war flavour.

William Stewart, journalist and biographer, was Scottish Secretary of the Independent Labour Party.

Mother's Sons William Stewart

'Killed in the war! My son, my bonnie laddie! Killed in the war!' She was a poor-looking, middle-aged woman, passing along one of our busy thoroughfares. She seemed dazed or demented, like a woman in drink, and if she was so I, for one, will not blame her. In her hand she held a crumpled scrap of paper, a War Office letter probably, and as she passed along the crowded pavement looking neither to the right nor to the left, but vacantly forward into vacancy, she kept mumbling to herself, 'Killed in the war! My son; he's killed in the war!' One of the great multitude of Rachels mourning for their children, and who will not be comforted. I wish I had not seen her, nor heard her. These women folk should be prevented from bringing their griefs out into the public streets. It is not seemly. It is treasonable almost.

A minute or two later and along the same street came the stirring music of the pipes and drums. The kilted band of the erstwhile peaceful tramwaymen, marching in martial array. Beating up for more mother's sons.

The Clyde Workers Committee strongly resisted labour dilution to increase production of armaments. As a result, David Kirkwood and other members were detained in Edinburgh for fourteen months in Calton jail.

Banished! Kirkwood and Other Clyde Shop Stewards Expelled from the West of Scotland—Taken From Their Beds

About three o'clock last Saturday morning the police, acting upon military instructions, visited the houses of six leading members of the Clyde Workers' Committee and arrested them. The names of the arrested men were:- David Kirkwood, A. McManus, J. M. Messer, S. Shields, J. Faulds, J. Haggerty.

We understand that Mr Faulds was afterwards released; but the remaining five were lodged in prison to await military instructions. These instructions, when they came, were to the effect that the arrested men were to be expelled from the West of Scotland and given a choice of residence at Edinburgh or Hawick, under police surveillance.

They chose Edinburgh and were transported there at Government expense, and as if to add the proper Siberian touch to the proceedings, the weather was bitterly cold and the snow was falling fast.

No charge! No bail! No trial! Men whose families have lived four generations in the same district, men whose personal character is unblemished, men who have the respect, the esteem and the confidence of their fellows, simply whipped off—as if we did not live in a free country!

Nothing since the war began has roused greater indignation in Glasgow, and on Glasgow Green on Sunday afternoon a collection of £12 was taken, and at the Metropole Theatre meeting at night a collection of £14 15/- was taken to raise a fund for the defence and maintenance of the dependants of these men while the necessity lasts.

A deputation has gone from the Clyde to interview members of Parliament, and before this appears in print, it is hoped that steps will be taken to bring pressure to bear on the Government to make at least a pretence of running this country on Constitutional lines.

The Press maintained a dignified silence on the whole business until Tuesday night.

Forward, 11 Sept. 1915 and 1 April 1916.

1917: Paddy's Market

For around 130 years Glasgow has had a place where second-hand clothing can be bought cheaply, now known as Paddy's Market and situated near the old Fishmarket. The present name derives from Irish involvement in this useful trade, and items that failed to find Glasgow buyers were shipped over to Ireland. This account of the Old Clothes Market, then situated near what is now the Salvation Army hostel in Greendyke Street on the edge of Glasgow Green, is by Peter Fyfe (1854–1940). As the city's Chief Inspector of the Sanitary Department, he fought hard for the removal of the notorious backlands in working-class tenement areas, especially in the East End. He trained as an engineer and joined the Corporation to oversee the building of the St Rollox Refuse Works before becoming Chief Inspector in 1885.

Of all the civic enterprises of the Glasgow Corporation, perhaps there is none which shows such a marked desire to meet the needs of the poorer part of her population than the Old Clothes Market in Greendyke Street, Calton. We are all more or less familiar with Dickens's description of Krook's rag and bottle warehouse in 'Bleak House.' We have several of these unsavoury 'stores' scattered over our teeming city, but here we have a roofed and galleried emporium covering over 2,300 square yards, leased out in stalls or stances to dealers in second-hand and worn clothing of every description. Eighty leaseholders, renting their stances at from 2s. 6d. to 12s. per week, exhibit their wares, rescued from the 'devil' or laniary machine of the flock factory. Where these are collected and whence brought to this place is one of the mysteries of the underworld of the city. Busy human 'ants' may be observed now and again scurrying out of closes with huge bundles on their backs, and, if followed, may be seen picking out the usable from the unusable, the woollen from the cotton, and generally classifying their wares for sale. Catching the 'crumbs which fall from the rich man's table,' they are the waste-preventers of the city, and thus not only serve themselves with a humble living, but help others, equally poor, to be served with still serviceable articles of clothing. Some of these 'collectors,' like those in higher walks of life, occasionally seek to make a 'corner' in such material. To secure a 'big stock' and wait for 'the rise' is the game of some rag-pickers as well as of market manipulators. One of them filled her two-apartment house four to five feet deep with rags and cast-off clothing, till Mr. Waddell and his fire brigade found her in flames one night, quenched her rags and her miserly ardour with cold water, and covered the back-court with the accumulation of years. When I saw her, she was wandering disconsolate and forlorn among the residue, and groaning inwardly over the evil fate which had overtaken her. Entry could never be obtained to her house, as knocking at her door gained no response. Even the house factor had never seen inside of it, as he informed me she was invariably prompt with the monthly rent, which she paid personally at his office two or three days before it was due. To such lengths do some go that their exercise of the virtue of thrift or the sin of cupidity brings them within the borderland of crime.

We are reminded as we pass along to Charlotte Street of the gigantic struggle for freedom and civilization which, in association with comrades drawn from every spot in our far-flung empire, our gallant lads of the 9th Highland Light Infantry are carrying on in the battlefields of Europe. It was on behalf of this now famous regiment that the first efforts of the Sanitary Department were made. So great and immediate were their demands for sleeping space that, before the echoes of Britain's war declaration had died on the air, we had cleared out the Old Clothes Market, and sprayed out every nook and corner of that great building with a powerful disinfectant, thus preparing a clean and healthful place of sleep for our local Highlanders. The deeds of Scottish valour have yet to be written fully in the annals of the most stupendous fight for righteousness the world has ever beheld, but we may be sure that those who learned the art of war in this building, and hardened their muscles by vigorous exercise on the Calton Green, will be found occupying a place of honour second to none, when the history appears.

One of the many barracks of a different kind of army meets our view as we wend our way up Charlotte Street. In the spiritual and moral struggles against the inroads of human weakness and vice, the Salvation Army have for many years taken a most active and honourable part. That they should have landed here in the old historic house of David Dale, one of Glasgow's great merchants and philanthropists, is of happy omen.

Peter Fyfe, 'A Tour in the Calton', from *Old Glasgow Club Transactions* (1916–17).

1922: Harry McShane and the Riot that wasn't

After the First World War Harry McShane was active in Glasgow and South-West Scotland organising the Unemployed Workers movement. Local committees contested the amount of unemployment relief money awarded by parish councils, and well-attended public meetings and demonstrations were held. In

October of this year ten Socialist (Independent Labour Party) MPs from the Clydeside area were elected on a wave of dissatisfaction with the post-war Coalition Government. Johnny (Milligan) was a founder member of the British Communist Party and a fellow-organiser with McShane of the Hunger Marches from Scotland in 1934.

One night I was booked to speak for the Anderston Unemployed Committee. When I got there I discovered that it wasn't an ordinary meeting but a boycott of a local picture-house; the manager had refused to let the committee have it free of charge for meetings. We held our meeting nearby in Hydepark Street, and from there I led the crowd up Argyle Street and round the back of the picture-house. There was a cordon of police round it, but I turned round and went backwards through it; the crowd followed and we smashed the police cordon (the people waiting to get in to the picture-house ran for it). Then we marched round the building and back to Hydepark Street to finish our meeting.

Everything was quite orderly, and Mrs Cameron got up to speak, when the police charged the meeting with drawn batons. We heard them shouting: 'Get Milligan and McShane!' I pulled Johnny against a wall, the police and the crowd ran right past us, and we went round the corner into a little pub and had a couple of half-pints.

The Gorbals crowd arrived after it was all over—I had sent for Allan Campbell, who was speaking at a Gorbals unemployed meeting. They had come ready for a battle and didn't want to go home. Finally we got them back to the south of the river. Afterwards, Johnny collapsed; we carried him to the local ILP rooms and from there he went to the Infirmary. At three o'clock in the morning we went to see him and found him demanding to be let out. He had picked up one of the old blue chemist flasks and was threatening them with it; I managed to get it off him when we were finally outside.

I was arrested the following day. They tried to keep me in prison without bail, but *Forward* took up the case and I was released on bail after eight days. The trial wasn't held until February 1923. The charge against another man and me was mobbing and rioting. In court a policeman, Sergeant Chisholm, claimed he was stabbed in the 'riot': as proof he produced a pair of trousers and a tunic and showed holes in them. But he hadn't been to a doctor, he hadn't been to hospital, and there wasn't a scratch on his body! He just couldn't explain how there was this big hole in his uniform but he hadn't felt anything until he saw it.

There was no proof at all of mobbing and rioting. In our evidence we pointed out that Mrs Cameron had been speaking on the platform at the time of the police charge, and obviously a peaceful meeting was in progress. Finally the sheriff asked to see Mrs Cameron; she came in—a big stout woman—and gave her evidence very clearly. The verdict was 'not proven' again, and I thought I had been fortunate.

Harry McShane, *No Mean Fighter* (1978).

1924: Housing on 'Red Clydeside'

There is a slightly hysterical note to this journalistic adventure by William Bolitho Ryall (1891–1930) into darkest Glasgow: 'I have come back from Glasgow with uncomfortable convictions', which were that unless something was done about the housing situation in the city there would be Red Revolution. Nevertheless, this is a graphic and gripping account of the backlands and ticketed houses of the slums of Glasgow. The population was now over one million and still growing. Much information was supplied by Patrick Dollan, who later became the city's Lord Provost (1938–41).

The Red Clyde, the smouldering danger of revolution in Glasgow, owing to the swift development of political affairs in Britain, has ceased to be a local anxiety, and become an interest and an alarm to the whole civilised world. The complacent days of trust in things as they are have gone since the world war and the Russian upheaval, and no State, however geographically remote, however seemingly secure in possession of an unshakeable constitutional system, can any longer be certain of immunity from violent, bloody change in its body politic. The world is no more than convalescent, politically, socially, economically. Revolution has grown virulently infectious, and any threatened outbreak in the very heart of the universal British Empire is as much a concern to citizens in other States as an outbreak of cholera in a central seaport; and a thorough understanding of its extent, history, causes, and likelihood of cure or progress is a necessity of high importance. England, the country immediately affected, knows this; has discarded the instinctive desire to blanket the Red Clyde, explain it away; and the bed-time stories of the censorship that served during the war, the comforting, airy explanations of the troubles that occurred there at that period, that the Glasgow workmen struck and rioted to the peril of their country's cause, were pacifist, anti-war, when even the Irish were volunteering, 'because of their high pay, and their spoilt selfishness,' are no longer heard with much patience.

There is something deeply wrong with the Clyde; the whole middle-class of England knows it, though hardly in detail; the motive is adequate, real, dangerous, that sends in repeated menace, to every successive Parliament, the same bitter group of extreme Left Members, irrespective of the changing political mood of the rest of the country, to kill with their fierce interruptions any restful optimism of the remainder of the House. The Red Clyde will remain the focus of English politics, until it has been cured, or definitely appeased; or until first Scotland, then industrial England, becomes fully infected by it, with momentous effects on Britain, the British Empire, and the rest of the world.

The mainspring of the trouble, the root grievance of the Clyde, is Housing. This is a simple term for a cancerous condition which, starting from the lack of space and light in the homes of the workers, festers and complicates itself, in numberless vicious circles, feeding on their Scottish vigour of character, their education, their stony wills; has developed into a political movement, quite apart from Marxianism, which threatens to harden into almost as rigorous an extremism as Leninism itself. The £60,000,000 necessary to make Glasgow entirely habitable by human beings would not end the matter, even if it could be provided. A swift grant of it might indeed, even now, whip their strongest argument out of the hand of the Red leaders and preachers of the movement; but even if possible in the present financial state of Britain, this grant would come too late to do more than delay the development, at present so leaping and rank, of this Clyde Socialism.

I have come back from Glasgow with uncomfortable convictions, after an unprejudiced examination of the frightful housing conditions of that city, which was helped by the most courteous facilities from the Corporation as well as full explanations and assistance from the chiefs of the Labour Party, the Clyde Reds themselves. I have seen the Housing scandal, the wide devastating crater of the movement; below it are volcanic forces with which the future must reckon. Shadowy yet in details, but already crystallised by two phrases, as fatal as the motto of the first French Republic, Liberty, Equality, Fraternity, a new Socialism, different from, but no less fierce and sincere then the Communism of Lenin, evolves on the Clyde. It is a Western Socialism, an unfatalistic Socialism, apt for Western peoples, which the stockyards of Chicago, the thrifty faubourgs of Paris, the conservative miners of the Ruhr, may one day hear of and understand. These Glasgow men have put at the base of their hard practical minds the two dogmas: 'Everyone must work,' 'A sufficiency for every worker.' They are not new sayings; I do not know that anywhere, at any time, they have been preached ruthlessly, unalterably by such men as these: these shipbuilders, artists in the geometry of iron, whose machines and whose ships carry the Empire of the seas; whom Kipling himself celebrated as the innermost strength of that Empire, men educated in the thorough, logical, desperately limited Scottish way, who have thus added to their Socialism, not the self-complacent innovations of Lenin, but the not less dangerous fire of fierce democratic convictions ingrained in their nation and passed down unaltered from generations of bleak Covenanting ancestors. They care as little for the consequences of their bald doctrine as did John Knox for his; and as little as he did will they temper it to the time or the obstacle. 'If our doctrine leads us to the instant expropriation of land for the worker, without compensation, or to the utter transformation of the economic system, we shall not shrink,' said Bailie Patrick Dollan, the Chairman of the Glasgow Labour Party, to me. 'We are going out for Social Justice.'

In mind of the first principle, 'Everyone must work,' Kirkwood, deportee and Member of Parliament, refused the invitation of the Prince of Wales on his visit to Glasgow last year. In virtue of the second, Glasgow must be rehoused. For the first meaning of this 'sufficiency' is a home fit to live in. At the present time, out of a population of 1,081,983, 600,000 people, that is, two-thirds, 'live in houses inferior to the minimum standard of the Board of Health' (Dollan), 40,591 families live in one-roomed homes, 112,424 families live in homes made up of a room and kitchen. There are more than 13,000 of these 'homes officially condemned by the Medical Officer of Health for the City,' but all but a round hundred of them are at present occupied. Only 32 one-roomed and 55 two-roomed apartments in Glasgow are empty as well as condemned. James Stewart, Clyde Member of Parliament, justifies himself from these figures in saying to me that his home city, Glasgow, is 'earth's nearest suburb to hell.'

William Bolitho, *The Cancer of Empire* (1924).

1929: H. V. Morton in Search of Glasgow

In his famous *In Search of . . .* series the *Birmingham Gazette* journalist Henry Vollam Morton (b. 1892) did not set out to be 'investigative' in the modern sense, but to observe and inform. His richly evocative portrait of Glasgow and the Clyde almost brings a lump to the throat, but although sympathetic, it stops short of the sentimental. He emphasises Glasgow's individuality—'it could not be any other city'—and obviously prefers it to Edinburgh, which he characterises as Scottish and Glasgow as cosmopolitan—the opposite of present-day opinion.

Glasgow on a November evening . . . .

The fog which has tickled the throat all day relents a little and hangs thinly over the city, so that each lamp casts an inverted V of light downward on the pavement. The streets are full of light and life. Pavements are packed to the edge with men and women released from a day's work, anxious to squeeze a little laughter from the dark as they move against a hazy blur of lit windows in which lie cakes, watches, rings, motor-cars, silk gowns, and everything that is supposed to be worth buying.

The sound of Glasgow is a human chatter punctuated by tram-cars—coloured in broad bands like Neapolitan ices—grating round a bend to Renfield Street. There is a sharp clamour of bells, the asthmatic cough of an express engine clearing its throat on the road to London, and most characteristic of all, the sudden yelp of a tug in a Clyde fog—the yelp of a terrier whose tail has been stepped on—as she noses her way down the narrow stream.

And the Glasgow crowds in perpetual and puzzling flux go, some home to flats in Pollokshaws and—wonderful name!—Crossmyloof, where the Queen of Scots once sat a palfrey; some to take the astonishing meal of high tea which Glasgow's cafés and restaurants have elevated to the apex of the world's pyramid of indigestibility (for I still cannot believe that tea agrees with fillet steak); some to dance for 3s. in surroundings for which we pay 30s. in London; some to the theatre; but most to drift up and down the golden avenues until the last Neapolitan ice takes them home to Camlachie or Maryhill.

I go on through the crowds. George Square—Glasgow's Trafalgar Square—which looks like the centre of the city but is not, lies in graduated greyness, rather empty, a little removed from the main surge of life, the splendid

Municipal Buildings wrapped in that same aloofness from the trivialities of a night which comes upon Westminster when Piccadilly is gay.

This and Trafalgar Square in London are the two most impressive and well-balanced squares in Great Britain. Walter Scott is its Nelson skied on a great pillar with his plaid over the wrong shoulder and a lightning conductor sticking like a dart from the back of his neck. Here, among stone horsemen, are some of Glasgow's few trees.

I am amazed by the apparent size of Glasgow. Her million and a quarter people are squeezed into a lesser space than that occupied by several other great cities, and this compression gives a feeling of immensity. You do not suddenly leave the main streets to plunge into dark and trackless valleys of the dead as you do in Birmingham, Manchester, and Liverpool. Here are miles of main streets, all wide, all marked by a certain grim and solid quality—shops as fine as any in Bond Street; clubs as reserved and Georgian as any in Pall Mall—and in a few yards you leave a street in which you could spend £1,000 on something for a woman's throat, to enter a street, equally broad and almost as well lit, in which perhaps the most expensive thing is a cut from the sheep whose corpse hangs head down, its horns in blood and sawdust . . .

This meeting of extremes is characteristic of Glasgow. The splendour of riches and the abjectness of poverty, seen so close together, appear sharper than in most great cities. East and west ends run into one another in the most grotesque way. In London, for instance, crowds are local. You know exactly the kind of people you will see in Piccadilly or Oxford Street. You know that the Aldgate Pump to Strand crowd at night will never go the extra yard to Cockspur Street; just as the Piccadilly-Leicester Square crowd will never cross the invisible frontier of Charing Cross. In Glasgow there are no frontiers.

This gives a rich and exciting variety to the crowds. My eyes are held by the passing faces. Sooner or later in the Bond Streets of this city, with their business heads under the biggest assembly of bowler hats in Great Britain and their crowds of perfectly lovely, fresh young girls, I shall see the stooped shoulders of some ancient wreck, the insolent swing of a youth with a cap over his eyes, the slow walk of a hatless woman from a neighbouring tenement bearing, much as the kangaroo bears its young, a tiny face in the fold of a thick tartan shawl.

This close-togetherness of Glasgow is one of its most important features. It means that a million and a quarter people live nearer the heart of their city than in any other social phenomenon of this size. This, I believe, explains Glasgow's clean-cut individuality. There is nothing half-hearted about Glasgow. It could not be any other city.

. . .

But Glasgow is—Glasgow. She is self-centred. She is the greatest, closely-knit community in Great Britain. She is the least suburban of all great cities. She has become the most populous city outside London without dissipating her individuality in distant suburbs; and in no other city of this magnitude do more people know each other, at least by sight. To know a man by sight in Glasgow is to ask him to have a coffee at eleven a.m. If the Clyde ever runs dry, sufficient coffee is consumed in Glasgow every morning to float the biggest Cunarder yet built.

There is a Transatlantic alertness about Glasgow which no city in England possesses. Glasgow can be almost oppressively friendly. In one thing is she supreme among the cities in Great Britain—accessibility. Her civic leaders and her business men are always ready to welcome the stranger. The important doors of Glasgow fly open to him. (I suppose if he is wasting time he flies out as swiftly as he entered!) I have found more senseless ritual, more pompous obstructionists in livery barring the way to some negligible grocer with a chain round his neck in a tin-pot English town than I have found in those marble halls where the Lord Provost of Glasgow directs the destinies of the 'second city'.

Glasgow plays the part of Chicago to Edinburgh's Boston. Glasgow is a city of the glad hand and the smack on the back; Edinburgh is a city of silence until birth or brains open the social circle. In Glasgow a man is innocent until he is found guilty; in Edinburgh a man is guilty until he is found innocent. Glasgow is willing to believe the best of an unknown quantity; Edinburgh, like all aristocracies, the worst!

But the great difference between Scotland's two great cities is not a cultural versus a financial tradition. It is something deeper. Both these are poses. Edinburgh pretends to be more precious than she is; Glasgow pretends to be more material than she is. Hence the slight self-consciousness of the one and the slight roughness of the other. The real difference between these two cities is that Edinburgh is Scottish and Glasgow is cosmopolitan. That is why they will always secretly admire each other; also why Edinburgh is definitely the capital.

Glasgow is a mighty and an inspiring human story. She is Scotland's anchor to reality. Lacking her, Scotland would be a backward country lost in poetic memories and at enmity with an age in which she was playing no part. Glasgow, facing west to the new trade-ways of the world, rose after the Union, calling to Highlands and Lowlands to forget old scores and to take a hand in the building of that new world which was to begin on a Sabbath afternoon in the spring of 1765 when James Watt walked over Glasgow Green occupied with sinful week-day thoughts. The new age began sinfully on that Sabbath, for James Watt had solved the problem of the separate condenser; and as he walked over Glasgow Green a changed world lay pregnant in his brain: a world of steel and iron, tall chimneys and speed.

. . .

If you have never seen the launching of a ship there is still a thrill in life for you . . . .

You go through the shipyard gates. Every one is smiling. They will not admit that they are excited. They will, in fact, tell you that it is all in the day's work, that they are so used to it that it is just a matter of routine, but—don't believe them! No man with a heart in his body could be unmoved by the birth of a ship; and when you have been hammering at her for eight months; when you have been sitting up in a bos'n's cradle playing hell with a pneumatic riveter; when you have been standing in the remote intellect of an electric crane swinging the proud body, plate by plate, into position—not excited? I refuse to believe it.

She lies, marvellously naked, high and dry on the slipway. She has no funnels, no masts, and no engines. Her bridge is there, unpainted and innocent of glass. High on her decks men run, shouting and peering over the edge of the steel cliff to the distant shipyard. Everything is ready, waiting for the Clyde.

Her stern, with its innocent propellers, is lifted high as a house above the water; five minutes' walk back along her hull, in the shadow of her forecastle head, is a little railed-in platform covered in scarlet cloth.

It is charming to see men who have riveted her flanks performing a last service by delicately knocking tacks into half a yard of red bunting!

The tide oozes on. Men look at their watches. Pretty girls arrive in motor-cars and stand in the shadow of workshops, gazing up at the ship, reading her name—*Empress of the East*, shall we say?—printed in big bronze letters high on the sharp prow. Groups of men in dungarees, who for eight months have worked on the ship, gather and gaze up too, laugh and joke and smoke cigarettes and admire the beauty chorus.

In the shadow of the hull men, creeping about in the mud like rats, loosen great blocks of timber until at the moment when the tide is high a few swift hammer blows along the length of her keel will send her downward to the water.

Every minute is now important. There is a laugh from the workmen as a fellow, high on the forecastle head, flings down a rope which dangles above the scarlet platform. But it ceases to be a common rope as it nears the platform: its last few yards are coloured red, white, and blue. An official of the shipyard, very important, mounts the steps of the platform bearing a bottle of champagne disguised in a tight overcoat of red, white, and blue ribbons. This he attaches to the hanging rope, and he stands there steadying the dangling bottle.

The time has come! The guests move out from the worksheds and mount the scarlet platform. The woman who is to launch the ship stands nervously fingering the hanging bottle.

'What do I do?' she whispers to the helpful official.

'Well, ye see, tak' the bottle like this and fling it har-r-rd as if ye'd break the ship and—try and hit this bolt-head!'

He walks forward and puts his finger on the steel plates.

The Clyde is high . . . .

A woman's hand in a brown suéde glove, trembling a little, holds the champagne bottle. The shipyard becomes silent! Work stops! Cranes become still! You can hear the hammering of other yards across the Clyde. The tug that is waiting out on the flood tide for the new ship sounds her siren three times in salute: 'Come along, come along, come along!' A piercing whistle rings out from somewhere, there is a great shout, the sound of hammers on wood beneath the ship, a tremendous air of frantic but invisible effort, and the vast monster seems suddenly to fill with life! She does not move; but you know that in one second she *will* move! In the tremendous suspension of that second the brown suéde glove tightens on the champagne bottle and a woman's voice says:

'Good luck to the *Empress of the East* !'

Crash! The champagne bottle hits the steel plates fair and square with a smothered tinkle of splintered glass, and great bursts of white foam fly left and right to fall like snow and to fizz a second and vanish on the scarlet platform; and now—off she goes! She moves! Hurrah! Good luck to her!

We see a wonderful thing! We see the great ship sliding backwards to the water! She makes no noise. The enormous thing just fades smoothly Clyde-wards, leaving behind her two broad wooden tracks of yellow grease. Silent as a phantom she is! Her stern takes the water, dips, dips, deep down. (Will she ever rise?) You watch her breathless as she dives into the Clyde to the distant sound of spray: and then her movement slows up as she meets the resistance of the water. She is almost afloat! She lies almost at the end of the two parallel grease tracks. She floats! She bounces gracefully and goes on bouncing, very high and light in the water, bouncing her great steel body as if enjoying the first taste of her buoyancy.

'Hurrah! Good luck to the *Empress of the East* !'

We lift our hats. Among a group of workmen an old man lifts his cap for a second as his eyes follow her out to the Clyde—lifts his greasy cap to eight months' wages:

'Good-bye and—good luck!'

But it is not yet over. As she floats we hear for the first time an unforgettable sound: it is the crack and creak of breaking wood, the falling asunder of the great timbers beneath her as she crushes them and drags them with her until the river all round her is alive with heavy spars, which leap up in the water beneath her hull.

Then suddenly gigantic iron chains, whose links are the thickness of a man's arm, begin to move. Until now they lay on either side of the slipway in twelve-foot heaps. They move slowly at first, but gather amazing speed. The mighty things roll over and over in clouds of dust and rust, and go bounding down to the riverside as if to pull the ship back to her birthplace, thundering after her, leaping through the mud until they take the strain, tighten out and hold her steady in the narrow stream . . . .

I stand there with the feeling that I have seen the coming to life of a giant, the breaking-away of all the shackles that held it from its element, and the glad acceptance of its fate.

I look down through the stark skeleton of poles which cradled her from the beginning, and I see her framed in the vista, still bouncing a little as if amused by the water—the symbol of Glasgow and the Clyde!

She will go to many places in her busy life, carrying the name of Glasgow across the oceans of the world. Men may love her as men love ships. On her bridge, so bare and inexperienced now, men will stand guiding her through storms to various harbours. She will become wise with the experience of the seas.

But no shareholder will ever share her intimacy as we who saw her so marvellously naked and so young slip smoothly from the hands that made her into the dark welcome of the Clyde.

H. V. Morton, *In Search of Scotland* (1929).

1930: Going to the Pictures—from Paisley to Partick

The author and editor, Iain Hamilton (1920–1986), was a reporter on the *Daily Record* in Glasgow in the mid-1940s. In 1947 he wrote the powerful ballad of a gang fight on Glasgow Green, 'News of the World', which presents a more violent aspect of Glasgow life in the 1930s than this nostalgic childhood reminiscence.

Apart from occasional week-end trips with my mother, longer visits to one or other of my relatives' farms, and the annual summer holiday, my favourite excursion was one which I enjoyed almost every Saturday afternoon for a year or two, with my grandparents. Although there were three or four picture-houses in Paisley which gave afternoon performances, they remained faithful, for some reason, to one in Partick—a district of Glasgow on the north bank of the Clyde in which they had lived before coming to Renfrew. Perhaps they simply enjoyed returning to a neighbourhood for which they still had great affection; perhaps they thought it more of a treat for me than simply going to Paisley, a straightforward journey to a town which, whatever its worthiness, lacked the glamour of Glasgow.

For Glasgow had that then for me, and has it still, in great measure. Golden Glasgow: misty, clanging, flaring, tumultuous city, its deep streets overhung by red and grey cliffs pierced by thousands of gas-lit windows, strings of coolies shuffling through the litter on the pavements, drunks in the gutters, luxury in the shop-windows, hills at the end of every street, the smell of the sea coming up from the tideway between ranks of cranes and rotting tenements and bringing a breath of life to the dullest air in the meanest alley. It would have been impossible for me then to imagine a city more splendid than Glasgow, and I still count it today the most romantic city I have seen.

There were two ways in which we could go to the picture-house in Partick and it was an agonising business to choose which it was to be. We could go by tramcar to the Ferry, cross the Clyde in the chain-bound tub whose vertical engine could be studied during the voyage, and on the northern bank take another tramcar straight to Partick. Or we could get off at Renfrew Cross and change into a tram that went eastward through the flat fields to Govan Cross where we would go down into the cable-drawn subway train and be carried under the Clyde to Partick. Both were journeys of much complexity and infinite variety, and no repetition could stale my intense enjoyment. Of the pictures themselves nothing much remains, but I can remember the high teas we used to have afterwards—the fish and pies and mounds of chips and teacups steaming.

Iain Hamilton, *Scotland the Brave* (1957).

1932: Compton Mackenzie's Rectorial Address

The 1931 Glasgow University rectorial campaign was remarkable for the election of a staunch Scottish nationalist, beating such candidates as Tom Johnston and Professor Gilbert Murray (849 votes to 110 and 581 respectively). In his inaugural speech Sir Compton Mackenzie (1883-1972) extolled the rights of small nations and described the rebirth of Scottish nationalism as 'a spiritual discontent rather than a political grievance'. He was, however, a strong supporter of the newly-formed Scottish National Party which sought political representation after the rejection of Home Rule by Westminster parties. During the 1930s the SNP enjoyed considerable popular support in the West of Scotland and gained its first seat at Motherwell in 1945. Compton Mackenzie only returned to Scotland at the end of his life. Clearly he found the Glasgow skyline inspiring.

When the Roman Empire broke up and Europe was ravaged by horde upon horde of barbarians from the East, almost the only light that shone forth into the bloodstained darkness shone from Erin and from the holy Western Isles of Alba. It may be that once again beside the Atlantic the souls of men will save themselves, and in saving themselves save the soul of man. It may be that this task is the supreme destiny of the Celtic race. I cannot but think that the rise of nationalism primarily in Glasgow is of tremendous significance to the potential force and endurance of the movement, for, though we must acclaim Edinburgh as the capital, the stern and masculine parent, Glasgow is the metropolis—the mother city. No other city is so representative of the whole country, and what is true of Glasgow is true of Glasgow University. Every criticism which is levelled against it may be levelled against Scotland itself. The virtues, faults, hopes, fears, ambitions, and dreams of the country as a whole are more completely expressed in this University than anywhere. Its very position in the midst of a crashing industrial turmoil and yet always within sound of the two voices of liberty, the voice of the sea and the voice of the hills, is a prefigurative symbol of our country's future.

A few weeks ago upon the Campsie Fells I gazed down at Glasgow. From a mass of dark cloud the sun, himself obscured from where I stood, sloped his golden ladders into that rain-washed city, which lay with all her spires and chimneys, with all her towers and tenements and sparkling roofs, like a vision of heavenly habitations. I have looked down over Athens. I have looked down over Rome. With beauty unparagoned the glory and the grandeur of the past have been spread before my eyes; but in that sight of Glasgow something was added which neither Rome nor Athens could give—the glory and the grandeur of the future, and the beating heart of a nation.

Address by Compton Mackenzie, on the occasion of his installation as Rector, January 1932.

1934: Lewis Grassic Gibbon on the Gorbals

Leslie Mitchell (1901–1935) was in Glasgow for a short time, working as an agricultural journalist. His essay, written under the pseudonym Lewis Grassic Gibbon, shows the kaleidoscopic impression the city made on him and how it affected his political beliefs: 'the vomit of a cataleptic commercialism' was one descriptive phrase he used. In 1934 Glasgow's population was 1,115,590, nearly at its peak. The Gorbals was already established as a new home for Eastern European refugees—a role it continued to play during World War II.

It is coming on dark, as they say in the Scotland that is not Glasgow. And out of the Gorbals arises again that foul breath as of a dying beast.

You turn from Glasgow Green with a determination to inspect this Gorbals on your own. It is incredibly un-Scottish. It is lovably and abominably and delightfully and hideously un-Scottish. It is not even a Scottish slum. Stout men in beards and ringlets and unseemly attire lounge and strut with pointed shoes: Ruth and Naomi go by with downcast Eastern faces, the Lascar rubs shoulder with the Syrian, Harry Lauder is a Baal unkeened to the midnight stars. In the air the stench is of a different quality to Govan's or Camlachie's,— a better quality. It is haunted by an ancient ghost of goodness and grossness, sun-warmed and ripened under alien suns. It is the most saving slum in Glasgow, and the most abandoned. Emerging from it, the investigator suddenly realizes why he sought it in such haste from Glasgow Green: it was in order that he might assure himself there were really and actually other races on the earth apart from the Scots!

'Glasgow', from *Scottish Scene*, by L. Grassic Gibbon and Hugh Macdiarmid (1934).

1934: George Blake on Glasgow's energy

Glasgow's claims to superiority over Edinburgh are usually argued by those who are unquestionably sons and daughters of the city. George Blake (1893–1961) was born in Greenock, but he is qualified to speak for Glasgow both for his editorship of the *Evening Citizen* during the 1930s and for the best-selling novels he wrote about the city. This cinematic look at the streets of Glasgow contains many sharp observations and an astute sense of the paradoxes that Depression-hit Glasgow could offer.

Glasgow is big—really much too big for Scotland. It sprawls. It has grown almost anyhow, without plan and without regard for tradition. That Glasgow is absurdly maligned would be a thesis very easy to defend. It is not by any means all degradation. It has its own vistas of wild beauty, its own grim dignity, and many unsuspected sweetnesses. Its ill-luck is to fail in any comparison of its amenities with those of the lovely city only forty miles away. Neither geology nor history has assisted it in this matter of looks. What the geologists call its clay drumlins give its West End an odd character of variety and even charm, and sentiment can see it as a City upon Seven Hills, with the storied Clyde cutting a silver filagree through the smoky maze of it. But these are mere possibilities forsworn. What it might have been is hopelessly overbalanced by what it is— square mile upon square mile of meanness and untidiness, of greyness and unnecessary squalor, of elements strangely diversified and quite unrelated. It is a city so chaotic that one despairs of discovering a generalisation to come within measurable distance of describing its quality. If it has the faults inherent in a fairly recent industrial growth, it has the interest of diversity. He would be a poor observer who did not see in Glasgow one of the most diverting communities in Christendom. But neither the most devoted loyalty nor the most exacting passion for accuracy could reasonably quarrel with the average stranger's impression of it as a grey and formidable city in its outward aspects.

This impression is curiously fortified by the dress and deportment of the people. The proportion of artisans and labourers to the total population being so high, their tweed caps and drab clothes sound a peculiarly low note in a subdued colour scheme. The business man of this strange city has an incorruptible devotion to the bleak rigidity of the bowler hat. Even in the height of summer the girls on whom one would reasonably depend for a touch of gaiety must wear over their most alluring dresses an overcoat of some forbidding sort. Such is one of the odd results of living where the climate is unreliable, if not so distressing as legend makes it out to be. And a more sombre effect of climatic instability is to be seen, as reinforced by overcrowding, in the low average standard of height among the people, in too many bow-legs and other symptoms of vitamin-deficiency.

Yet it may confidently be maintained that here is the liveliest community in Scotland. This fantastic mixture of racial strains, this collection of survivors from one of the most exacting of social processes, is a dynamo of confident, ruthless, literal energy. The Glasgow man is downright, unpolished, direct, and immediate. He may seem to compare in this respect with the Aberdonian, but in him there is none of that queer Teutonic reserve, which is so apt to affect human intercourse with the native of Buchan. That he is a mighty man with his hands, the world knows and acknowledges; that he is nearer the poet than his brothers in the other cities is less obvious but equally true. He has the 'furious' quality of the Scot in its most extreme form. He can be terribly dangerous in revolt and as terribly strong in defence of his own conception of order. He hates pretence, ceremonial, form—and is at the same time capable of the most abysmal sentimentality. He is grave—and one of the world's most devastating sardonic humorists.

This is to look at Glasgow largely in terms of the working man; and that is justified by his predominance in the social scheme of the untidy city of the West. Glasgow's large and respectable bourgeoisie we shall encounter later on, just as we shall see how the generality of Glasgow people manifest themselves in various social directions. It is enough just now to note the large, coarse untidiness of this city by the Clyde, and to observe why there should exist between it and Edinburgh a notorious jealousy. It is common form to regard that jealousy as a joke, but it can be a deadly reality. The graceful capital of tradition must resent this upstart phenomenon of the West, so much richer, so much more practically powerful than itself, so inveterately provincial; and Glasgow in its turn must feel aggrieved that the seats of all formal authority are in the relatively small city of the East that can give itself so many airs and is yet, in the Western view, so unfaithful to the Scottish realities.

The jealousy is as significant as it is real. It symbolises the clash of Teuton and Gael, of the Scotland of tradition and the Scotland of hard and ugly fact. And it is just typical of Scottish life that one of its most dramatic features should be a schism. The race seems to thrive on differences, on contending, in the Stevensonian phrase, 'for the shade of a word.' Many a good Scots cause has been lost through the absurdities of this inter-city rivalry. It may, in a detached view, have been the accomplished fate of Scotland to lose its soul in niggling quarrels.

George Blake, *The Heart of Scotland* (1934).

1935: Edwin Muir on the Living Dead

Edwin Muir (1887-1959) was brought to Glasgow from Orkney at the age of 14, from a farming community to a city of nearly a million people in its Edwardian industrial heyday. Muir never lost a feeling of culture shock from his Glasgow experiences. Yet he was converted to Socialism there and later wrote a novel with a Glasgow background, *Poor Tom*. Although Muir left the city in 1919, he returned fifteen years later to write a long chapter of his *Scottish Journey* which is principally concerned with the slums and unemployment. The contrast with the bustling city he remembered was indeed striking.

There was a time when if a man looked round him he could get work of some kind; but now for tens of thousands there is nothing but 15/3, 23/3, 27/3, 29/3, or whatever the figure may be, and nothing they can do can alter these cast-iron hieroglyphics, which are a sort of black charm keeping them in a state of semi-animation and making them a race of 'the dead on leave,' 'die Toten auf

Urlaub,' to use Rosa Luxemburg's phrase. Most of these unemployed men in Glasgow are as honest and decent, and when they have money of their own, as generous as one has any right to expect them to be. They are excellent workmen whom society has deprived of work, good fathers whom society will not allow to provide for their families, cheerful companions who live in a world where they cannot afford even the little harmless amenities which make companionship twice warmer. Their life now is a long and dreary Sunday; their hands have grown useless; their skill has dropped from them; their days have turned into an unending, inconclusive dream. The effect of one, or two, or five, or ten years of waiting for work can be seen in their attitudes as they stand at the street corners; the very air seems empty round them, as if it had been drained of some essential property; they scarcely talk, and what they say seems hardly to break the silence: the strongest impression I received of Glasgow was one of silence. In the centre of the city people are still busy, or seem to be so; but when one goes down the Clyde, to what used to be the busy shipbuilding quarter, there is hardly anything but this silence, which one would take to be the silence of a dead town if it were not for the numberless empty-looking groups of unemployed men standing about the pavements. I noticed that even the children seemed to make less noise than they used to do, as if silence had seized upon them too: or it may have been simply that they were insufficiently fed.

It was a very hot bright day when I went down to see the shipyards that once in my life I had passed every morning. The weather had been good for several weeks, and all the men I saw were tanned and brown as if they had just come back from their summer holidays. They were standing in the usual groups, or walking by twos and threes, slowly, for one felt as one looked at them that the world had not a single message to send them on, and that for them to hasten their steps would have meant a sort of madness. Perhaps at some time the mirage of work glimmered at the extreme horizon of their minds; but one could see by looking at them that they were no longer deceived by such false pictures.

I was on my way to a shipbuilding office where I had once worked for several years. During my time there had been twelve clerks in it; they had now shrunk to six, and the six were on half-time and half-pay. Like the unemployed they were all sunburnt, since they spent half of their days in enforced leisure. The office had always been a pleasant one to work in; for the cashier, an old gentleman now dead, had for fifty years or so resisted the importunities of travellers for newfangled devices such as adding-machines and filing systems, and had stuck to the methods he had found in operation when he entered the office as a junior clerk. When that could have been I have no idea, probably about 1860. We were all proud of him, and grateful for the way in which he left us to ourselves: I have never been in a little community where such an idyllic and quietistic atmosphere reigned. Something of it still remained when I paid my visit. So my old friends, instead of being embittered by the bad turn of shipbuilding, were philosophic and resigned. Nevertheless, it was sad to revisit the place and remember the time when it had been filled with hope: a hope which in it, as in a hundred other workshops and offices in the Clyde, is now hardly more than a memory. Thousands of young men started out a little over twenty years ago with the ambition of making a modest position in the world, of marrying a wife and founding a family. And thousands of them have seen that hope vanish, probably never to return for the rest of their lives. This is surely one of the most astonishing signs of our time: the disappearance in whole areas of society of a hope so general at one time that not to have it would have seemed unnatural. As for the generation of unemployed who have arisen since the war, many of them are not even acquainted with this hope.

Edwin Muir, *Scottish Journey* (1935).

1935: Tommy Lorne

Tommy Lorne (1890–1935) is generally reckoned to have been one of the greatest Glasgow comics; between the wars he was, for Albert Mackie, 'the funniest man on the stage'. He was actually born in Kirkintilloch but grew up in Glasgow. Like many Scots comedians he was most appreciated in his native land, with his greatest local success in pantomime at the Royal Princess's Theatre in the Gorbals (now the Citizens'). He died suddenly in 1935 of double pneumonia, at the height of his career—the previous year he had had his own summer show at Dunoon and pantos in Inverness, Edinburgh and Glasgow. G. S. Fraser, discussing the people of Glasgow in 1958 (*Vision of Scotland*), wrote: 'They are affable and talkative, with an accent which, while nobody could say it has poetic beauty, lends itself very aptly to the work of the great Glasgow comedians. In such a comedian as Tommy Lorne Glasgow probably expressed a great deal of itself'. He further commented on Colm Brogan's piece on Lorne: 'Tommy's actual words, when he folded his hands on his stomach, were—being Irish and devout, Mr Brogan does not give them—"In the name?"'

  The pastoral comics are all more or less divorced from reality. The other kind, the industrial comic, is nearer the bone. The greatest of these was the still lamented Tommy Lorne. Tommy's real name was Hugh Corcoran. He was bred in one of the most wretched slums in Europe and he knew Glasgow under the skin. The Clyde for him and his like was the stretch of water which separates the mortuary from the Gorbals. His best days as an artist were spent in the Gorbals. It is not a pretty neighbourhood, nor is it oppressively Scotch. Kosher meat is much in demand, and the pubs have names like Rooney. The local colour is Red.

  The Princess pantomime begins in December and it stops in early summer. It doesn't go in much for Tiller Girls or transformation scenes, but it does try to be funny. Tommy gave impersonations there that will still be talked of by senile persons in 1990. He was a tram conductor on an all-night car and a continuous dancer with enormous bandages on his feet. He was a very individual Dame. Tommy was tall and angular, and when he was dressed as a woman he was mostly bones and two mournful and apprehensive eyes. His Dame was a weel-daeing' working-class woman, with a lot of jerky dignity, determined not to be put on, but finding the world too much for her. She had beautiful squeals of indignation and moments of outraged stillness when she mutely asked Heaven if this or that outrage could be, and only the mobile lips and trembling fingers witnessed to the turmoil within.

Tommy's hands were wonderful. In moments of conscious innocence and triumph, they were folded (in white gloves) on his stomach, where they lay like doves asleep. When suspicion of some indignity entered the Dame's mind they stirred, and when shocks of nervous excitement went through her body, every finger had a separate and hysterical life.

Popularity was Tommy's downfall. He went to the Royal in Glasgow and then to Edinburgh, in among the Tiller Girls and the Grand Finales. But he had marvellous moments up to the end. In his last Glasgow pantomime he sat, as Dame, on a log with a love-lorn maiden. The poor Dame described her romance with a gentleman friend many years ago. With coy giggles and nudges she told how they would go to a field and push over a cow to get a warm place. But Fate took the gentleman friend away. As the Dame began to hint at the sad end, her mouth trembled and her fingers shuddered with woe. At last, her face simply melted. It was very delicately done.

There was nobody quite like Tommy. Glasgow could bear the loss of all her M.P.'s and town councillors with Roman fortitude, but the sudden death of Tommy Lorne was a cause of real public grief. It was sad to think that we would never again hear about the woman who kept the wee pie shop in Lumphinans, or watch the tall figure of the Dame standing awkwardly and uncertainly rigid, with occasional subsidences, like a camp chair. Life was the poorer for everybody.

Colm Brogan, 'The Glasgow Comedians', in *Scotland—1938* (1938).

1937: Glasgow as seen by an Englishwoman

Cicely Hamilton (1872-1952) first visited Glasgow as an actress before the Great War; she returned as a kind of female H.V. Morton, adding Scotland to the series of countries (Germany, France, Russia and Italy among others) 'as seen by an Englishwoman'. This account was written 'for the uninformed English reader' and was concerned with aspects of Scotland that did not normally attract the attention of a visitor. Her viewpoint could be described as Conservative feminist. While she thought that, obviously, slum clearance was a good thing, she is not so happy about the aspects of social control by the Corporation that she sees involved—in fact, among the peripheral housing schemes there came to be 'desirable' ones, like Knightswood, and 'undesirable' ones, like Blackhill. The arguments rehearsed here—over unemployment, housing schemes, high-rise blocks, domestic drudgery—are still to be heard fifty years later.

By courtesy of officials of the Public Health Department I was guided to one or two of Glasgow's notoriously insanitary streets and introduced into several of their typical dwellings. All the tenants, when questioned, confessed cheerfully to bugs and, judging by the state of some of the woodwork, rats were no strangers to their domiciles. Needless to say, these prize specimens of Glasgow slumdom had been condemned by the sanitary authority; their occupants, so soon as a clearance scheme was ready to receive them, would move to decent surroundings in the suburbs, and the evil-smelling tenements, left to their vermin, would fall to the pick of the housebreaker. In one domicile we visited, the pick of the housebreaker was already at work farther down the block that contained it; and the occupying family, packed and ready to depart, were only awaiting the arrival of the barrow which would convey their household goods to a new and more sanitary dwelling. Some of their household goods—their bedding—had already been removed by a sanitary inspector; it would be restored, at the new and clean abode, after due disinfection against vermin. Bedding, however, is not the only means of transport for vermin; they can be conveyed from house to house in other articles of furniture as well as in wearing apparel; hence it is the business of local health visitors to keep an eye on migrating families and urge them to special efforts in the way of watchfulness and cleanliness. The office of health visitor in slum and slum-clearance districts must be anything but a sinecure; it stands to reason that men and women who have dwelt for years, perhaps all their lives in the squalid surroundings of a Glasgow rookery are likely to need persevering instruction in the arts of domestic cleanliness; and it says much for the health visitor, as well as for the average ex-slum family, that the authors of a report, issued on completion of Glasgow's forty thousandth new house, are able to state that 'the response to the improved environment and better accommodation has been phenomenal, fully ninety per cent of the rehoused tenants in slum areas showing in every way a decided improvement.' The ten per cent residuum, one concludes, must be borne with and, so far as possible, prevented from becoming a nuisance to their cleaner-living neighbours.

One little woman whom we called on in her slum would, I suspect, need a good deal of attention from the health visitor before she discarded the sluttish habits acquired in her years of squalor. She was a friendly little soul, with a sloping forehead and unwashed face, who, like most of her fellow-slum-dwellers, seemed quite pleased to be called on; the mother of three grubby infants under school-age—one of them in arms, one old enough to stand and stare at us, one crawling on the unmade family bed where, in the unrestrained manner of infancy, it had recently obeyed a call of nature. There were two more absent at school, the mother told us; these latter presumably, being better clad and washed than their younger brethren—the education authority would see to that, providing at least the necessary footwear. A query with regard to the husband and father brought the all too frequent reply that he was out of work; the income that he and his family obtained from the public purse being thirty-nine shillings a week. Whereby, as in other like-situated households, one glimpsed a problem affecting more than Glasgow and Glasgow's slums; the problem of the man of no particular skill who may find himself, when at length he gets a job, little, if at all, better off as to money than when he draws his dole in idleness.

. . .

And, in some instances—though not in all—preference for the unearned income is not likely to be lessened when the unemployed man, with his family and furniture, are removed from a vermin-ridden, one-room tenement in Charlotte Street to an exemplary and far more extensive dwelling on one of the new estates that Glasgow has erected. To a flat, as we should call it in England—a house, as they call it up there—complete with living-room, bedrooms, scullery, bathroom, and entrance-hall; and for which the rehoused tenant, in a good many cases, will pay a lower rent than he paid for his evil-smelling slum. The tenants of a two-roomed abomination in one of the condemned blocks told us that their rent was ten shillings a week; for less than that sum more fortunate families are established in well-built flats of the type above described . . . . Hardly necessary to state that these latter rents are not economic; the families who pay them are receiving a subsidy from the ratepayer.

. . .

According to the *Glasgow Herald* of May 30, 1936: 'In the last ten years the Scottish local authorities have built over 133,000 houses, the equivalent of a town half the size of Glasgow, and it is expected that by the time they have completed their housing programmes, they will have rehoused about a third of the total population of Scotland!' To these housing activities of the country Glasgow has contributed her full share; in the year 1919 it was estimated that the needs of the city amounted to 50,000 new dwellings, and sixteen years later, in September 1935, the Housing Department of the Glasgow Corporation celebrated the opening of its forty-thousandth house—while subsidies have been granted for over 10,000 additional dwellings, erected by means of private enterprise. If Clydeside slums are a byword and reproach, the Clydeside of to-day, by its building schemes, is striving to make atonement for its past disgrace of neglect. To revisit Glasgow after several years' absence (as I did recently) is to realize how swiftly and widely the city has expanded her borders. Growth of population, as well as slum clearance, has necessitated housing schemes on a generous scale; hence the planned and ordered suburbs that have thrust, and thrust deeply, into yesterday's woodland and field. I have heard this encroachment on the open regretted, and not only for aesthetic reasons; I was told of material causes for regret—that much of the land that has been eaten up by the insatiable city was good farming land, a source of supply to the country. (The same thing, of course, is happening on the outskirts of many other cities.) It was

H

a pity therefore (my informants urged) that slum-clearance schemes should have taken the form of new suburbs; it would have been better for Glasgow, and the country at large, if the farming land of the neighbourhood had been spared and tenement blocks had been erected in central districts, on the sites that had been cleared of slums. If the blocks had been several stories high, as they are elsewhere, it would not have been necessary to build all these new suburbs; and the rehoused citizens, it was added, would likely enough have preferred this alternative, had it been offered them; when a man had his dwelling in central Glasgow, he was usually nearby his place of work—there was less to be spent in fares and not so long a journey night and morning . . . . All that may be true but there remains a real difficulty; where do you bestow your ejected slum-dwellers while you tear down their rookeries and replace them with new blocks of flats? By the present system of suburban expansion, there is no need to find temporary quarters for the tenant of condemned property; his new home is made ready before he is ejected from the old.

In all departments of modern urban life planning is an urgent necessity; urban life to-day is on too vast a scale to be left haphazard to its own unhindered growth, its own experimental devices. Like all human activities, however, planning, large-scale planning, has its drawbacks, whereof perhaps the chief is its tendency to monotony; municipal estates, by whatever city they may be erected—and along with their advantages of cubic space and modern convenience—are apt to suggest an atmosphere charged with dullness. It is not only the regimented look of the houses, set down neatly, according to plan; with no trace of individual taste or guidance, of adaptation to the varied needs of their owners. To the making of a beautiful city goes an element of growth, and there is no suggestion of growth about a housing scheme; it is a ready-made article, turned out of the municipal factory, and as such—in its beginnings at any rate—lacking in many of the daily interests and small excitements that diversify the day in the older quarters of a town. These older quarters may be shabby and insanitary, but in and around them are the interests and excitements of a life more varied than that of the regimented suburb; as a rule they are nearer than the regimented suburb to streets with a traffic of crowd and vehicle. Nearer also to shop windows, where variety of content is an antidote to street monotony; and to another and valued variety of cheap places of amusement. In the new and sanitary estate, on the other hand, shops will be comparatively few and sometimes almost lacking—and as for a vista of lit window and display of fashion, that may mean a journey by bus. Then, in all likelihood, there will be small choice with regard to entertainment; one accessible cinema in lieu of half a dozen. And the streets themselves, being purely residential, will afford little interest in the way of passing traffic.

Women, it is obvious, must suffer more than men from the tedium of life on new suburban estates; stay-at-home women, that is to say, whose duties to their families confine them to their own neighbourhood. Men who leave home in the morning and return to it only when the day's work is over will be less irked by the blankness of their dormitory suburb. A friend of my own—a woman who was formerly a trade-union organizer—and with whom I once discussed this aspect of suburban housing schemes agreed and more than agreed with my views on the depressing effect of their monotony. She went so far as to designate one of the newest and tidiest of our London housing schemes as a set of little prisons for women! Well-appointed little prisons where a woman's sphere was indeed the home, since there was nothing to interest her outside it! While a woman doctor I met in Glasgow, whose acquaintance with slums and their tenants is extensive, also knew of cases where the occupants of well-found municipal dwellings regretted their insanitary streets. She told me of women who had been moved from that slummiest of Glasgow districts, Anderston, into subsidized dwellings, fitted with modern conveniences; but who, to her knowledge, were bent on deserting their clean and spacious quarters and returning to Anderston's familiar squalor, so soon as they could find vacant room. What those who are seeking to do good to their fellows sometimes forget is that one man's meat is another man's poison, and the hardships of one type of mind, the pleasurable comforts of another; it is probably no more than a minority of our countrymen who object to noise as a daily accompaniment of life, and although to some of us privacy is an absolute need, others delight in close-huddling and find privacy hard to endure.

. . .

There is one Glasgow housing scheme which is surely ideal in the matter of providing both interest and amusement for its inmates; and that, strange to say, is a building—a hostel—in the Carntyne district which provides cheap lodgement for women, and elderly women at that. I say it in no spirit of feminist acrimony, but simply as a fact that inquiry will verify, that it is not usual to consider the interest and amusement of elderly females until the needs, in that direction, of (*a*) males and (*b*) children and young persons have been satisfied in every particular. Hence my astonishment at this Carntyne hostel which, as I have said, is an ideal residence for ladies of the pension age; supplying them, for the sum of five shillings a week, with a self-contained flatlet where cooking and cleaning can be done to the best advantage, as hot water is on tap night and day. In addition, at the end of a passage, a communal bath and a communal washhouse is at the service of every half-dozen inmates; I was told, however, that these particular facilities were not much sought after—having plenty of hot water ready to hand, the old ladies prefer, as a general rule, to scrub both themselves and their garments on their private premises.

Considered as lodgings at five shillings a week, the flatlets are more than good value; but, in addition to the benefits already enumerated, they have an advantage peculiar to themselves which must rouse the envy of municipal tenants with domiciles less fortunately situated. All the windows in that hostel—thirty-four in number—look out upon a greyhound racing track; so that free, gratis, and for nothing those happy old ladies have a comprehensive view of proceedings for which others have to plank down their shillings. And this sporting prospect enjoyed from the windows is not only an interest in itself—it brings other interests into the lives of the hostel's occupants. The racing season means frequent visits from their children and grandchildren —who, but for the dogs, might be tempted to neglect their elderly relatives . . . . I cannot help suspecting that this advantageous residence was allotted in error to old ladies; the officials responsible being unaware of the amenities which might have been placed at the disposal of (*a*) masculine or (*b*) juvenile Glaswegians.

One of the inmates who kindly permitted a call and inspection of her domicile was an old Irishwoman, understood to be the doyenne of the hostel. When asked if she was satisfied with her present quarters, she qualified her affirmative by stating that it had been dull there lately; for some reason or other the track had been closed and there had been no racing for weeks—but she was glad to say it was beginning again in a day or two. Another Irish inmate, by origin of Belfast, was, she informed us, smartening up her clothes for July the twelfth—which the Orangeman of Glasgow still celebrates with banner and with drum . . . . It may, or may not, have been a coincidence that in the slums and slum-cleared tenements we inspected that day the majority of the occupants were bearers of Irish names—in the first of the new housing blocks in which we set foot there was Connor on one side the hallway and Curran on the other. Irish names are more than frequent in the region of industrial Scotland; but their prevalence and its effect on the national life needs more than a paragraph at the end of a chapter; it is important enough to require a chapter to itself.

Cicely Hamilton, *Modern Scotland as seen by an Englishwoman* (1937).

1938: Glasgow Speech

The speech habits of Clydeside have been commented upon long and often, usually by perplexed outsiders. The following extract is from a survey of the language and idiom of Glasgow schoolchildren aged 5–12 based on the impressions of their teachers. However, it soon develops into a list of linguistic features that should preferably be eradicated or toned down by classroom example. Although its general tenor would probably not be acceptable today, the survey marked a step forward in recommending more emphasis on oral work in schools. A more recent phonetic study concluded that there are very wide variations within so-called Glasgow dialect which depend on age, sex and social class. Adult speakers are often inconsistent, varying their idiom and vocabulary according to each situation.

What Glasgow Speaks

In most cases Glasgow pupils enter the schools with one language only, the Central Scottish Dialect, and they proceed to learn to write Standard English.

As the result of education the vernacular is gradually eliminated from written work, but it persists in colloquial use.

The Central Scottish Dialect is the medium of expression naturally employed by the Glasgow child who may interrogate the teacher during a Dictation lesson with such a question as, 'Whit cums ofter "after"?' In the playground children who try to speak Standard English are generally laughed at, whilst in the class-room a lapse into the mother-tongue is greeted with hilarity. Thus, the boy who during the dinner-interval maliciously created a stampede of his classmates by the cry of 'Polis', that same afternoon caused much amusement in the school-room by reading, 'Sir Robert Peel founded the *Polis* Force'.

What Glasgow Thinks

Fear of ridicule and abhorrence of affectation combine to stultify efforts to obtain clear enunciation and to eradicate debased forms of the vernacular. Children usually hear little else than a Scots dialect and so they come to regard Standard English as artificial. To speak properly requires not only a departure from the normal pronunciation but also forethought in selection of words. Hence when they endeavour to use Standard English, they feel self-conscious. In such moments they tend to lapse into the mother-tongue, much to their dismay. In the presence of visitors or inspectors they are sometimes inarticulate, at other times silent. They know that their ordinary mode of speech will be criticised, and at the same time they lose their self-possession because they feel they cannot glibly perform in the other language. Adults can understand the parallel position of a grown-up suddenly called upon to recite to his friends and an important stranger. To his distress the unpractised reciter discovers that all eyes are focused on him; he becomes alarmingly aware that he is not sure of the words; with dismay he recollects he must adopt an 'elocution voice'; and he is certain that the only outcome of the ordeal is that he will make a fool of himself.

The handicap involved in the realisation of limitations and deficiencies can only be abolished by constant oral practice in the use of 'proper English'. Class teachers are convinced that too much written work is demanded where oral work is weak. Complaints are made that written composition 'is an obsession with some headmasters and inspectors who sometimes apparently think that teachers are slacking if their classes have not a composition in the book every week'.

In Glasgow the time has come when those responsible for education must ask: 'Which is more important—the written or the spoken word?'. The answer must depend on the needs of the children; conditions vary in different parts of the city. Yet, for the larger part of the school population the greater need is correct speech.

Proper Speech Suspect

A rapid improvement in oral expression would be possible if public opinion was favourable, but the attitude of Glasgow people towards speech must be changed before an extensive and speedy alteration can be made. The child who has been accustomed at the dinner-table to conveying peas from the plate to his mouth with the aid of his knife, is apt to suffer from embarrassment in polite society when a new instrument, the fork, has to be employed and when the peas seem to be endowed with unnatural powers of agile locomotion and tantalising elusiveness. Most adults could tell of similar experiences undergone in their callow days when they were acquiring on the installment plan the Book of Etiquette. To the average person, 'the correct thing' is the right thing: 'the rules of the game' are unquestioned. The great trouble in Glasgow, however, is that in speech the mass of the population do not look upon the careless speaker as breaking the rules or upon the proper speaker as a normal person. At a football match the individuals in a crowd who would simultaneously give voice to the fierce yell of 'Foul!' before the referee had time to blow the whistle, take no exception to breaches in the rules of grammar or to ill-usage of language, and would almost unanimously dub a correct speaker as a 'Swanker'.

'Broad Scots' Not Bad English

This attitude of people towards proper speech, not confined to Glasgow alone, is due to a variety of causes that are not so easily dismissed as by saying offhand that slovenliness, ignorance and ill-breeding produce the improper enunciation and the idioms characteristic of Glasgow speech. The Glasgow people who use 'Broad Scots' are using not a debased form of Standard English but a dialect derived from a sister dialect to those from which Standard English has descended. Central Scots forms part of the Northumbrian or Northern English Division of languages: Standard English is a blending of the Midland and Southern English dialects. This kinship of the Central Scottish Dialect to the sister speech has been to its detriment and disadvantage. While in the Lowlands bad habits in grammar-usage have been formed, condemnation has been so general as to label the diction and idiom of Broad Scots as vulgar and uncouth.

Report on Glasgow Speech by the Educational Institute of Scotland (Glasgow Local Association) (1938).

1938: The Old Firm

Rangers (founded 1872) and Celtic (founded 1887) are the two most famous—and successful—teams in Scottish football. Their dominance of the game over the last hundred years led to their 'partnership of opposition' being dubbed The Old Firm—a 1904 cartoon on the Glasgow Charity Final is captioned, 'What, you two again!' However, their monopoly has recently been challenged by teams from the East Coast, like Aberdeen and Dundee United. It was the New Year game at Ibrox on 2 January 1939 between Rangers and Celtic that saw the biggest capacity crowd ever for a league match in Britain—118,576 spectators.

The Old Firm, it need hardly be said, are Celtic and Rangers. Their monopoly and the nature of their rivalry have no parallel in football outside of Scotland. With them, as with the worshippers under the melancholy steeples, the Battle of the Boyne is still a matter of lively dispute and recapitulation. Racial, historical and religious considerations inflame the excitement of the supporters. In fact, a Celtic-Rangers match is as much a contest of supporters as of players. They occupy different ends of the park and shout at each other. The Celtic fans are much given to hymn-singing. The Rangers, being less religious but more politically-minded, encourage their champions by songs which celebrate ancient deeds of battle and massacre. In the good old days when ricketties and bugles, painted steel helmets and banners, added a fine gaiety of sound and colour to the proceedings, the scene was very lively indeed. The violence of the rivalry among the supporters is very remarkable indeed. Sometimes it leads to fights and arrests. It is exceedingly profitable for both clubs.

In post-War years Rangers have won the League championship fourteen times out of eighteen, which is a virtual monopoly. On the other hand, they developed a habit of losing the Scottish Cup so abruptly and unexpectedly that it looked as if they were letting the precious object fall out of their hands. In 1920 they were beaten by a fledgling First Division club after drawing twice, and that was astonishing. Next year, they got into the Final and were most unexpectedly beaten by Partick Thistle. The year after, they were in the Final again with Greenock Morton, a team which would not be considered to have any chance with them in a League match. To make things quite hopeless for Morton, their star player had to call off, and it was said that the management thought so little of the team's chances that they did not bring a single bottle of wine against the possibility of having to fill the Cup. Yet, quite early in the first half the Rangers were bunching together nervously in the field and a supporter on the terracing lifted his bugle and dismally played, 'It's all over now.' The musical mourner was justified in the event. It is also said (though it sounds too good to be true) that Morton borrowed a couple of bottles from the Rangers to fill their trophy.

Worse was still to come. Rangers drew Celtic in the Semi-Final when Celtic were doing very badly indeed. It was now obvious that Rangers had the Cup jitters, but they always play best against their old rivals, and the disparity in form was so glaring and well-established that even the usually confident Celts took the field in a very anxious mood. But they beat the Rangers five-nothing. It was nothing short of a rout. Outside the main gate of Hampden, broken-hearted Rangers supporters made a bonfire of their flags: it was the dark night of the soul. Year after year, Rangers went down in one stage or other of the competition. It became a national joke. Famous Rangers players, laden with international honours, retired from the team without a single Cup medal.

When success came, it was doubly sweet, for they met and overcame Celtic in the Final. The Princess pantomime had a comic sketch that year of Rangers as Cup winners. Naturally enough, the Christmas pantomime was still running when the Final was played in April, and the comedian came on to the stage, wearing a Rangers jersey, and carrying, not the usual comedy prop, but the Cup itself, the genuine article. There was an enthusiatic uproar. It would be pleasant to think that the ranks of Tuscany could scarce forbear to cheer, but when it comes to cheering the other side, Rangers and Celtic fans can forbear without difficulty.

Colm Brogan, 'The League and the Cup', in *Scotland—1938* (1938).

1938: Unemployed, Orangemen and Hibernians

The Aberdeenshire journalist John Robertson Allan (1906–1986) was perhaps more accustomed to dealing with country life *(Down on the Farm, Farmer's Boy)* but here he turns his sympathetic eye on some of the oddities of city life. Glasgow has always been a city of contrasts, and Allan's vignettes of street processions amply point this up, also neatly encompassing two old bogies: politics and religion.

Once on a November afternoon I was walking along Buchanan Street about half-past four o'clock. It was a busy day: hundreds of fashionable women were trafficking among the shops and the business men were returning from or going to the coffee-rooms. There was an atmosphere of money and well-being, the sort of thing that makes you feel pleased with yourself as long as you have a few shillings in your own pocket. Then a procession came up the street, with blood-red banners, that swayed menacingly under the misty lights. These should have driven the women screaming into the basements of the shops for they bore legends in praise of Moscow, warnings about the wrath to come. 'Communists,' the word flew along the pavements. But no one screamed. The men that carried the flags were broken beyond violence by the prolonged misery of unemployment and could not sustain the menace of the legends. The ladies in the fur coats could look without fear on the procession, for it was not the first stroke of revolt but another triumph of law and order. A dozen constables were shepherding the marchers, and they were such fine big men and stepped along with such manly dignity that they themselves were the procession. The unemployed seemed to have no community with such defiant banners, such splendid constables, and they may have known it, for they walked without any spirit, as if they realised they had no place in society, not even in their demonstrations against it. The procession turned into George Square. The unemployed dismissed and went home wearily to their bread and margarine. The constables eased their uniform pants and went off to the station with property and privilege resting securely on their broad shoulders. It was just another Glasgow afternoon.

Then some months later I was looking out from the window of a coffee-house in Argyle Street about seven o'clock of a Saturday evening. I heard fife music; then a procession came out from St Enoch's Square. It was a company of

Orangemen, or some such Protestants, in full uniform, back from an excursion in the country. They passed, an army terrible with banners, and comic, as men that have a good excuse for dressing up. They had just gone by when a new music came up to us and a new procession appeared, coming from Queen Street Station. They were Hibernians, or some other Catholic order, also returning from a day in the country; terrible and comic also, after the fashion of their kind. Orangemen and Hibernians! we said to ourselves. What will happen if they forgather? Being wise youths and having some pleasure on hand, we did not follow to see. But we met a man some time later that night who swore he had been present. The Hibernians, he said, discovered that the Orangemen were in front, so they quickened their pace. The Orangemen, hearing also, slackened theirs. Some resourceful and sporting policemen diverted both parties into a side street and left them to fight it out. After half an hour, when all the fighters had thoroughly disorganised each other, bodies of police arrived, sorted the wounded from the winded and despatched them to their proper destinations in ambulances and plain vans. That is the story as it was told to me and I cannot swear that it is true in every detail; but it might have happened in Glasgow that way, and I doubt if it could have happened in any other town. Such incidents give Glasgow afternoons and evenings their distinctive flavour.

J. R. Allan, 'Sketches for a Portrait of Glasgow', in *Scotland—1938* (1938).

1938: The Empire Exhibition

The 175-acre Bellahouston Park was the scene of the 1938 Empire Exhibition. From Thomas Tait's 300-foot steel tower visitors could gaze down on 'a city of palaces and pavilions designed in the simple lines and curves typical of modern architecture and knit together by wide avenues: a city of light, colour, spaciousness, spectacle and gaiety' (according to the Exhibition handbook). Much of the gaiety was provided by the giant Amusement Park described here. Other novelties included a Highland clachan, with its own post office, and an Indian restaurant, as well as the national pavilions. 13½ million visitors attended the Empire Exhibition despite appalling weather; perhaps people sensed it was to be the last opportunity for a carefree time for years to come. Tait's tower was rapidly dismantled in case it became a landmark for enemy bombers.

Everywhere were gadgets for turning you upside down, rolling you round and round, shaking your liver, in short, putting you in any position other than the normal one. Here man (and that means woman too) is twisted, thrown, bumped and shaken, and he likes it. If you doubt me, go and see for yourself. Watch him come off the most fearsome-looking machine smiling and happy, and asking for more and getting it. No wonder that poets sing of the wonderful Spirit of Man.
    Come with me into the Stratoship, a cigar-shaped 'aeroplane' that seats

about six or seven. It is attached to a long arm and has a propellor. When you are securely strapped into a cage arrangement, off you go, the motion being something like a plane beginning to rise. It's all very pleasant—and then your 'plane' suddenly rolls right over, and before you know where you are you're sitting up gasping—and then over you go again.

The subtlety of this thing is that it doesn't turn over with unfailing regularity. You are all prepared for a roll and it doesn't come. You go round smoothly again and decide that there are to be no more rolls, and at that moment over you go again. And everybody loves it.

If the Stratoship is a thrill, the Rocket Railway is even more thrilling. I'm not sure whether the more exciting thing is to travel on this railway or watch it going round. It goes round in a deep pit. You've probably seen that act known as the Wall of Death in which a motor-cyclist goes round a 'well' at a tremendous speed. This is the Rocket Railway on a smaller scale.

As the train gathers speed it climbs higher and higher up the side of the well or pit until the passengers are all sitting sides-up. It doesn't seem possible, I know, but believe me it does happen. I could not help wondering what the driver of the train feels about it. You go on once or twice but, remember, he goes on all the time. Does he end the season with a lop-sided view of life, and find the ordinary method of train travelling flat, stale and unprofitable?

After the Rocket Railway I felt the need for something less exciting, so I went in to see the giraffe-necked ladies, who sat in a comfortable cabin on the floor of which a baby played. The neck rings, I was told, are never removed.

Then I made for the Octopus via the crooked house. No, I didn't go into the house. A laughing sailor (a most realistic dummy figure) sits above the door and rocks with laughter. Little Audrey had nothing on him. She merely laughed and laughed and laughed, but he laughs and laughs and laughs *ad lib*. And everybody else laughs. I tried not to but it was impossible. Soon I was holding myself, and I decided not to go into the house yesterday for I had laughed my fill, and any more might have been dangerous.

Now for the Octopus. It is a machine with long steel arms reaching into the air. On the end of each arm or tentacle—there must be about 20 of them—is a chair that holds two. The passengers are carefully fastened in, and the Octopus begins to waggle its tentacles. Up they go, down they go, and all the time the seat is revolving. It may not be your form of enjoyment, but you are in the minority, for it was highly popular yesterday. As one man came off, after several rounds, his eyes were sparkling, and he said, simply: 'It's a wow!'

'All Play & No Work!' by Argus, *The Evening Citizen*, 5 May 1938.

1939: Evacuees

There was official recognition that war with Germany would mean many industrial towns taking terrible punishment from the Luftwaffe bombers. In the

Spring of 1939 the city's primary school children were divided into groups of thirty and the term 'evacuees' began to be used. Then during September 1st–3rd, just as Hitler was about to invade Poland, 120,000 Glasgow children swiftly left in trains going to reception areas as near as Ayr and Renfrew but as far afield as Perthshire and Aberdeenshire. The exercise was faultlessly planned but not very effective, since more than 75% of the children had drifted back to Glasgow by Christmas and a second evacuation had to be arranged for the heavy bombing of 1941. The evacuees were unable to adjust to rural life and found the diet unfamiliar: boiled eggs were singled out as being particularly hard to take.

At the schools where evacuation did not begin until late in the forenoon there was something like a rush on the trains. Many of the children had obviously got together their belongings in a very short time. The persons least affected by the partings were the children themselves. Most of them were happy and gay, as if they were going away on a picnic. A postman, leaning over a railway bridge to watch them getting into a train that would take them to the peace of the moors, remarked—'After all, they don't know what they're being sent away to avoid. And it will be best if the authorities can manage to keep them from ever knowing.'

There was no hitch, no congestion and little or no hindrance to citizens going about their business. Arrangements worked, in the words of an official, 'like clockwork'. But at Strathaven, Lanarkshire, where only a little over 500 evacuees turned up out of 1600 scheduled for the town, a 'revolt' broke out among a large number of mothers, when they learned from billeting officers that individual families could not be accommodated in one house, but must split. Some of the mothers had as many as seven and eight children—some were toddlers and others were still being carried in arms. They came from the Kinning Park district of Glasgow, and had been up as early as five o'clock in the morning.

At the Town Hall, one of the four receiving centres, harrassed billeting officers endeavoured to persuade the mothers there was no alternative but to allow some of their children to be taken to other homes. 'We won't leave our children. We'll take them back to Glasgow rather than be separated from them. They will cry their eyes out if they are taken from us', chorused a number of flushed and excited mothers.

After waiting five hours, two mothers decided to take the law into their own hands. They walked out of the Town Hall with nine children between them, determined to get back to Glasgow. As they wandered through the town, a Strathaven resident stopped them and learned of their plight. He took them into a restaurant and ordered a meal for the two families. The two mothers broke down and wept, and after they had finished their meal and rested, they boarded a bus for Glasgow.

Realising that it was impossible for everyone to be accommodated in the same house, other mothers of large families ultimately gave in to the billeting officer and by the early evening everyone was satisfactorily billeted. No difficulty was experienced in billeting unaccompanied children but residents in some houses scheduled to accommodate as many as six or eight persons definitely refused to take the children if the mother was with them.

Glasgow's evacuation organisation was brilliantly successful. Special trains to carry the departing children slid alongside the station platforms and left again with their loads only a few minutes later. The trains were leaving in some cases only a quarter of an hour after the leaders of the children's procession reached the station entrance. The railway staff handled the evacuation with less trouble than an ordinary holiday rush would have caused.

Mothers of Glasgow, standing outside city schools or walking with the evacuation processions to the stations, watched red-eyed with tears but bravely quiet, struggling to hide their feelings as their children disappeared behind the station barriers to the waiting trains. 'See you soon' was all that most of them said.

'Smiling children set off on new adventure', *The Bulletin*, 2 September 1939.

IV

Altered Images (1945 to the present)

Introduction

In the combined euphoria and scarcity of the post-war years the Glasgow Question reasserted itself. The Clyde Valley Plan (1946) foresaw a city drastically depopulated, surrounded by Regional Parks, 'overspill' New Towns and Recreation Centres. The Corporation's own City Plan showed a new radial metropolis with massive suburbs—modern, logical and nightmarish in its assumptions.

A new Glasgow was to emerge eventually containing features of both Plans. The massive depopulation to New Towns and elsewhere did take place, huge areas of older tenements were demolished to make way for new housing, roads or just leisure space. The city's boundaries strained against the 'green belt' to accommodate vast peripheral housing schemes. The skyline bristled with a succession of high-rise towers, the only assumed solution to Glasgow's chronic land shortage.

After the inter-war stagnation, Glasgow was now to become the place for trying out the latest orthodoxies on urban renewal. Much was undoubtedly effective—living conditions were substantially improved just by reducing the densities of people (from nearly 500 people per acre to an average of 160 within the space of twenty years). But there were also considerable costs associated with rapid change.

Gone were the insanitary conditions conducive to ill-health and social malaise so startlingly revealed when Clydeside children were evacuated in 1939. The improvements in health were dramatic, mainly due to the the National Health Service and new drugs, although better health education and initiatives like the mass X-ray campaign were also effective in reducing endemic diseases. Working conditions also improved, with shorter working hours and longer, paid holidays. There was a major expansion in higher education and vocational training.

The colourful, unpredictable pre-war times were being replaced by a planned future where many would live miles from the urban centre in singularly bleak Corporation housing schemes. Home-owners increasingly fled to suburban pockets outside the city boundaries until (in the mid-1960s) less than 20% of Glasgow's housing was owner-occupied. The birth of the area-based Housing Associations in the 1970s provided more private rented accommodation and began the tenement restoration that has so changed the city's outward appearance.

It is ironic that the political leaders of a Labour fiefdom for more than fifty years should in the 1980s have overseen the recent major upsurge in private housebuilding and improvement, mainly financed from Scottish Office money under a Conservative government. In other areas like provision for the arts, environmental improvement and inner-city regeneration the District and Regional councils are also involved to a remarkable degree.

The spectacular civil engineering achievements of the 1960s and '70s have helped to make a cleaner, greener Glasgow that is almost unrecognisable to the exile returing from America or Australia. The achievements have involved the clearance of 85,000 tenement houses and the complete obliteration of many working-class districts. Of the many Crosses that were once focal points of the city, only Glasgow Cross and Bridgeton Cross have retained their identity, saved by the GEAR Project which has transformed the neglected East End. In hindsight, perhaps the 1968 hurricane only presaged a man-made destruction of stone and mortar on a far greater scale.

The rapid decline of Glasgow's heavy engineering and fabrication industry was another factor—in 1947 nearly half of Britain's steam locomotives and 90% of her sewing machines were still being produced on Clydeside. Few could have predicted the speed with which the past would be written off, a process temporarily halted by events like the UCS work-in. In the 1980s Glasgow's role has become that of a dependent, in Professor Checkland's phrase 'a deficit city to an extent greater than most, drawing upon the general resources of a nation and the EEC'.

Out of every decline comes a form of regeneration. The derelict land and buildings of former economic might are adapted—Templeton's huge carpet factory thrives again as a small business centre; abandoned docks and quays make way for riverside housing and the Scottish Exhibition Centre; the loss of 200,000 people leaves space to build landscaped factories for the high-technology 'industries' that must generate the city's future wealth; the inexorable reduction in Glasgow's daily papers has opened the way for community-based weeklies as well as a strong market for local radio and new media like cable TV.

The city's future is clearly not as workshop to the world, a role that effectively ceased before the turn of the century. Contructive Contraction is now the guiding principle, an intense concentration upon the abiding assets of what is still a great conurbation of more than $^{3}/_{4}$ million people. Much has disappeared that was, in hindsight, worth preserving, but much more remains. It is therefore appropriate that many of Glasgow's writers and artists are concerned with the means and the effects of change, both as physical manifestation and psychological trauma.

1946: C.A. Oakley on the Glasgow Man

Charles Oakley (b. 1900) drafted much of *The Second City* before the outbreak of World War II. During the war years he became Regional Controller for the Ministry of Air Production in Scotland and Northern Ireland. After the war the book was completed in a few months before the author became Scottish Controller to the Board of Trade, concerned with encouraging new industry into Scotland. His background in industry dates from 1918 when he came to Clydebank to serve an apprenticeship at John Brown's. Here he tries to pin down the typical features of the various classes of Glasgow male, often a baffling mixture of reserve and belligerence, hardheadedness and nostalgia.

A great many people have been grateful for having, at a hazardous moment, a Glasgow man on their side. In matters concerning his own self-interest—or, at least, what appears to him to concern his own self-interest—he is a realist and an opportunist, ever, like Kennedy Jones, with his eye on the main chance. With his roots in the soil, he has a good understanding of his fellow-men, and he can usually be depended on, as Sir John Moore was when carrying out the retraining of the British infantry soldier, to concentrate on what really matters while handling those under him humanely. He drives the men in his charge, but mixes with them, and is never 'stand-offish'.

To what extent is the common impression that he is a solitary man really accurate? He likes to be alone, is reticent, and does not mix so readily with his fellow-men as the Englishman does—the Glasgow 'pub' is a dismal place, quite lacking the warm geniality of the London pub—but he is, nevertheless, the better host. Scottish hospitality has a world-wide reputation, and the American and Dominion troops, who spent their leave in this country made no secret of their view that they were better looked-after in the North than in the South. Yet the Glasgow man lacks the social graces—he is reluctant to say please, thank you, I'm sorry, or excuse me—and he is apt to push people out of his way rather crudely and often unnecessarily. He glories in being outspoken, sometimes without realizing that an inaccurate or ill-advised remark is not rendered any the less inaccurate or ill-advised by being candid.

The outstanding weakness of some Glasgow people is perversity. Contra-suggestibility is found in every community throughout the world; but, alas? the percentage of Clydeside people, who seem disposed to do the opposite of what is suggested to them, is on the high side. As a recent Medical Officer of Health for Glasgow remarked, 'the people of Glasgow are inclined to be thrawn'. They always want the one brand of toothpaste not in stock, to ride on the crowded tramcar rather than on the empty one behind, to go among the Celtic supporters at a football match and cheer for the Rangers. Their predilection for jay-walking in busy streets is probably the most unfortunate feature of their social behaviour. Believing that he has a prior right on the roadway to automobiles, the perverse man expects them, even if the traffic lights are in their favour, to make way for him, and he will walk scowling in front of motor cars, daring their drivers to knock him down. Thus he makes visiting motor-ists—including those who might consider building new factories in Glasgow—ill-disposed towards his city on their first contact with it—and first impressions have a habit of lasting.

Perhaps this unreasonableness has its origin in the Glasgow man's endea-vour, a worth-while endeavour, to preserve his individuality. It has many good and even fine phases. In integrity, for instance. The reputation of the Scottish insurance companies in the United States is still high because, unlike some American companies, they did not haggle over claims at the time of the San Francisco earthquake. And it is worth noting how often the Glasgow man, who has had a business failure, succeeds later in meeting his creditors in full. Sometimes his children do it for him, years after his death. The goods he makes are of first-rate quality. The last battle in the struggle between craftsmanship and mechanized production is likely to be fought in Glasgow. Pride in personal appearance can be seen in any city street. The Glasgow business man and his clerks and typists are usually better dressed than their opposites in London—although the latter are sublimely unconscious of their relative and, indeed, actual dowdiness. Contrast, too, the bearing of the Glasgow bus drivers and conductors in their tidy, well-pressed green suits and that of the mussy London bus drivers and conductors.

The Glasgow man's concern about his appearance arises from his self-consciousness. In comparison with the extraverted Southern Englishman or Lancastrian the Glasgow man is highly introverted. He is, for instance, shy about singing in public and, as J.H. Muir remarked, he would not for his life lower himself to be seen in a tramcar blowing his child's nose. But he is much the more likely among parents to take that child on an annual visit to the pantomime and, when he grows older, to give him the better start in life.

The Glasgow man has the reputation of being stubborn, and wits sometimes tell stories about the awful spectacle to be seen when two Glasgow men push their chins in each other's faces, both actuated by the necessity for maintaining profound and inviolate principles. Much of this misrepresentation is nonsense, although the Glasgow man does not have the Londoner's sense of compromise, and the lack of it is apt to be a handicap in the conduct of his affairs. Yet he often derives great moral force from his principles—witness, for instance, the courage of the Covenanters and the sacrifices made by many who took part in the Disruption of the Established Church. He came out of his stand against professionalism in sport with a great deal more dignity than his opposites in England. And, although he is quite capable of being astute when arranging a deal, he is not a 'smart alick' or a 'double-crosser'. The word of the Glasgow business man still stands perhaps a little higher than the word of the business men of certain other towns.

Whether the Glasgow man is more intelligent than most people in Great Britain is debatable. He thinks he is, and speaks about the intellectual limitations of some others, including the Cockney, quite patronizingly. He really *does* seem to be more alert mentally, and he is on the whole unquestionably better educated. He has the tidier mind and the greater capacity for grasping a logical argument. His methods are the more direct, and he has a commendable dislike of fuss, sham and humbug. He does not waste time. Indeed, the stigmata of the Glasgow man used to be given as—besides the turned-up trousers, the 'hard hat' and the umbrella—that he was always in a hurry.

It is sometimes said of the young Glasgow salesman that, if left to 'pick up his job', he does badly, because his individualism makes him resent having to be servile. He allows himself to get irritated with and to argue with difficult customers. He cannot see that his primary job is to sell goods, not to indulge in across-the-counter combats for verbal supremacy. Yet Glasgow men have become some of the finest salesmen in the world. The explanation is probably that the more intelligent Glasgow salesman grasps the point that he can gain ascendancy over awkward and even hostile customers by subtly guiding them to do what he wants, and that he can have excellent relationships with them while getting them to comply, largely unwittingly, with his wishes . . . The successful Glasgow man can become, even if nature has not built him that way, the warmest of men. The best chairmen at social functions and the wittiest after-dinner speakers are usually London Scots, most of them Glaswegians or Aberdonians.

The same point can be made about the Glasgow man as a factory operative. He has the reputation of being difficult to handle, and team work undoubtedly comes less naturally to him than to some others. But, if well led, there are few people who march so steadily in step with their fellows as the Glasgow lads. The fact that the Glaswegian is an individualist must always be recognized; but we would point out that, although the characteristic feature of the Glasgow man's play in most sports is individualism—at soccer, for instance, he likes dribbling because of the satisfaction he derives from being able to get the better of his opponents by his own endeavour—the part he played in making Rugby a team game should be remembered. And if the persistent inability which the Glasgow dissenters to the Established Church have shown to agree among themselves be mentioned on the one side, the cohesion shown in the Scottish associations of employers and of trade unions should be mentioned on the other. It is sometimes said of the Glasgow worker that, while he has the capacity to do a better job than most other workers in Great Britain, he often lacks the inclination to do so. That might be, however, a reflection on the ability of some of his managers. Most Glasgow men and women in industry not only can turn out an excellent job, but actually do so.

Some of the criticism of the Glasgow worker comes from a failure to make allowance for his caution. More than once a manager from other parts, reduced to despair by his workers stolidly maintaining that the way in which he wanted a job done was impossible, has been gratified to find some hours later that they have carried out his instructions, slightly modified, perhaps, but modified to their improvement. Others have at first been disappointed to find their new Glasgow employees learning their jobs more slowly than would have happened in London or in Manchester. But, after a month, they observed that steady progress was being made, and before long were delighted because the outputs of the Glasgow workers, both in quality and in quantity, had gone ahead of the outputs on comparable work elsewhere. And they stayed ahead.

C.A. Oakley, *The Second City* (1946).

1946: Unity Theatre and *The Gorbals Story*

Glasgow Unity Theatre was set up in 1941 to stage committed left-wing plays. After the war a 'professional' company existed for a few years, taking drama to new audiences both in Glasgow and on tour. The company's greatest success was *The Gorbals Story* by Robert McLeish, an artist on *The Bulletin* newspaper. First staged at The Queen's music hall theatre, Glasgow Cross, it was transferred to London's West End, and a film was later made. The play introduced a welcome note of realism in language, subject matter and stage presentation into the jingoistic world of post-war theatre. Under the heading 'Glesca Comes to Toon' a London theatre critic conveyed some of the initial impact.

Playgoers who are—as they should be—a little weary of The Mayfair Story, The Chelsea Story and The Home-Counties Story should go to see Mr. McLeish's play and get a profound shock and a strange thrill.

For this is Glasgow, the slummy, swarming core of it, presented with honesty, frankness and verisimilitude.

A baby is born. Its mother dies. A young unmarried couple make love. Young married couples seek a home, hopelessly. An old drunk comes close to fortune and then discovers he has forgotten to post his pool coupons. Nothing—as we say—happens. It is all a mere matter of life and death.

But let me declare that the middle hour of this play, the heart of it—after its slow beginning and before its arbitrary conclusion—is the very stuff of human drama.

This is the music of humanity, not still and sad as the poet declared it, but rich, raucous, clamant, tingling, coarse and thwarted. There is no sentimentality here. Its sheer avoidance makes the single love-scene all the more poignant.

The pair envisage that halcyon impossibility, a home of their own. The young tough (with his razor in his pocket) is drunk enough to imagine 'a kettle on the bile, a big orange ca-at purr-r-r-rin' awa' by the fi-ire.' And repudiation of the vision comes not from the boy but from the girl: 'Ach awa', man, and doan't be da-aft!'

These middle scenes have a throbbing interblend of comedy and tragedy. Howard Connell is the funniest stage-drunk since Arthur Sinclair's Paycock. And I should think there has been nothing quite like the violent true-Glasgow dialect heard on the London stage ever before. It is delivered with gusto by the brilliant Glasgow Unity Players. It made first-night ears quiver, eyes pop, and boiled shirts wilt. And anyone who imagines this dialect to be overdone should be told that, on the contrary, it has been considerably toned down for London consumption.

Scottish Theatre Archive, Glasgow Unity cuttings book.

1947: Naomi Mitchison's Two Faces of Glasgow

Here the Scottish writer Naomi Mitchison (b. 1897) airs some trenchant views on Glasgow politics and people, although like other contemporary post-war observers—G. S. Fraser, J. B. Singer—she saw through the smoke to the fire, and felt too that something better must rise from the ashes. This extract comes from the notes to her novel *The Bull Calves*, the background to which is covered by her recently published wartime diaries.

But if the north bank of the Clyde is Highland, the south bank is Lowland, the contact there is with weaving and mines. Keir Hardie was an Ayrshire man; he began and led the I.L.P. whose great days were Glasgow days. The mixture has never quite coalesced, nor has either side made much effort to understand the other. Lack of this understanding has induced the Labour Party in Scotland to behave from time to time with a really remarkable stupidity and tactlessness.

But the hierarchies of Transport House do not really fit into the Clydeside pattern. We still have our anarchists and there are still almost as many minority socialist parties holding meetings and putting out publications as there are minority Protestant Churches. The tradition of both Kirk Sessions and ceilidh lend themselves to doctrinaire arguings. Probably Marxism has found a readier home on Clydeside than anywhere in England (it is arguable that the English feel more deeply and talk less than the Scots). Yes, we like the talk fine; some of the folk who have most notably wasted their own and other people's lives by heady talk, have been from hereabouts. Yet in the end we grow impatient, since, unlike the Irish, the Highland Celts are at bottom disconcertingly, even unpleasantly, practical. The class war in Glasgow was organized in a skilled, practical and even disciplined way. There are plenty on Clydeside to remember John MacLean, though his published speeches read as badly as forgotten sermons. It is at least likely that the organization of Shop Stewards would not have appeared odd to a Highlander of two hundred years before.

I know Edinburgh well enough. I feel easy there in my birthplace, the beautiful northern city, the half alive, emptied capital, the lilac-smelling squares of the New Town, the great amethyst shadow of the Castle Rock. Yet now, surely, I know Glasgow better. And I am always in two minds about this Glasgow. Edinburgh has two faces, one of beauty and order and the possibility of civilization: the other of conservatism and the dead hand—a little enthusiasm over the preservation of past beauty but none over the creation of new beauty along new lines. And Glasgow also has two faces. Neither is of beauty or order. It is a disgustingly ugly town, a huddle of dirty buildings trying to outdo one another and not succeeding, an overgrown village with no decent architecture except Blythswood Square and a few half-forgotten terraces, its ancient buildings hardly to be seen through the mess and squalor that surrounds them. Glasgow, 'the most uniform and prettiest' town that Burt saw on his eighteenth-century tour! The population is as ugly as the buildings. Walk down the Gallowgate; notice how many children you see with obvious rickets, impetigo or heads close clipped for lice, see the wild, slippered sluts, not caring any more to look decent! There is something queerly inappropriate about their bobbed heads, since shortened hair should either be elegantly dressed or else glow and wave with brushing; they have no money for hair-dressing, no energy for brushing; they went down with their men into the hell of unemployment and vile housing. They do not speak any real variety of Scots, but a blurred, debased English, or—since 1942—American. They lost everything, even the courage and solidarity that stopped London from panicking desperately during the blitzes, as Glasgow panicked in 1942. The other thing that will give you a good scunner in Glasgow is any place where the prosperous Glasgow businessmen congregate to eat—or drink. They have full as little use for beauty as those out of whose bodies the profits were made.

But yet through all one's anger against Glasgow, there is the other side. It is alive, it is full of hope and people wanting to be educated, wanting to try out something new, even though they don't rightly know what it is. And it is friendly—dirty and friendly and hospitable as a great slum tenement building or a Highland clan stronghold two hundred years ago. And it might be great and beautiful.

Naomi Mitchison, *The Bull Calves* (1947).

1948: The Humour of Glasgow

These thought-provoking observations were made by an Edinburgh-educated Canadian writer. As an exercise in stereotyping they can easily be disagreed with, but Augustus Muir makes a valiant attempt at getting to the root of the mutual antipathy between the two cities.

How different is the surface of life in Glasgow! The folk there are more like Londoners: they meet you half-way, they are quick, mercurial, ready-witted. they have an easy, friendly way with them: there is an intimacy even in the singing lilt of the Glasgow accent. And the humour of the two peoples is different. I should describe Edinburgh humour as slightly more grim and salty, with a deeper basis of realism, grappling with life rather than adorning it, with a readier response to the macabre and the incongruous, preferring metaphysical lapses rather than a glorious slip upon a piece of orange peel. Perhaps the humour of Glasgow shows a more fluid imagination; I think it is rather more nimble, has more of a sparkle; there is more of Falstaff's deep belly-rumble in Glasgow laughter. Is the difference due to climate: Edinburgh with its dry cold, its keen air, its occasional easterly haar that blows in from the North Sea; Glasgow with its gentler air, its moisture? Is the difference due to a greater proportion of Gaelic (including Irish) blood in Glasgow veins? You will hear that Glasgow lays more stress upon the power of money, Edinburgh upon the power of intellect: but at least it is discernible that Glasgow wears a more convivial smile, seems more determined to enjoy life than the city in the east, is more 'easy-come easy-go', and wears a jaunty feather in her bonnet, leaving Edinburgh to her mortar-board. Glasgow has fixed her route and knows where Destiny is leading her: she is pleased that Edinburgh should remain the capital city.

Augustus Muir, *Scottish Portrait* (1948).

1955: The Glasgow Bourgeoisie

The poet James Burns Singer (1928–1964) was born in New York but was brought up in the Glasgow area and worked in the Marine Biology Laboratory in Aberdeen from 1951 until moving to England in 1955. He published two collections of poetry and a vigorous prose book on fishing, *Living Silver*. This piece on Glasgow, while perhaps more balanced than Gibbon's or Muir's depiction, is nonetheless a strong, imaginative portrait, with an affection for the city's contradictions, matching Alexander Smith's description of a century before in *A Summer in Skye*.

Imagine therefore a city with a frontier of smoke, billowing inwards, fluffing outwards, as smoke will in the slightest breeze, and you will have some picture, though vague yet accurate, of the shape of Glasgow. Within that frontier everything is even more blurred than its edges. There is indeed a centre, the City centre, but it is backed on the North by some of the gentlest streets and most silent tenements that can be found in the whole area, and, apart from this central blob of tumult and business, and some sprawling suburbs, there are few distinctions. Residential areas meander confidently to the front door of industrial establishments. Slums and slums clearances lie like entangled lovers. Quietness collides with the sooty clank of traffic (This last aspect too may be accounted for by the geological structure, for the steep side of a drumlin is no easy place to build a tram-line or drive a yellow bus). But, whatever the reason, Glasgow is not the sort of zoned and centred city which is typical of Western Europe. Neither is it, like London, an enormous collection of little villages, each with its own highly individual character and some of them inflated into looking like the capital of an Imperial Power. No, Glasgow is homogeneously mixed, so that almost any square mile of it could be taken as representing the whole. The delightful way in which parks have been sprinkled like spots of green pepper throughout the amalgam is only a special instance of this peculiarity.

This vagueness in the boundaries is far from being limited to the boundaries of the city. It is found also in society, especially among the dominant middle classes. Petit bourgeois, grand bourgeois, bourgeois of all sizes, from the stately gentleman who offers you his assistance in fiddling those income-tax people to the little lady who informs you from behind a bundle of false teeth that nobody understands how difficult it is for the artist to keep his integrity, they are none of them very sure about the nature of society and they are all jealously uncertain about their own particular place in it.

In rabid contrast to this is the assured certainty with which the working classes judge their position, and I have always thought that I could detect an element of envy in the conventional hostility of the Glasgow bourgeois to their 'inferiors.' I can well remember how, at a meeting of a University political club, the scion of one of our families of senior colonial officials began to address his audience of incipient lawyers and scholiasts with the words: 'I presume that all of us present are members of the working class.' This admiration extends far beyond the level of undergraduate discussion. It can be found, under various guises, in industry, commerce, and the professions. Perhaps, indeed, it would be true to say of Glasgow, as of no other city in the Commonwealth, that a working class origin is there an advantage rather than a drawback to the ambitious young man.

The bourgeoisie attempts to make up for its lack of political and intellectual vigour and for the makeshift nature of its internal social categories by the universal device of snobbish exclusiveness. But, as I have already mentioned, this process is undermined by a certain amount of equivocation as to what precisely is to be regarded as a social asset. The envy, no matter how it may be disguised, that the middle class feel for the proletariat serves further to confuse the categories by which they try to cover their social nakedness. Poor Mrs A. is never sure which of her numerous accomplishments is *the* one—entitling her to the exalted position we are all so willing to concede to the good lady. Is it that her husband earns £3,000 p.a. and goodness knows what not in expenses? or maybe it is because she managed to get a B.A. after five years at Oxford? Or perhaps in the end she really deserves our esteem because grandfather, the old rogue, was a common journeyman who came up the hard way? According to the reason that happens to be uppermost in her mind, she fidgets about from one social grouping to another until each comes to think that she is far too free with her invitations and acceptances. Each group, as a group, would probably prefer to exclude her, yet as individuals they would never dream of suggesting such a thing since, as individuals, they are all in a similar situation. Thus, for all the feline concentration with which it is pursued, the art of being a successful snob in Glasgow is a rather unsatisfactory—almost a pathetic—imitation of the practice of England and the continent. The same could be said of all the attempts of the Clydeside bourgeoisie to be artistic.

There is a partial escape from it in the University. Even more than the other Scottish Universities, Glasgow retains its original character as the home of the 'lad o' pairts'—though, with the benevolent apparatus of local authority grants to aid them, an ever-increasing proportion of the lads and lasses have very few 'pairts.' Nevertheless, it can be said that in the work of instruction and the attitude of lecturers there is absolutely no class bias—not even that slight prejudice in favour of the brilliant proletarian to which I have already referred. In some undergraduate circles there is a tendency to exclusiveness but this is so slight, and so justifiable, that even it forms a pleasant contrast to the virulence of the outside world. In spite of this, however, it is impossible to treat the University seriously as a cultural influence *in* the city. Glasgow is too big for the University to exert more than the most tentative of civilising influences, and even within it the demands of practical science—engineering, medicine, teaching—are so great that the Arts, scientific or otherwise, tend to be swamped by a plethora of students who need a pass in order to get aboard one commercial band-wagon or another. Yet, within these strict limitations, there are men who do their great best to nurture that understanding of ourselves and others which is the only conceivable reason for our being here at all.

It would be impossible to over-estimate the extent to which students can be affected by such men, yet in the nature of things they can affect only a very few. No matter how extensive the educational system may become this number can never be substantially increased, for it is to a small minority that the unique qualities of their teaching reaches through. The majority is content to get over its exams, with Honours if necessary, but still to miss the point. Yet even this majority is but a small fraction of the population of the city. The remainder must learn from the city around them and it is it they must come to understand. Although it cannot rival its professors in subtlety or in delicate wisdom, the city is able to compensate to some extent by the size of what it does present and the urgency of its own presence.

I remember discovering this on the railway. It was in Buchanan Street Goods Station, 'the biggest in the country,' where I was employed for about three months. A huge parallelogram of steel and stone, it contains four or five large sheds, and was populated by hundreds of motor-lorries and a small infinity of very well-mannered horses. Railway trucks jolted down sidings to the main line. Motherwell, Lanark, Wishaw, names of places. Box cars open to the weather, refrigerated Italian models, dark covered waggons on steel wheels. And men smoking at back of them, in hiding under grotesque industrial objects. And a foreman prodding sensitively forward in search of dodgers. The tiny two-wheeled barrows would melt away beneath the loads they carried and the porters too would disappear behind them, so that boxes would come, emerging into domes of yellow light, square, oblong, spherical, huge tubes of linoleum, precarious piles of carbuoys, waltzing raggedly everywhere as though on their own initiative. I remember it now in all its variety of curses and cubes, the loitering over a fag-end and the abrupt surge of well-being as I found myself able to manage a heap of steel that seemed ten times my size, and I remember that as I watched some enormous pyramid wrapped in brown paper come cartwheeling towards me, I would ask myself with genuine wonder: Who wants this? Who could want anything so odd? And why?

Of course, I never found out, as I have never been able to discover why anybody ever wanted a city like Glasgow, or wanted to raise all those buildings and put people unceremoniously into them. Perhaps nobody did want it. Yet it was done. The buildings were erected and some of them demolished, the people were born and some of them were broken, and it was men who did it all.

Sometimes, though, remembering the mythical city of my childhood and my attempts to cure some adults of their belief in it, I remember the retort of one of them: 'Where there's smoke, there's fire.' And there is fire in Glasgow, a destructive element which gives off light and heat. From the industrial Aurora of Dixon's Blazes to the warmth in a smile across the counter, there is a consuming energy at work. It is at the heart and at the periphery. It is in all the apparently aimless trundling hither and thither of things that no-one can see the point of. Perhaps there is none to see. Perhaps the point is in the shifting, in the way things move and are moved by people who find no sense in them, people who change and are changed into the strangers they will never understand.

Burns Singer, 'Glasgow', *Saltire Review* (Spring 1955).

1957: X-Ray campaign against TB

Thirty-seven mobile radiography units were used in an intensive five-week campaign to identify as many TB carriers as possible in the city. The X-ray stations, some in vans visiting housing schemes, offices and factories, were manned by volunteers. Glasgow deaths from pulmonary tuberculosis were the highest in Britain (25 per thousand of population), but the 1957 campaign resulted in 715,000 people being screened. Media coverage and a weekly prize draw of X-ray cards ensured a good response, and the exercise was repeated in most other large cities, using the Glasgow campaign as a model. The following letter was sent to every household, signed by the city's Medical Officer of Health.

Dear Fellow Citizen,

I am writing to you about a matter of the greatest importance to yourself, your family and your city.

On Monday, 11th March, the city will launch a Mass X-ray Campaign which will last for five weeks and will be the greatest ever attack on tuberculosis.

During these weeks there will be an X-ray unit close to your home, and **everyone over 14 years of age should go for an X-ray.** This applies to the old as well as the young. There will be no undressing, and all results will be entirely confidential.

Of those X-rayed only a very few will be found to have anything wrong; but we must X-ray the many to find the few. It is those who are suffering from this disease and not having treatment who are the danger. I should like to stress, particularly for parents and grandparents, that only by going for an X-ray can you make sure your home is safe for children as well as adults.

Wonderful new treatments have greatly improved the outlook for patients with tuberculosis. More and more people are back at their old jobs completely cured within a few months. For those who require hospital treatment beds are available, and there will be financial help help for those who need it, during both treatment and convalescence.

Take this chance to check up on your health and make sure every member of your family over 14, young, middle-aged or old, does the same.

Please help us by completing the enclosed card and handing it to the voluntary worker who will call on you within the next few days.

Yours sincerely,

(Sgd.) Wm. A HORNE.

Glasgow's X-Ray Campaign against TB, Report by Town Clerk's Department, Glasgow Corporation.

1958: Jack House on Pubs and Dancing

These accounts of Glasgow's most popular indoor amusements in the post-war era are by that most percipient of the city's observers, Jack House. The wealth of incidental detail they contain shows how much social attitudes have changed in the interim. Of course, nearly all large dance halls have since closed. Today's equivalents, the discotheques, occupy less space whilst emitting at least as much sound. Hugh Macdiarmid described Glasgow pubs as 'Frowsy and fusty enough to suit my taste', but by now the evil reputation of the city's licensed premises (720 of them in 1983) should have withered away.

Dance Halls

Dancing is tremendously popular in Glasgow and there is a higher proportion of dance halls to the population than anywhere else in the British Isles. The standard of dancing was considered, up till 1940, the best in Britain. Experts now say that the standard has deteriorated because of such 'foreign' influences as the arrival of American soldiers and sailors. Although the standard may have deteriorated, the number of dancers is still enormous, and many of the patrons of the big ballrooms attend four or five times a week. In a recent broadcast from Barrowland Dance Hall in the Gallowgate, a girl said that she danced seven nights a week—six nights at Barrowland and Sunday night at a special dance club.

There are more than 30 licensed dance halls in Glasgow, and a large number of small halls where dances, as distinct from 'dancing,' are held. No dance hall in Glasgow is licensed for the sale of alcohol, and trouble is sometimes caused by young men bringing in bottles secretly and drinking from them in the lavatory. This is sternly discouraged. The occasional fights, followed by police court appearances, on Friday and Saturday nights are most often caused because doorkeepers will not allow 'drunks' to enter.

Dennistoun Palais holds 1,700 dancers and is the biggest dance hall in Glasgow. The Plaza is renowned as the place where family parties go, particularly for twenty-first birthday celebrations. 'Jiving' is not encouraged in any of the big dance halls, but one, the Locarno, has experimented in having a special space apart for 'jivers.'

Many private and club dances are held in Glasgow, in hotels, Masonic halls, community centres and church halls. Less than 30 years ago most churches would not countenance dances, and church youth clubs held what were euphemistically called 'socials.' At some of these the number of dances was restricted to, say, four. But there was no restriction on 'games,' so the organisers would include The Grand Old Duke of York, the Eightsome Reel and items of a similar nature as games. Each of the four dances lasted for at least a quarter of an hour. Nowadays church youth clubs are, in the main, unrestricted, and no longer have to call their dances 'socials.'

. . .

Pubs

Glasgow public houses have been indicted for many years for their lack of social amenities, particularly as compared with the standards of Southern England. There are 1,083 pubs in Glasgow, and it is probably true that about half of them do not reach the English standard. It must be said, however, that all of them have reasonable lavatory accommodation, which is far ahead of the English standard.

'Perpendicular drinking' has been said to be the trouble with Glasgow pubs, and it has even been suggested that the Glasgow invention of square-toed shoes was to enable the Glasgow man to get closer to the bar. (Square-toed shoes were invented by Mr. Alexander Somerville, who left his money to found the St. Mungo Prize, which amounts to approximately £1,000 and is awarded every three years to the person who has done most for the city in the three preceding years.)

But many Glasgow pubs now have lounges, mostly 'modern' affairs of chromium, concealed lighting and imitation leather in scarlet or bright blue. These lounges are for both sexes, and the price of drink is generally slightly higher than in the ordinary bar. There are still a fair number of pubs in Glasgow where women are not admitted, and it is only in pubs at the top and the bottom of the social scale that women are allowed to stand or sit at the bar.

Whisky, in spite of its price, and beer are still the most popular beverages in pubs, and visitors are still surprised at the Glasgow man's addiction to the 'Hauf an' a hauf pint'—a half glass (or nowadays it may be a 'nip') of whisky, and a half pint of beer. In some of the lower quarters of the city, whisky is thought to be too dear, and the customary combination now is a glass of cheap red wine and a half pint of beer. Pubs which sell this combination are known as 'wine shops,' and are not notable for their amenities.

Drinking habits have improved considerably in the slum districts of the city. During the 'depressed' years of the early 1930's, there were two drinks known as 'jake' and 'red biddy.' These were mixtures of methylated spirits and cheap red wine. It was said that a favourite practice of drinkers who wished to achieve oblivion as quickly and as cheaply as possible was to attach a tube to the gas bracket on the stair landing of a tenement and allow a 'whiff' of the gas to enter a glass of milk. While it is known that this was done, it was not a general practice at all, and it gained fame because it was mentioned in newspaper reports.

Scent drinking was popular at one time, and is still known in Glasgow. Any cheap scent will satisfy the addict, but the favourite for years has been an Eau de Cologne, which costs about sixpence for a small bottle.

Before World War II experts on oblivion said it was possible to be drunk for a fortnight on 10½d. At that time the addict could buy sixpenceworth of spirits of salts (forbidden now) from any chemist. He also bought a large bottle of lemonade, which then cost fourpence ha'penny. Into the bottom of a tumbler he put a very little spirits of salts, and filled up the tumbler with lemonade. When he swallowed this mixture he rapidly became unconscious. As soon as the addict had regained consciousness (a period of time depending on the proportions of the two ingredients in the concoction), he took a glass of water. The action of the water made him drunk again. Once again, when he recovered, he took another drink of water, and kept on drinking water until it no longer had any effect. He then made a new mixture of spirits of salts and lemonade and started the process all over again. By ringing the liquid changes in this way, he could—it was said by experts in the matter—remain drunk for two weeks.

This sort of extra-mural activity has nothing to do with the Glasgow public houses. Possibly the most remarkable feature of Glasgow pub life is its geography. Glasgow Town Council do not look with favour on the provision of licences in new suburbs, and there are also some residential districts which use the Local Veto to 'protect' their area. Thus, in the Exchange Ward of the city there are 231 licensed premises for a population of 23,872 (one for every 108 persons living in the ward); in the Gorbals there are 112 licensed premises for a population of 40,525; in Maryhill there are 17 licensed premises for a population of 25,744; in Dennistoun there are four for 27,902; in Provan one for 21,010. And there are no licensed premises at all in three wards—Whiteinch, Knightswood and Cathcart.

In one street in the East End of Glasgow, the Gallowgate, there are 66 pubs. Many of the people who lived round the Gallowgate are now living in newly built Glasgow suburbs which have no pubs at all. At present the majority of men who have 'flitted' to a new suburb and who like a drink travel to their former neighbourhoods and use the pubs with which they are familiar.

There are strict rules in Glasgow pubs against singing, music (apart from that provided by a radio set), and any other game but dominoes and draughts. These restrictions, plus 'Temperance' propaganda, have given rise to the prevalent idea that most Glasgow pubs are mere 'drinking dens' and have no social function. While this is true of a small proportion of Glasgow pubs (and particularly the 'wine shops'), the amount of social activity in pubs used by working-class men is considerable. Many of these men do regard the pub as a club.

Some Glasgow pubs have an annual outing to the country or the sea. Customers pay a small subscription every week, and a committee arranges the details. An outing held by the customers of The Wee Man in the Gallowgate, for example, was to Rothesay on a Sunday. Some 50 men turned up at the Central Station. The rendezvous was the gentlemen's lavatory beside Platform 13. There each man received tickets allowing him a half glass of whisky or a bottle of beer, and had time to have a drink before the train left for Wemyss Bay. The party travelled in reserved coaches each labelled The Wee Man. They varied widely in age, but most would be between 30 and 40. They carried with them cases of whisky and beer, two footballs, a trumpet, a wig and false moustache. As soon as they boarded the steamer at Wemyss Bay, they started a concert, in which the trumpet, the wig and the false moustache were all used.

At Rothesay they went straight to a large hotel and had luncheon. Two 'buses were waiting outside the hotel and immediately after luncheon took the party to Ettrick Bay. There they played football, paddled, and took part in various forms of athletics. A temporary bar was set up and those who had tickets left were able to have a drink. Then the 'buses took the party back to the hotel for high tea, which was followed by speeches and 'harmony,' when most of the songs and choruses which had been sung aboard the steamer were sung again.

On the journey back in the steamer the party held yet another concert on the deck, and a large number of day trippers from Glasgow not only joined in the singing but also provided several individual 'turns.' Perhaps it should be stressed here that steamer bars do not open on a Sunday, and that the high spirits were not artificially inspired.

This kind of pub outing should not be confused with the Sunday outings arranged by some groups of Glaswegians who want to take advantage of the 'bona fide traveller' law and who hire 'buses to take them on a tour of country hotels for the purpose of drinking.

In recent years a number of well-known footballers have become associated with Glasgow pubs as proprietors or managers. Football is the principal subject of conversation in any Glasgow pub, so footballers' pubs are generally popular. In at least one of them there was the additional attraction that the customer could be photographed receiving his drink from the hands of his hero.

Jack House, 'Community Life', from *The Third Statistical Account of Scotland: Glasgow*, edited by J. Cunnison and J. B. S. Gilfillan (1959).

1958: End of the Line for the Trams

The heyday of the Glasgow trams was before the First World War, when fares were still ½d a mile and the network stretched from from Dalmuir to Uddingston and from Giffnock to Bishopbriggs. But by the 1940s the Corporation were introducing trolley and motor buses which were quieter and less likely to cause traffic snarl-ups in the city centre. When Liverpool scrapped its trams, Glasgow bought the Green Goddesses as an economy measure to keep the service going. But during the 1950s the network was inexorably pruned. In 1958 the *Glasgow Herald* commented favourably on the plan to phase out the tramway system by the early '60s, but this writer had different hopes.

It is not uncommon in Renfield Street, for instance at the rush hour, for several blocks to be jammed solid with tramcars, so that when the lights change, traffic cannot move forward, because the next block is full. Among the worst places for congestion are Clyde Street and the Broomielaw, at the approach to the bridges; Argyle Street, between Hope Street and Glassford Street; the stretch of Hope Street beside the Central Station, where there are three sets of traffic lights in less than a hundred yards; Renfield Street; the lower part of Buchanan Street; and Sauchiehall Street, between Renfield Street and Cambridge Street. A survey by the Road Research Laboratory indicated that the average speed of traffic through Central Glasgow was appreciably slower than through Central London, with its wider streets and less frequent junctions. A recent report would suggest that the position is getting worse, for whereas the Road Research Laboratory gave the average speed attainable in early 1952 as about nine miles per hour, a Corporation spokesman stated in September, 1957, that this had fallen to seven miles per hour.

. . .

Within the city and a number of immediately surrounding areas, public road-passenger services are provided by the Corporation Transport Department, which operates trams, motor buses, trolleybuses and the municipal Underground Railway. Glasgow is still the great stronghold of the tramcar, and in fact it now has about half the trams still operating in Britain, though even here they are beginning to be displaced. The compactly built nature of the city made it well suited for tramway operation, which needs a dense traffic to make use of the higher carrying capacity of the trams, and thus spread their higher maintenance and capital costs over more passengers. Even in 1955–56, when a number of tram routes had already been abandoned, out of a total of 661 million passengers carried on the system, the trams still accounted for 367 million, as against 215 million on the motor buses, 44 million on the trolleybuses and 34 millon on the Underground.

Nevertheless, it has been becoming increasingly clear in recent years that a change will have to be made. Although Glasgow has about 300 modern bogie cars, nearly all built since 1938 and many of them almost brand new, it also has about 600 old four-wheeled cars, some of which are up to fifty years old. The decision to scrap these has already been taken, and once they are replaced the modern Coronation cars will then be due for replacement. According to the Transport Manager's figures, the capital cost of replacement of the old trams by modern trams would be £11,230,000, as against £5,539,000 for motor buses and £7,412,000 for trolleybuses. Certainly, the average life of a tram is much greater, but against this must be set the need to reconstruct the track.

At the time of writing the controversy is still raging in the local press, for the Glaswegian has a strong attachment to his 'caurs', with memories going back to the model service they gave in the days of the late Mr Dalrymple before 1914. It is true that a tram holds more people and that you can read in it. It is true that modern trams on good track can be comfortable, and if it were possible to run coupled, single-deck cars at high speeds on their own tracks, as in some Continental cities, there might be much to be said for them. But this cannot be done in the Glasgow streets, and meanwhile the trams cause congestion and their rails and cobbles make the streets bumpy and dangerous for other traffic. Moreover, though trams last longer than buses, they are route-bound and their services cannot easily be adapted to changing traffic needs. Already Edinburgh and Dundee have replaced their trams and Aberdeen has also recently done so, while in most of the English cities they have either disappeared or are on the point of doing so. Whatever the final decision in Glasgow, however, they are likely to remain for another twenty years or so.

J.F. Sleeman, 'Transport in Glasgow', in *The Glasgow Region* (1958).

1960: The Cheapside Street Fire

Until fairly recently in many Scottish towns and cities whisky bonds were situated close to shops and housing. Early in the evening of March 28th 1960 smoke was reported rising from a warehouse on Cheapside Street (now the line of the Kingston Bridge northern approach road) which contained more than one million gallons of whisky and rum in casks. Although the first fire engines arrived within three minutes, the seat of the fire could not be located and shortly afterwards the warehouse erupted. The situation was not brought under control for another ten hours, by which time it was discovered that nineteen firemen (from the Glasgow Fire Service and Salvage Corps) had been lost in the blaze. No other lives were lost, but it was the worst Fire Service disaster in peacetime. In the 1960s many of the city's fire stations, some nearly 100 years old, were replaced with new buildings. This extract is from a report on the fire.

... the crews and appliances now located in Warroch Street (i.e. at rear of premises) were continuing to investigate the earlier report by the civilian that flame had been seen issuing from the upper level windows of the Bonded Warehouse sections, and for such purpose the turntable ladder was brought into operation to allow examination of all upper levels including the roof area, but no trace of flame could be observed.

At about this time the Managing Director of Messrs. Arbuckle Smith & Co., Ltd., arrived at the scene, he having been in town when he was attracted by Fire Service appliances proceeding due west whereat many premises owned by this firm were located, and his natural curiosity prompted him to follow on perchance any of his premises being involved, which in fact proved to be so. With this knowledge of the layout of the premises, and in response to a request by Fire Service personnel who explained their difficulty in gaining access to the apparent location of the fire, he took them to the rear of the premises in Warroch Street and there directed the attention of Fire Service personnel to the emergency doors located at ground level and positioned one to each of the three sections forming the main building—i.e., No. 1 Bonded Warehouse occupying the centre section, with No. 2 Bond on its north side and the Tobacco Bond on its south side.

Under his guidance Fire Service personnel broke down one of the timber emergency doors, and thus entry was gained to the building, but it was soon realised that there was no sign of fire or smoke in this section, and indeed that they had entered the Tobacco Warehouse. No doubt the excitement of the situation confused the Managing Director in his well-intentioned assistance.

Fire Service personnel then proceeded to the next rear door which would have taken them into the rear of No. 1 Bonded Store, but as this door was metal-lined and bolted internally, it proved difficult to force an entry despite the use of heavy axes, etc.

Some little time prior to this, firemen in Warroch Street saw a glow of flame through the ground floor window of No. 1 Bond, and accordingly a charged hose line operating from a hatch ladder was directed into the area of flame. The flame was unique both in respect of its colour and position. It had the characteristic purplish-blue colouring associated with alcohol, and was located on the underside of the first floor—that is the ground floor ceiling.

. . .

As the Assistant Firemaster gave the instruction to radio for further assistance he was approaching the fire location from the south end of Cheapside Street when an explosion occurred, whereby the front and rear walls of the No. 1 Bonded Warehouse were blown outwards into Cheapside Street and Warroch Street respectively.

. . .

Due to the extensive dimensions of the premises with frontages in Cheapside Street and Warroch Street, it was not at first realised that the explosive forces had a through-and-through effect causing collapse in both streets simultaneously. There was no prior warning whatsoever of an impending explosion, and all witnesses suggest that the type of explosion was unique in so far as the sound was not violent as with detonation, but was more like an echoed 'Whoosh' followed by the thud of falling debris. The impression was one of the sudden release of high pressure.

Martin Chadwick, Firemaster, *Report of the Glasgow Fire Disaster* (1960).

1960: The Appeal of the Merchant City

The 'British place-taster', Ian Nairn (c. 1925–1979), after his visit to Glasgow, lamented that 'it is usually only the slums that receive the publicity'. During his four-day study of the city's principal streets and buildings he was strongly impressed by the Merchant City area, then under threat from the Inner Ring Road proposals (see 1971). This area, stretching from High Street/Saltmarket to Union Street/Jamaica Street, contains most of the city's pre-Victorian buildings. Nairn is not correct in every detail: Duke Street prison had been demolished the previous year. He also makes the Tolbooth Steeple ('The Cross') a century too old and neglects to mention that it and the Merchants' Steeple are only surviving remnants of larger buildings. His account perceptively contrasts this jumble of churches, markets and warehouses with the later Victorian town-planning to the north and west. Thirty years after Nairn, as new, domestic uses are found for old buildings, we are beginning to appreciate the Merchant City again.

Glasgow was a shock to me. It was only my second visit, and I had expected something like a vast Scottish mixture of the worst of Leicester and Liverpool, with a few outstanding buildings embedded in it. Instead I found what is without any doubt the most friendly of Britain's big cities, and probably the most dignified and coherent as well. In looks it is much more like the best parts of some American cities—Boston or Philadelphia—than anywhere in England; but a walk along any of the streets will show the difference. In America (this is no idle generalization, because I have pounded many miles of American urban sidewalk) the average casual contact is unpleasant, a mixture of indifference and neurosis. Any Glasgow walk is inflected by a multitude of human contacts—in shops, under umbrellas (there *is* a good deal of rain in Glasgow), even from policemen—and each of them seems to be a person-to-person recognition, not the mutual hate of cogs in a machine who know their plight but cannot escape it.

. . .

Glasgow is so coherent and so strongly patterned that it is worth while to describe it chronologically. Medieval Glasgow was at the east end of the present city, running down from the cathedral to the river. The cathedral I want to leave until last, except to say that it is one of the best Gothic buildings in Britain; all the rest has gone except one moderate house (Provands Lordship) on the west side of Cathedral Square. High Street, the medieval axis, is an astounding mixture of utilities, the roaring underbelly of coherence: it contains a passenger station, two goods stations, a gaol, a waterworks, and (at the corner of Bell Street) the best warehouse in Glasgow, the Bell Street Stores, a six-storey stone monolith so sheer that pilasters and drainpipes an inch or so thick are sufficient punctuation. The Bell Street front is very slightly curved, providing the same effect as entasis in a Greek column.

Bell Street is next door to Glasgow Cross, a splendid five-ways *non sequitur* of traffic, without benefit of traffic lights or policemen (in all seriousness the anarchy is probably as efficient here as any sort of traffic control). The Cross itself is sixteenth century, and only just reprieved from demolition; with two other steeples it just about represents Glasgow between John Knox and the Act of Union. One, the Tolbooth, is just a jolly bit of fun; the other, the Merchants' Exchange, is a deliberate design, done by Sir William Bruce who built Holyrood Palace, the three receding stages with their homely proportions a faint, distant echo of Amsterdam. There is far more Continental influence in Scottish architecture (first French, then Dutch) than there ever is in English, just as Glasgow and Edinburgh frequently look more European and more metropolitan than London.

With the eighteenth century Glasgow's story stops being a matter of individual buildings and becomes a kind of topographical epic with the buildings as incidents, good though they are. Until the breakdown of classical traditions (which in Glasgow was not until the eighteen-eighties) the whole sum of building is the struggle to get a style which matches the Glaswegian spirit at the same time as money is available to build it (this, I suppose, in its feckless way, is a kind of universal truth). It is like a Beethoven symphony played over 150 years, and this working out in time has power that superimposes itself on the topography. At every street corner you know where you are in time as well as in space—not as an antiquarian exercise but through the living pattern of the city. Where Newcastle is superimposition, and the pattern is the shock of contrast, Glasgow is one organic growth like a vast forest tree. And lucky accidents caused it to grow tree-like up and out in one direction, to the west.

. . .

The whole city took it up in about 1820, and moved westward along the steep slopes of the ridge running parallel to the Clyde. The plan was, more or less, a grid laid across the hillside, and hence there is the exciting San Francisco pattern of almost level streets along the slopes and extremely steep short streets up and down them. Every building gains in effect by being seen from underneath on the next road downhill. St. Vincent's Church and the Art School, which will appear later, both exploit this. Blythswood Square is the set-piece, but really this is an architecture of perspectives not of enclosures (the opposite of Edinburgh) and it is the total effect of a half-mile stretching into (usually) the mist that is so magnificent—Bath Street or St. Vincent Street. It is even serviceable enough and tolerant enough to make a fine marriage with unabashed commercialism (a very different thing from forcing tidiness on to a cheerful hegemony) and so Sauchiehall Street, the Oxford Street of Glasgow, has a sparkle and a scale that I have never met in any other honky-tonk street (and not only never met: I would have said it was impossible). One of the nicest things about looking at towns for a living is that you realize, eventually, that nothing is impossible. Here for once, the gridiron plan is really working for its living.

Ian Nairn, 'Britain's Changing Towns V', *The Listener*, 27 October 1960.

1965: Edwin Morgan on Glasgow Culture

Twenty years before Glasgow District Council's 'Miles Better' campaign the poet Edwin Morgan (b. 1920) noted the portents in this brave attempt to find indicators of change in the city's lifestyle. The cultural stirrings have now become a whirlpool: the Buchanan Street complex is nearing reality; STV's Theatre Royal (originally opened in 1895) has been restored to its former splendour by Scottish Opera; in the Gorbals almost everything has been demolished except the Citizens'; the Close Theatre has gone, but there is now the Tron; and the facelift of the city's buildings has proceeded apace. The writer's less than total enthusiasm for conservationists ('Prop up's the motto. Splint the dying age,' he later wrote in *Glasgow Sonnets VII*) should, however, be noted.

Anyone who has lived for a while in Glasgow knows that it isn't all rivets and razors and that as far as entertainment and culture are concerned—on a year-round basis, and discounting such bonus events as the Edinburgh Festival—it's possibly better off than any city outside London. Yet the image persists of a grim place and an uncouth folk: a fearsome porridge stirred up from vague recollections of *No Mean City*, *Miracle in the Gorbals*, and the tartan tammies, ricketies and raucous cries of our periodical descent on Wembley. There's some truth in the image. A certain forthrightness in Glasgow behaviour is not to be got over, and can cause trouble. A young man taken to court recently for assaulting a bus conductor in Argyle Street admitted the charge but is reported as having said:

I was sitting beside my wife and not bothering anyone. My feet were in the passageway and he asked me to get them in. When I wouldn't he kicked them in. I waited till my wife was off the bus then I hit him. I thought he deserved it.

And certainly it wouldn't be Glasgow without the highly animated scene in George Square at half past midnight on Saturday or Sunday morning, when a gay but wild mob hot from the dancing fights its way into the all-night buses bound for the huge Drumchapel housing estate. On one such occasion I heard a struggling matron, swept along in the torrent, cry in the anguished tones of Kelvinside: 'It's just disgraceful! Where are the police?' This got a big laugh. Someone cried. 'Are you kiddin'?' I could see two policemen grinning in the background as they watched over this commonplace operation. It's fun, life in Glasgow, so long as you don't weaken!

But the bad days of the gangs of the Twenties and Thirties, which cling like burrs to the image of Glasgow, are over, and Gorbals itself, though many slums still remain in it, is being steadily transformed, demolition by demolition, into the impressively spaced bastions and towers of Sir Basil Spence and Sir Robert Matthew. Clusters of white 'scrapers' (as Glaswegians familiarly call them) are pushing up everywhere out of the grey (or more often black) Victorian sprawl. The redevelopment plan, involving 29 areas of the city and the eventual construction of over 200 tower blocks, with the highest flats in Europe among them (the 31-storey Red Road massif, now taking shape), is staggeringly ambitious. A Glasgow Hilton has been discussed; it would certainly not be out of place. Redevelopment has concentrated on housing, since slums were and are Glasgow's major social problem. But we are to have an arts centre too, on the site of Buchanan Street goods station: a complex which will probably include a large concert hall (to replace the Scottish National Orchestra's former home in the St Andrew's Halls, gutted by fire), a civic threatre (for general and amateur use), a smaller theatre (for the Citizens' Theatre company, whose Gorbals premises are scheduled for demolition), an exhibition gallery, and a restaurant.

These are plans, and plans are signs and wonders. But what sort of reality have we got to meet the plan? There seems no doubt that things are beginning to stir again culturally in Glasgow. New art galleries are springing up and the active Glasgow Group of painters recently started a Glasgow Group Society (members get a 20 per cent discount on works purchased) which testifies to growing public interest. This year has also seen a renewed awareness of Glasgow's architecture. As more and more buildings are cleaned and 'treated for starlings', and as the smokeless zones begin to spread, the forgotten splendours of the Victorian city emerge again from the grime. The New Glasgow Society was inaugurated in April (behind the specially floodlit columns of 'Greek' Thomson's extraordinary church in St Vincent Street) to keep an eye on our Victoriana and at the same time to 'encourage high standards of architecture and town planning in the Glasgow region'. These two aims aren't always compatible, and there have been battles between preservationists and developers, but at least buildings are being discussed and looked at again.

In music, there's the growing success of the Scottish Opera Company, marked this year by an ambitious and powerful performance of *Boris Godunov*, to add to the regular concerts and proms of the Scottish National Orchestra.

For those who prefer Beatstalkers to John Ogdon, the open-air lunch-time concerts in George Square are ready with scenes of mad enthusiasm. At one of these pop concerts in June, the fans forced the performers to flee and take refuge in the City Chambers, losing bits of their clothing on the way.

As for theatre, one must always rejoice cautiously, but it does seem that the worst days of recession and closing down are over. We have lost the Empire to the property developers, and the Royal is now the headquarters of Scottish Television. The surviving theatres rely on a standard diet of revue, musical, pantomime and light play, with occasional visits from Sadler's Wells or the Royal Ballet. A pungent native humour, reductive and extravagant, is kept going by comedians like Rikki Fulton and Jack Milroy, Lex McLean, Clark and Murray, and a show will be advertised as 'the biggest laugh since granny's ceiling fell in'. In straight drama, there have been two interesting developments this year. One is the decision of the Citizens' Theatre (which celebrated its 21st birthday in 1964) to start an experimental offshoot called the Close Theatre Club, in premises seating about 150, 'up a close' beside the parent company; this is expected to begin production in September. The other is the emergence of Glasgow University's Arts Theatre Group, playing in the university theatre, as a spearhead of intelligently produced drama.

Traditionally, you think of Glasgow as being dancing mad, fitba' daft, and fond of its pint. But the pattern is changing. There's no doubt as much dancing as ever, and the sharply-dressed queues still shuffle into the brilliant portals of the Locarno and the other big ballrooms. They are lured by day as well as by night, with lunch-time disc sessions. But the beat, jazz and folk clubs offer the strong competition of a more intimate atmosphere. And then there's the *Maid of the Loch* on its 'showboat cruise' up Loch Lomond, with two bars if the jazz makes you dry: five hours for eight-and-six, not bad? Glasgow is still very much a football city, but 'the gemme' isn't the obsession it once was when there were fewer alternatives. Geodesic domes over Hampden and Ibrox might help to repeople the terraces, but there's still television and 10-pin bowling to pull in another direction. Neither standing shivering nor standing drinking seems quite so much in the inescapable order of things as it once did. New pubs, new restaurants, new hotels have multiplied in the last few years, and Glasgow has found itself liking Chinese, Indian, Italian and Scandinavian food as a sudden extension of its naturally embracing and now very cosmopolitan soul.

But however Glasgow changes, it seems likely to remain a place of strong character. I've seen and liked a lot of cities, from Paris and Moscow to Cairo and Beirut, but there's a peculiar quality about Glasgow (it certainly isn't charm) that fascinates and leaves its indelible mark. It's partly the lingering violent mythology of the slums and the gangs and the sagas of the shipyards, partly what survives in things like the Orange Walk, which with its banners and sashes and songs and trot has become folk art, a social ritual deprived of much of its religious bitterness. It has something to do with the paradox that a city which is in some ways very sophisticated (much more sophisticated than Edinburgh, for example—Edinburgh is a city which has never eaten the apple, but Glasgow has, and although it is deeper in sin it is readier for grace) is at heart rough, careless, vulnerable and sentimental, its people using and expending freely everything a modern city has to offer, not out of civic-mindedness but for purposes of sheer human enjoyment.

The Christmas lights are a case in point. Glasgow boasts that its Christmas decorations are 'the best in the country'. I'm inclined to agree with the claim. Sauchiehall Street, Renfield Street, Buchanan Street, and Argyle Street—the main shopping routes—are canopied with a fantastic glitter which culminates in a riotous kinetic centrepiece in George Square. There are special buses in the evenings to 'see the lights'; the shops do a roaring trade; people come in from far and near and the streets are blocked with cars. This image of the great dark industrial city blazing with a source of simple widespread pleasure—something childlike in the enjoyment, yet something fitting in the extravagance of the display—is one that appeals to me very much, and it's perhaps the one that most nearly shows the soul of the place.

Edwin Morgan, 'Signs and Wonders', *New Statesman*, 13 August 1965.

1968: High-rise Living

As large areas of tenements were cleared they were in some cases replaced with multi-storey flats, making a dramatic impact on the city's skyline. The earliest tower blocks were little more than ten storeys, but by the mid-60s the 31-storey Red Road flats were under construction. Although high-level living is now judged to create as many social problems as it solves, the first Corporation tenants were delighted with their new homes—although some problems were already apparent. These passages are taken from a summary of findings from 15,000 interviews with high-rise dwellers in the city. There is a reference to Hurricane Low Q which, with gusts of 102 mph, brought down more than a thousand chimney-heads and left thousands more houses with tarpaulins as roofs for years to come. It took place in the early morning of Monday January 15th.

Many families were enormously set up, almost awed with their high flat when they first saw it and they continued to point out its physical attractions even when they had been there for some years. Its brightness, airiness and modernity were a fantastic contrast to the gaunt and gloomy places so many had lived in previously. To have a bathroom outweighed even the dream kitchen or the under-floor heating. A mother pointed to her 3-year-old who, acustomed to being washed in the sink, would splash about for ever in this lovely shiny bath. They showed the snow-white toilet next to the bath and some recalled the horrors they had known, maybe a murky, unlighted den off a stone passage outside the house. The snugness of one's home matters a lot in a Northern climate, and comfort was a word constantly in use by people of all ages, children as well as pensioners. The flat's cleanliness was another thing they talked of. The place was practically dust free and shoes brought little dirt into the home since the approach was via lift hall, lift and across the polished tiles of the floor hall. They also considered that health should benefit from the cleaner atmosphere though there is considerable uncertainty as to how far the air really is purer. Evidence about the possible effects of height above ground in relation to air pollution from smoke, sulphur dioxide, etc, suggests that in periods of high wind almost any variation is possible. Decrease of pollution with height is most evident in periods of general calm. The tenants themselves also pointed out that when the children played outside the block they got more sunshine here than they did in the old streets where the 60-feet-high tenements cast such long shadows. The powerful electric lighting about the block's entrance and of all the common areas was cheerful compared to the wan and minimal bulbs on the stairs of the old tenement. Then too the flat was so convenient. There was no coal to get in and no grates to clean. The low ceilings and swivel-hung windows saved lugging a stepladder about, and you tipped your rubbish into a chute instead of having to hump the bin up and down stairs. 'You can do the week's wash, get Billy up, have dinner ready and be done for the day easily between 9 and 12.' Another satisfactory feature of the flat which almost every adult referred to spontaneously was the view. In the old home they had so often looked out on to a dreary street or the broken-down washhouses of a back close. 'Now we look out and see shrubs and things.' Even should the nearer prospect be dullish, the distant one was nearly always fine and it could be breathtaking— a sweep of perhaps 15 miles, or even a glimpse of Arran, 40 miles away. 'I could sit a couple of hours looking at the lights,' said an elderly man.

The actual height of their block, the sheer drop, did not seem to worry the tenants. Perhaps because those who were nervous about such things had excluded themselves. On the other hand, there seemed to be some feeling that 10 floors or so was the desirable limit. At a pinch one can walk up this number of flights and it is just possible for adult and child to maintain a brief bawled conversation with each other.

. . .

Facilities for laundry aroused a good deal of adverse comment. Just a few blocks had communal laundries on the ground floor, the only suitable place because of the weight and noise of the equipment needed. There was no overt demand for the communal laundry and no strong evidence that it had the social assets ascribed to it in the case of some of the high flats in, for example, London and Sheffield. The tenants' real problem was not the washing as such, which could readily be done inside the flat or at a laundrette, but getting things dried. There were many nostalgic memories of 'our lovely old drying green'. The blocks had various types of drying areas for shared use that were semi-open to the air. These might be up on the roof, or at the base of the block, or on intermediate floors. Or each floor might have a locked electric drying cupboard with a meter. Some had an electric cupboard inside the flat. Most tenants approved the Councils' ruling that balconies should not be used for (visible) drying—'you can't have towers draped in underclothes'. On the other hand even if the flat had its own drying cupboard this was insufficient for a sizeable wash, and shared facilities gave endless troubles over theft, vandalism and rows with other users.

. . .

Complete breakdown due to an external cause such as an electricity failure or a strike is one of the hazards that faces the lift user. Glasgow's 1968 hurricane cut off the electricity in certain blocks. At Red Road some families had the alarming experience of walking down to the ground floor, the children terrified because unfamiliar with the shadows cast by a candle. A few months later a strike of maintenance men meant that, in a number of cases, one of the block's two lifts was out of action for up to three weeks. One mother told how she had to lug a pram and toddler up 18 flights; on another estate a man walked up and down to a 17th floor four times in one day; in another case an invalid had stumbled down 9 flights, unaided but for her two sticks. The lifts also vary in their basic reliability, in the efficiency of their firm's servicing, and in the caretaker's ability to deal with the minor troubles he is authorised to handle.

Any block with a high proportion of children is especially vulnerable. There is always a critical stage, the early days of the block's occupation, when both the children of the block and those of the vicinity 'play the lift', using it like a super yo-yo. Trouble also tends to occur when the load is heavy, i.e. when school comes out, and during the holidays. Another strain is caused by the small child who can only reach the button by jumping, using a stick, etc. One real sinner, in that he holds up the lift, is the milk boy who props its door open with his crate while he collects from perhaps 16 flats. Or on a quiet floor footballers have been known to use the lift cage for a goal!

The necessity to use a lift can have odd repercussions on the tenant's daily life. Somehow one needs to be tidy if going in the lift. Thus it deters people from popping out in their slippers for the odd bit of shopping, or seeing what the kids are up to. Or again, there is the pensioner who, if he has to use the lift, won't bother to take a turn round the estate before the evening sets in. The occasional whiff of fresh air, and the occasional brief spell away from the rest of the household, are useful in terms of health and temper: but they have gone as far as the 'typical' flat-dweller is concerned. That the lift may even dictate the pattern of the tenant's day was shown in the case of the mother who never went out in the afternoon because of the risks of the early evening queues which meant she could not be sure of getting back in time. She was also liable to incur black looks if her pram stopped others from squeezing on to the lift, a matter that did not make for good relationships within the block. The lift's uncertainties had other repercussions. People spoke of the difficulties doctors had in getting to their patients because of lifts not coming, or out of order, and of workmen who went away disgusted with their jobs not done.

Pearl Jephcott, *Homes in High Flats* (1971).

1968: Anatomy of a Gang

The high point of the Glasgow street gangs was the 1930s until the newly-appointed Chief Constable, Percy Sillitoe, incarcerated most of the leaders (as he had preciously done in Sheffield). The 1930s gangs were sectarian, perpetrating much of their violence at football grounds or dance halls. By the 1960s the gangs were amorphous, performing the tribal function of providing security and some form of identity in featureless housing schemes or decaying inner city areas. The close mouth and the street corner were traditional gang meeting-places: most people saw only the spray-painted slogans. Here a journalist who made contact with a Townhead gang is struck by the aimlessness of its members.

There are about 150 YY Shamrock, hard children who hang around Dundas Street and Parliamentary Road, an area of betting shops, cheap cafés and cigarette kiosks near Queen Street railway station and the main bus station, before Sauchiehall street begins. The core, 30 to 40 strong, stopping women in the street and cadging cigarettes, jumping on the back of moving scooters, are mostly unemployed, sporadically violent and dangerous—but still with the bravado which is only the steel-plating of the very immature young.

Peter is 17, and produced a new, stolen breadknife as credentials the second time I met him. He has short, fluffy hair and a large area of acne spots along his jaw. He scratches himself when he talks to you, and his arms push into the air in short jerks. He has a job as a pipe insulator, but gets away early and is usually in Dundas Street by the afternoon. He says his mother and father are happily married, that he had a happy childhood, and is happy now. He has served one short borstal sentence for breach of the peace, and been fined once for breach of the peace and once for theft of a scooter.

He says he joined the Shamrock 18 months ago because he couldn't walk down the town without being attacked by other gangs. 'Now we're the top and we don't need to protect ourselves. Carrying weapons is just a habit, like smoking or drinking. Everybody wants to be a big name. It's fighting for the sake of fighting. You feel good inside when you're chasing them and all, and batter them with bottles and slash them with razors. They deserve it. They wouldn't feel sorry for me if they set about me, so I don't feel sorry for them.'

Peter hates queers, men who interfere with children, smartly-dressed toffs, and the police: 'Most of these toffs, their old man's a lawyer. Not many people start off poor and get money. The Glasgow police have been watching these Yankee movies too much, driving about in their Jaguars and sunglasses. They all want to be Yanks. 'Put your hands up against the wall,' they say in an American accent.

'I'd like to go to elocution lessons to learn how to talk, and buy clothes and just go about drinking and all that. I'd like lots of birds, not just one. With money you can go anywhere with nobody to stop you. The coppers aren't going to tell you to move on and pull you up in front of birds all the time. I'd like to be a guy who is in charge of the underworld, a big top nut, or Lee Marvin. He is cheeky. I like him; he is a kind of rough diamond, but he is always smartly dressed.'

. . .

The meeting place of the Real Mental Shamrock used to be a bar nicknamed 'Munnie's', in Castle Street. I was introduced by a drunk called King, who claimed to be a member of the team and offered to protect me—for money, of course. His personality had deteriorated too far for him to belong to any group, and I never saw him again. But when he tried to make me frightened of the Shamrock it was because *he* needed to believe they were dangerous: the power he attributed to them was the only mental weapon he had left against whatever other powers threatened to overwhelm him. Later, a barman at 'Munnie's' said: 'You're frightened and I'm frightened. But they're frightened too. The difference is that they don't admit it.'

'Munnie's's was closed down by the time I left Glasgow, although it may since have reopened. The Shamrock drank in the pub during the Glasgow Fair holiday at the end of July, and by the beginning of the second week their money had run out. They owed the pub over £30, and stock was missing: they had stolen bottles over the counter behind a barman's back, and he, through fear or stupidity, had sold them rounds of drinks at something like quarter-price. One night after closing time they broke into the pub and got away with a few bottles of sherry and spirits. Half of it was stolen from the empty house where they dumped it overnight, and next morning they sat in the pub discussing how to move the remainder in a van with no brakes. Two policemen, whom you learn to smell in such a setting, were standing a few feet away. The following night the Shamrock broke into the pub again. Their profit from the two operations was about £20.

It is hard to be objective about the Real Mental Shamrock. I liked them, the way you tend to like most of the people you talk to at length, particularly if you sympathise with them because they are mentally or economically depressed. I was lucky to meet them when they had even less money than usual, and were grateful for the drinks I bought them. But they gave me a lot more, relatively, than I gave them. Once in the team you share what you have, and it is only when group finances are nil, and there is no dole or wages due to anybody, that they turn to thieving. Their technique, as the 'Munnie's' incidents showed, is less than immaculate.

. . .

The real test of your attitude towards people like the Shamrock is how you react when you are threatened by them. One night in George Square a group of them were arguing about a petty incident with the Fleet, going over the rights and wrongs of something too trivial to loom in anybody's mind. Then one lashed out at me, blind drunk, shattered by some anger he did not understand: 'You, standing there smiling, wanting your story. You'll get it all right, but it'll be what happened to yourself you'll be writing about.'

I had been smug for 10 days, proud of making contact with the gang and getting them to trust me, shaking my head over their sad backgrounds. Now the aggression was turned on me, and my pride was hurt because the rest of the gang were watching and I could think of nothing to say or do.

Immediately, anger made me look at the other side of the coin: other people with the same backgrounds as the Shamrock did not use weapons or thieve or waste time as if it was water. They were Shamrock because they were weak and selfpitying, not because they had no choice. So one of these yobs, a bit of dirt, ignorant and worthless, was threatening *me*, and if I had been able to get him beaten up or destroyed or put inside I would.

Any relationship I made with the Shamrock was artificial and shortlived. Any understanding I gained would not generate enough tolerance to let them threaten my pride or comfort. Until I gain the tolerance there will be the the

Shamrock, and me, and the gulf between us. And the police? What do they think?

'We are aware that there is a group called the Shamrock operating in the city,' said Sir James Robertson, Chief Constable of Glasgow. 'We have had occasion to deal with members of the group on a variety of charges.

'Our attitude must be repressive. Violence must be treated severely. I could not have any sympathy for violent manifestation of protest against society.'

Ken Martin, 'Anatomy of a Contemporary Gang', *The Observer Magazine*, 1 December 1968.

1971: Motorway City

With the opening of the Kingston Bridge in June 1970, leaping 470 feet across the Clyde in a single span, Glasgow became a motorway city. After the opening of the Clyde Tunnel in 1963, a Highway Plan had further recommended the building of an Inner Ring Road to relieve through-traffic pressure on the city centre. Six years later the western and northern parts were built, and the east flank was due to proceed down the High Street on stilts. The glacier-like effect of the IRR on surrounding buildings is noted here by two architects in writing about Lord Esher's report on conservation in Glasgow. The conservationist viewpoint, as articulated by bodies such as the New Glasgow Society, became increasingly heard in the early 1970s and the east flank proposal was shelved. (The Kingston Bridge now carries 115,000 vehicles a day, approaching its official saturation point.)

Since the war, planning in Glasgow has been characterised by a ruthlessness of purpose unmatched in the UK. The problems of slum housing, increasing dilapidation of tenements and traffic congestion made urgent action essential, and for this reason Glaswegians let the various departments have their head. It is only now that they are beginning to see what they have let themselves in for as the full horror of comprehensive development areas and the motorway plan become physical reality. Indeed so total has this programme been that in Glasgow at least CDA has stood for 'comprehensive *demolition* area'. Certainly many authorities made mistakes in the immediate post-war years in their anxiety to solve pressing needs, but there is disappointingly little indication that Glasgow housing and planning policies have learnt anything in the intervening 25 years.

The original road plan dates back to 1946, and was confirmed with some modification by Scott Wilson & Kirkpatrick's 'Highway plan for Glasgow' in 1965. The plan is for a double-ring system linked by several radial routes, and the inner ring—the north and west section of which is practically complete—passes right through Glasgow's central areas. At one point it runs 30yd in front of Glasgow's principal library—the Mitchell. In its path it removed Charing

Cross shopping centre, part of Garnethill and most of Anderston. This western part of Glasgow, especially Sauchiehall Street, is now in such a serious state of shock that it could die: shops and offices remain unlet, streets dirty and uncared for.

However, that half is built. What really matters now is whether to the south and east the motorway should (or can) be stopped leaving just the outer ring. This east flank is aligned up Glasgow High Street, removing from its path two Adam buildings, a 1751 chapel and Charles Rennie Mackintosh's Martyrs' School. As it crosses the Clyde at a height of 60ft, it will overshadow the Justiciary Courts (Starke 1806), ruin the views and scale of St Andrew's Square and make a nonsense of the 17th century Tolbooth and Merchants' House Steeples: at its upper end it will cut off the cathedral from the city to which it gave birth.

This eastern flank joins the M74 which has been aligned through Glasgow Green at the heart of the old city. Here a motorway interchange is planned, virtually annihilating Britain's oldest civic park and increasing the social polarisation between east and west. Were this flank constructed, those who could afford to would abandon east Glasgow; and further deterioration of an already neglected area seems inevitable. Conversely we may be sure that the planning department would never have dared align a motorway through Glasgow's *west* end park—Kelvingrove.

Recently the city corporation began to demonstrate its concern for both the Glaswegians and for the Glasgow which remains. It commissioned Lord Esher's report, produced an exhibition, 'Glasgow 1980', of its achievements and intentions, and it is currently advertising for the post of environmental officer (at a salary over £4000). Unfortunately 'Glasgow 1980' reveals no shift of attitude; there is still pride in its 'highest flats in Britain' and 'over 100,000 houses demolished to make room, above all, for roads'.

It is in this context that Lord Esher's report appears; fundamentally it could blend into official Glasgow policy without curdling. The motorways haunt his report, as they do Glasgow: rarely mentioned but ever present. He has taken this ring as the determining locational factor in considering potential conservation areas. Only when a motorway goes slap through the middle of some of them does he protest, and even then but mildly: 'The proposed outer ring motorway is a serious threat to this whole area of fine townscape (Drumbreck-/Crosshill, Pollokshields and Strathbungo): its alignment will need most careful consideration.' We can infer from this that his specific task was to pick up the bits that remained after the motorways and CDAS had been completed. This impression is reinforced by his division of Glasgow into two—the 'central area' within the inner ring road, and the 'suburban areas' outside. Apart from the fact that it's impossible to tell where this 'central area' lies precisely, as all motorways have been omitted from the conservation report's map, the lumping together of the widely varying areas within the inner ring girdle as 'central Glasgow' and the remainder as 'suburban Glasgow' implies either a severe ignorance of the city or a directive from Glasgow Corporation.

That the corporation asked Lord Esher to cary out a conservation study for Glasgow is welcome; and despite the many omissions of the report itself, its positive recommendations for the selected conservation areas should be implemented without delay. The public interest which Lord Esher's study has drawn upon Glasgow may possibly induce the corporation to have more care for the environment in the future. After all, as Lord Esher says, it is the finest surviving Victorian city.

Charles McKean and J.M. McKean, 'Motorway City', *The Architects' Journal*, 27 October 1971.

1972: The New-Look Gorbals

In the late 1950s, as an approach to reducing inner-city overcrowding, Glasgow was divided into 29 Comprehensive Development Areas (CDAs). This meant rehousing everyone (usually in peripheral housing estates or in New Towns) and bulldozing large areas of tenements. Demolition began on Laurieston-Gorbals CDA in the early 1970s. One of the streets affected was the imposing Abbotsford Place, built as part of an affluent suburb in the 1830s but by the 1950s in spectacular disrepair and grossly overcrowded. Today's Gorbals has less than a quarter of its 1950s population, and most of them live in multi-storey blocks—often in overcrowded conditions once again. The fashion for rehabilitation came too late for Abbotsford Place. Here some of the residents reminisce about the street's past glories, prior to their departure.

Woman—Cleland Street (20 years in Gorbals).
Aye, I'll have to go. I don't want to go but I'll have to go. I've got a good house. (*Would she like to move to a modern flat?*) No, I would not. Just look at those houses over in Crown Street. The rooms are too small—look at all those wee windows. And concrete stairs inside your house! I work as a home help in one of these multi-storeys and they have these big long corridors from here to (*gestures about 100 yards*), and all these wee doors, it's like a prison. You expect to see the prisoners coming out to empty—you know. Look at that one over there (opposite the Citizen's)—I don't know what it'll be like when it's finished but just now it's a thousand windows . . .

There's no companionship, you know. I might see you in the lift today, and then I wouldn't see you again for a month. But I'll have to go just the same. I wouldn't mind one of those new houses up at Mount Florida.

Newsagent at Centre Street (25 years in the same shop).
Oh, I'll be glad to see it go. Well, it's progress isn't it? (*Do you really think it's progress?*) Well, no, to be honest I don't. The people here dread the high flats. I mean, we have all these planners and they build these schemes and there are no

amenities, there are no public toilets and the roads are not wide enough for the traffic—where's the planning in that? Just take around here—there were four schools around here at one time, now the last one's closing in June. There were four newsagents in this street and we were all making a living. Now I'm the only one left. There'll be no shop left here at all—the people'll have to go over to the shopping centre at Eglinton Street. They'll be at the mercy of the supermarkets then . . . . *(Would you take a shop there if it was offered?)* No, I would not. Do you know what the rent and rates are? You can be £50 per week before you put stock into a shop. *(What do your customers think about moving?)* Well, they vary. Some are glad to go, some are sorry.

(If people had been consulted, would the district have been redeveloped in the way it has?)
No, no. Certainly not. They don't mind the maisonettes, the three- and four-storeys, but they wouldn't have had the highrisers.

(Will anyone be sorry to see the Gorbals go?)
Oh yes, the Gorbals was a famous place, you know. A lot of famous people came from here—Benny Lynch, Johnny McGrory . . . . It was a friendly place, your door was never shut. There were fights, yes, on a Friday night, but not knives, not viciousness like now. I went to Centre Street School and my pal went to St. John's and once a year, on St. Patrick's Day we'd have a fight and the next day we'd be the best of friends again. *(Will you look for another shop when this one comes down?)* No, no, I'll be packing up. Twenty-five years serving the public is enough!

Pensioner, Abbotsford Place.
The houses are rotten—too many years on them. Do you know I pay £4 for a couple of rooms here, here's my rent book if you don't believe me. *(Later she showed us her flat—two dank ground-floor rooms, one huge and impossible to heat and a kind of large scullery divided into cooking and washing areas. Everything scrupulously clean. She explained the rent by saying it was called a farmed house)* I want an old person's flat in a new block, that would suit me fine.
Of course, these were beautiful houses once. I lived in Norfolk St. when I was a girl and Abbotsford Place was all doctors then. But there's been nothing done to them for years—I suppose they could be done up but they'd be too big for us. An old person's flat, that's what we're looking for.

Old lady, 44 years in Main St., Gorbals.
(What do you think of redevelopment?) I think it's great. But there's some'll miss it. There's some go away from here and then they want back. No, I'll not be going for a while yet. They'll not be pulling down this building for at least six year. They'll maybe be moving me out before that—feet first!

Glasgow News, No. 14, 15–29 May 1972.

1972: UCS—A Place in History

In 1971 only five shipyards remained on the Upper Clyde—John Brown's at Clydebank and four others in Glasgow. Although huge losses had accumulated over the years, covered by government guarantees, profits did at last seem imminent—particularly with North Sea oilfields being rapidly exploited—when the Conservative government initiated a policy of letting 'Lame Ducks' go to the wall. In the summer of 1971 a liquidation of four of the yards (Yarrow's had been sold off) was recommended, then a later plan suggested retaining only two. The strong support the Upper Clyde Shipbuilders work-in received throughout Scotland eventually forced the Department of Trade and Industry to put up £35 million for the formation of an amalgamated Govan Shipbuilders. As a result only a few hundred jobs were lost. Early in 1972 shop steward Jimmy Reid addressed a mass meeting, arguing that all four yards must be included.

Around the UCS there are wider implications in the fight against redundancies and closures. We saw the greatest public demonstrations of the working class this century in Scotland in that march to Glasgow Green, where it is estimated that 80,000 people participated and hundreds of thousands stopped work. That's what has been happening. And alongside that there was the dialogue in the first instance with the government. These were not negotiations. Because negotiations imply that redundancies and closures are negotiable on our part. They are not negotiable. Our stand has been that one of the great weaknesses in the trade union movement in recent years has been the preparedness to consider negotiations on redundancies.

With the demeaning spectacle that always accompanies that—discussions on who goes out the door first, who gets stabbed in the back, who gets sold out, what happens to the blood money of the workers whose jobs are lost. All the rest of the demeaning, undignified experiences we've seen far too much of, particualry in the West of Scotland in the last ten years.

So there were no negotiations with the government. There was a preparedness to talk, and we've indicated that we will talk to anybody, but no negotiations that carry implications of redundancies. We totally reject that. We reject the attitude and the mentality that lies behind it.

. . .

We are reaching a crucial stage in this fight. This campaign can be successful but there is a need for optimism and confidence.

IT CAN BE WON.

But I tell you to win any fight you have to have the workers in the yard or the factory concerned resolved to fight to the end and win. In the absence of that you can get all the decisions you want but there can be no final victory.

We have this in abundance in UCS. No movement, no fractures, no cracks in the unity. Whatever is said and written in the future I've never seen a better bunch of fighters than the UCS workers have demonstrated themselves to be since the end of June of this year.

Victory is important not just for us. There is now a tremendous feeling of responsibility on our shoulders because we have become the symbol of the fight against policies of redundancies and closures.

Defeat, or a settlement tantamount to defeat, a compromise which means the selling out of jobs, will have a harmful effect on all these workers who have been inspired to fight redundancies and closures.

On the other hand, success in UCS will have a regenerating effect on the whole working-class movement. We have to say that, and we have to fight along these lines, because there is now little doubt that since the general election unemployment has been used as an instrument of government policy. They rejected an incomes policy, but the strategy obviously was to create such a pool of unemployment that would make an incomes policy unnecessary.

These people do not control this economy however. Having begun a process with the deliberate objective of creating mass unemployment, they are finding out that the creaky economy isn't like a car speeding downhill. You don't just slam on the brakes and it works.

For the brakes are not working. And they find they cannot stop and start this creaking economic vehicle at will for their own political ends.

So increasingly people have begun to understand the need for solidarity with the UCS workers and those in the forefront of this battle; the need to support them to a successful conclusion. In all the complexities, one thing has remained—and will remain—constant. A solution for the four yards and for the workforce.

Jimmy Reid, *Reflections of a Clyde-Built Man* (1976).

1973: Humour as Survival Kit

Glasgow is not alone in using humour as a defence mechanism to fend off a sometimes unappreciative outside world. Yet even in an age of supposedly upward social mobility one notably resilient feature of the Glasgow temper is an irresistible urge to squash pretension in any shape. As a way of reasserting social cohesiveness in times of affliction this 'A kent his faither' attitude is perhaps justifiable. But all too often it is used as a means to avoid confronting anything novel or unfamiliar. Here Cliff Hanley, writer and entertainer, looks at the many sides to Glasgow humour, with a few examples.

Humour is the product of hard times, and Glasgow humour, if such a thing can be isolated, is hard stuff. It does, I think, have a particularity, both in attitude and in rhythm, and the reason for the success of American comedians in Glasgow during the great days of variety is that American comedy (which is often American-Jewish comedy) is closer in pace and acid content to Glaswegian than either is to southern English.

The archetypal Glasgow keelie is a gallus man—gallows-man to the purist of language—and this description itself is hard to explain; jaunty, reckless, what-the-hell, voluble, scruffy and several other things. We may sometimes be amused, but we are rarely impressed. The ultimate in sceptical derision is a Glaswegian nodding his head and saying, 'Aye, that'll be right'.

Some of his humour is as much 'in' and incomprehensible to outsiders as Parisian argot jokes. The great Bud Neill, whose cartoons held the city in thrall for a generation, is often untranslatable and inexplicable. One Glasgow bird yells to another Glasgow bird, 'Haw Jennifer, ma kirby's fell doon a stank!' This demands a vast mental hinterland of Glasgow styles and manners.

Bud Neill acknowledged the influence of the goonish American artist Bill Holman, and his drawings were often spattered with obscure notices: on the wall of a pet shop the stark legend 'Budgies repaired'; in a grocer's window the alluring announcement 'Nice cheap messages'; and outside a filling station 'Tyres blew up wi' fresh air nice'.

For that matter, the late Tommy Morgan could convulse an audience by simply saying 'Clairty!' and there is no point in trying to explain this. His humour was firmly in the hard, subversive, proletarian tradition of the city, still maintained by performers such as Rikki Fulton and Jack Milroy and Johnny Beattie.

One of his favourite stories, which he never told on stage, was a long tragic epic about a man on the dole during the depression (a great source of Glasgow humour, the depression). This anguished citizen, driven nearly mad by the chorus of his starving children, 'Breid, daddy, breid', went out to collect his money and bring back a loaf, was absent for hour after hour while the children carried on chanting and his wife became distracted.

When he came back, soaked by the rain and breadless, he had experienced a tragedy too deep for words. Badgered and cajoled by his wife, he finally cried: 'Have you no' seen the paper? The Prince a Wales has fell aff his horse'.

The pretensions of the great attract a fair amount of quiet Glasgow acid. A carter stopped at a pub and asked an amiable-looking man to watch his load for a minute. 'My man, do you realize I'm a bailie of the City of Glasgow?'. 'Aye okay, but surely to God I can trust you wi' my horse.'

Apart from his taste in actual jokes, the Glaswegian relishes the bone-hard feel of language—a face like a torn melodeon, a bowler hat sitting like a pea on a dumpling, away and bone-comb your oxters. When a football idol returned to play in the city with a newly-acquired paunch, one of his fans shouted from the terracing: 'Tell us who did it, Jim, and we'll make her marry you!'

Ah, football, of course, a hard fact compounded by the ancient Protestant-Roman Catholic war. This, thank God, only distantly echoes the bitterness of Ulster and perhaps Glasgow's humour is the cooling unguent. There are endless religious stories, enjoyed impartially by both factions.

A man went into a pub in a Rangers stronghold and asked if they served

Catholics. Influenced, perhaps, by the fact that the man was leading a live alligator, the barman assured him that they served anybody. 'Okay. A pint for me and a Catholic for my pal.'

I have no doubt that the splendid cruelty of these tales is an escape valve rather than a stimulus to violence. The legendary violence of the city is a fact, but however much we detest it, it is probably an inevitable product of the sheer energy that makes Glasgow vibrate below the threshold of violence, the energy that creates its peculiar humour.

A Rangers fan at the cinema seeing *The Robe* told a friend that he would have to leave because the slaughter in the arena was making him sick.

'Stop worrying—in these old days all the Christians were Catholics.'

'Is that a fact? Hey, what's that lion up to, sittin' there doin' nothin'?'

Above and beyond factionalism we still joyfully clasp our totem of pure aggression, and its classic expression is certainly the experience of a Roman encampment somewhere in the Borders, where the garrison preparing for the final invasion were exasperated by a gallus, shilpit bauchle of a Glaswegian who kept poking his head over the wall and shouting insults and then vanishing northwards.

A hundred hand-picked legionaries were sent in pursuit. Three days later the sole survivor staggered back to the fort, several limbs short, saluted the commander and fell dead with the chilling words, 'Sir, it was a trap—there were two of them'.

Glasgow's economic fortunes have gone up and down like a yo-yo over the past two centuries, but most of the time, for most of the people, life has been hard and often hopeless and the humour is made to match.

It is a commentary on the brute reality of life and a clue to the city's character. But, more than that, in a grim situation the joke is a survival kit, and we have a million of them.

Cliff Hanley, 'A drop of the hard stuff in humour', *The Times* (Glasgow supplement), 18 May 1973.

1974: Govan's 'Wine Alley'

Wine Alley was the local name for an early slum-clearance scheme built in 1934 to house 500 families mainly from the Gorbals. The 'village' of Govan felt threatened by this invasion of outsiders. Although as a low-rent Rehousing Estate the houses had only the most basic amenities, there was resentment that they had not been offered to Govanites. Rumours spread about the nefarious activities of the Wine Alley residents, and soon people were applying to leave. In the early 1970s Sean Damer, a Dubliner working with the Corporation Planning Department, was intrigued by the scheme's evil reputation and rented a flat there for nine months to see if it was truth or folklore. Here he entertains a conference on the subject of 'Deviancy' with an account of his stay.

At the present time, the social picture of Wine Alley seems typical of a Scottish manual working-class housing estate. The scheme is ordinarily very quiet: during the day there are peaks of activity between eight and nine when the children are going to school and the men to work, and between about four and six when the children are home from school and the workers are returning. At this latter time there are hordes of children in the streets engaged in all the traditional street games described by the Opies, large 'mums' hang out of the tenement windows, yelling at the children and each other. Younger mums come back from the shops with their prams and messages and gather in small knots at the street-corners for a gossip. The teenage boys play energetic games of football wherever they can find a flat space, and dribble in and out of the groups of skipping girls. In the evenings during the week the scheme is very quiet; the children are generally off the streets by nine o'clock during term time, and all that is to be seen in the occasional group of two or three men going to the pub. At the weekends, life is more hectic. The men go to the pub at lunch-time and then to the match and then to the pub again. Then they return with their 'carry-outs' and parties break out. These generally degenerate into a soulful shambles around two or three in the morning, and it is possible to sleep again. The overall tone is unmistakably Glaswegian—this is evident from the decibel-war between record-players blasting out the war-songs of the Rangers and the Celtic, and also from the wine bottles in Monday morning's bins. But it has to be stressed that not every family by a long shot is involved in these drinking and singing parties. While they do happen practically every Friday and Saturday night, they only occur then, and it is a minority of families who sponsor them, according to my observations. In short, Wine Alley gives all the appearance of a fairly ordinary Glasgow manual working-class community—a somewhat battered but cheery place to live.

However, observation of a more systematic nature soon introduced some modifications of this superficial picture of a 'community'. In talking to locals I was frequently asked: 'What do you want to come and live in a dump like this for? I'd get out of it if I could.' Others said, in a phrase which seems to be international: 'Ah'll tell you whit thi place is, it's a dumpin-ground, they just dump all the riff-raff here now.' The contemporary perception of 'riff-raff' is something very like the Corporation's definition of the 'problem tenant': someone whose behaviour gives strong offence to his neighbour; behaviour which is associated with violence, drunkenness and noise. A local woman put it graphically:

'There are young men, an the great thing in their lives is this game they play: tig with hatchets. They're a' chibbed and if yer no chibbed yer no good. They think this is great. These are the ones ah'm telling you about. They don't stay at this end of the scheme, not near it. But they'll come up that road and you can watch for yoursel.

I was told of many incidents which were illustrative of the behaviour of riff-raff, and indeed a neighbouring family was sometimes pointed out to me as falling into this category. But the point is that even with this neighbouring family, the behaviour which was condemned occurred only occasionally; it was a case of *incidents* rather than pattern. I found the riff-raff, the 'anti-social' families, very nebulous people indeed; this is not to deny that 'anti-social' families exist in Wine Alley, but what I would stress is that they exist in different forms at different times for different reasons. The family which was near me, and which was occasionally pointed out to me as anti-social, only behaved in an uproarious way at weekends. On Friday and Saturday there were wine-drinking and singing parties in the house, and these not infrequently wound up in yelling matches and occasionally a fight. But during the week the husband and wife lived very conventionally, and indeed the man was well-known and liked. Noise was the main anti-social phenomenon in Wine Alley, and sometimes it could be very noisy indeed, but I honestly doubt whether it was any noisier than the student area of any large city on a Saturday night.

The quality of the noise, so to speak, was what could be disturbing: from time to time the din was constituted by a fight or by screamed and intimate obscenities. But I repeat that my observation confirmed that these were incidents, rather than the norm. Further a researcher clearly does not go around asking people if it was true that *they* play tig-with-hatchets, but my respondents pointed out two families who by repute contained the really hard men in the scheme, men who were alleged to have committed all sorts of violence in earlier years. But although both families did have a male member 'inside' doing long sentences for crimes of violence, their day-to-day style of life was eminently respectable, and, in one case, even a trifle elegant. The remarks of the informant *vis-à-vis* the hatchet merchants are, I feel, expressing a more generalised fear of the extrovert and boisterous behaviour of the local teenage boys, who, with the exception of about four well-known boys who were never out of trouble with the police, were, as far as I could determine, conventional working-class kids who preferred a game of football to a fight. But like their peers elsewhere, they were prone to tell anybody who chided them to 'eff off' in no uncertain terms.

Sean Damer, 'Wine Alley: The Sociology of a Dreadful Enclosure', *Sociological Review*, Vol. 2 (1974).

1974: *The Scottish Daily News*

In March 1974 the Beaverbrook newspaper group closed its printing plant in Albion Street, folding the *Evening Citizen* and printing the *Scottish Daily Express* in Manchester. A quarter of the 2,000 made redundant determined to resist closure, putting their money into a new co-operatively run daily paper. Launched in a blaze of publicity, with financial backing from the Labour government and also from publishing tycoon Robert Maxwell, the *Scottish Daily News* soon lost circulation and plunged into debt. As the demand for advertising revenue became desperate, the radical aims of the workers' co-operative were diluted and Maxwell closed down the operation after six months. This graphic account of the first issue going to press is by two journalists.

By eight o'clock on the Sunday evening of the launch, May 4, the tempo which had been quickening throughout the day reached frenzy. The production cycle of a newspaper reaches a jagged pinnacle in the hour before copy deadline for the first edition and that time has the visual appearance of a silent movie with a soundtrack added by Stockhausen. Typewriters hammer, phones jangle, nerves shred, voices are never below one hundred decibel level, radios tuned into police and fire brigade frequencies cackle metallically, copy boys weave between crashing lunacy picking up and dispatching copy. On launch night there were several added constituents, the neon presence of several television crews and the periodic appearance of voyeur-celebrities slowly and obstructively coasting through the melee. The players, sweating under arc lights, smoking incessantly, downing cups of coffee, giving off malevolent vapours, coped with it all—even the dribble of sparkling ladies who minced through, glasses of drink in hand, *en route* to watch the button being pushed to start the run.

Tony Benn, the Industry Minister, was there, as was Robert Maxwell, the latter doing the introductions and the guided tour like a proud father—Allister Mackie seeming to be pulled along in the slipstream. Jimmy Reid, the left-wing UCS shop steward, flanked Teddy Taylor the right-wing Tory MP for Cathcart. William Wolfe, the chairman of the Scottish National Party, nudged Matt McGinn the Glasgow folk-singer and bard to the *Daily News*.

The splash story in the first edition concerned a pretty young girl who had 'died' in a car crash and after being brought back to life had gone on to become a moderately successful model. The headline 'IT'S GREAT TO BE ALIVE' exemplified the mood of the 500 workers who provided their own 'we proved them wrong' piece which ran alongside. It was a poor splash story, particularly for a newspaper which promised to be 'bright but never trivial', more suited to the couthie *Sunday Post* market than a thrusting, finger-on-the-pulse entrant into the daily paper market.

. . .

After all the subbed copy had been sent down the suction tube to the caseroom below where it was set into type, journalists began drifting down to the machine room where a tight crowd was gathering to watch the first paper come off the co-operatively owned presses. The crowd swelled as the projected deadline, 9.50 p.m., approached. Production workers, their part in the operation finished, joined the jostle as the last stereo plate trundled along rollers set in the metal floor of the press bed, crowding in on the nucleus of Robert Maxwell, Allister Mackie and Teresa Docherty, the paper's first public investor, who would push the button to set the rotary presses running.

Television crews, from 'World in Action' and the BBC, turned their radium-blue focus on the hub. As the klaxon sounded the all clear, Allister Mackie popped open a bottle of champagne, glasses were filled and handed up to men hanging from the catwalks above. One or two voices shouted 'Let's beat the *Record* on to the streets', two men embraced emotionally while others shook hands, Robert Maxwell roughly pulled Teresa Docherty's face into the full fluorescence of the TV lights before she pressed the button feeding the reeled paper through the inked rotary plates until it came out at the other end, chopped and folded into into sixteen broadsheet pages, as the *Scottish Daily News*.

It was good to be alive!

Ron McKay and Brian Barr, *The Story of the Scottish Daily News* (1975).

1979: East End Renewal

In 1976 incredulous newspaper readers in Glasgow learned of the launching of Glasgow Eastern Area Renewal (GEAR). Covering 4,000 acres of the city, stretching north of the Clyde east from the Green, it was the most ambitious attempt at urban renaissance in Western Europe. With the aim of arresting economic decline, improving the environment and attracting new industry, GEAR was masterminded by the Scottish Development Agency (SDA)—a move that was criticised by those who feared the wishes of East-Enders would be overlooked. Certainly major facilities, like parks, sports and leisure centres, have been provided, imaginative uses devised for noteworthy buildings, and the whole area extensively facelifted. Creating a new non-industrial base for the East End will be a long-term task, however, as the writer of this supportive article appreciated.

It is an irony that the journey into Bridgeton Cross takes one into the wastelands which have become today's monument to the industrial revolution which James Watt and his colleagues began.

People are scattered over the hinterlands of the world with family roots deep down in this unpromising ground, and it raised some men of mettle and a communal spirit to be envied. In truth, they never had much in the way of worldly possessions, but were terrors in defence of their city. Right now it is the most appalling mess, enough to make even strong men weep amidst its ruins. And yet this very month all the powers-that-be are meeting to approve what has been called 'a strategy for salvation' and it will cost all of £160,000,000 to breathe new life into the East End.

When I went over to study the plans, and share the dreams of social workers involved in this imaginative and massive scheme, they protested that it would be unusual for readers of 'Scottish Field' to be interested in such a thing.

Extraordinary really, because this is the very heritage and fabric of Scotland—a fundamental piece of history, and it is also our future. Of course we care!

Think of all the memories Scots have carried away from the East End, through the Victorian era of steam and ironworks, trams and railways. The Cross where so many New Years were brought in together, Barrowland for the dancing and Sunday bargain stalls, Parkhead the home of the Celts raised up above the whole area on a pedestal as the people wished it.

The East End was once the industrial powerhouse of Glasgow—and that means Scotland. It grew in the early 19th century as offshore oil has boomed in the North-East today, through cotton and textiles at Bridgeton, metal-work and engineering at Beardmore's, Parkhead, Arrols of Dalmarnock, and Napier's in Camlachie, which led the shipyards of the Clyde. There used to be thousands of people staying in the area; an average of three to a room. Since 1951, however, 100,000 people have left . . . only 45,000, mainly elderly, still remain. Unemployment exceeds 20%—the worst in Britain. It is a sad story.

Hopefully, though, a dramatic change sets in from now, so that soon the returning visitor will wonder whatever happened to the erstwhile Victorian powerhouse. It will be replaced by an entirely new and modern inner city, with another generation to restore the community of old. The work is being planned by 'GEAR'—Glasgow Eastern Area Renewal, a fearfully unwieldy but well-meaning amalgam of councils and developers who are showing a proper concern for restoring not only habitations but also morale to a place almost beyond hope. They are doing sterling work and this article is intended to publicise the fact, for too many writers have poured forth their scorn and it is unfair.

There is much that is imaginative afoot now in the East End, notably in what are ludicrously under-stated as 'environmental improvements',—a ponderous way of saying that the backcourts are being cleaned up, trees planted, and the place made less ugly. Decent homes are going up, a real effort made to attract new industries and retrain people to new skills, and, strangely in these times, poverty is being tackled realistically with an army of social and welfare workers seeking out the needy. There is still a heap of pride in the East End.

There is a lot more happening: the familiar facade of the Royal Infirmary, centre of the city's health care, has even now a £25m replacement topped out behind it. The old schools in which the basic three R's were taught by rote are being modernised with special attention to something called 'the problem of language disability' which might well mean having a good Glesca tongue for a' I ken. They are also pulling down disused cinemas and putting up sports centres.

The nostalgic amongst us will be relieved to know that the planners intend to leave The Barrows much as they have always been, although some improvements are under consideration, and the local corner shops are being given top priority, even if there is a supermarket planned for Shettleston and new shops in Baltic Street.

The future success of Glasgow's East End seems to me to look secure, if only for one major reason: the special spirit and flavour of the area permeates right through the plethora of development plans and schedules. Those who have remained in the area manifestly carry on old traditions, so that their wishes and memories are an integral part of the blueprint. They do say it will take three decades to put back what the end of the steam age has taken out, but it would be no surprise if micro-electronics did not achieve a miracle much quicker than that.

'Glasgow's East End—A Place of Dreams', *Scottish Field*, February 1979.

1984: *The Observer* is surprised

The 1980s saw Glasgow making a determined bid for its own tourist trade rather than depending on stopover visitors. Despite the nearness of Edinburgh, the new Regional Tourist Board seems to have attracted both hotel developers and new visitors, often expatriates from North America. At the same time the success of the District Council's *Miles Better* campaign has given the city's refurbished image exposure south of the Border. The approval of travel journalists is also needed. Here one of the most influential writes about three days spent in Glasgow at the invitation of the National Trust. Apparently the response to this article was unusual: 'Scots all over the world wrote to me. A woman in San Francisco said it made her cry'.

I hope it's true about realising you know nothing worth knowing being the beginning of wisdom. Because if it is, I'm set to rival Erasmus.

For example, I've just been to Glasgow—for the first time: some sort of record for a north countryman of my age—and got all illusions shattered.

From what I'd heard, it was a grimy city, pitch dark three months of the year, wetter than Manchester and lawless. The only time the streets were safe was when they were empty, such as on a flag day. Drunks in woolly berets with pom-poms cutting up innocent passers-by with broken bottles.

This turns out to be incorrect, or very nearly. Flanks of high-rise flats on the outskirts don't appear particularly welcoming (although the minute tenement flat at 145 Buccleuch St, that the National Trust for Scotland has has rescued and opened to the public—four at a time—suggests that family life, even in those cramped conditions, may have had compensations). But much of Glasgow looks as neat as an Edwardian housemaid, a bit like suburban Vancouver, in fact, which itself is modelled on what I imagine Guildford to have been like around 1935.

Glasgow taxi-drivers help you with your luggage and you can hardly believe you are in a British Rail terminal at Central Station, the absence of squalor being unnerving. You might as well be in Zurich. And I haven't seen so many young men wearing suits and ties for years, not even in Tokyo. It's a sign of

Glasgow's roaring sophistication that the new owner of the North British Hotel is an *Egyptian*, like the owner of the Ritz in Paris.

A streamer on the City Chambers alleges that IT'S MILES BETTER IN GLASGOW, a dig, I took it, at Edinburgh, now relegated to being no more than an old stick-in-the-mud. (Glasgow expects to receive more visitors in 1984 than the capital.) There's nothing to touch Edinburgh's Georgian glory, or, if there is, not obviously, because Glasgow is an Industrial Revolution phoenix with appropriate architecture, overbearing at first sight until much delectable detail, now revealed as the result of cleaning, suggests that the citizens, though outwardly dour may not have been just the tight-fisted, severe Covenanters it suited their purpose to make themselves out to be.

Furthermore, the city is perched dead centre of fine surroundings and sights, like a cock on a midden. Great estates and fine mansions are two-a-penny, castles such as Culzean, looking ready to dive into the sea but still where Robert Adam left it, are rarer but more impressive. There's the sweet delight of Loch Lomond where you can hear what silence once sounded like. And a rich profusion of gardens. Greenbank, part of Glasgow city now, is a garden of rooms, so that you can walk, as it were, from bedroom to parlour and on into the kitchen.

Only the majestic Clyde saddens. The sight of the Scott Lithgow shipbuilders yard, looking cornered and misunderstood, is baffling. All you can spot is the submarine fleet, creeping out to sea on NATO patrol as if carrying a guilty secret, great, black monstrous objects containing God-knows-what vicious toys, more frightening than the Loch Ness monster.

'They say the port's dead,' I said to a Glaswegian. 'Why is that? Commie dockers: unions?' That's what you hear in England.

'No, road transport's put the ships out of business. Even tea comes overland now *from India*.'

Culturally, Glasgow's a freak, having achieved the seemingly impossible and opened a new art gallery. The Burrell Collection of textiles, furniture, ceramics, stained glass and pictures is inconveniently situated unless you have your own transport and is in danger of being overpraised but it's a triumph in the present political climate.

Edward Mace's Travel Talk, *The Observer*, 6 May 1984.

1984: Mayfest

During the 1970s Glasgow's reputation as a desert for highbrow culture came suddenly unstuck. Scottish Opera and Scottish Ballet had already located their headquarters in the city. The Citizens' Theatre also had a major re-fit, but now awaits a facade to match its international reputation. Smaller-scale venues for the performing arts were provided by the Third Eye Centre occupying a 'Greek' Thomson warehouse, Glasgow Arts Centre a disused school, and the Tron

Theatre Club undertaking a gradual but imaginative conversion of the Laigh Kirk. Local premises like Bridgeton's Dolphin Arts Centre also allowed Glaswegians to become actively involved in the arts from an early age. Mayfest, which began in 1983 with support from trade unions, commercial sponsors, local councils and the Arts Council, is the latest manifestation of the city's welcoming attitude to the performing arts. Described as 'cheap and cheerful', it has succeeded in getting enthusiastic audiences for a wide range of offerings.

What finally brought Mayfest into play was a happy coincidence of interests. Certain prominent local trades-unionists had long felt that a Labour stronghold like Glasgow should be celebrating Mayday with some kind of people's festival. The city's District Council, Labour-controlled, was keen to explore any avenue that would contribute (preferably in a non-elitist way) to the cultural life of the city and, at the same time, help burnish a long tarnished national/international image. Though financial help would, perforce, be limited, the District Council were eager to give whatever practical backing they could . . . several trades unions agreed to chip in . . . and Feri Lean rose to the challenge and volunteered to organise the event.

That first Mayfest, held in 1983, was a heartening, talked-about-for-ages success. Feri, determined to get her acts together, travelled to and fro across the globe to find and sign up talent. Does that sound frightfully glamorous? Well, of course, it wasn't. Lean times were had in flooded Zagreb, Amsterdam theatre was seen through a veil of tear gas. But come the First of May the show went on.

Groups from Yugoslavia, Italy, Germany, USA and France played alongside Scottish companies, drawn together on a shoe-string budget of £100,000. Average attendance was 77% with 28,000 tickets sold during the two-week period. And, at the end—the most difficult trick in showbusiness—the books balanced.

One thing, however, had not worked out to the satisfaction of the organisers. The aim had been to provide a people's festival that would not only appeal to, but also *reach*, all sections of the community. Because events had been staged in city centre venues, those living in the city's peripheral housing schemes—particularly the poorer families there—had been virtually excluded. The low-paid and the unemployed who live in these decaying dormitories can hardly afford the bus fares into Glasgow at the best of times. Transport *and* the cost of a ticket? It just wasn't on for most of them.

. . .

If audiences for community events in the city were disappointingly small—and oftimes composed of friends of the cast—the quality of the work performed was promising. Strike Back Theatre, a group of unemployed from Springburn, reminded those who saw *I'll Cry Tomorrow* that a mere thirty years before, their area had been alive with small industry and modest hopes. The destruction of the railway works and the demolition needed to let the motorway power through regardless had left Springburn on its uppers. Depressing, yes. But the situation was sparked with humour. A Glasgow play that had something to say to Glasgow people. Mayfest, by bringing this, and other projects, into the public eye, had taken an important step in the right direction.

Mary Brennan, 'Their Very Own Mayfest', *Drama* 4, 1984.

1985: Easterhouse

Easterhouse is one of Glasgow's four major peripheral council estates (known as Schemes) which were developed during the 1950s as part of the city's slum clearance and overspill programme. By the mid-1960s Easterhouse, comprising thirteen separate estates, had provided a much-improved standard of housing but it had also become known as a 'problem area' with widely publicised delinquency and vandalism. Although the size of a town, Easterhouse lacked shopping facilities, social provision and employment opportunities. In 1977 the Easterhouse Festival Society was set up and now runs its own newspaper, employs community artists, organises employment ventures and encourages creativity within the different communities that make up the Scheme. A new area initiative, backed by the city and Strathclyde region, aims to give the 50,000 inhabitants of Easterhouse more say in its management and future.

In the beginning, they were housing estates pure and simple. But they were often as large as small towns. Kirkby, on Merseyside, had over 60,000 people, and Easterhouse in Glasgow well over 50,000. The people who went there were often those in the most urgent need of re-housing—such as large families and the unemployed. So by the early 1970s, the estates had already become recognised as poor and overcrowded. Often, half the population were under 15. For years there were few if any shops, pubs or services of any kind. They quickly became notorious. The *Z-Cars* image of Kirkby is the best-known example.

But what has happened to the outer estates in the recession-hit 1970s and 1980s, at a time when the inner cities have had some benefit from special urban programmes? To try to find the answer, we at CES Ltd, an independent urban research centre, have just completed a national project on outer estates. We took Kirkby in the Merseyside metropolitan district of Knowsley, Glasgow's Easterhouse, Hull's Orchard Park and the East Middlesbrough estate as our examples. The project was funded by the four local authorities. Our report is published this week.

We found that, as national unemployment has risen, so the living standard in the outer estates has dropped markedly in comparison with the national average. Income levels are lower, and unemployment higher, than the inner city areas which are designated for special help.

The tables show that unemployment is nearly three times the national average. On other indicators, such as the proportion in low-skilled groups, the outer estates we studied have higher levels of 'deprivation' than the inner cities.

As local factories lost markets and their technology became obsolete, there were closures, dilapidation and dereliction. The new wave of investment in high tech factories, in warehouses and in small enterprises is taking place well away from the outer estates. It is situated in prestige hi-tech parks, in enterprise zones—and some in the inner cities themselves.

The very size and isolation of these 'towns,' often miles away from city centres, means that they have much less disposable income circulating than the inner city. No one commutes into the outer estates to office jobs or shops, as they do into city centres. There is little trickling-down of income from more affluent suburbs.

These are one-class towns, much more so than some inner city areas. They lack the intermingling of 'gentrifying' liberal professionals or a rich multi-ethnic culture. They are solidly working class. They still have many skilled workers who used to work in the nearby industrial estates, but on average half their population is in semi-skilled and unskilled social groups. This is considerably more than the inner areas.

The jumble of old buildings and derelict sites you see in the inner cities are completely absent. There is an almost eastern European monotony. Almost every building and every piece of land is owned by the local authority. Perhaps 70 per cent of households receive some part of their income from the state.

Contradictions abound. There are often vast and green open spaces, which are put to little use, and are criss-crossed by informal muddy footpaths and scattered with litter and rubbish. The low-density layout puts many people out of easy reach of shops and jobs. But there are also overcrowded maisonettes and terraces, with no private spaces or gardens. Neighbours can hear each other through the walls, or cannot find their own front door easily. Gangs of youths come streaming past bedrom windows. Despite the long distance to other areas, over 70 per cent of households are without a car.

There are some peculiar phenomena. Where else are there mobile shops regularly patrolling residential streets? In what other low-income areas are there long lines of taxis drawn up outside the (usually meagre) shopping centre (four sharing a taxi is cheaper and easier than catching a bus)?

Some of the underprovision seems grotesque. At one point in our study, there was no single functioning swing to serve Easterhouse's several thousand children. People living in damp, mould-ridden flats and houses can still 'pay' (through social security) a rent of £25 or £30 a week, almost the same as for a house in perfect repair.

It is well known that many families cannot 'subsist' on the present level of benefits, especially since the rise in fuel prices, rents, food and other basic items. But here we are seeing the emergence of whole communities which have sunk to a kind of subsistence economy. There is less and less cash circulating, no land market, little or no market for consumer goods, and no competition.

Some shops can extract high monopoly prices. Even the leverage which the residents used to have over public authorities through their rent payments has been reduced as cash benefits have been replaced by direct paper transactions between public agencies.

This is not simply inequality of income and living standards between different areas. It is the emergence of two entirely different socio-economic systems. In the rest of the nation there is a market economy. On the outer estates there is a local economy which subsists entirely on state provision and administrative fiat. Resentment grows in proportion to the sense of powerlessness.

Andrew Broadbent, 'Estates of Another Realm', *New Society*, 14 June 1985.

1985: The Scottish Exhibition Centre

The opening of the Scottish Exhibition and Conference Centre (SECC) in September marked the beginning of a drive to attract large conferences and trade exhibitions to Glasgow. From the outside the complex is not very appealing, but the huge space inside (uncluttered by supporting pillars) is divided up into a range of spaces suitable for a modest product launch or a mega-star pop concert. In 1988 the Glasgow Garden Festival takes place across the river, on the site of Princes' Dock, linked by a footbridge to the SECC. This 'celebration of Glasgow's rejuvenation' will contain a host of attractions, including a yacht marina, a maritime museum and a number of theme gardens that will transform this blighted area of riverside. Here journalist Ruth Wishart inspects the newly-built SECC and learns of plans to transform the docklands.

For months it most resembled a futuristic legoland, sections of tubular walkway protruding from the defiant bright orange of its outer aluminium panelling.

But with the additions of parking facilities with their distinctive lighting poles, the completion of the concourse area and its outer piazza the Scottish Exhibition and Conference Centre suddenly emerged as a very dramatic whole down on Glasgow's Queen's Dock.

The 64 acre site has its formal opening in November during a hastily re-scheduled Motor Show when The Queen will provide a suitably majestic blessing and the main concert hall will be named in her honour.

The SECC is a £30 million pound investment in a part of Glasgow which will undergo a remarkable facelift in the space of a very few years.

For immediately across the river from the centre is the site of 1988's International Garden Festival, 12 acres of which will remain permanently landscaped after the addition of new housing in a riverside complex.

Funded by the Region, the District, the SDA and the major financial institutions it's a bold attempt to put Glasgow and Scotland in the major league as a conference and exhibition venue and its first year diary includes the Modern Homes Exhibition, The Commonwealth Games Conference and Exhibition, The Ski Show, Computer Show and arts events from the Proms to the Circus.

Indeed when Nellie the elephant packs her trunk and says goodbye to the Kelvin Hall she can look forward to a season in premises which have installed personal flush toileting arrangements for animals notorious for leaving a powerfully lingering reminder of their visit.

But in truth these are merely the bread and butter of a complex whose financial jam will only come from full recognition in the international market place.

Thus far it has attracted one major international conference. CIDESCO is a 27-nation event geared to the medical side of the health and beauty market, and Glasgow went to Helsinki to pitch for it successfully against strong bids from Spain and Israel.

And of the eighty plus enquiries about facilities currently being dealt with, over a quarter are from abroad which marketing director Bob Saunders describes as 'an outstandingly good percentage'. But he acknowledges that having set his targets high in the first instance, he still has a massive hill to climb in terms of competing with some very classy European venues not even to mention London which survives as the most popular conference centre in the world.

His problem, as he frankly admits, has been an inability to market the SECC as agressively as he would have liked until the final piece of the jigsaw is allowed to fall into place.

That is the provision of what are known in his trade as 'break-out facilities' . . . the laying on of smaller meeting areas adjacent to the main complex delegates can move to in between the major sessions or at their conclusion.

In the case of the SECC these are to be in a custom built hotel already planned into the site, but for which planning permission was briefly delayed because of opposition from the existing Glasgow hoteliers.

Bob Saunders finds it difficult to disguise his irritation at what he considers the shortsightedness of their hostility which he overcame by means of presenting them with some irrefutable financial logic.

It goes something like this. At every conference venue it is calculated that the benefits run in a ratio of one to nine. In other words for every £1 expended at the centre, £9 is spent in the local community.

The current figures are that for accommodation, taxis, eating and shopping each delegate can be expected to spend £90 per day in the city where the conference is being held.

On that basis Saunders has calculated that the business which could accrue from the existing enquiries is worth some £28 million.

There were 51 sites considered in all for the centre, and Clydeside won out because of a fairly unique set of advantages including its proximity to the motorway, expressway, major rail and air links and other city centre hotel accommodation. It has to be said that the rest of that area is not at the moment the world's most aesthetically pleasing eyeful, but the Garden Festival will change much of that.

Scotmedia, 5 September 1985.

1986: Billy Connolly and the European Capital of Culture

In October 1986 Glasgow was nominated by the Minister for the Arts, Richard Luce, as European Capital of Culture for 1990 (Edinburgh came fifth)—a fitting culmination of the decade's Miles Better campaign. In some quarters this news gave occasion for displays of rampant chauvinism (see the *Evening Times* for 20 October 1986), but here Billy Connolly, who himself has done more than most to put Glasgow on the map, merely indulges in a quiet 'bout of civic pride' in his home town.

An áctor friend of mine told me once of how he returned home to Glasgow after some success on the London stage and decided to visit the Italian café where he frittered away his youth. The owner, Tony, was still there, hidden behind the wooshing and grinding cappuccino machine. He gave my friend a warm welcome and, drying his hands with his ever-present tea towel, asked him what he thought of the place. Had it changed much while he he had been away pursuing fame?

My friend cast an eye around the sea of Fablon and Formica and found it much the same. There was one obvious addition, though: a horrendous painting covering one wall, in gaudy colours unknown in nature, depicting a shortbread-tin Highland scene, a loch with mountains, complete with unlikely looking wildlife—eagles, deer, badgers, pheasant and haggis. Below the painting sat the café's only other customer, a dishevelled individual, his head in the soup, snoring and bubbling furiously between mumbled swear words.

The owner then asked my friend the question he had been dreading. Pointing to the garish wall, Tony said: 'Well, what do you think of my muriel?' The best response my friend could manage was a blurted 'Eh it's very nice, Tony.' No sooner had the words left his lying lips than the soup drinker in the corner uttered his judgment: 'Very nice, ye say? Very nice? Ye call that a muriel? Christ, Venus de Milo would turn in his grave if he'd seen that!'

Thus goes the best piece of artistic criticism I have ever heard; a thumping piece of honesty which the Sunday review pages would do well to emulate. Of course, it was uttered in the midst of that cultural centre of Western civilisation, Glasgow. What is this I hear you say in the cultural deserts of London, Birmingham, Bristol and Manchester—tish, bah, pooh, bosh and figs?

The reason for my bout of civic pride in my old home town is that, in an unusual display of wisdom, Richard Luce, the arts minister, has nominated Glasgow as a centre of cultural excellence, and not before time.

For too long Glasgow has languished under the shadow of Edinburgh. In the minds of those who award prizes and tributes to cities and the like, Edinburgh has held a sort of franchise on the beauty department of Scotland's cultural heritage; a fact that has caused a great deal of sand to lodge in the collective Glasgow craw.

Glasgow, this city of 70 (yes, 70) parks and open spaces, has long resented its image as the blackspot of Europe. For many years it has been a victim of documentary film-makers who, when short of evidence of marauding gangs terrorising the wide-eyed and innocent populace, were not above slipping some unemployed youths a couple of bob to impersonate the same.

To deny Glasgow's violent past would, of course, be less than sensible. However, it seems to me the right approach would be to build on the more positive side of Glasgow's character.

Glasgow scored a cultural dropkick a few years ago when it refurbished the Theatre Royal—a great Victorian music hall which had been sliced up, groaning all the way, into a television studio eventually wrecked by fire—and made it the home of Scottish Opera. In a world that seems obsessed with building car parks and high-rise office blocks this came as a real shock.

. . .

My own love of things cultural arises from a mistake of geography, really. I was born and spent my formative years in Partick, most famous I suppose for Partick Thistle, a football team of somewhat mixed fortunes—an English friend once remarked on hearing the result Partick Thistle 2, Motherwell 1: 'My goodness, I always thought that they were called Partick Thistle Nil'.

At the front of Kelvingrove Park in Partick is the Kelvingrove Art Gallery and Museum, where, on many a Sunday, my sister Flo and I would go for an afternoon's cultural absorption and a slide on the highly polished floor.

Some talented buyer in the Glasgow council had purchased Salvador Dali's Christ of St John on the Cross, causing quite a furore at the time. I have always been grateful to that person, for I spent many happy hours looking at that painting. It has instilled in me a love of Salvador Dali and, more important, surrealism in art and in life in general that has pleased and fortified me many times in my travels.

As a special treat, I would be taken every couple of years to the People's Palace, a truly great folk museum at Glasgow Green. This, the most alive museum I have experienced, is dedicated to Glasgow's history and life-style, without denying the humour of the place. It suffers greatly at the hands of the press and the less enlightened members of the council because of the shadow thrown over it by its wealthier cousin, the Burrell Collection, affluently housed in Pollok Estate.

Personally, I preferred the Burrell Collection when it was in boxes in various warehouses, disused schools, and abandoned churches. My father would point out one of these schools solemnly. 'That building holds treasures,' he would say, and I would stare at the sooty, grimy place, suitably impressed.

The culture of my Glasgow is a living, working, singing and laughing culture. It is a culture of a city renowned for toughness born of adversity. If this type of toughness upsets you, I would advise you to stay clear of Glasgow.

It is a culture that has been fought for and won by dedicated men and women, not always citizens of Glasgow. People like Giles Havergal of the Citizens' Theatre, John Cunningham and Sandy Goudie in art, Alasdair Gray and Carl MacDougall in literature, Liz Lochhead in poetry, Elspeth King in the museum department, and Sir Alexander Gibson and Bill McCue in music.

My only hope, when an honour has been placed on such richly deserving shoulders, is that the louder and more shrill trumpet-blowers of the Scottish press can be blanketed by the calmer members. The time for trumpet-blowing and naive pleas for recognition has long gone. If you are lucky enough to have been born there, or smart enough to wish to be there, then the time has come to be quietly pleased.

Billy Connolly, 'I'm telling ye, we're the Big Yin of arts', *The Sunday Times*, 26 October 1986.

Some Further Reading

Anderson, Iain F., *Scottish Quest* (1935)
Annan, Thomas, *Old Closes and Streets: a series of photogravures 1868-1900* (1900)
Beattie, William, *Scotland Illustrated* (1838)
Bell, J.J., *The Glory of Scotland* (1932)
Berry, Simon, 'The Greening of Glasgow' (*Scotsman* 23 June 1984)
Bostock, E.H., *Menageries, Circuses and Theatres* (1927)
Boyle, Jimmy, *A Sense of Freedom* (1977)
Brennan, T., *Reshaping a City* (1959)
Brogan, Colm, *The Glasgow Story* (1952)
Burgess, Moira, *The Glasgow Novel* (2nd ed. 1986)
Burrowes, John, *Front Line Report* (1981)
Chambers, Robert, *The Picture of Scotland* (1827)
Checkland, S.G., *Scottish Banking: a History 1695-1973* (1975)
        The Upas Tree: Glasgow 1875-1975 . . . and after 1975-1980
        (1981)
Connolly, Billy, *BC: The Authorized Version* (1976)
Cullingworth, J.B., *A Profile of Glasgow Housing* (1965)
Ferguson, T., *Scottish Social Welfare 1864-1914* (1958)
Ferguson, T. and Cunnison, J., *In Their Early Twenties: A Study of Glasgow Youth*
        (1956)
[Frame,?], *The Philosophy of Insanity* (1947)
Freer, Walter, *My Life and Memories* (1929)
Gallacher, William, *Revolt on the Clyde* (1936)
Gibson, John, *The History of Glasgow* (1777)
Glasgow Municipal Commission on the Housing of the Poor Report (1904)
Glasgow Presbytery Report of Commission on the Housing of the Poor (1891)
Gomme, Andor and Walker, David, *Architecture of Glasgow* (1968)
Hanley, Cliff, *Dancing in the Streets* (1958)
Harvey, Mrs Margaret and McLeod, Miss, *A Medley of a Decade* (1899)
House, Jack, *Music Hall Memories* (1986)
        Pavement in the Sun (1967)
        Square Mile of Murder (new ed. 1976)
Jephcott, Pearl, *Time of One's Own* (1967)
Keevins, H. and McCarra, K., *100 Cups: the story of the Scottish Cup* (1985)
Kellet, J.R., *Glasgow: a concise history* (n.d.)
        The Impact of Railways on Victorian Cities (1969)
Kohl, J.G., *Travels in Scotland* (1844)
Laidlaw, S., *Glasgow Common Lodging Houses* (1956)

Lipton, Thomas, *Leaves from the Lipton Logs* (n.d.)

Lockhart, J.G., *Peter's Letters to his Kinfolk* (1819)

MacGregor, George, *The History of Glasgow* (1881)

Marr, Robert A., *Music for the People* (1889)

Meehan, Patrick, *Innocent Villain* (1978)

Middlemass, R.K., *The Clydesiders: a left-wing struggle for parliamentary power* (1965)

Morgan, Edwin, *Poems of Thirty Years* (1984)
       'Glasgow Writing' (*Books in Scotland* 15, 1984)

Moss, M. and Hume, J., *Workshop of the British Empire: Engineering and Shipbuilding in the West of Scotland* (1977)

Munro, Michael, *The Patter: a guide to Glasgow usage* (1985)

Oakley, C.A., *The Last Tram* (1962)

Patrick, James, *A Glasgow Gang Observed* (1973)

Pennant, Thomas, *A Tour in Scotland* (1790)

Percy, W.S., *Strolling through Scotland* (1934)

Power, William, *My Scotland* (1934)
       Should Auld Acquaintance (1937)

Reed, Sir E.J., *Report on the 'Daphne' Disaster* (1883)

Robertson, George Gladstone, *Gorbals Doctor* (1970)

Roxburgh, J.B., *The School Board of Glasgow 1873–1919* (1971)

Saunders, Donald *et al*, *The Glasgow Diary* (1984)

'Shadow', *Midnight Scenes and Social Photographs* (1858, repr. 1976)

Sillitoe, Percy J., *Cloak without Dagger* (1955)

Slaven, Anthony, *The Development of the West of Scotland* (1975)

Smout, T.C., *A Century of the Scottish People 1830–1950* (1986)

Urie, John, *Reminiscences of Eighty Years* (1908)

Wardlaw, W., *Recollections of Ebenezer Wardlaw* (1841)

Whyte, Hamish, ed., *Noise and Smoky Breath: an illustrated anthology of Glasgow poems 1900–1983* (4th imp. 1986)

Wilson, John, 'Glasgow Revisited' (*Janus* 1826)

Worsdall, Frank, *A Glasgow Keek Show* (1981)

INDEX